A Deserter's Adventures

Dom Felice Vaggioli

Translated by
John Crockett

University of Otago Press

Published by University of Otago Press
PO Box 56/56 Union Street, Dunedin, New Zealand
Fax: 64 3 479 8385; Email: university.press@otago.ac.nz

ISBN 1 877276 11 1

Printed through Condor Productions Ltd, Hong Kong

Contents

Acknowledgements

First I wish to acknowledge the generous support of many people to enable this translation to be prepared and published.

In particular, my thanks are due to Rev Bruce Bolland and Marian Nee of the Catholic Diocesan Archives, Pompallier Centre, Auckland; the assistance of the Benedictine archivists, Dom Beda Paluzzi OSB of Subiaco, Dom Angelo Galletti OSB of Parma, and Abbot Bruno Marin OSB and the community of Praglia monastery; don Bruno Bertoli and research staff of the archives of the cardinal patriarch of Venice and Katy Hannan-Sabella, who carried out research in Italy on my behalf; Rory Sweetman for his essay and additional notes; David Simmons, retired ethnologist, once again a source of inspiration and knowledge, and finally, Wendy Harrex, managing editor of University of Otago Press, and Linda Pears for their dedicated, inspiring editing.

For permission to use photographs, I thank the Catholic Diocesan Archives, Auckland.

JOHN CROCKETT

This translation is dedicated to Dom Felice Vaggioli OSB, determined scholar and fearless monk, to the cherished memory of Adelinda Malatesta, and to my dear daughters, Emily and Julia.

The first page of 'Verso il Nostro Destino'/'Towards our Destination' (Chapter 1) in Vaggioli's manuscript.

Introduction

While translating the second volume of Dom Felice Vaggioli's *Storia della Nuova Zelanda e dei Suoi Abitatori* (published as *History of New Zealand and Its Inhabitants*),[1] I received a New Zealand government research grant enabling me in 1996 to visit Benedictine monasteries in Italy in search of Vaggioli archival material. Before leaving New Zealand, I wrote to the ancient monastery of Subiaco for possible leads. I received an encouraging reply from its archivist, Dom Beda Paluzzi, OSB. He not only offered to introduce me to appropriate persons in the Congregation's North Italian monasteries, but enclosed a photocopy of a brief biography of Vaggioli, taken from a collection of historical essays marking the Congregation's centenary.[2] I was particularly interested in the footnotes indicating archival sources. Mostardi, Vaggioli's biographer, provided a summary of his writings, which included his *Storia della Nuova Zelanda e dei Suoi Abitatori*, described by Mostardi as 'two large scholarly volumes',[3] and an unpublished manuscript entitled 'Le Avventure di un Refrattario descritte da lui Stesso' ('A Deserter's Adventures, an Auto-biography'),[4] which I anticipated would be a vital source of information. On my visit to Subiaco, Dom Beda proved to be as hospitable and helpful as he had indicated in his letter, among other things arranging my visit to Praglia monastery, which contained the manuscript I was seeking.

Both the monasteries of Subiaco and Praglia enjoy the status of national monuments *(monumenti nazionali)* because of their cultural heritage importance. Their libraries are funded and staffed jointly by the Italian government. I had scheduled a week in Praglia, mainly to examine the manuscript mentioned above. On my arrival, the state archivist brought me the five bound volumes of the work. Two of the volumes contained nearly three hundred pages describing Vaggioli's experiences as a missionary in New Zealand between 1879 and 1887. I asked the archivist's permission to photocopy some of the material. He refused, saying the manuscript was too fragile to be photocopied and that I would have to take notes by hand. I feverishly set to, in an endeavour to copy as much information as I could. In the meantime, however, I had established a rapport with the monastery's head archivist, Dom Callisto Carpenese, since deceased, who was keenly interested in my project. Towards the end of my stay, he asked me if I would like any of the manuscript photocopied! I replied – 'The whole New Zealand section'. He said that would be no problem and that he would also arrange for it to be couriered down to

Rome, where I would later be staying. I was thankful that Church and State were not entirely in accord on this occasion.

At that time, my research was related primarily to backgrounding Vaggioli's *Storia della Nuova Zelanda*. I had hoped, during my visit to Italy, to obtain my own set of the two volumes.[5] Dom Callisto informed me, however, that very few copies existed because of the British government's request for the work's suppression on the basis of its stinging criticism of the effects on Maori of British colonialism. To verify this allegation, for which there was no documentary evidence, Dom Callisto advised me to visit his Benedictine confrère, Dom Anselmo Bussoni, at the monastery of San Giovanni Evangelista in Parma, where the volumes had been collected, housed and later destroyed.

On my arrival, Dom Anselmo confirmed the story, stating that as a young monk in the same monastery, he had witnessed their destruction over time. Elements of the two accounts puzzled me, however, particularly the sequence and timing of events. When I made a subsequent private research visit to Italy in November–December 2000, I tried again to contact Dom Anselmo. In Dom Anselmo's temporary absence from the monastery, another monk, Dom Angelo Galletti, replied to my email. He volunteered a summary of events which, fortunately, helped to put the pieces of the puzzle together. His statement is probably the closest one will get to the truth regarding this extraordinary episode:

> ... It was I who spoke to Dom Callisto Carpenese[6] confirming that the British authorities, through diplomatic channels, had had the volumes of Dom Felice Vaggioli's *Storia della Nuova Zelanda* removed from circulation because they considered it unflattering towards England. We have still not been able to find written evidence of this diplomatic request, but it would have occurred before 1930. Some of my confrères affirm that it would have happened at the beginning of the Fascist period. I, however, believe it would have been at the turn of the twentieth century. The destruction of the books would have been initiated within the monastery to get rid of an encumbrance. The volumes were slowly destroyed from the 1930s to the 1950s. We kept only one copy, held in our monastic archives.[7]

Besides Mostardi's biography and the Praglia manuscript of Vaggioli's autobiography, the other major source of information regarding Vaggioli was a large collection of letters I was shown when I visited the Monastery of Santa Maria della Castagna in Genoa in 1996.[8] These were letters Vaggioli had written from Gisborne, the Waikato and Auckland to his superiors in Italy. I discovered a smaller cache of letters from Gisborne and Coromandel on my second visit to Praglia monastery.[9] There is also, however, tantalising anecdotal oral information about Vaggioli from some Maori sources. Kaumatua I have consulted have told me that he had a significant, sustained, informed and close relationship with Maori, and was known as Ta Waho[10] on the East Coast and also as Whetaui, a transliterated version of his name.[11] This is an aspect of his life which has evoked controversy in Maori circles, not helped by the fact that

Vaggioli himself paradoxically makes little mention of involvement with Maori in his autobiography or letters, while Part 2 of the first volume of his *Storia della Nuova Zelanda* provides a 540-page scholarly, detailed study of Maori life and customs, including Italian translations of *waiata, pihe* and *karakia*.[12]

BIOGRAPHICAL NOTES

Domenico (Felice being his professed name) Vaggioli (1845–1921) was a Benedictine monk of the Cassinese Congregation of the Primitive Observance. He was born in Bastia, Tuscany, on 8 November 1845. When he was thirteen, he entered Pontebosio Seminary. On reaching the age for military service, according to Mostardi[13] he felt a reluctance to take up arms and became a conscientious objector, fleeing his home territory, the duchy of Modena, and hiding in the Lombardy/Veneto region, which was under Austrian rule. This event gave rise to the title of his manuscript autobiography, 'A Deserter's Adventures'. That same year, 1863, Vaggioli entered Praglia monastery, beginning his novitiate on 15 January 1864. He was professed a religious on 29 June 1865, the last person to do this before the suppression of religious orders in Italy by the government.

The threatening annexation of Venetia and the 1866 law of suppression placed Vaggioli in extreme peril. During the night of 24 June 1866, instead of going to matins, Vaggioli and some other monks took the train to Austria, seeking refuge in Lambach monastery in upper Austria, clearly out of reach of the Italian government. He was later sent by his superior to the monastery of Pierre-qui-vire to learn French and practise austerity. The bracing regime included a mainly vegetarian diet, observing a strict rule of silence, sleeping robed on boards, and daily farm work, which apparently affected his health but strengthened young Vaggioli's will.[14] It was also intended that he would later be sent to form a new religious community in Monaco, but this did not eventuate. On 8 December 1871 Vaggioli took his solemn vows as a religious and on 24 February 1872 he was ordained a priest. In 1876 he was sent as a missionary to the island of Gerba in Tunisia to work in a mostly Muslim Berber community. There Vaggioli studied local languages and sought to establish good relations with Muslims and local Jews. Missionary life was not easy. Abbot Romarico Flugi cited Vaggioli's need to sail sixty miles in a dhow to get to confession as one illustration of the obstacles his Benedictine missionaries faced.[15]

In 1879 Vaggioli's superiors decided to send him to New Zealand. Abbot-General Dom Nicola Canevello's original intention was to select Vaggioli for India,[16] but Fr Adalbert Sullivan, the Pro-Visitor of the English Province, persuaded him to change his mind and send Vaggioli instead to New Zealand. Even in these early days, Vaggioli had a low opinion of the man who would later be his superior in New Zealand: 'How could the cornerstone and Superior of the new mission be the man who had completely ruined the English Province?'[17]

Out of obedience Vaggioli accepted his new posting, but not without foreboding: 'I went to New Zealand believing that our mission would not succeed, and things did not work out well. After seven years I returned to Europe to avoid witnessing the mission's collapse.'[18] The reason he gives here is at odds with that of ill-health, which he later repeatedly pleaded to his superiors. In the context of Vaggioli's on-going criticisms of Fr Sullivan's chronic mismanagement of mission finances, it offers a more convincing explanation for his return.

Vaggioli accompanied to New Zealand a fellow Benedictine priest, four lay brothers and the newly appointed Catholic Bishop of Auckland, Archbishop Steins SJ, on board the *Ringarooma*. On 23 December 1879 they reached Auckland. A year later they were followed by another six monks, mostly from the Ramsgate Bendictine community in England. Newton, in Auckland, was assigned to the Benedictines as their main centre. At the beginning of 1880 Vaggioli was appointed as Gisborne's parish priest, much to his consternation, as his knowledge of English was minimal, gleaned mainly from a small English–Italian dictionary he had purchased in Malta en route to New Zealand. A Mr Tierry, a French school teacher, fortunately befriended Vaggioli and tutored him in English.

The Gisborne mission was in considerable debt because Fr Chastagnon, Vaggioli's predecessor, had built a large church with the help of loans. As he reports in 'A Deserter's Adventures', Vaggioli managed to clear the debt within two and a half years, making the final payment to the Bank of New Zealand in June 1882. By October that year he was recalled to Auckland by his superior, Fr Adalbert Sullivan, to apply his financial acumen to a greater debt: on St Benedict's church in Newton. Vaggioli patiently worked on this task until January 1884. However, the stress involved severely affected his health. In October 1884 his doctor advised him that he had heart disease and might not have long to live unless he had complete rest. Vaggioli took a brief holiday in the Waikato and his health improved. On his return to Auckland, he asked Fr Sullivan to release him from his financial responsibilities; the request was reluctantly granted.

Vaggioli had his Order's permission to return to Europe, but Fr Sullivan was opposed to it. Vaggioli put his terms to Sullivan. Either he allow him to go to a less strenuous mission in New Zealand, or he would return to Europe. Towards the end of January 1885, Sullivan appointed Vaggioli to Coromandel, which had been without a resident priest for six months. Though enthusiastic and working with his typical dedication, Vaggioli found that Coromandel was not an easy posting. His health again deteriorated, exacerbated by the rugged environment, extensive travelling and the unpredictable torrential weather. In his sojourn as Coromandel's parish priest, Vaggioli gained considerable popularity among his Catholic parishioners, and also apparently with local Protestants. When he resigned his position, he received an emotional send-off and generous farewell gifts from Catholics and Protestants alike, an untypical occurrence for those sectarian times.

On 25 July 1887, after a brief stay in Auckland, Vaggioli left New Zealand, never to return. Back in Italy, he assumed the important post of Abbot Visitor of the Italian province of his order in October 1888. While engaged in this role he also began to write his two-volume *Storia della Nuova Zelanda e dei Suoi Abitatori,* which he published at his own expense in 1891 and 1896.[19] Vaggioli left his position as Abbot Visitor in 1896 and concentrated on his writing. From 1910 until his death on 23 April 1921, foreseen by himself some twelve years previously,[20] he occupied the prestigious position of Superior of San Giorgio Maggiore monastery in Venice. His funeral was presided over by Cardinal La Fontaine, Patriarch of Venice, who preached the eulogy.

Vaggioli's final days were carefully recorded in the monastery's chronicle. His doctor's diagnosis was stomach cancer. On his death bed, he begged his fellow monks' forgiveness for any lack of charity or inattention to the Benedictine Rule on his part. His chronicler commented that Vaggioli was, in fact, a stickler for the Rule and would freely and frankly reprove confrères for transgressions. After a period of delirium, Vaggioli briefly rallied, as though, according to the chronicler, 'struck by a marvellous vision',[21] and then died.

A DESERTER'S ADVENTURES

In the preface to his autobiography, Vaggioli goes to some lengths to explain his self-description as 'a deserter' in a favourable light. His rationale is presented here in his own words:

> The term *'deserter'* [*refrattario* in Italian] used in the title of my autobiography is not strictly accurate, because it describes someone who, having gone before a military board and been passed as fit, then escapes to another country to avoid military service. I should really have used the expression *failed to report for military service (renitente alla leva).* This term applies to a twenty-year-old male who does not physically appear before a military board, nor recognise government authority. Because of this failure, he is declared by the authorities as *having failed to report for military service.* In common parlance, the two terms are used interchangeably, and I have followed this convention. But strictly speaking, they are not synonyms. I consider that I failed to report for military service rather than that I deserted.[22]

In modern terms, without wishing to detract from Vaggioli's clear distinctions, he could be seen as a conscientious objector, though he did actually evade conscription by fleeing into the Veneto region, not then under Italian authority. He describes his motive for desertion or 'draft dodging' in detail in a later section of the autobiography (p. 180):

> I had been considered a deserter by the new Italian government because in 1865 I did not present myself before a board for military service. I was, however, already a professed religious under the Austrian government, which then ruled the Veneto region. This act[23] violated the ecclesiastical and civil laws of preceding governments. I was so incensed that I decided to emigrate rather than obey an unjust law.[24]

The actual autobiography comprises five bound volumes in unpublished manuscript form, housed, as mentioned earlier, in Praglia monastery near Padua in northern Italy. Books One and Two cover the period from Vaggioli's birth in 1845 until 1863. Book Three is entitled 'The Deserter, A Missionary in Africa' and Book Four 'The Deserter, A Missionary in the Antipodes'. Book Five has the title 'The Deserter's Return to the Cloisters'. There is a slight complication in that the New Zealand section of the autobiography actually spans both Books Four and Five. This section was begun in 1909 at Subiaco and completed in 1911 in Venice. In my translation I have treated this section of the autobiography as a complete and separate work, though retaining Vaggioli's chapter titles. I have included the final section describing Vaggioli's departure from New Zealand as the final part of chapter nine, rather than the beginning of a new chapter made by the author in the original manuscript.[25]

Vaggioli's autobiography, unlike his *Storia della Nuova Zelanda,* is not written as a scholarly study for a general, discerning audience. It was, however, written for *an* audience, rather than as a personal diary, and is characterised accordingly with occasional references to the 'reader'. My surmise is that Vaggioli considered his colourful life and exotic experiences, particularly as a missionary, to be of sufficient interest to engage a wider audience than his fellow monks, but one that was conservative, Catholic and partisan, like himself. The Italian manuscript has never been published in its original language and thus the translation of the New Zealand section into English is the only part to have seen the light of day.

Vaggioli's copperplate script is a translator's delight. His prose style, however, lacks the elegance and economy of his *Storia,* possibly because it was not polished for publication. In 'A Deserter's Adventures' Vaggioli is opinionated, patronising and garrulous. Yet the force and individuality of his personality is constantly apparent in his writing, and there is an immediacy which is particularly vivid in his recall of disputes and dramatic events experienced in New Zealand. In my translation, I have 'tightened' (edited) the text when Vaggioli, in my view, was driven towards unnecessary repetition. But in all other respects, I have tried to be faithful to the original text. The other problem arising from this being a previously unpublished work is the absence of a clear chronological structure. I have added approximate dates to the chapter titles to help the reader.

DOM FELICE VAGGIOLI, THE PARADOX

Vaggioli's lifetime spanned a period of huge change. The controversial monk embodied many paradoxical elements inherent in the degree of upheaval caused by the dismantling of absolutism and the emergence of a modern state. Dramatic change was nowhere more evident than in Italy itself, which passed from a hybrid collection of kingdoms, principalities and fiefdoms to a single unified state in the wake of the Risorgimento. Steeped in the traditions and teachings of the Catholic Church and entering the Benedictine Order in his adolescence, Vaggioli viewed the emergence of modern secularism and socialism with loathing. The dismemberment of the Papal States, the unification of Italy and its concomitant anti-clericalism were anathema to him, and he continued his personal crusade against secularism in colonial New Zealand. Yet, throughout his life, Vaggioli maintained a lively curiosity about the modern world, studying and embracing its technologies and avidly utilising its advancements in communication. As a young monk, he studied French and German, using the latest learning methods. In New Zealand, in spite of being almost immediately plunged into an English-speaking environment, Vaggioli quickly learnt the language, eventually gaining a reputation as an eloquent preacher. He embraced journalism with a similar enthusiasm and quickness, instantly recognising the connection between the medium and the message, and becoming an advocate of the Catholic press in New Zealand. Curiosity, considerable intellectual ability and a strong sense of justice led him to write his massive two-volume *Storia della Nuova Zelanda* on his return to Italy. As an outside observer, he was able to present what he saw as an unbiased view of the corrosive effects of British colonialism on the disenfranchised Maori, the indigenous population, and offer an insightful critique which had to wait a hundred years to be matched by modern scholars. In later years Vaggioli, as Abbot Visitor for his order, introduced electricity to Subiaco monastery, literally taking it out of the dark ages.

As he frequently noted, Vaggioli suffered from ill-health. His self-discipline, however, reinforced by the principles of monastic rule, enabled him to achieve considerable feats as a monk, missionary, reformer and writer. The completion of the *Storia della Nuova Zelanda* was carried out under the most difficult circumstances, written when the other monks were asleep. Vaggioli placed himself under a punishing regime and at times he appeared to be as stern and hard on others as he was on himself. But the autobiography also frequently reveals a compassionate side to his nature, illustrated, for example, by his seeking out the distraught Fr Breikan, his confrère, who had been heartlessly ostracised by the Benedictine community in Newton and left to fend for himself at Puhoi, an impoverished rural settlement outside Auckland. Vaggioli sensitively befriended this psychologically fragile man and eventually arranged his repatriation.[26]

Vaggioli's sense of independence is the trait which, in my view, most represents his personality, allowing full rein for a quixotic individualistic surety and sharpness from an unexpected quarter. While he was recognised throughout his life for his frankness, it was his independence of spirit which at times alarmed and confounded his superiors, fellow priests and parishioners, and anyone who had the misfortune to affront or challenge him. He was unafraid to speak for himself as himself, without losing sight of the fact that he was a monk. His clear, logical mind and absolute certainty regarding his Catholic faith and values made him a formidable force. As a young monk, he had been criticised in Rome for forthrightly expressing his own view that the Gerba mission should be retained by the Benedictine Order. It was expected that a monk would be submissive. Vaggioli wryly commented, on learning of the criticism, that he would regard it as a compliment and a quality that he would happily take to the grave.[27] His forthrightness was appreciated in many circles in colonial New Zealand and he was even invited to stand for Parliament in Coromandel, an invitation he declined.[28]

Vaggioli is now known mainly for his *History of New Zealand and Its Inhabitants,* but he died with a realisation that his book had not gained the wide audience he had hoped for it. He may, however, have gained considerable solace from a letter from Gisborne he retained in his personal correspondence. It was from a close friend, Mr Jennings, a member of his parish committee, lamenting on his young daughter's behalf, Vaggioli's departure from Gisborne:

'You will not credit me when I tell you that our little Mary never goes to bed without saying her prayers and her last words are God bless Father Goli.'[29]

JOHN CROCKETT
Auckland, May 2001

Felice Vaggioli and Colonial Catholicism in New Zealand

As the s.s. *Ringarooma* berthed in Auckland at 2 a.m. on 23 December 1879, a large crowd waited patiently to greet its most distinguished passenger, Walter Steins, the newly appointed Catholic bishop. Among his entourage was a 34-year-old Italian Benedictine priest, Felice Vaggioli. Despite the hour, many of these folk then accompanied Steins and party to the Bishop's residence in Ponsonby, where the Hobson Band played 'Home, Sweet Home' on a lawn specially decorated with pretty Venetian lanterns.[1]

The joy and relief felt by Auckland Catholics at finally having a bishop to lead them was also evident in the several addresses presented at a formal reception the following evening. As one speaker remarked, the diocese had 'been deprived of an episcopal head for some five or six years.'[2] This long interregnum had begun when Bishop Croke returned to Ireland in 1874, after which the Auckland diocese was turned down by a variety of religious orders. Following his appointment, Steins, a Dutch Jesuit and former Archbishop of Calcutta, had immediately arranged for assistance from the Cassinese Congregation of the Order of St Benedict. It agreed that its English Province should staff the diocese for a two-year trial period, after which time both parties could decide whether the Benedictines should take it over permanently.[3]

The New Zealand mission gave the Benedictines' English Province a new focus for its enthusiasm and a chance to recover from a spectacular financial disaster during the 1870s. The Auckland diocese had itself undergone a similar collapse under its first bishop, the Frenchman Jean Baptiste François Pompallier, a situation only partly rectified by his Irish successor, Thomas William Croke. Felice Vaggioli's autobiography gives us a rare insight into these events. The account of Pompallier's problems with the Marists and his fondness for the bottle draws on stories told by clergy who had lived through these events.[4]

While Vaggioli's verdict on Croke's careerist approach to his Auckland sojourn has been confirmed by modern scholarship, his dismissal of the Irishman as an 'unsuccessful bishop ... not suited to this mission' seems rather harsh.[5] The Italian priest gave higher marks to those leaders he knew personally, but in fact all colonial Catholic bishops faced similar problems, not least the vagaries of an unstable economy, prone to boom and bust. Much depended on their administrative skills and ability to generate financial resources. Pompallier spectacularly lacked the first, while Croke had plenty of the second. As well as his private wealth, Croke was fortunate enough to arrive when the Thames goldfields were beginning to produce their riches in abundance.[6]

The need to ensure that their burgeoning diocese was adequately staffed often led Catholic bishops to rely on itinerant priests. In 1867 the Bishop of Wellington, Philip Viard, defended this practice to his ecclesiastical superior. 'On all sides I was loudly implored for priests and the Society of Mary could not furnish them ... Must souls be abandoned? Could we refuse the subjects Providence sent us?'[7] Even apart from those 'renegades' described by Vaggioli, missionary priests were usually strong personalities unused to and resentful of close episcopal supervision, and if dissatisfied easily able to find a place in a neighbouring colony. In an attempt to secure a regular supply of clergy, bishops often chose to contract with powerful religious orders, who prized their independence. Relations frequently turned sour: the Marists left Pompallier, the Franciscans fell out with Croke, while the Benedictines made life difficult for their confrère, John Edmund Luck (Bishop of Auckland 1882-96).[8]

This said, Vaggioli was correct to accuse Croke of having 'a jaundiced view of religious orders'.[9] The explanation for his attitude lies at the heart of the conflict raging within colonial Catholicism in these years.

The British Empire was to Irish Catholics what the Roman Empire had been to Jews and early Christians – the alien organism by which a faith was carried to the four corners of the earth.[10] During the nineteenth century Irish bishops and clergy fostered a distinctly Irish expatriate culture among their immigrant flocks. Behind this phenomenon was the so-called 'devotional revolution' in post-Famine Ireland, associated with the reign of Paul Cullen, Cardinal Archbishop of Dublin.[11] As a result, the Irish Catholics, lay and cleric, who peopled Britain's colonies, brought an aggressive, ultramontane Catholicism in their cultural baggage.

For men like Thomas Croke, rival Catholic traditions as represented by the Marist and Benedictine orders were seen as more dangerous to the Catholic faith than the Church's avowed enemies. After his arrival in Auckland, Croke commented privately that 'an Irish Bishop was not sent here a day too soon. Had there been more of a delay, I fear the faith would have died out altogether.'[12] His fellow Irishman, Patrick Moran (Bishop of Dunedin 1869–95), was equally dismissive of the efforts of the Marist missionaries in his diocese. 'The Frenchmen are good men and respectable priests, but they have the interests of their order, as they call it, to attend to, and in doing so they appear to me to have satisfied themselves with saying their prayers.'[13] Croke and Moran plotted to carve up New Zealand between themselves, before the former's premature departure for a more exalted field of action as Archbishop of Cashel (1875–1902). This coincided with a distancing by the Vatican authorities from Irish ecclesiastical politicking, which was expressed in the appointments of a number of English and Italian bishops to Australasian sees.

The years Vaggioli spent in New Zealand (1879–87) witnessed an ecclesiastical arm-wrestle over who would be chosen as archbishop, which Catholic see would become the metropolitan and who would control the newly-created bishopric of Christchurch. It was largely a battle between Wellington and Dunedin, although the Auckland clergy made desultory attempts to push the claims of their own diocese.[14] Rome's eventual decision was a crushing blow to Patrick Moran and the Irish secular clergy throughout the country. In May 1887, the English-born Marist Francis Redwood was appointed as head of the newly established ecclesiastical province of New Zealand, with yet another English Marist, John Joseph Grimes, named as Bishop of Christchurch. The disappointed Irishmen attributed their reverse to an anti-Irish plot by English government officials active in Rome, and accused their rivals of aiming to denationalise Irish Catholic colonial youth.[15]

Such charges reflected a heightened ethnic consciousness within Irish Catholic communities overseas, responding to turbulent events in Ireland during the 1880s. A newly formed Irish Parliamentary Party, led by Charles Stewart Parnell, adopted obstructive tactics in the House of Commons to promote the demand for Irish Home Rule. Their cause was complicated by the Irish Land War (1879–82), with its attendant boycotting, landlord shooting, and sporadic rural violence, all of which was reported in lurid detail in the colonies. In May 1882 came the gruesome killing of the newly appointed Irish chief secretary, Lord Frederick Cavendish, and the under-secretary, T.H. Burke. The Phoenix Park Murders were carried out by the Invincibles, an extremist society of Fenian background, but many wrongly suspected Parnellite complicity.

While the Catholic press followed Irish events closely, the issue was brought most alive for New Zealanders by the visits of Irish nationalist politicians: John and William Redmond in 1883, John Dillon, Thomas Deasy and Sir Thomas Esmonde six years later. The Redmond brothers, both members of the British Parliament, had a rough time in Australia, with many halls and theatres closed to them, and prominent Irishmen keeping their distance.[16] Irish Home Rule was widely regarded as a threat to imperial unity. Passions ran high on both sides. Colonial Catholic leaders whose misfortune it was not to be Irish needed to be especially careful when handling this thorny issue.

In early 1883 Vaggioli's new boss and fellow-Benedictine, Bishop John Edmund Luck, stepped blindly into this minefield. Despite a declared sympathy with Ireland's past woes, he knew little of the country save as the graveyard of his family's wealth.[17] Appalled by the violence of the Land War, the English-born Luck was deeply suspicious of secret societies and itinerant agitators. He described John Redmond as 'a diplomatic agent whose mission is to work on the national feelings of the Irish colonists and implicate them in the meshes of political leagues and parties.'[18] He discountenanced the Redmond mission and instructed his clergy to keep their distance. 'I do not see the wisdom or utility of mixing oneself up, in an adopted country, in the feuds and strifes of the land of one's birth, especially when the land of one's adoption is at the very antipodes of the field of action.'[19]

Luck's stance earned him the poisoned tribute of the *New Zealand Herald* as 'an Englishman first, a Catholic afterwards'. His Irish flock was less favourably impressed. Several deputations urged him to alter his position, which was subject to hostile comment in the Catholic press. Stories of his anti-Irishness spread rapidly in New Zealand and abroad.[20] This was less than fair to Luck, who denied any wish 'to impose my own opinions on anyone', and refrained from condemning the Irish National League, the organisation currently being promoted among the Irish at home and abroad.[21] While Luck did not attend John Redmond's lecture, neither did his fellow bishops, Moran and Redwood.[22] Archbishop Goold of Melbourne also issued a circular 'instructing his priests to avoid identifying themselves with political movements or agitations'.[23] Luck was better attuned than Vaggioli to the Holy See's disquiet at recent Irish developments, which was regularly expressed in formal censures (albeit prompted by English diplomatic pressure).[24]

Accused of anti-Irish bigotry, the new bishop received little help from his Benedictine confrères who knew him better. On the contrary, as Vaggioli recounts, they were not above using the issue to discredit him.

They had several reasons for welcoming Luck coolly. Some, who had been his rivals for the mitre, believed that he would judge them harshly. Men used to exercising authority over him found it hard now to be his subjects. Adalbert Maria Sullivan (also known as O'Sullivan) is the villain of Vaggioli's autobiography. On probation as heir apparent to the Auckland see, despite his earlier misdemeanours, he plunged into an ambitious property deal, amassing large debts, before fleeing his responsibilities. Vaggioli warned Steins that Sullivan had done all this before; Luck did not need telling, as it was his patrimony that Sullivan had squandered on property speculations in Ireland, almost wrecking the English Province in the process.[25]

Vaggioli was the exception among Luck's confrères, attributing his 'foolish' action over the Redmond mission to inexperience and ignorance, rather than malevolence towards the Irish nationalist cause.[26] He urged Luck to follow the example of the Bishop of Wellington, Francis Redwood, who made a fetish of his Irish sympathies.[27] Redwood's nuanced approach to the subject was apparent when tutoring his friend Grimes on the delicacy needed in any reference the bishop-elect might make to Irish politics:

> A feeling ... against you as being not Hibernian enough, in fact anti-Hibernian, has been strongly expressed in the New Zealand Tablet, and there are some who may be rendered cold in your regard on account of it. So be particularly cautious in your speeches and sermons, letters, etc., to say nothing against the Irish, but imitating

Cardinal Manning, always have some kind thing to say in their favour, and if possible, express your sympathy with them in their exertions to obtain Home Rule.[28]

Luck gradually altered his stance, a shift made easier by British Prime Minister W.E. Gladstone's conversion to Home Rule, which then gained respectability in colonial eyes.[29] He partially redeemed himself in late 1889, when attending a public lecture given by the Irish MP John Dillon.[30] Six years later he was reported to have 'warmly received' the ex-Fenian founder of the Irish Land League, Michael Davitt, who was, however, more favourably impressed by Luck's Anglican counterpart, W.G. Cowie.[31]

Luck was not the only one to be surprised by the fervour of Vaggioli's Irish nationalism, or by the depth of his knowledge. After two years of special study, the Italian priest felt confident enough to lecture the aristocracy of Church and State on the subject, also to make it the keynote of occasional public speeches. He listed his many sources – 'books, periodicals, British, Irish and American journals, as well as Australian and New Zealand publications'[32] – but it is more likely that Vaggioli's Irish creed was a by-product of his crash course in the English language, his poring over the Catholic newspapers, the *Freeman's Journal* and the *Tablet*, both of which gave their readers a weekly defence of Ireland past and present.

Vaggioli believed that his historical judgement was 'totally impartial', but his version of Irish history is romanticised and highly coloured. 'Ireland has been denigrated, reviled and plundered by the British Government, which since 1540 has used all the means within its power to make it Protestant, but without success.'[33] His corrosive critique of British misgovernment in Ireland recalls similar strictures on the authorities in New Zealand in his *Storia della Nuova Zelanda*. Vaggioli was a man of firm beliefs and equally firm prejudices. He liked the Irish, was impressed by their religious devotion and grateful for their generous acceptance of him. He was aware of their human weaknesses (male drunkenness, female proclivity to mixed marriages), but minimised them. While his autobiography provides savage evidence of the failings of the Irish colonial clergy, he placed the model of heroic faith witnessed in Ireland before his parishioners to motivate them to do their religious duty.

Why did the Irish Catholics, among others, respond to him? Vaggioli would not have been the first 'foreign' priest to be frozen out by an unwelcoming Irish flock. His fearless advocacy of Irish nationalism merely highlighted his many other qualities. Once he had overcome the handicap of not knowing a word of English, Vaggioli proved to be fluent and persuasive in speech and writing. He was obviously a man of education and culture, one who impressed Protestants. He became involved in colonial life, managing to be fiercely partisan and also community-minded. His nose for intrigue overcame a belief that priests should stay out of politics. In the 1881 East Coast election he helped to secure the return of a Presbyterian over a Catholic candidate. He could himself have been Gisborne's Hibernian branch president or even Coromandel's member of Parliament.[34]

Vaggioli sheds a great deal of light on New Zealand Catholicism in the colonial era. He shows how deeply ethnic stratification affected all the Catholic religious orders, and especially his own. Censorious of his colleagues' failings, on which he kept Rome well briefed, he regularly predicted the failure of the Benedictine mission in New Zealand. He has given us rare details of the life of a colonial Catholic missionary: duties, income, and concerns, even diet. Also a valuable insight into Catholic ecclesiastical politics and the Irish Catholic sub-culture: its concern with respectability, avoiding scandal, being able to look the Protestant neighbour in the eye; its problems of drink, poverty and transience; the prevalence of mixed marriages and their cause; the survival of the Irish 'wake', which as in Ireland frequently turned into a drunken shambles.

In some ways Vaggioli's autobiography resembles a snapshot album of late nineteenth-century New Zealand by a perceptive Italian visitor. He disapproves of drunken Irish Catholics and immoral British Protestants (especially those living in Auckland), the sights of Rotorua recall Dante's Inferno, while the Coromandel mines bring the Roman catacombs to his mind. Vaggioli was a hard man to ignore. He relished controversy, taking up his pen to fight against Freemasonry and secular education, for state aid to Catholic schools and in defence of the Catholic missions.[35] Naturally, he is the hero of his own story: he confounds his enemies, tutors his social and religious superiors, performs financial miracles, and wins converts to his faith. In his account of the demise of the Benedictine mission and of the *Freeman's Journal* there is more than a hint of 'après moi le déluge'.

RORY SWEETMAN
Dunedin, June 2001

A Deserter's Adventures
by Dom Felice Vaggioli, OSB

NEW ZEALAND BOUND

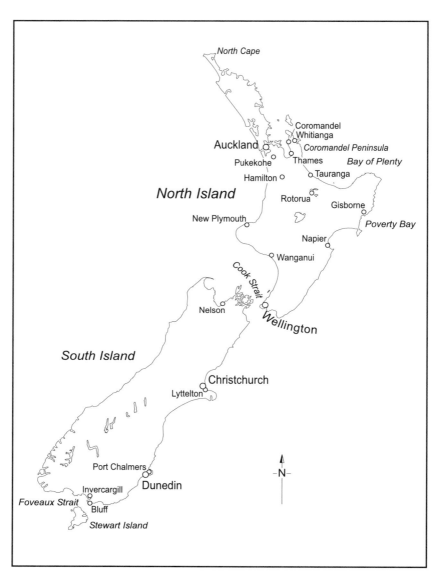

Map of New Zealand showing places mentioned in the text.

NOTE: Throughout the text, Vaggioli has converted pound sterling values into francs. The conversion rate he used was £1 = 25 francs.

CHAPTER ONE

Towards Our Destination
(8 TO 23 DECEMBER 1879)

SUMMARY. − 1. Aboard a new steamer. − 2. Second class − a proper pigsty! The lay brothers join us in first class. − 3. Terrible weather and seasickness. − 4. At Bluff, southern extremity of New Zealand. − 5. Dunedin. − 6. Christchurch. − 7. Wellington, the colonial capital. − 8. Napier. − 9. Gisborne. − 10. Tauranga. − 11. We safely reach our destination. − 12. Evening reception. − 13. *Storia della Nuova Zelanda.*

1. When we reached Melbourne's main wharf we were shown the steamer on which we were to embark for New Zealand.* The voyage from Melbourne to New Zealand's first port of contact at the bottom of the South Island traversed 18 degrees latitude east, or 1080 miles (1998 kilometres). Three steamers plying from Melbourne and Sydney provided a weekly postal service between Australia and New Zealand. The Melbourne vessel travelled to the southern tip of New Zealand, then up the coast, stopping at every port as it voyaged north. Clearing North Cape, it went on to Sydney, Australia. The Sydney steamer did the opposite run, heading for the North Cape of New Zealand, travelling down the east coast of both islands and then leaving for Melbourne. The New Zealand 'Union Jack' Company provided this maritime service, as well as a coastal run through another company.†

I can't remember the name of the steamer we boarded.‡ It was a solid iron, approximately 2000-tonne vessel, and squat, ugly and cramped. It had only first and second class. First class, which we priests occupied, was reasonably well-appointed and clean with three and four-berth cabins. Our lay brothers occupied second class. Once I was on board I went to see my cabin and inspect my luggage to ensure that nothing was missing. Finding everything intact and in order, I went back on deck to view the impressive port. At about four the steamer weighed anchor for New Zealand. Towards seven it cleared the narrow, treacherous harbour mouth. It was a beautiful, calm evening.

---

* The reference is to the fellow Benedictine priest, four lay brothers and the newly appointed Catholic Bishop of Auckland, Archbishop Steins, who accompanied Vaggioli on his voyage.
† The reference is actually to the 'Union Steamship Company' which includes the Union Jack in its ensign.
‡ The reference is to the s.s. *Ringarooma*.

2. My companions had gone to sort things out in their cabins and the lay brothers went down to second class to find their berths. I was the first to complete my unpacking and return on deck. Shortly afterwards Br Joseph joined me. I asked him if he was happy with his berth and whether everything was fine. Crestfallen, he replied, 'It's shocking … it's a proper pigsty! You can't sit anywhere. There's nowhere to eat. No beds, no cabins, only filthy straw mattresses tossed on the floor! This is so-called second class!'

I expressed my surprise and disbelief, but he replied, 'See for yourself. You'll find out that the situation is even worse than my description.'

The Jesuit lay brother, equally distressed, joined our conversation. He said that it would be impossible to live in such squalid conditions, which were suitable only for animals. I couldn't disguise my incredulity. The two lay brothers then said, 'Come and have a look. You'll see that we're not exaggerating.'

'I'm coming right now,' I replied. 'Lead on. I'll follow you. You know the way.' They led me towards the bow, to the entrance-way to second class. I peered down through the hatch into the squalid interior. It was stinking and filthy! The staircase was flimsy and perpendicular. Aghast, I exclaimed to my companions, 'This can't be second class. It must be the ship's boys' and sailors' quarters.'

'No, no,' they replied, 'it really is second class! The steward put our luggage down here and this is where we were taken when we presented our tickets.'

I simply could not believe that this was second class. I clambered down the rickety staircase to the pigsty below. I noticed two men standing. One of them, a passenger, was eating out of a mess-tin. The other was a steward. I turned to them and spoke in French, 'Is this second class?' 'Yes,' they replied, as if it were of no consequence. I ventured into the squalid surroundings, and my companions followed me. I was dumbfounded. Second class here was much worse than poor emigrants' fourth class. The floor was dirty and strewn with rubbish. There was a small rough, filthy table three metres long and a metre wide with four or five wooden forms in a corner of the room. The rest of the area was divided into three compartments which each had wooden bunks two metres high, four metres long and a metre wide, with no privacy. Straw-filled sacks, rather than mattresses, and blankets lay on the floor. That was the bedding. There were no pillows, sheets or pillowslips. I came down to earth with a jolt! Only poor beggars could expect such conditions. I said to my companions, 'You can't stay here! It's absolutely disgusting! I'm going to talk to the archbishop and get you shifted.' We left and returned on deck.

I immediately went to the prelate and described to him in detail the conditions in second class where the brothers had been put. His Lordship was incredulous, not having come across squalid conditions in second class in any postal or passenger steamer he had been on before. The lay brothers, however, confirmed my description as absolutely true. Seeing he was still unconvinced,

I urged him to go and see the pigsty for himself. Then he would appreciate what second class was really like. He went down and shortly afterwards returned. He confirmed that it was not fit for the lay brothers. The good bishop spoke to the captain and had them transferred to join us in first class. He paid the difference. All the Union Company's second class is the same.* The bishop said that it was designed as a deliberate means of exploitation, forcing passengers to transfer to first class, ensuring handsome profits for the company.

3. The weather continued to be pleasant near Van Diemen's Land, or Tasmania, south of Melbourne, but once we entered the Pacific Ocean the situation changed. The mighty ocean demonstrated its ugly mood and capriciousness. There was nothing *pacific* about it. New Zealand lies in the Pacific Ocean, east of Australia and a thousand miles from it at its closest point.

On the first evening the sea was calm and I ate in the dining room with the others. But soon afterwards my stomach felt unsettled, and I decided to retire earlier than usual. At nightfall I turned in. The steamer pitched and rolled throughout the night. I intended to get up early as usual the following morning, but my stomach was still queasy. I felt like being sick, so I stayed in bed. Meanwhile, the ship ploughed on through mountainous seas, causing crockery to break and crash everywhere. The rest had to be secured or it would all have been smashed. I got dressed about 9 a.m. and went on deck to see what the weather was like. A strong, chilly nor'easterly was buffeting the ship. It was raining hard and the sky was leaden. Wind gusts whistled through the rigging and the white-capped sea was menacing. Waves crashed over the bow, drenching the deck and sending spray over us huddled at the stern. My stomach was heaving and I felt so cold that after a few minutes I returned to my cabin. Still in my clothes I went to bed hoping my stomach would settle. At ten o'clock I joined the others for breakfast. There were few passengers in the dining room because many were ill, like me. I tried to drink a little soup to gain some strength but after a few sips I had to rush out and throw up. Bed was the only answer. For the following two or three days I just lay there. The only food I could eat was a piece of dry bread. Stewards brought me meals but I refused them.

The captain said that the weather wasn't too good, but nothing exceptional. According to him this was not unusual weather for the Pacific Ocean. I thought it was terrible! The steamer would normally cover between 330 and 350 miles a day in calm seas. We had rough weather for four or five days and it made much slower progress. On the first day it travelled only 180 miles, on the second 125 miles, on the third 160 miles and on the fourth about 205 miles, as I recall. Then the wind subsided, the sea became calmer and the steamer speeded up.

* Union Steamship Company.

4. Finally, thank God, on 16 December 1879, the morning of the eighth day of our wretched crossing, we reached the first port at the bottom of the South Island. Bluff provided a fine sheltered harbour. It was not a town or village as such, just a few houses scattered around the port and a miserable hotel. The houses were wooden. There was little sign of cultivation and the few plots I saw were small and neglected. A stretch of land extended south and south-east, enclosing and sheltering the harbour. The captain said we would be stopping for four hours to deliver mail and parcels to the train for the towns of Invercargill and Dunedin and unload goods for Bluff.

Many passengers went ashore, some to take the train for their destination and others to stretch their legs and go for a walk. We, too, disembarked for a stroll since it was fine, though a little windy. The bush near the port was cleared, but further beyond it was hilly and forested. The island was mountainous, alpine and still covered in virgin forests. I was not impressed with Bluff and its soil seemed quite poor. The railway, too, was wretched, with a narrow gauge track and no barriers. The station was a miserable wooden shack. At eleven the excuse-for-a-train, with its passengers and mail, departed for Dunedin on a six-hour journey. It would take our steamer about twenty hours. About 12.30 we returned on board for an hour's lunch. Fortunately, after so many days of forced abstinence, I was able to eat. I certainly needed to because I felt very weak. At 2 p.m. the steamer left for Dunedin.

5. It was a further 950 miles nor'-nor'east from Bluff to Auckland, our actual destination. Our journey would take another five or six days, including the various stops up the east coast. The weather was much improved. The wind had dropped considerably, but there was still a swell and the ship rolled slightly. The calmness of the Indian Ocean, however, was a thing of the past. At least I was able to keep something down and take a stroll on deck, in spite of the chilly weather, because the day after leaving Melbourne I had put on all my thick underwear to keep me warm.

About 11 a.m. on 17 December we reached Port Chalmers, near Dunedin. The steamer docked for six hours. Mons. Steins, our two English priests and lay brother decided to take the train to Dunedin and pay their respects to Mons. Moran, the Catholic bishop. Br Joseph, the Jesuit lay brother and I stayed behind. The town of Dunedin was situated on a large plain, about fourteen miles away by rail. It was concealed from the port by surrounding hills. Dunedin's population was about 35,000. As soon as the passengers had disembarked on to the wooden wharf and were seated in the cramped carriages, the train departed.

There was a volcanic hillock about a hundred metres high near the wharf where the steamer berthed. About thirty houses facing the port were scattered on its slopes. It was a settlement in the making. Streets were marked out, but most were rough and hardly begun. There was only a carriage-way leading to the port and it too was rudimentary.

The two lay brothers and I disembarked and climbed half-way up the hill to observe the surrounding countryside. From our vantage point to the far side of the harbour were beautiful, lush fields; very pleasant, I thought. We also admired a few remaining groves kept perhaps as shelter for sheep and cattle. About 4.30 p.m. our trippers returned, accompanied by the Bishop of Dunedin, a small man about fifty years old. We paid our respects and shortly afterwards he and his secretary returned by train to Dunedin. Our steamer was soon on its way again.

6. Once it left the port the ship headed for the town of Christchurch, 180 miles away. I can't remember when we reached Lyttelton harbour, connected by a few miles of rail to Christchurch. As I recall, we arrived at Lyttelton by dusk on 18 December. The town's population was about 30,000. It did not have a Catholic bishop and was part of the Wellington diocese, administered by Marist priests. It was later made a diocese under the Marists. The steamer berthed for just over an hour to unload mail and cargo and soon departed for Wellington, about 180 miles away.

7. I remember reaching Wellington, the colonial capital, about 10 a.m. on 20 December. While not large, the harbour was beautiful and crescent-shaped. The town was built around it like a vast amphitheatre. It was very pleasant and attractive with good roading and some fine reinforced concrete buildings. But most of the houses were wooden because of frequent earthquakes in the area. The population was about 45,000.

As soon as the steamer berthed, we disembarked and went to pay our respects to Mons. Redwood, Marist Bishop of Wellington, and the priests living with him. The Catholic mission was in a very fine location in the centre of town. We were warmly welcomed by the bishop and three priests. We then visited the Catholic cathedral, a large, mostly wooden building, the Marist brothers' substantial school, and the residence of the bishop and missionaries. The bishop offered us refreshments and we then had a small tour of the town.

Wellington is the seat of the colonial government with two chambers, an upper and a lower house. Parliament Buildings is entirely built of wood.* As I recall, it comprises three large buildings three or four storeys high, connected by passages, and is the largest wooden building in the world. Because the steamer was running late, it sped up unloading and departed about 4 p.m.

---

* Vaggioli has mistaken Government Buildings for Parliament Buildings.

8. We continued steaming up the east coast. While there was still light I stayed on the deck looking at the continuous thickly forested North Island coast. The following morning, about 9 a.m. on 21 December, we entered Napier harbour. The steamer stopped for only half an hour to unload mail and a small amount of cargo on to boats which came alongside, and it then continued on its journey. Napier was a township of about 5000 inhabitants. I tried to see it from the ship, but a hill near the shore blocked my view. I could only espy three or four houses scattered near the shore.

9. At dusk the steamer entered Gisborne harbour, or Poverty Bay, a long, wide, well-sheltered bay, but with sand bars at its northern end where the settlement was located. It was impractical to build a wharf and steamers had to stay out to sea. This was the first port we reached which was part of Bishop Steins's Auckland diocese. The settlement, with a population of about 2500 inhabitants, was on a plain near dense hilly bush to the north and a fertile valley to the west. The steamer anchored for about an hour. Once it had unloaded mail and cargo it set off again as nightfall began to cover the land with shadows.

10. At about 11 a.m. on 22 December we entered Tauranga harbour in the Bay of Plenty. It was long, narrow and dotted with dangerous reefs, only some of which appeared above the water. About a kilometre from the port entrance we noticed the hulks of two ships which had come aground some years before, serving as a warning to sailors to be watchful. After half an hour's slow passage through the channel the steamer dropped anchor about 200 metres off the small European settlement of Tauranga to unload mail and cargo. The local Catholic missionary, an Irish Franciscan monk, immediately rowed out and came on board to pay his respects to his new bishop. He stayed and chatted with us until our departure. The friar was a small man dressed like an English clergyman. He would have been more than fifty, but strong and energetic. After nearly two hours the steamer set off again. Its next stop was Auckland, our destination, where it would berth for two days before continuing its voyage via North Cape to Sydney, Australia. At Tauranga I saw native Maori for the first time. They were olive-skinned, tattooed, intelligent, well-proportioned, strong, vigorous and of average height.

11. My overall impression sailing up the east coast of New Zealand was of an extensive country with mountain ranges, virtually uninhabited, uncultivated and covered in bush and virgin forests. The captain told us that we would reach Auckland about midnight, but it was 2 a.m. before we berthed. About midnight a lighthouse beacon indicated that we were about to enter Auckland's large, impressive harbour, but darkness prevented us from seeing its attractive coast and islands. After steaming along the harbour for an hour we passed a

Archbishop Walter Steins SJ arrived in Auckland with Vaggioli, to take up his position as the new bishop.

promontory and could see the town, illuminated by gas lighting, spread out over dark hills. The port stood out even more brightly. At 2 a.m. on 23 December 1879 the steamer berthed at the large wooden wharf and we disembarked. After a forty- eight day voyage from Malta to Auckland, we had finally reached our destination safe and sound. We had left Malta on 4 November and arrived in Auckland on 23 December. I was grateful our odyssey was over.

12. A telegram had been sent from Melbourne that the Bishop of Auckland and missionaries were on board the steamer. Parishioners had been waiting in expectation from the morning of the twenty-second. But a further telegram from Tauranga dashed their hopes of welcoming us that day. We were greeted at the wharf by the vicar-general, local priests and about fifty prominent Catholics. Carriages were drawn up and, after exchanging greetings, we were driven to the bishop's wooden residence in Ponsonby, an Auckland suburb, about two kilometres from the wharf, which had been made ready to receive us. Shortly after our arrival, about 4 a.m., we retired. An official reception was to take place at 11 a.m., as I recall.

St Patrick's Cathedral, Auckland, from Hobson Street, c. 1884. The reception welcoming Mon. Steins to Auckland took place here.

13. In describing my adventures I will not allude to the ancient or modern history of New Zealand, nor refer to the native Maori history, religion, customs, war conduct, etc. They are fully described in my *Storia della Nuova Zelanda*, two large volumes in Italian, published between 1890 and 1895 by Fiaccadori Press, Parma.*

* The reference is to Vaggioli's two-volume *Storia della Nuova Zelanda e dei Suoi Abitatori*. The first volume is a natural history, including a comprehensive study of Maori life, language and customs. The second volume is a social history, from the European discovery of New Zealand to the mid 1880s, providing a critical view of British colonisation. This second volume has been translated into English and published by University of Otago Press (*History of New Zealand and Its Inhabitants*, 2000).

CHAPTER TWO

In Auckland
(LATE 1879 TO EARLY 1880)

PART 1. THE TOWN OF AUCKLAND

SUMMARY. – 1. Its location and size; the harbour. – 2. Population of town and suburbs. Churches, public buildings, denominations. – 3. The Catholic bishop's residence. Catholic churches. The Sisters of Mercy convents. – 4. Commerce. – 5. My overall impressions, good and bad.

1. Auckland is situated at approximately 37 degrees longitude south and 175 degrees latitude east. The town is modern, its planning begun only in 1850.[*] It has a distinctly English character because nearly the whole population are British subjects: English, Irish and Scottish. Auckland is spread across and down the slopes of six or seven hills which can be seen on clearing the last promontory of the harbour. The landscape dips, rises and widens out to the north-west, reaching about 100 metres above sea level. Centuries ago the hills were small volcanoes. About three-quarters of a kilometre further to the north is Mount Eden, a large extinct volcano, about 400 metres high, flanked by hills to the east and west.

The town is spread over six kilometres from east to west and it is about two kilometres in a direct line from the coast to the slopes of Mount Eden. Most of the town is within sight of the clear, tranquil harbour's northern promontory.[†] The majority of houses were wooden, except for a few buildings, such as banks, shops, etc., near the port, which were brick or reinforced concrete. Most of the roading was still unfinished, except for the three main streets and crossroads in the business and port areas. They were well made with wide footpaths. Houses were spread out throughout the town. Only in the main commercial area near the port were houses and shops crammed together. Further beyond, houses had a small front garden and a vegetable patch or lawn at the back.

Auckland harbour is one of the largest and most beautiful in the world. One could really describe the Hauraki Gulf as a huge harbour, about fifty miles long and thirty-five at its widest part. It could contain the naval fleets of the whole world within its sheltered waters. The town, however, uses only the nearest part of the harbour as its port. This is sufficient, even if trade were to increase a hundred-fold.

---

[*] Vaggioli was aware that Auckland had been established by Governor Hobson as capital of New Zealand in 1840. cf. Vaggioli, *ibid.*, p. 100.
[†] The reference is presumably to North Head in Auckland.

2. By 1879 the population was about 52,000, and it was continuing to increase slowly with the arrival of new migrants. Most were Protestants, about 40,000 in all, comprising some sixty different denominations. There were approximately 10,000 Catholics. A few hundred Jews were residents, mostly successful merchants and bankers. There were also just over 200 Chinese working as market gardeners. The town had an Anglican bishop, a fine, well-educated man. He believed that Christ's true Church was the Roman Apostolic Church. He did not convert to Catholicism simply because the Catholic Church could not offer him the stipend and salary his parishioners and the Church Missionary Society paid him. If he recanted his errors, as a family man he would lose his means of support and find himself in a parlous state, as he later confided. There were about thirty Protestant churches, but some were simply a rented room in a private home.

There were five Catholic churches, both small and large. The cathedral near the port was built of black volcanic stone. The rest, like Protestant churches, were wooden. Most of the Catholics were Irish, but there were also about fifty Englishmen and Scots and a few more Italians, mostly non-practising, especially the southerners. Finally, there was a small number of equally lax Frenchmen. Catholics, in general, were poor labourers, soldiers, artisans and domestic servants. But there were some shopkeepers, and some comfortably off, but not wealthy, families. The Irish were generally devout and loyal, practising their religion to the best of their ability. The whole town had only five Catholic priests. The vicar-general had the Parnell parish. Three priests were attached to the cathedral and were responsible for the rest of the town. One, while a parish priest, was also proprietor and editor of the *Freeman*,* a weekly journal. Another cathedral priest said daily Mass for the Sisters of Mercy in Ponsonby, and on Sundays two went out to say Mass, one at Newton and the other elsewhere. There were only two Sunday Masses at the cathedral.

3. The bishop's residence was about 1500 metres from the cathedral, in the north-east corner of the town, in the suburb of Ponsonby. It was an old wooden house set in nearly a hectare of grounds and framed on two sides by tall eucalyptus trees planted about 1855, when the house was originally built. The single-storey dwelling, with a verandah running along the front and sides, had six or seven rooms, besides the kitchen and two servants' attic quarters above the four main rooms. On the same site, fourteen or fifteen years later, Mons. Luck, OSB, laid the foundation stone for a fine, brick episcopal residence.

Across the road, about a hundred metres south-east on the lower slope, the Irish Sisters of Mercy had a large, beautiful two-storey convent and chapel set

---

* Vaggioli was a regular correspondent to the *New Zealand Freeman's Journal,* which played a vital role in the cultural life of the Auckland Catholic community from 1879 to 1887.

on a three-hectare site. The sisters ran a girls' boarding school and also taught the local Catholic girls. Four sisters taught boys and girls at the cathedral. In addition, five or six sisters ran the Parnell parish convent for children living in the town's south-west area. Below the Ponsonby convent was an orphanage for about one hundred girls. The colonial government had gifted the land and assisted in the construction of the building, as well as providing an annual subsidy. Private donations were also made. The sisters were in charge and provided free education to the girls, most of whom were Catholic. The nuns had other small convents in five diocesan missions outside the town.

4. Auckland was a thriving town. It had about thirty shoe manufacturers, producing approximately 300,000 pairs of shoes annually. Much was exported to the Pacific Islands. Hides and sheep skins were also exported. Clothing and blankets for natives were manufactured. A considerable amount of timber was exported from the town and district since kauri grew only in the north. All the wooden colonial homes were built of this excellent material, which was also exported to Australia and England. Large quantities of kauri gum, which was used for varnish, etc., were sent to England and elsewhere. Two of the main exports, however, were wool and Waikato coal. Other export items were preserved meat, smoked fish, gold dust and ingots from the Thames and Coromandel mines. Imports, more than doubling exports, mostly came from England, enriching the mother country. Sailing ships and steamers berthed daily in Auckland on their importing and exporting rounds. Only Dunedin, in the South Island, was a bigger commercial town.

5. The town's harbour location is picturesque – indeed, beautiful. The North Shore opposite would soon be a town too. I liked Auckland's pleasant, healthy climate, which is somewhat similar to Italy's. Evening temperatures are generally ten or twelve degrees cooler than during the day. It was 23 December when we arrived, and summer. People were feeling the heat. I, however, was cold. I kept my winter clothes on and slept under three woollen blankets! That was nothing compared to hearing everyone speaking English and my not being able to understand a word. Between 1866 and 1867 I had learnt a little German but forgotten it through lack of use. How would I learn English?

Part 2. The Bishop's Reception: 23 December 1879

Summary. – 1. The Catholic community's desire to hold a formal reception for their new pastor. – 2. Carriage procession from Ponsonby to the cathedral. – 3. The cathedral. – 4. Reception at the cathedral. – 5. Addresses by the clergy, laity, daughters of Mary, Irish Society, etc. The prelate's reply. – 6. Luncheon with the clergy in the cathedral presbytery.

1. When the local clergy and parishioners learnt that the bishop was on his way from Australia, they decided to hold a formal reception for him at the cathedral as soon as he reached Auckland. Missionaries of the diocese and the vicar-general met with a committee of prominent Catholic laymen for three days to plan the reception. The committee concentrated on the practical details of preparing the cathedral and grounds, transport, etc., while the priests attended to the rest. There was consternation, however, when the steamer was two days late, because most of the missionaries had to return to their posts on 23 December to prepare for Christmas ceremonies. They decided that if the bishop arrived during daytime on 22 December, the official reception would be held immediately after he disembarked. But since we arrived in the early hours of the following morning, it was to be left to the bishop to decide the day and time. Mons. Steins, when informed, decided to have the reception the same day, at 11 a.m., so that the missionaries could leave that afternoon for their missions.

2. The reception was very well planned and went like clockwork. At about 9 a.m. Mons. Fynes (the vicar-general), the local clergy and missionaries, and two new priests hoping for admission to the diocese, arrived at the bishop's residence. Finally, the six committee members drew up, followed by the other carriages. There were fourteen priests and seven of us, including our lay brothers. Altogether, with the committee, we numbered twenty-seven. At exactly 10 a.m., the twelve four-seater carriages, each drawn by two horses, assembled. The bishop and vicar-general sat in the first carriage. We priests and lay brothers were next, then the local missionaries, and finally the committee members and prominent laymen. When we were all seated, the carriages set off, filing along the main thoroughfares or streets of the town, taking a circuitous route from the bishop's residence to the cathedral. Even at a trotting pace, the trip took nearly an hour. We proceeded along the length of Grafton Road, down Queen Street, the main commercial street, almost to the wharf. We then turned left up a slight incline. At the top, about 100 metres from Queen Street and 400 metres from the quay, stood the cathedral.

3. The cathedral, built of volcanic stone, had a plain interior and exterior. It was T-shaped with a single nave, and about thirty metres long and twelve wide.

The ceiling was wooden, not stone, and at the far end was the main wooden altar. A railing enclosed the sanctuary. On the Epistle side was a side altar and on the Gospel side a small sacristy where priests vested for Mass.* The cathedral had been built about 1860 by Marist fathers and was the only stone building in that part of town.† It did not have a belfry. The approximately 200-kilogram bell was mounted on four conical beams, supported by wooden trusses. This was, and still is, the most typical and economic kind of belfry in English missions, especially in country districts.

Eight years later, under Mons. Luck, OSB, successor to Bishop Steins, the cathedral more than doubled in size. The old church became the transverse arm of the new Roman cross design. A sanctuary and apse could not, however, be added, because a main street blocked the way. The entrance, which previously was east, was faced north and a fine brick belfry was erected above the main porch of the new cathedral. The beautiful wide single nave and wooden ceiling features were kept in the new design. At the rear were the main altar and two side chapels. The sacristy was enlarged and the old entrance became the new cathedral's side entrance. In 1889 three church bells were placed in position. Mons. Luck had bought them in Italy, where churches were destroyed in the name of progress! But in the Antipodes they were erected to represent true freedom and progress, values traduced by the anti-Christian Masonic clique, which made out it was cultured and Catholic!

4. Four other carriages joined the procession en route. When the cortege reached the precincts of the cathedral, it could not advance because of the throng of parishioners. They were blocking every street into the cathedral, which was already full. The carriage conveying the bishop had great difficulty moving through Cathedral Square because it was packed with men and women of all ages and station. The rest of us followed on foot behind the prelate's carriage, moving at a snail's pace. Finally the bishop alighted and approached the cathedral porch, where the parish priest and two curates were waiting to welcome him. Mons. Steins removed his cape, revealing a lace surplice and violet cope. He received the aspergillum from the parish priest wearing a plain surplice, and he blessed the clergy and congregation. The processional then began. The cross-bearer and acolytes led, followed by the clergy. The bishop was in the rear with the vicar-general on his left. They made slow progress to the altar because the congregation not only filled the pews but spilled out into the aisle, and they could only proceed in single file. The committee members followed

* Signifying respectively right (Epistle) and left (Gospel).
† The reference is to St Patrick's Cathedral, also described in Vaggioli's *History of New Zealand and Its Inhabitants*, p. 301. The cathedral was built under Bishop Viard's supervision and consecrated on Sunday, 19 March 1848.

the prelate and sat in reserved seats near the sanctuary. The clergy, our three lay brothers and the bishop entered the sanctuary and prostrated themselves before the Blessed Sacrament. At the same time the choir, accompanied by the organ, sang the hymn *Ecce Sacerdos Magnus*, etc.* The cathedral was decked out with streamers and garlands of flowers. At the end of the hymn, the vicar-general said the customary prayers for the reception of a new bishop.

5. When this was completed, speeches of welcome began for the pastor who had come from so far away to care for them. Mons. Fynes, the vicar-general, was the first speaker. He read out his address, which was written on embossed parchment. On behalf of the diocesan clergy, he expressed his pleasure that after some years absence, the diocese once again had a leader.† On their behalf, he pledged loyalty, obedience and devotion to parishioners' salvation. His speech was in English. I didn't understand a word, but later it was explained to me. The other speeches were also in English. The bishop gave a brief reply, expressing his hope in the clergy's full support. He thanked them for their warm welcome, hoping that with their cooperation the diocese would again flourish. Father Walter McDonald, the cathedral administrator (in missionary countries, missionaries including secular priests are called 'Father'), read out another address on behalf of the local clergy, and again Mons. Steins made a brief reply. The Catholic Member of Parliament made a speech on behalf of the laity of the diocese and the prelate replied. This was followed by the address of the president of the Irish Catholic Society.‡ Finally the director of Catholic schools delivered a speech. In his final address, the bishop congratulated everyone and encouraged them all to persevere as loyal and obedient sons of the Church. The reception concluded at 1.30 p.m. with the benediction of the Blessed Sacrament.

6. At 2 p.m. the committee gave a sumptuous luncheon for the bishop, ourselves as new arrivals, and the local clergy in the cathedral presbytery, a single-storey dwelling with three smallish rooms. It housed two or three priests who were responsible for three-quarters of the Catholics living in the town. The committee members also joined us for lunch and everything went very well, in an atmosphere of blessed rejoicing and merriment. Champagne was served and we drank to the Pope, Queen Victoria and the bishop, who replied to the toast. After our repast we had coffee and at about 4 p.m. the carriages which had brought us took us back to the bishop's residence in Ponsonby.

* 'Behold the Great Priest', etc., an Old Testament reference.
† The Auckland diocese had been without a bishop for four years, from 1875 to 1879, following the translation of Mons. Croke to archdiocese of Cashel, Ireland.
‡ The 'Irish Catholic Society' presenting the address was the Hibernian Australasian Catholic Benefit Society, of which Vaggioli later became a member. It was an offshoot of an Austrian, rather than an Irish, organisation.

Part 3. The Auckland Diocese

Summary. – 1. The first Catholic mission in New Zealand. – 2. The first Apostolic Vicar and Bishop of Auckland. His remarkable missionary zeal. – 3. The Devil at work. The prelate's desolation. The bishop's niece ... his resignation. – 4. Mons. Croke, the second bishop. Quarrels with the Franciscans. They quit the diocese. – 5. Auckland without a bishop.

1. The Auckland diocese is huge, more than one-third the size of Italy. It comprises nearly two-thirds of the North Island and outlying islands, and stretches from 34 to 39 degrees longitude south. By 1879 this enormous territory had scarcely more than 100,000 European inhabitants and about 30,000 native Maori, of whom 5000 were Catholic. Their missionary was Dr James McDonald, the cathedral administrator's brother. There were some 25,000 European Catholics in the diocese. Europeans had fourteen missionaries. Outside Auckland there were seven mission stations. Three were near the town: Onehunga, Otahuhu and Drury. The fourth was in the Waikato. The other three were on the east coast, at Thames, not far from Auckland, Tauranga and Gisborne. That is how the diocese was divided up by the time of our arrival in December 1879.

2. From 1814 Protestant missionaries came from Australia to New Zealand. Their predecessors were British and American whalers hunting the abundant whales in New Zealand. In the eighteenth century they had been virtually undisturbed because the natives' ferocious cannibalism meant that very few whalers risked approaching New Zealand waters. Any whites who landed were massacred and devoured. Nevertheless, Europeans slowly began to settle in the Bay of Islands in the far north of the North Island. By 1840 there were about 2000 European inhabitants, mostly whalers. They included two or three Catholic families. The French Government considered occupying New Zealand, but when the British Government discovered this, it sent orders to Australia for New Zealand to be occupied and declared a British colony. In 1846,* the Holy See appointed Mons. Pompallier, a Frenchman, as Titular Bishop and Apostolic Vicar of Southern Oceania, excluding Australia. The vicariate included several Pacific islands as well as New Zealand. It was assigned to the Marist Order, recently founded in Lyons, France, of which Mons. Pompallier was a member.†
He departed from Europe accompanied by four Marist fathers. Two priests were left on a Pacific island,‡ while he and the other two priests continued on

---

* In fact, 1836.
† Pompallier, while associated with the nascent Society of Mary, was not a member.
‡ This account is at variance with that recorded in Vaggioli's *History of New Zealand*, where he states that Father Chevron and a lay brother were left on the island of Uea or Wallis, and Father Chanel and a lay brother on the island of Futuna, *ibid.*, p. 81.

and landed in the Bay of Islands in 1848.* They immediately set to work with great zeal to convert the native Maori. Later, with the increase of the European population through migration, New Zealand was separated from the Vicariate of Southern Oceania, which was assigned a new vicar. Mons. Pompallier eventually became Bishop of Auckland, the seat of his episcopate, about 1852. As the harvest of native converts began to increase significantly, the bishop was able to recruit more than thirty missionaries from France. He dispatched them to various tribes. There were about 60,000 natives in his diocese and approximately 20,000 in the rest of the colony. The zealous bishop travelled extensively encouraging missionaries and his flock, and in less than ten years more than 30,000 Maori embraced Catholicism.[†] Even Protestants admired the prelate's inexhaustible energy and ready spirit of self-sacrifice for others and consequently he found general support. The Marist missionaries also toiled day and night for pagans' conversion, living in their midst and exposing themselves to every privation the natives endured. When Mons. Pompallier became aware that Wellington's European population was also increasing, he sent down his vicar-general and two Marist fathers to support European Catholics and convert local natives. He made him vicar of the area and about 1860 he was appointed Bishop of Wellington.[‡]

3. To assist him, Mons. Pompallier accepted the offer of help of one of his nieces, a French nun. She especially wanted to work among Maori women. She accompanied the bishop, teaching and demonstrating a singular zeal for their conversion. Things in the diocese progressed well until about 1860. Around this time the Devil caused mischief and a strong disagreement arose between the bishop and superior-general of the Marists in Lyons. The bishop wanted the missionaries to work individually among native tribes. The superior, however, saw the grave perils they faced living with the Maori, sleeping with them in their homes, bodies pressed promiscuously around the fire.

He decided that this was not suitable. He also believed it was not appropriate for missionaries to be scattered in isolation. They should be living in pairs in huts of their own. The views of the two men were plainly incompatible and

* In fact, 1838.
† Pompallier himself gives two different figures: 25,000 in his *Succinct and Precise Report on the Catholic Mission in New Zealand and Especially on the Diocese of Auckland*, Paris, 1859; and 8000 by 1857 in his *Annual Report to the Sacred Congregation of Propaganda Fide*. (cf. Crockett, John, *Bishop Pompallier and the Foundation of the Auckland Diocese (1841–1868)*, unpublished Licentiate Paper, Urban College de Propaganda Fide, Rome, 1971). Vaggioli's claim is thus much exaggerated.
‡ Viard went to Rome for his consecration, returning to Wellington, his bishopric, on 1 May 1850, as recorded in Vaggioli's *History, ibid.*, p. 142. These inaccuracies would indicate that Vaggioli was writing from memory.

strong friction developed between them. The bishop's preoccupation was the good of the mission. He was little concerned about the Marists' Rule and he was casual about how he used the Marists. Their superior, however, was deeply concerned about their well-being. He wanted them to observe their Rule and have some accountability to him. Since the two men were unable to come to an agreement, the Marists' founder ordered his missionaries to quit the Auckland diocese and take up new posts in Wellington. As a bishop, Mons. Pompallier was no longer a member of the Marist Order. Suddenly stripped of three-quarters of his missionaries, he was devastated. Where previously he had more than thirty missionaries, he was now left with half a dozen secular priests! The mission was practically deserted! Words cannot describe the bishop's anxiety and desolation. To remedy the disaster, Mons. Pompallier left for Europe as soon as possible to search for new recruits to the diocese. He found a few in Ireland and France, but insufficient to meet the need. He then approached the Franciscans and their general gave him about half a dozen priests, mostly Italian and a few French. He returned with his recruits but was disappointed in the numbers. The prelate was demoralised because of the Marists' desertion and the insufficiency of priests in the diocese. He began to drink heavily to drown his sorrows, but never to the point of inebriation. Previously he had always been very temperate. His drinking, however, even in the midst of these trials, did not affect his conduct or judgement.

Meanwhile, the Devil was again up to some nasty tricks. This time he used the prelate's niece as his pawn.* For many years she had worked zealously for the conversion of souls, living in the bishop's residence and accompanying him on his missionary journeys to Maori tribes. But then the Devil used her for his evil designs. The wretched woman seduced a young priest living in the bishop's house. She had become infatuated with him and led him into sin. She, naturally, did not breathe a word, but the priest made a full confession to the bishop, describing the lengths she had gone to to seduce him and lead him to transgress. You can imagine, dear reader, the enormous suffering this caused the poor bishop. To assuage his grief he drank more heavily, but not to the point of intoxication. Aware, however, that the diocese was languishing, he sent his resignation as Bishop of Auckland to Rome. It was accepted. He left New Zealand on a French naval vessel and returned to France where, burdened with sorrows, he died a few years later.† These events were recounted to me by missionaries who were with Mons. Pompallier in Auckland.

* The bishop's niece is identified as Lucie by E.R. Simmons in his entry on Bishop Pompallier in the *New Zealand Dictionary of Biography,* vol.1. She accompanied Suzanne Aubert to New Zealand. Simmons makes no mention, however, of the incident described above.
† Pompallier retired to the village of Puteaux, near Paris, where he died on 21 December 1871.

4. A few months after Mons. Pompallier's return to Europe, Mons. Croke, an eloquent Irishman, was appointed. He accepted the position, not because he welcomed being a missionary, but as a stepping-stone to an appointment to an Irish bishopric. In Bishop Pompallier's time, missionaries wore the soutane inside and outside the presbytery. But when Mons. Croke arrived, he ordered them to dress like English and Irish Protestant clergy, wearing trousers, waistcoat and top coat. Mons. Croke had a jaundiced view of religious orders. Mons. Pompallier had placed two Franciscans at the cathedral. He stationed a further two in Thames and the rest in other missions. The new bishop demanded to use them as he saw fit, without reference to their superior.

About this time goldmining began in Thames, and people flocked in. The mission prospered through generous donations. The bishop decided to remove the Franciscans and replace them with secular priests. The monks resisted, maintaining that Mons. Pompallier had assigned them the mission, and since there was nothing to criticise them for, there was no reason to remove them. The bishop accused them of sending tithes for their upkeep and extra donations to their general, when they should have handed them over to him for diocesan expenditure. But even though the accusation was true, they were entitled to do so because the money was given for their upkeep. Instead of spending it on themselves, they went without to support their order. Since Mons. Croke was opposed to the Franciscans, his secular clergy followed suit. Consequently, quarrels often occurred between them, especially at the cathedral,* which had two Franciscans and two or three secular priests. One day on the pretext that the secular priest was to say Mass before the friar, a heated argument developed and they hit each other on the head with their chalices! In 1883, Fr McDonald showed me one of the dented vessels which had been used as a weapon! Because of the altercations with Bishop Croke and his secular clergy, about 1866 the Franciscans' general recalled all his monks,† except an Irish Franciscan,‡ whom the bishop wished to remain. This was the missionary, mentioned earlier, whom we met on 22 December in Tauranga.

Mons. Croke was not really successful as bishop. He was not suited to this mission. He managed to recruit only a handful of missionaries and accepted unsuitable priests who would later cause problems. He himself admitted that he did not like Auckland and wanted to return to Ireland. After five years as Bishop of Auckland, the Holy See appointed him Archbishop of Cashel in Ireland where he remained until his death, between 1895 and 1898.§

---

* St Patrick's Cathedral, Auckland.
† The withdrawal occurred, in fact, in 1874.
‡ The reference is to Fr Mahoney.
§ In fact, he died on 22 July 1902.

5. After Mons. Croke left Auckland, the diocese remained without a pastor until 1879, when Mons. Steins was appointed. Meanwhile the Wellington and Dunedin dioceses flourished, particularly the former through the Marist fathers' zealous efforts, while Auckland barely managed to survive because of the dearth of missionaries. Mons. Croke made his report on the Auckland diocese to Propaganda.* The cardinal prefect believed the best way to revive it would be to reinstate a religious order or congregation, since secular priests were not available. In fact, Propaganda offered it to the Marists, who had originally managed it so successfully, but they refused, declaring they lacked sufficient religious. It was then offered to the Jesuits, Lazarists and other religious orders. All declined. Meanwhile, under the direction of the new vicar-general, Mons. Fynes, the diocese continued to languish and, with the assistance of only a few new priests, it could not fully meet parishioners' spiritual needs. Mons. Steins, a Jesuit, was then appointed. He tried unsuccessfully to get his order to accept the diocese. Finally, the priests from our English province accepted it on a trial basis.†

PART 4. MONS. STEINS SETS TO WORK

SUMMARY. – 1. Mons. Steins's personality. His aims for the mission. –2. Missionaries' meeting. – 3. Establishment of the Newton mission in town. – 4. He sends two newly arrived priests to Coromandel and Puhoi. – 5. Mons. Steins's error of judgement regarding renegade priests misrepresented by their referees.

1. Mons. Steins was an elderly missionary, about sixty-eight years of age. He had spent thirty-five years in India, ten as a simple Jesuit missionary and another twenty-five as Archbishop of Calcutta. He was wise, prudent, holy and reflective. He had an affable and considerate disposition. He not only knew how to run a mission but also how to set one up or get it back on its feet. His only concern was the glory of God and the good of souls entrusted to his care, and his many years' experience as Archbishop of Calcutta made him the right person to restore the new mission. The prelate's aim was to have the diocese back on its feet within two years and provide it with a stable administration and sufficient priests. Before leaving Europe, Mons. Steins was appraised of the state of the Auckland diocese and he wanted to do his best to set things right. He requested Fr Adalbert Sullivan, who had been appointed superior, to bring as many priests as he could to accompany him to New Zealand. He said that I and the two other priests I mentioned earlier could go with him,‡ and that

* The Sacred Congregation of the Propagation of the Faith; that is, the Congregation responsible for the missionary activities of the Roman Catholic Church.
† The Ramsgate community of the Benedictine Order.
‡ That is, with Bishop Steins.

two other priests in Adelaide (Australia) could also be sent immediately. He would then arrive with further priests. There would, thus, be a dozen priests available within the first year.

The bishop also wanted Fr Adalbert to come out immediately but he hedged, saying that as inspector of the English–Belgian province he could not come out straightaway, having to sort out the order's affairs. He promised that he would follow in a couple of months. Meanwhile, he would obtain more missionaries for the diocese. The truth, however, as it later transpired, was that he did not want to come until he was appointed Bishop of Auckland, as he had been promised by the cardinals' commission. Mons. Steins was not content with fine promises. He wanted action; that is, for Fr Adalbert to come out immediately, and assist him in administering the diocese. He wanted to see if he was not only capable of ruling his monks but managing the diocese. If he could demonstrate his capability, Mons. Steins would then propose to the Holy See that he be appointed bishop. Much to the bishop's annoyance, however, he had to wait until Fr Adalbert had sorted out his affairs in Europe. Until Fr Adalbert's arrival, the bishop had also to act as our superior.

2. As soon as we reached our destination, the prelate had lengthy private discussions with the vicar-general and other missionaries, especially Fr Walter McDonald, the cathedral administrator, to gather clear information about the missionaries, missions, parishioners and their needs. On 27 December, Mons. Fynes hosted a luncheon in his Parnell presbytery for the missionaries of the town and district, in honour of the bishop and his fellow-travellers. A few days later Mons. Steins reciprocated. All the clergy attended except Chastagnon, Gisborne's priest. He wrote that he could not attend because he needed to work on the church's debt, but that as soon as he had collected the money he would come. An Irish priest and a Dutch priest, who had recently arrived in the colony seeking admission to the diocese,* also attended the lunch. The repast was generous but not extravagant. After the meal we took coffee in another room where the conversation continued and those who smoked could do so. I couldn't understand a word, so contented myself with observing people's behaviour. The missionaries behaved with dignity and decorum.† But the same could not be said of the two newly arrived priests. Cassidy, the Irishman, seemed serious, rather withdrawn, guarded and awkward. He appeared to be putting on a front

---

* Vaggioli later explains the peculiarities of priests presenting themselves as candidates for admission to a new diocese (cf. pp. 26-28).
† There is some confusion in Vaggioli's use of the terms 'missionary' (*missionario*) and 'priest' (*prete, sacerdote, secolare*). At times the terms are used interchangeably, but more generally a distinction is made between *'missionario'* as priest of a religious order and *'secolare'* indicating a secular priest. It would be difficult to clarify the meaning in each context Vaggioli uses it.

Fr Walter McDonald, St Patrick's Cathedral administrator.

and not being genuine. The Dutchman, on the other hand, was garrulous and worldly and I noticed he was partial to wine. But I kept my observations to myself.

3. Newton, situated in the north-west part of the town, had a wooden chapel with a small belfry in the Catholic cemetery grounds. It was on a corner near one of the main roads. A cathedral priest said Mass on Sundays for the parishioners and returned for benediction in the evening. Nearby was a Catholic secondary school run by a Catholic lay teacher and two others. At the beginning of January 1880, Mons. Steins placed my two colleagues, Frs Downey and O'Gara, in charge of the parish and school. Newton was made a separate mission, especially because of its centrality. The bishop wasted no time and rented a wooden house near the cemetery for the priests and lay brother, Adalbert, and sent them immediately to Newton. They were put in charge of parishioners living in the south-west, near the railway station connecting Auckland to the Waikato.

4. Cassidy (the Irishman) and the Dutch priest, whom I mentioned previously, arrived in Auckland, three or four weeks before us, hoping to be appointed as priests to the diocese. I don't know where they had been previously. Their papers, as was customary, contained neither good nor bad comments. They simply stated: *nulla censura irretitus.**

The vicar-general and cathedral administrator favoured their admission to the diocese because of the shortage of priests. They decided to leave it to the

* 'not guilty of reproach' (Latin).

bishop to make the decision after his arrival. The vicar-general and Fr McDonald maintained that since being in Auckland their conduct had been beyond reproach. Mons. Steins listened and accepted the priests without demur. He sent Cassidy to the Coromandel mission, which was without a priest. He dispatched the Dutchman, who also spoke German, to Puhoi where there was a small settlement of about four hundred German Catholics.* Their behaviour, however, was reprehensible. Cassidy turned out to be a lecher and drunkard, and the Dutchman also drank excessively. They were eventually ordered out of the diocese.

5. The bishop was indeed a saintly man, intent on seeking the good of the diocese and the parishioners. He was, however, unaware that the situation regarding priests in the British colonies of Australia and New Zealand, as in the United States of America, was different from colonial India. There were priests in America who were given to drinking and other vices. When they had done the rounds of American missions and been expelled, they went on to try their luck in Australia and New Zealand. They repeated their tricks, with the same result. Many returned to America, and on it would go. This very rarely occurred in India because there were few Europeans. They were native missions. The funding was provided by Propaganda.† Moreover, these renegades were not interested in bringing natives to God but only in furthering their own ambitions and satisfying their passions. The prelate was ignorant of this and he was thus duped into accepting the two priests. The main blame, however, should be placed on the cathedral administrator. He was well aware of the situation, but through misplaced charity and pity he recommended that the bishop accept the misfits.

Part 5. Two New Renegades!

Summary. – 1. My temporary residence at the bishop's. – 2. I say daily Mass for the Sisters of Mercy. – 3. Sr Bernarda. – 4. Two new priests from the Wellington diocese in Auckland. – 5. Providentially, the truth about them is discovered. – 6. I ask Sr Bernarda's permission to tell the bishop what I know.

1. As I mentioned previously, my three colleagues were appointed to missions by the bishop. Not knowing English, I was useless. Consequently Br Joseph and I remained at the bishop's residence with his assistant. Mons. Steins suggested that we study English, but how could we learn without a teacher? It was impossible and I told him so. While in Malta, I had bought a small Italian–English dictionary, but it was practically useless without a pronunciation guide.

* Actually from Bohemia.
† The inference is that there was not the luxury of a European population's financial support to permit that kind of living.

And as soon as I heard words I promptly forgot their pronunciation. The bishop hired a layman who knew a little French to come two or three times a week to give us an hour's language lesson. But even so I made scarcely any progress, forgetting the words. I stayed at the bishop's until the beginning of February 1880.

2. Immediately after my arrival in Auckland on 23 December 1879, I began to say daily Mass for the Sisters of Mercy. Their chapel was opposite the bishop's residence. The bishop made this request to free the cathedral priests from an extra duty. I was happy to do anything for the mission and willingly accepted the task. Normally on Sundays and holy days of obligation, the bishop or another priest would say the second Mass and preach to parishioners who might attend. I said the first Mass at about 7 a.m., as on weekdays. There were always parishioners present. After Mass, Mother Superior invited me into the parlour for coffee and breakfast. I simply had coffee with milk and plain bread, since I did not indulge in finer fare. She quickly realised that I did not speak English and summoned Sr Bernarda, an elderly nun, to keep me company. She was about sixty or seventy years old and spoke French fluently. She had been a French teacher in the convent.*

3. Old Sr Bernarda limped a little, using a walking stick. She suffered from rheumatism in the changeable climate. She had been in New Zealand for many years, and had served as superior in their Wellington convents. Sr Bernarda had been in Auckland for seven or eight years. She strictly observed the Rule and was devout, pleasant and kind-hearted. She was devoted to others and determined that missionaries should set the best example as Christians. Mother Superior asked her to come to the parlour, her health permitting, to keep me company when I had coffee after Mass. She generously acquiesced, and hardly ever missed an occasion, chatting with me for a quarter of an hour or so. This afforded me considerable pleasure and I gained much detailed information about the diocese and people from the nun. I was also able to ask her the English for key words. In fact, often our conversations would extend to half an hour or more after I had coffee and the good sister spoke freely with the best intentions of the diocese in mind.

4. Soon after Christmas 1879, two secular priests arrived in Auckland from the neighbouring Wellington diocese. They had the requisite *discessit*, or permission to resign given to priests wishing to leave, with the customary 'free from censure' clause. They said they had come for a retreat with the priests of the diocese

* Sr Bernarda, aged about sixty-five in 1880, was a former superior of Wellington convent. She was Mary Bernard Dixon, who had nursed in the Crimea War, based in Wellington 1861–73, then returned to Auckland, dying in 1895.

since they heard the bishop was taking it. But their real intention was to seek acceptance into the diocese, because they did not want to stay in Wellington. Accordingly, they went to see the cathedral administrator, Fr W. McDonald, who was only too aware of the diocese's great lack of priests. Being gullible and obliging, he promised that he would do all he could to get the prelate to accept them.

Fr McDonald spoke to the bishop several times about the new priests. He mentioned their intention to go on retreat and that they had left their posts because the Bishop of Wellington did not want secular priests, only Marists, in his diocese. They heard about this and decided to leave. The bishop was sorry to lose them, etc. Mons. Fynes, the vicar-general, on the other hand, was more perspicacious and shrewd. He had no intention of taking responsibility but left it for the bishop to decide, guided by the Lord. I had heard of the renegades' arrival and that they had been introduced to the bishop by the administrator. But the bishop did not discuss with me whether to accept them or not. I thus did not concern myself with the matter, simply presuming that they were good priests. As far as I knew, the bishop was willing to accept them into the diocese, but he wanted to think it over. He needed to have more information about the missions and needs of the diocese.

5. One morning, about halfway through January 1880, I was having coffee at the convent when Sr Bernarda asked me if it were true that the bishop intended accepting the two priests as intimated to her by Fr McDonald. I told her that I knew nothing of this, since the bishop had not confided in me regarding the matter. Moreover, since I did not understand English, even if he had discussed it with the vicar-general and Fr McDonald, I had no knowledge of it. I did say, however, that I was aware that the latter would move heaven and earth to get them accepted into the diocese.

'I would be really upset,' said Sr Bernarda, 'if they were accepted!'

'Why do you say that? Do you know them?' I replied, surprised at the degree of intensity of her distress and repugnance. I realised that there was more to it.

'I know one of them very well. When I was in New Plymouth, he was the local missionary. I don't know the other priest, but I often heard him being discussed. He was the missionary at …' She mentioned the place, but I can't remember it.

'You obviously know something about them. Please tell me about their behaviour.'

'Their conduct,' she replied, 'left a lot to be desired. It was common knowledge that they often got drunk. There were also widespread rumours that they led licentious lives.'

'Are you absolutely certain?'

'I myself saw the New Plymouth priest drunk several times, and the other apparently was the same. I never witnessed any loose-living, but there were many who would vouch for it. Others denied it. Enquiries were then made, which supported the negative comments because they came from reliable sources.'

'Why wasn't the Bishop of Wellington informed about their behaviour so they could have a chance to mend their ways?'

'He was told. He summoned and reprimanded them. They promised to change. He suspended them briefly so they could alter their ways, but when they returned to duty they got up to their old tricks. From what I gleaned from our local sisters, their misbehaviour continued and Bishop Redwood dismissed them, replacing them with Marist fathers.'

'But I heard their bishop gave them good dimissory letters. Am I to believe he would lie and give good testimonials to unworthy priests?'

'You shouldn't give credence to dimissory letters,' she replied. 'No one takes any notice of them. They are general statements, simply indicating that the priest is not under censure, and that's all. If they don't get good dimissory letters, they are stuck in the diocese.'

This was startling news to me!

'When misfits learn of a new bishop's arrival, they seek him out, hoping to be admitted to his diocese, because they are unknown to him. This practice is nothing new.'

I was glad to hear the truth from Sr Bernarda but dismayed about their behaviour.

6. After reflecting, I said to the nun, 'Would you mind if I mention what you've told me to Mons. Steins?'

'No, not at all. Go ahead. That's why I told you. But don't mention my name. I wouldn't like him to know the information came from me.'

'I understand, but it's unlikely that the bishop will believe me. He knows that as a foreigner I don't know English or what's happening in the colony, especially among the clergy. He'll ask me where I got my information from. How will I reply? That I got it from a very reliable source. He'll surely want to know the person's identity. What am I to say?'

'I see. Yes, you're right!'

'We're dealing with matters which affect the Church and souls. The bishop needs to know. But all in strict confidence.'

'Very well, if it's necessary, let the bishop know I told you, as long as it's in confidence.'

'I'll do that. But what about the other two priests accepted by the bishop? Can you tell me anything about them?'

'I don't know them and I've heard nothing, except that the cathedral administrator speaks very highly of them.'

Part 6. Should the Renegades be Accepted?

Summary. – 1. The bishop is inclined to accept the new priests. – 2. I ask him if he has all the facts. – 3. I urge him not to accept them because of their unsuitability. – 4. Their dimissory letters are in order. – 5. How reliable are American and colonial bishops' dimissory letters? – 6. What would I do if I were Bishop of Auckland? – 7. How do I know that the two priests are unsuitable?

1. After my discussion with Sr Bernarda, I hastened to Mons. Steins to ascertain whether he had accepted the two Wellington diocesan priests. 'Not yet,' he replied. 'I need to think it over and have them wait a little. The diocese urgently needs priests and I don't know how to meet the demand!'

I told him that I had heard that the cathedral administrator promised them he would get them accepted into the diocese, and that he was right behind them.

'But it's not up to him,' the bishop replied. 'It's my responsibility. In fact, I am thinking of accepting them, but I still haven't made up my mind. I'm taking my time. I don't want to make a mistake.'

2. I asked the bishop if he had the necessary information. He replied that their dimissory letters were in order; that Fr Walter McDonald and their parishioners had spoken highly of them and that the vicar-general was willing to accept them on trial. I asked him if he had written confidentially to the Bishop of Wellington for full information. He said that he hadn't and that he didn't intend doing so once he saw that their dimissory letters were in order. 'They are not laudatory,' he added, 'but they don't mention any misconduct.'

'I should hope not,' I exclaimed, 'but …!'

'They won't shine as missionaries,' continued the bishop. 'They're just average. But they're capable of some good, and there's such a shortage of priests.'

3. At this point, I said to the prelate, 'Excuse me, Excellency. I've heard from a most reliable source that the two priests are neither men of integrity nor moderation, but a source of scandal. I beg you not to admit them. They will only harm souls.'

Mons. Steins was startled by my entreaty and annoyed by my serious accusation. 'You can't converse in English. What can you say about them when you don't even know them?'

'That's indeed true, Excellency. Even so, I know the priests did not set a good example and have acted scandalously in their diocese right up to the present. Surely, they would behave the same here.'

'Very well, give me reasons for not accepting them. I want facts. Carry on, I'm listening.'

'I believe there are two main reasons. First, the Wellington diocese is short of priests; admittedly, not as much as Auckland, but it certainly has none to give away. If they were fine, upright priests, the bishop would have done everything in his power to keep them after their years of service. Instead, he is packing them off because they're not suitable. Second, they would have stayed in Wellington if they could, because they would be better off financially than in our poorer Auckland missions. This all proves my point.'

4. 'Father, this looks like prejudice to me. Where's your clear evidence? You might even be right, but your reasons aren't substantiated, and I need clear proof.'

I didn't reply and caught myself half-smiling.

The bishop continued, 'I have thoroughly examined their dimissory letters and there's no mention of misconduct or any censure. You couldn't say they were expelled from their diocese.'

'But then why have they left their posts and come to this poor diocese?'

'It's not unusual for people to get tired of being in the same place and want a change. They think they'll feel better if they move. Permanency is a rare thing, even for missionaries.'

' You could be right, Excellency, but I'm not convinced. If they were worthy, upright priests, their bishop would have given them better missions for their talents rather than lose them.'

The bishop replied that in practice it didn't work out that way, especially where there was a difference of opinion with the bishop. I said that since dimissory letters contained nothing specific, you couldn't put much faith in them. They simply stated that a priest had not been excommunicated or suspended. They said nothing about their moral character or suitability as priests.

5. Mons. Steins replied, 'If a priest given a dimissory letter is known to be licentious or to have caused scandal, it would need to be mentioned so that other bishops would not be deceived. If the Bishop of Wellington has made no mention of any reprehensible behaviour, that's a sign that none exists.'

'I agree with you, Excellency, that bishops issuing dimissory letters should mention good or bad behaviour. This is undoubtedly true. But, in fact, they hardly ever do. And that's just how it is. There are two reasons for this. First, if they stated the truth, priests would not leave their diocese, because they would be aware that no other bishop would accept them. Second, bishops act out of misguided compassion, hoping that these priests will mend their ways elsewhere. This is how bishops free themselves and their flocks from scandalous priests.'

I continued, 'Many newly appointed bishops in the United States of America, Australia and other British colonies are often duped by dimissory letters sent by other bishops.' I told him this (and repeated it three years later to Mons. Luck) to help him see that dimissory letters which generally state that the person is without censure are irrelevant. I explained to the prelate:

1) If a priest's misbehaviour is drawn to his bishop's attention, he may reprimand him two or three times. Should he persist, he is suspended *ad tempus** and requested to go on retreat. If this has no effect, he is again suspended, removed from his parish and encouraged to leave the diocese to avoid causing further scandal.

2) An incorrigible priest, however, won't leave his diocese (and he can't be forced out by the bishop) unless he has a proper dimissory letter, even vaguely expressed, with which he can obtain a parish or mission in another diocese. The bishop, faced with the unpleasant alternatives of either issuing the requested dimissory letter or having to put up with him continuing to cause scandal in the diocese, resigns himself to the lesser evil. If the priest is suspended, he lifts the suspension so that he can write that the priest is not under censure or suspension. Armed with this document, renegade priests can finally leave the diocese and rush off to work in another diocese where they are not known. Initially, they behave themselves and even show enthusiasm and dedication, and a willingness to accept any posting. But, in fact, they beguile the new bishop with deceit, to conceal their defects, claiming, for example, that they grew tired of staying in the same place, that they were disillusioned by the tepid response of their parishioners to their earnest efforts, that their bishop did not appreciate them enough, as shown by others being given the best missions while they were appointed to the most unpopular, remote, difficult ones, etc.

3) Experienced bishops knew that such excuses were made by deceitful priests and that neither they nor their letters were worth a pinch of salt. No matter how pressing the need for missionaries, they would rather leave their missions depleted than accept newcomers they adjudged unsuitable. New bishops, however, hoodwinked by the rogues, would believe them and take them on. They would then rue their decision and try to get them removed from their diocese. To do so, they had to give them the same kind of letter, or wait until they moved on.

4) And lastly, American and colonial bishops who have upright, exemplary priests do everything they can to support them and retain them in their diocese. If, in spite of this, such a priest decides to leave, his bishop gives him a good report, mentioning all his merits. But this kind of situation rarely happens.

6. Mons. Steins heard me out but then replied with irritation, 'You make too many generalisations. You would say that any priest coming from another diocese is unsuitable. In practice, it's not like that. And, besides, it's not easy to know whether someone is suitable or not.'

* 'temporarily' (Latin).

'I agree, Excellency, and given the difficulty, I would ask applicants why they left their mission to come here.'

'I've done that and tried to get all the information I could from the vicar-general and Fr Walter.'

'I wouldn't stop there. I would go a step further. I would want to write confidentially to the priests who had taken their place to give full information on their behaviour, for the good of all concerned. They would be assured of confidentiality and their report would be credible.'

'I understand that Fr Walter McDonald has done just that.'

'There's a final step. I would write a strictly confidential letter to the Bishop of Wellington asking him for the whole truth. What was their behaviour like in their missions, to identify any vices, and why they left, it being on his conscience, with God as his judge, to tell the complete truth. I would assure him that his information would remain confidential. I would then be sure that the bishop was telling me the full story about the two priests to avoid compromising his conscience and risking damnation.'

The good bishop listened to me in silence. I continued: 'I am just as keen as you, Excellency, for the missions here to prosper, but I would not want flawed or scandalous priests. I would rather missions went without priests. That would be the lesser evil.'

7. The bishop was silent, as though perplexed. He then asked, 'How did you find out that the two priests are unsuitable? Who told you? What exactly are they accused of?'

'They are accused of being drunkards and lechers.' I then told him what Sr Bernarda had mentioned to me. 'I gained this information from a very reliable source. Actually, she did not want her name revealed, but given the seriousness of the accusations, I told her I was bound to tell Your Excellency everything, and, if required, to reveal her name. And given Your Excellency's specific request, I need to tell you that my source is Sr Bernarda, an elderly Sister of Mercy in the nearby convent. She knows one of the priests well because they were in New Plymouth together. The other priest was often talked about when she was there.'

The prelate listened in silence, startled by my revelation.

'Now that you know, Excellency, where my information came from, why don't you speak to the good sister? I'm sure you'll learn even more. I'm convinced she's speaking the truth.'

'I still haven't accepted them. I need to think it over carefully before I do.' With that, the bishop ended the discussion and I took my leave.

Part 7. Destined for the Gisborne Mission

Summary. – 1. Fr Chastagnon, Gisborne's parish priest. – 2. He decides to build a large wooden church. – 3. Bankruptcy of the Scottish Glasgow Bank; Gisborne's commerce ruined. – 4. Chastagnon, unable to repay the debt on the church, is determined to leave Gisborne. – 5. His ruse to secure his departure. – 6. The bishop grants him permission to transfer. The bishop selects me for the post.

1. About the middle of January 1880, Fr Chastagnon, a French secular priest, arrived in Auckland and stayed at the cathedral with the administrator. Shortly afterwards, he paid his respects to the bishop. He said that he could not come earlier because he had to work on the debt on the church and was helping his parishioners to clear it. He stayed six or seven days in Auckland, visiting the bishop several times and twice dining at his residence. Chastagnon was a small man, about thirty-five years old, with a limp because of a foot deformity. He was, however, physically strong and fit. He had been living in New Zealand for some time. He came out as a sub-deacon at the time of Mons. Pompallier or Mons. Croke, probably the latter, who ordained him a priest.

Chastagnon had been some years in Gisborne, Auckland's most distant mission. The approximately 400-mile voyage south by steamer from Auckland via Tauranga took about thirty hours to reach Gisborne, in Poverty Bay. Chastagnon was a good, zealous, upright, well-respected missionary. When he first arrived, the situation was critical. The priest who had been there a year or two before had hung up his soutane and taken up with a Maori woman, marrying her. He went up to North Auckland with his lover, settling among the Maori. The priest's name was Simpson. Drink led to his downfall! In my time he was a coachman living in Auckland with his strumpet! The scandal set Protestant and Catholic tongues wagging. Another missionary was sent temporarily to Gisborne and then Fr Chastagnon arrived. In the beginning things weren't easy for him but eventually his good character soothed Catholics and Protestants alike.

2. It was probably about 1873 or 1874 that Chastagnon was sent to Gisborne. The settlement's population was about 1800, of whom about 150 were Catholics. The whole district had only about 2000 Europeans, including 200 Catholics. The rest were Protestants of various denominations. Several Maori villages were scattered throughout the area, with about 3000 to 4000 natives. In my time, there were only three Catholic Maori families. The white population was mostly British, the most well-off being Scots and then the English. The Irish were the poorest, being mainly market gardeners, labourers, farm hands or servants. The Scots were keen to stimulate the district's development. They obtained a loan of 25 million francs in instalments from the Bank of

Glasgow.* The Scottish settlers then bought or leased land from the Maori at scandalously low prices for grazing cattle, sheep and horses. Land thus began to be cleared for fields, pastures, etc.

With the bank's large loan all kinds of businesses were set up. Banks, houses, shops, stores, hotels, etc., were built. Construction in the district began on roading, bridges, farms and sawmills. There was work for anyone who wanted it. The daily pay rate rose up to twenty-five francs a day. Even a menial labourer could earn at least fifteen francs a day. Poor Catholics, who lived by their labour, did very well. Others were attracted to the district and soon Gisborne had a further 300 workers.

The original wooden church could accommodate the local Catholics, but Fr Chastagnon believed that the population and trade would continue to grow. He decided to build a new wooden church for a congregation of 1000, assuming that businesses would continue to prosper and in a short time parishioners could pay off the building cost. Construction of a new church was discussed at several meetings and approval was given. It was to be built in the English Gothic style. Bank loans at nine and a half per cent interest were obtained, and the new church was built on the site of the demolished original church. It had a Latin cross design with a single altar, a corrugated iron roof and a beamed and boarded ceiling. There was a large Gothic window behind the altar and a carved wood sanctuary. The two wings also had Gothic windows, while the nave had three small windows on each side. The choir loft above the entrance and portico had a high round Gothic window. Apart from the sanctuary, the rest was not lined. Fr Chastagnon planned to do that later. The church was consecrated and dedicated under the same name of *Stella Maris* (Star of the Sea) as its predecessor.

Chastagnon collected several thousand francs from the faithful before construction began, but since this was clearly not enough, he needed to borrow some 30,000 francs from banks. The actual cost of construction rose to about 40,000 francs. He hoped that, with God's help, the parishioners' contributions would pay off the debt within four or five years, which would have happened if trade continued to flourish. By 1876 the church was partly completed and further collections continued for the debt. Fine pews were commissioned and forms were used as seating in the meantime. The altar was furnished with a crucifix and small glass candlesticks. The missionary's portable Mass kit provided the other items and the women's guild made a few altar cloths.

3. Things went well until the end of 1878 when the situation was turned upside down, plunging Gisborne into despair. At the beginning of 1879 the telegraph

* Vaggioli refers to this bank variously as the Bank of Glasgow and the Bank of Scotland. His usual description is the Bank of Glasgow in Scotland (*Banca di Glasgow in Iscozia*).

office received the message: 'Bank of Glasgow declared bankrupt, deficit £6 million' (or 150 million francs!). England, but even more so Scotland, was thrown into panic over the catastrophe. A vast number of families, with all their savings in the bank, were ruined. But Gisborne was truly dealt a mortal blow because its citizens owed the failed bank 25 million francs. The bank's creditors appointed liquidators to salvage as much as they could by putting pressure on debtors to pay up. The many Scottish debtors in Gisborne were also ordered to pay, but this was easier said than done, because they had little ready cash. They sent what they could, which was still insubstantial, because most of the 25 million had gone into purchasing land, livestock and building houses, shops, etc. They informed the liquidators they could not just sell off everything to pay back the loan because there weren't sufficient wealthy landowners or speculators to buy even half. They would have to be patient and accept being repaid slowly. Otherwise they too would be bankrupted and ultimately the bank's creditors would lose out. This was true and the liquidators agreed, realising that their proposal made sense. They did not let the matter rest there, however. They sent an agent to Gisborne with full powers to take charge, cut costs to the bone, reduce staff, and not only to prohibit any further expenditure or new enterprise, but to cut back wherever possible. He was to retrieve all the money he could and send it regularly back to Scotland. The agent scrupulously carried out his orders.

There were significant consequences. One of the biggest Scottish merchants in Gisborne, who had a loan of £300,000 (7.5 million francs) and more than 300 employees, had to lay off 200 staff and a few months later another seventy, leaving him with just thirty. Another trader with 100 staff had to lay off eighty-two. A third who had more than fifty employees had to reduce his work force to just six men, and other employers were similarly affected. Suddenly work was not available and the daily rate of pay dropped to between seven and ten francs, less than half it was before. Even so, work could not be found. At the same time, rent, clothing and food (apart from meat) stayed high. Workers who had saved money over the previous years, seeing there was no more work and they could not support their families, quickly left Gisborne for better prospects. Catholics, mostly poor Irishmen, with no land of their own or work to be had, suddenly found themselves in a desperate situation. With no money they could not take their families away. They accepted any kind of work, no matter the pay, to avoid starvation.

4. Fr Chastagnon was in a terrible predicament. There was still a debt on the church of more than 20,000 francs and a crushing 2000 francs a year interest. He decided to try to transfer to another mission to wriggle out of his embarrassment. He knew that he would not be able to pay off the debt, which would keep increasing with interest. It would not be easy, however, to escape and quit the debt because the new bishop would not let him transfer until it was

substantially reduced. How could this be achieved when the approximately 300 Catholics in the area were finding it a struggle to survive? There was plenty of goodwill, but that was not enough. The Church owed the Bank of New Zealand £480, or 12,000 francs, and the Union Bank of Australia £12, or 300 francs. About £300, or 7500 francs, was owing on the organ, pews and the foreman's, carpenters', traders' etc. unpaid bills. And there were other debts. By the end of 1879 total debts amounted to approximately 21,000 francs.

To resolve the situation and secure his release, he held several meetings with his parishioners. They could not pay, so he asked them to write out promissory notes redeemable within six months. They refused because they could not guarantee them then or in the future. They would give the little they had and that was that. He agreed to a subscription, putting himself at the head of the list. I'm not sure how much Fr Chastagnon collected. Parishioners gave as much as they could, probably about £100 (2500 francs). He then paid the bills of some creditors who threatened him with court action and would not have let him leave Gisborne. He also paid £20 (500 francs) to the Bank of New Zealand, reducing its debt to £460 (11,500 francs).

5. Since Chastagnon was unsuccessful in substantially reducing the debt, he visited a number of better-off Catholics and urged them to write promissory notes so that the bank could show its Auckland managers that the debt was not so large and would be repaid. When the parishioners refused, he said, 'This is really just a formality. I know you can't meet these amounts, but that doesn't matter. If you don't have the money, the bank can't force you to pay. You'd be doing me a great favour and it wouldn't affect you.' He was so insistent that eventually several agreed. One man signed a note for £50 (1250 francs). Two others made over £25 each. Another four wrote notes for £10 and several others promised £5. In total, more than £200 (5000 francs) was promised. The priest collected the notes and went to the Bank of New Zealand, but he did not present them. He simply asked for a statement. The debt was £460. He then went to the Union Bank, where the debt was £12.

6. About mid-January 1880, Fr Chastagnon sailed to Auckland with his bank statements and promissory notes to see the bishop. He showed him the documents and apprised him of the church's finances. He led him to believe that the debt owing to the two banks totalled £472, as well as a few trifling accounts for four pews. In round figures the total debt was £500 (12,500 francs). Fr Chastagnon then showed the prelate the promissory notes, saying, 'Here are about £200 in promissory notes which will be honoured within six months, reducing the debt to approximately £300 (7500 francs) – a paltry sum, which will be repaid in no time at all.' The bishop praised his dedication and energy and expressed amazement that an impoverished Catholic congregation of a mere 300 souls could achieve

so much in the middle of a severe depression. He could not praise the poor people enough. This report came to me through Chastagnon and Gisborne Catholics.

Once he had convinced the bishop that the debt was not worth worrying about, Chastagnon asked to be transferred to another mission. He pleaded that he was tired of the debt, his health was affected and he needed a rest. He was ready to go anywhere where there was no church debt. Chastagnon also reported on Gisborne to Fr McDonald and the vicar-general, and they too lauded his efforts. He asked them to endorse his request for a transfer to an easier mission. They promised their full support in view of his merits. The bishop promised to try and meet his request. He spoke with the vicar-general and cathedral administrator. They told him that Fr Chastagnon was an outstanding, dedicated, hard-working priest who had done much for Gisborne and deserved a favour. They discussed where to place him and it was decided to give him Pukekohe, about twenty miles from Auckland. A replacement in Gisborne had to be found, and they decided to send me. While Chastagnon was still in Auckland, the bishop told him of this decision. He was to prepare for his departure from Gisborne, and I would be sent to replace him as soon as possible.

PART 8. MY APPOINTMENT TO GISBORNE

SUMMARY. −1. I am in the dark about the bishop's discussions with Chastagnon. − 2. The prelate tells me that he is thinking of sending me to Gisborne. − 3. I am not impressed. My reasons. − 4. Our discussion. − 5. I suspect that Fr Chastagnon is in financial difficulty. − 6. The bishop decides to send me to Gisborne. Out of obedience I accept.

1. Over lunch and dinner the bishop spoke to the lay brothers and myself of Fr Chastagnon's dedication in building a fine large church and paying off nearly the whole debt. I had not been privy to all their discussions. Twice the bishop entertained him to lunch, but they spoke in English and French about insignificant matters. Fr Chastagnon spoke to me personally a couple of times about his mission. We used French. He told me about building the church and the debt. He saw me once more before leaving Auckland and mentioned that he had asked the bishop to transfer him so he could recuperate. His Lordship agreed. Chastagnon said he was sorry to be leaving such good people, who, while extremely poor, were so well-intentioned, but for his health he had to. I asked him why, since he had started the project, he wouldn't see it through and stay until the debt was repaid.

'The debt's nothing to speak of, just £300,' he said, 'and I need to recuperate. The bishop has approved my transfer to another mission – Pukekohe, I believe.'

'Who is going to replace you?'

'I'm not absolutely sure, but His Lordship intimated that it would be you. I'm sure that if you are sent, you'll be fine and enjoy it.'

'I can't go. I can't speak English. I'd be no use. I don't believe the bishop's considering me for any post at the moment, including Gisborne. I'd have to learn some English first.'

2. A couple of days later, after Fr Chastagnon's departure, Mons. Steins mentioned to me all the good he had done and his request for a change. He felt that he could not deny him this and that he needed a well-earned rest.

'Who will you send to Gisborne, Your Excellency, to replace him?' I asked.

'Well, I have to send someone. You're the only priest available. I'm considering sending you. What do you think of that?'

'If I knew a little English, I wouldn't hesitate. But I don't. I'd be useless. I could only say Mass, as I do here. I wouldn't be able to function as a missionary.'

'True, in the beginning. But after a short while, by dint of circumstances, you'd start learning the language. If you stay here, you won't make much progress in English because you can still speak Italian or French.'

'I'd be no use to the parishioners. I wouldn't be able to understand them or they me. They wouldn't be happy with you, Excellency, for sending them a useless priest.'

'This happens all the time in the missions. People recognise that missionaries are sent where they are most needed and that they might have to learn the local language on the spot. If I had another priest available, I would send him, but I don't. There's only you. Think it over. Don't be upset about the language difficulty. You'll pick it up quickly. I have to use you because of the need.'

'I will think it over, Excellency, but I still don't think it's practical, given my total ignorance of English.'

3. I was dismayed with the bishop's proposal. I could see his point that, forced by necessity, I would learn English more quickly there than in Auckland, but he was wanting to send me to a place where I would be the sole priest and not able to communicate. I would surely be faced with enormous difficulties, given my ignorance of the language. This would be due to no fault of my own but of the person who considered putting me in such a terribly embarrassing position. I also believed that the parishioners would be upset with the decision. Besides being critical of my ignorance, they would be annoyed with the bishop. I also felt that my reasons for not wanting to go had been neither understood nor acknowledged by him. In the final analysis, however, I had to capitulate. He had no one else to send. Pukekohe was without a priest. He couldn't abandon Gisborne. In his position, I would have made the same decision. Nevertheless, that didn't solve my problems. God had His own intention, however, while I

wanted to act in accordance with common sense and human wisdom. He uses the clumsy, inept instruments that we are to remind us that of ourselves we can lay no claim to good or glory.

4. Two days later, after speaking with the vicar-general and Fr Walter, the bishop summoned me and came immediately to the point: 'I have decided to send you to Gisborne because I have no other priest available. I not only hope but am convinced you will be successful and do well. You're an experienced missionary. You won't have any problem.'

'If the Holy Spirit were to grace me miraculously with a repeat of Pentecost things will be fine, but otherwise, I'm not so sure.'*

'Experienced missionaries don't need miracles, but if one were needed, God would provide. You'll see that in no time at all you'll understand and be understood. Cheer up. It'll be fine.'

'Excellency, I'd like you to know that English isn't the only problem. I've also heard that the church is saddled with an enormous debt. What can I do about that? I'd be no use whatsoever.'

'Don't worry. It's only a small debt of about £300.'

'Well, how will only two hundred poor parishioners pay it off?'

'Little by little,' the prelate replied. 'There's no urgency and it's not a lot of money. Besides, Irish Catholics are generous and Fr Chastagnon will sort it out. You won't have to concern yourself.'

'I believe, Excellency, that the debt is much greater than you have been led to believe.'

'No, no,' he replied. 'I myself have examined the bills and when the promissory notes are honoured, there will be only £300 to pay, not a lot at all.'

I had heard that Fr McDonald was very pleased that the bishop was sending me to Gisborne. I understood that he wanted to get rid of me and remove me from the bishop's side because I was opposed to the acceptance of the two priests I mentioned earlier. Once I was gone he could persuade the bishop to admit them to the diocese. My suspicions were confirmed by the Jesuit lay brother. I was annoyed, but I didn't say anything to the bishop.

5. When the bishop said the debt was only £300 I was incredulous and expressed my scepticism. 'If the amount is as you say, Excellency, and easy to repay, why does Chastagnon now want a transfer? I rather believe he can't pay it and he wants to take off. He wants to extricate himself from the mess he has created and embroil someone else.'

'That's a very harsh judgement of a fellow priest,' Mons. Steins sternly

---

* The scriptural allusion is to the visitation of the Holy Spirit on the apostles in Jerusalem, giving them the gift of tongues. Acts 2:4.

replied. 'He's been a long time in Gisborne and worked very hard. Now he wants a change to recuperate. I think it would be unfair to deny him his request.'

'Maybe, Your Excellency, but I must say I don't put much faith in the reasons he has advanced. In my view, a priest who has worked hard in his mission becomes even more attached to it. If he were happy, he would not want to leave. That he has asked you for a transfer indicates there is something serious behind his need for a change.'

'Not everyone thinks like you. There's no need to be so suspicious without good, clear evidence. Do you have any proof of your suspicions?'

'No, Excellency, I have no actual proof. My point is that it may not be exactly as Fr Chastagnon has said, and that there could be other, undisclosed motives for his eagerness to leave Gisborne.'

6. After our long discussion, Mons. Steins concluded, 'I have listened patiently, sincerely and openly to all your reasons and objections. I acknowledge some difficulties, but anyone would face them anywhere. What priest wouldn't have something to contend with in his mission? The difficulties you raise are not serious enough to make me change my mind about sending you to Gisborne. I have to. I have no one else. I'm sure you will do well within a few months and we'll both be happy, and I'm pleased that …'

'Are you saying, Your Excellency, that you do want me to go to Gisborne?'

'Yes. That will make me very happy.'

'As a dutiful priest, I will go wherever you desire. You are my superior, Excellency. You have the right to command, and it's my duty to obey.'

'Excellent. Well said. You agree then to go to Gisborne?'

'Yes, Excellency, but on one condition.'

'Namely?'

'That it be on your conscience and you take full responsibility for any messes I unwittingly make through my ignorance of the language?'

'Yes, yes,' the bishop immediately replied. 'I'll take full responsibility, but I'm sure none will occur.'

'Well, then, Excellency, there's nothing more to say except to quote St Paul's words to our divine Master, Jesus Christ, "I will place my trust in your word." I will go to Gisborne. I have nothing to add.'

Part 9. Preparations for Departure

Summary. – 1. Forced to dress like an English clergyman; my distaste. – 2. We are provided with new clothing. – 3. I agree with the Jesuit lay brother about the two priests from the Wellington diocese. – 4. Farewelled by friends. – 5. Packing. – 6. En route to Gisborne. – 7. We disembark at Gisborne.

1. I mentioned earlier that when Bishop Pompallier was Bishop of Auckland he wanted his secular clergy to wear the soutane and members of religious orders their habit both inside and outside the presbytery. This, in New Zealand, afforded them protection and distinguished them as Catholic priests. Mons. Croke abolished this practice and insisted they dress as priests did in England and Ireland. They were to wear the soutane only in the presbytery or church. Outside they had to wear black trousers, a waistcoat, knee-length coat, a clerical collar and top hat. This secular style did not suit me at all. I would dearly have preferred to continue wearing my habit inside and outside; strange looks from Protestants wouldn't have worried me. But I was told that I would have to do the same as everyone else.

2. Mons. Steins asked me if Br Joseph and I had brought this other kind of clothing with us. I replied that we hadn't because in Africa we always wore our religious habit. In Auckland we had been wearing the same habits for more than three months. Although they were practically new when we left Gerba,* they had become worn and faded after the long voyage. I asked Mons. Steins if we had to dress like the other clergy when we were outside.

'Yes, you must,' he replied. 'But Br Joseph is to wear ordinary clothes.' I told him that I would be sorry not to be able to wear my habit outside. But he said that I had to do the same as other priests, and conform to the law which in England prohibited the religious habit being worn outside the presbytery. I obeyed the bishop's wishes. The bishop had Fr McDonald fetch a Catholic tailor to take our measurements. A few days later he brought Br Joseph and myself good quality, well-made suits. I was provided with black trousers, waistcoat, coat and a clerical collar. The suit cost £15 (375 francs). I got my top hat from a hatter's for thirty-two francs and my boots cost eighteen francs. In Europe they would have cost less than half that, but in New Zealand clothing was very expensive because most of the material was imported from England at a high price. Br Joseph Ricci's suit was also woollen. It was not such good quality, but still well-made and hard wearing. Practically speaking it was the kind of suit worn by a man in the street, even down to the hat. His outfit,

---

* Vaggioli was first appointed as a missionary to the Tunisian island of Gerba from 1876 until 1879, when his superiors decided to send him to New Zealand.

The only known photograph of Vaggioli wearing a clerical suit, c. 1880.

including his shoes and hat, cost 250 francs. Mons. Steins paid for our suits and told us to get single tickets for the steamer to Gisborne from Fr McDonald. The tickets cost £5 each (250 francs for both). The bishop paid our expenses on the understanding that Fr Adalbert Sullivan, our superior, would reimburse him when he arrived from Europe.

3. I regret not being able to remember the name of the Jesuit lay brother, also an Italian. He was a good, affable, deeply religious man. When we had a little free time we would get together for a chat. He thought a great deal of me and I felt the same towards him. There were no secrets between us and we supported each other, sharing our burdens and difficulties. He was very upset that the bishop was sending me so far away because he said that I was the only person he could confide in as a friend. The poor man was intimidated by the bishop and was sorry he had agreed to accompany him because at his age of nearly sixty-eight he was made to work too hard. He had to go three or four times a day to the central post office, which was about two kilometres from Ponsonby, and he was hardly ever given money to take the tram.* I mentioned to him

* Literally, 'horse-drawn tram' (*l'omnibus a cavalli* in Italian).

about the behaviour of the two priests from the Wellington diocese wanting to be accepted. I knew he was the soul of discretion and wouldn't mention a word to anyone, not even the bishop. I asked him to do everything he could to prevent their admission to the diocese. In any case, I told him to keep me informed, and if the bishop did accept them, to write to me immediately. I would then inform Propaganda in Rome. He promised he would and he kept his word.

4. A couple of days before our departure for Gisborne, Br Joseph and I went to say farewell to our Newton confrères. They were pleased to see the back of us because, as I have mentioned elsewhere, they didn't like Italians. From Newton, we went by tram to the vicar-general's in Parnell. I thanked him in French for all he had done for us and he received us very cordially. On our return we visited the cathedral priests and by evening we returned home. The following morning after Mass I thanked Mother Superior for her and her sisters' kindness to me. I particularly praised Sr Bernarda for her consideration. She acted as my interpreter. The sisters were upset about my departure because I had been reliable and said Mass punctually for them in a devout, simple, dignified manner. They also mentioned that I did not draw it out, taking only twenty-six minutes. I was rather surprised at their comments, realising how carefully the good sisters had observed my every action. 'Now that you are going,' Sr Bernarda said, 'we will have to rely on the cathedral again to provide Mass for us and we'll have no guarantee about punctuality. God grant us patience.'

5. We poor monks did not need long to pack. My trunk contained a few books, my portable altar and underclothes. It had hardly been opened since my departure from Africa. I had left things practically intact in anticipation of my next posting. The other suitcases were quickly packed. We had only our personal laundry and the clothes we had brought from Gerba; just a few simple, cheap, well-worn items. I had bought only a hat to wear when riding or in the rain because I didn't want to ruin my fine silk top hat which cost about thirty-two francs. In the trunk I also placed the carrier for my altar kit, which I would use for saying Mass in various places in the mission, assuming that the Gisborne church would have everything necessary for liturgical functions. I never thought of bringing with me from Africa pillowslips, towels, cutlery, napkins, etc. for my future home. I imagined that whichever mission I was sent to would have everything needed. On the morning of our departure, a horse and cart took our luggage to the steamer we would embark on for Poverty Bay, as the Gisborne district is called.

6. We left on a Thursday, at the beginning of February. It would have been between 6 and 8 February. We were to depart from the bishop's residence at 11 a.m. Just before then, the Jesuit lay brother bade us farewell. He was terribly upset, and wept like a baby. His Lordship came out, urging us not to be distressed

and saying that everything would be fine. We asked him for a blessing. He obliged, embraced us and saw us to the front door. The Jesuit lay brother asked him if he could accompany us to the steamer. He agreed. A coach, brought by the cathedral administrator, was awaiting us at the entrance. After a further blessing from the bishop, the four of us entered the closed carriage and immediately set off for the wharf. We arrived in just over half an hour.

The steamer was a large 2500-ton vessel providing a service between New Zealand and Australia. It had come from Sydney two days previously and would return to Melbourne after coasting New Zealand. First class was pleasant, clean and comfortable, but second class, as I have already mentioned, was a proper pigsty, used by few passengers. The voyage from Auckland to Gisborne was 360 miles, or 666 kilometres, with a stop at Tauranga, in the Bay of Plenty. The weather was fine, but the Pacific Ocean had its own mood. As soon as we were out of the harbour, the steamer started to roll and I felt nauseous. I couldn't eat a thing until we reached our destination. For the whole forty hours it took to reach Poverty Bay, I ate nothing and spent most of the time in my cabin. Br Joseph, however, was unaffected and spent the day on deck. At 9 a.m. on Saturday, the steamer dropped anchor in the bay, near Gisborne.

7. Before we entered the bay, stewards came and took our luggage and that of a dozen other passengers on to the deck. Meanwhile row-boats came out to pick us up and take us ashore. The trunks were loaded separately. We and four other passengers took our suitcases and clambered into a row-boat manned by two sailors. They began rowing us towards the landing.

The only Gisborne landing place was by the banks of the Waipaoa river, near its outlet. The river mouth entrance was difficult because it was particularly shallow at low tide, causing considerable turbulence. Sometimes boats sank there. The least one could expect was a drenching. Fortunately it was only a short twenty-metre stretch before entering the gentle waters of the river. We were lucky that particular day because the sea was quite calm and high tide had been only an hour before. We negotiated the passage with very few jolts and getting just a little wet. An hour's steady rowing took us to the wooden jetty on the right bank of the river. We had landed in the small settlement of Gisborne.

Above: St Mary's Church, Gisborne, soon after erection in 1879.

Left: Fr Stephen Chastagnon, Vaggioli's predecessor as parish priest of Gisborne.

CHAPTER THREE

I Land Myself in a Mess
(1880)

PART 1. ARRIVAL

SUMMARY. – 1. Our arrival in Gisborne. – 2. We go to the church. – 3. Welcome at the presbytery. – 4. Tour of the settlement. – 5. The settlement of Gisborne. – 6. Gisborne valley. – 7. My first Sunday in Gisborne.

1. Fr Chastagnon and about a dozen prominent Catholics were waiting for us at the landing, as well as many children and onlookers curious to see the new Catholic missionary. Fr Chastagnon introduced me to his parishioners, who welcomed me with considerable pleasure and warmth. Our luggage was taken and carried to the presbytery, which was only about 300 metres from the jetty. It was a hot day, being February, which is summer in the Antipodes. The sun was shining and the weather was settled. Chastagnon spoke to us in French and the others in English, acting as our interpreter. I began to actually experience how horrible it was not to know English and to have to rely on an interpreter. How would I manage after Fr Chastagnon left? The very thought made me desolate, but I tried to brush it aside. In the presence of such good folk I simply had to put on a brave front. They greeted me very warmly, welcoming me with words I couldn't understand. I was so distressed, I almost burst out crying.

2. After the welcome and greetings we went to the church next to the presbytery for a brief visit to the Blessed Sacrament. I could not say Mass, because feeling sick on the boat that morning, I had had a cup of coffee.* I fervently prayed for the Lord to come to my aid. I felt absolutely lost and useless with my lack of English. I begged Jesus to help me and implored Him to ignore my worthlessness and send His Holy Spirit to my aid. As the church was dedicated to Our Lady, Star of the Sea, I prayed to her to be my guide, support and strength in my depth of ignorance and ineptitude!

3. After our visit to the Blessed Sacrament, Fr Chastagnon took us to his small wooden presbytery, which was only about twelve metres from the church, enclosed with a picket fence. When we left the church, most of the parishioners who had accompanied us, took their leave. Only three or four came to the

---

* Having broken his fast, Vaggioli would not have been able to say Mass.

presbytery and we went into the small drawing room. The house, which had a covered verandah, was single-storey, comprising a drawing room, a dining room, a study, two bedrooms and a kitchen in the rear. Fr Chastagnon served refreshments and we spent half an hour chatting, with him interpreting.

4. After the pleasant midday lunch, Fr Chastagnon took me on a thorough inspection of the church, inside and out. The interior was not completely lined but the exterior was finished. It was a large handsome church built in the Gothic style, typical of New Zealand churches. He then took me to meet Mr Butt, manager of the Union Bank of Australia. He was tall and slim and about thirty-five years old. He was a Protestant minister's son, but his wife was Catholic. The bank was on the ground floor, with accommodation upstairs.

For all intents and purposes, Mr Butt was more Catholic than Protestant. He never went to his own church but would come to ours, frequently attending Mass and vespers with his wife. He was one of our most dedicated, competent singers. His wife was a good, devout Catholic. They were, however, upset at not having children. We then moved on to the Jennings', an excellent Catholic couple with a baby. They had a tobacconist's shop in the main street and their own home was behind it. Fr Chastagnon then took me to visit another two or three prominent Catholic families, including the O'Mearas, an Irish family with grown-up children. Finally we strolled through the township to give me an overall impression.

5. The township of Gisborne was built on a level strip of land, bounded by a deep river running north and south-east. South-west, a shallow, stagnant stream separated the spur from the rest of the large harbour. To the west the land led to the beautiful, wide valley of Poverty Bay. It got its name from Cook, the English navigator, from his first visit when the natives refused him supplies. At the south-east end, by the landing, the spur was only 200 metres wide. But a mile to the west towards the valley, it was more than 700 metres wide. The settlement was spread along this strip of land, but most of the main buildings and houses were near the landing. Most private homes and public buildings were wooden, except the Bank of New Zealand and a three-storey store, which were concrete.

There were four churches. The Catholic church was about 200 metres from the landing, the Anglican about 600 metres, just off the main street, the Presbyterian 700 metres away on the same street as the Catholic, and the Wesleyan was 200 metres from the Anglican church. All four churches were large wooden buildings, but the Anglican was the biggest and most beautiful. All were in debt. The Catholic church's actual debt was about £750, the Anglican £650, the Presbyterian £400 and the Wesleyan about £390.

The township boasted a fine post office, a registrar's office, custom-house, court, town hall, police station and government primary, secondary and technical schools. There were three banks, two large concert halls, five big hotels, about a hundred shops of all kinds and two printers. One published the *Poverty Bay Herald*, the daily newspaper, and the other two papers, one fortnightly and the other twice weekly. There were about fifteen lawyers, half a dozen public notaries and four or five doctors. The township's European population was only about 2500. To the east, however, just over 500 metres from the landing, was a native Maori village with about a thousand inhabitants. To the west, about a kilometre from the settlement, there was another small native village, with about a hundred Maori.

6. The Gisborne valley extended west of the township in an almost triangular shape. It was about nine kilometres long, bordered on the west by a mountain range, and was about nine kilometres wide from north to south. There were European homesteads in four areas of the valley, as well as two government primary schools and three hotels. At the north-west corner was the settlement of Ormond. It had about 400 European inhabitants, a court-house, government school, two large hotels and some shops.

Native villages were also scattered through the valley, with an overall population of about six or seven hundred. A river flowed through with its outlet into the harbour. The soil was a mixture of mountain and forest detritus and alluvial deposits. By 1880 nearly all the fertile land had fallen into European hands and was in pasture, intensively grazed for horses, cattle and sheep. European grass seed was sown. Seed produced sold at 6.2 francs a kilo and annual exports realised an average of 375,000 francs. It was much sought after because it was the finest in New Zealand.

New Zealand had an Upper and a Lower House.* It was divided into counties, except for towns. Each county had the right to elect a European Member of the House of Representatives (MHR) for a European population of over 9000 inhabitants. Otherwise, two counties could elect one. Cook County, in which Gisborne was situated, was huge. It was about 500 kilometres long and 250 kilometres wide, with only 7500 Europeans scattered over about fifteen settlements. Combining with a portion of Wairoa County's population, it comprised 10,000 inhabitants, and was able to elect its own MHR.

7. Two days after our arrival in Gisborne, being Sunday, Fr Chastagnon went to Ormond in a trap to say Mass. At ten-thirty he returned to Gisborne. At 11 a.m., after the singing of the *asperges,*† I began to celebrate Mass. The

---

* At the time New Zealand had a Legislative Council, or Upper House, and a House of Representatives, or Lower House. The latter is referred to here.
† The reference is to the solemn blessing with holy water before the beginning of the traditional Latin High Mass. ('Wash me clean of my guilt, purify me from my sin.' Psalm 51.)

accomplished choir sang the 'Kyrie' and 'Gloria'. After I read out the Gospel, Fr Chastagnon approached the altar and I sat down. He gave the sermon, but I didn't understand a word. Later he explained to me that he made a farewell speech, mentioning that I had been sent to replace him. He reassured and encouraged the congregation, etc. After his address, I continued saying Mass and the choir sang the 'Credo', 'Sanctus' and 'Agnus Dei'. Most of the women left at the end. The men stayed behind to have a meeting about Fr Chastagnon's departure. I didn't participate because I couldn't understand what was said. I said my prayers of thanksgiving and retired to the presbytery for a cup of coffee, feeling depressed about the dismal future. The meeting ended at midday and Fr Chastagnon came home. At 7 p.m. there were sung vespers, a sermon and benediction of the Blessed Sacrament. Fr Chastagnon wanted me to sing vespers, but I declined and he had to officiate. He then gave a brief sermon, the service ending with benediction. The women left while the men stayed in church for another meeting, which I also attended. They read out a farewell speech to Fr Chastagnon and presented him with a purse of money for his journey, as a token of their affection. He made a brief speech of thanks. They then individually paid their respects and the meeting ended.

Part 2. I Try to Clarify the Situation

Summary. – 1. A parish visit through the valley. – 2. Distasteful custom of offering spirits as hospitality; my argument with Fr Chastagnon. – 3. I request Fr Chastagnon take me to the bank to find out about the debt. – 4. Another trip. – 5. I ask Fr Chastagnon to stay; he is impatient to leave. – 6. His departure for Auckland.

1. Over the next few days, Fr Chastagnon took me to visit Catholics living in Gisborne. He wanted both to introduce me to them and see where they lived, and to bid them farewell. He was to depart on the next steamer, which was due the following Friday. We visited every Catholic family in the valley. We went in the mission trap drawn by its sturdy horse. Everywhere we were welcomed with open arms. They all offered us spirits. I had no intention of drinking spirits during the day. This was a Catholic custom, especially among the Irish, who had brought it from the old country with them. When a priest paid a visit, whether morning or afternoon, he had to be offered alcohol, such as whisky, brandy, rum or wine. They generally offered whisky or brandy. Even the poorest family had a bottle of some kind kept for the priest. I knew the damage this evil custom caused and consequently I always refused alcohol, saying that I didn't like spirits and they affected my health. Fr Chastagnon and most missionaries would accept at least a small glass in every home they visited. They were used to it, but I was not, and I had no intention of starting.

2. This custom was very harmful and I was determined not to accept alcohol, even if I was thirsty. Parishioners were very surprised, and asked Fr Chastagnon if I preferred something else. I told Fr Chastagnon to tell them that I had a sensitive stomach and alcohol did not agree with me. My refusal was in the interests of my health. To tell the truth, this was really just an excuse. Often I did feel thirsty and would have liked to have a small drink, but I didn't want to get used to this dangerous custom. So I put up with being thirsty, realising that if I asked for a drink of water, I wouldn't get one. Fr Chastagnon also urged me to take a tot, saying that it would do me good. I held my ground even with him. In one home we had the following conversation:

'If you won't accept a drink,' he said, 'you'll offend these people's hospitality.'

'Why would they get upset and be offended?'

'Because you'd be refusing their generosity.'

'I do appreciate that, but I have to think of my health. I'm not used to taking alcohol outside meals. It upsets me.'

'But you could just have a sip to show your appreciation of their hospitality. That would do.'

'No, I can't and I won't. They shouldn't be offended.'

'But all priests accept at least a tiny drop, including me. Why can't you? It won't do you any harm.'

'That's not true. You and other missionaries are used to it. I'm not. It doesn't affect you, but it would me. You go ahead. Not me.'

'You're the first missionary I've ever met who won't accept their hospitality.'

'Be that as it may, that's how I am. I won't take what harms me. However, there is another reason. I see this custom as extremely dangerous for missionaries. They could easily become habituated to alcohol and become drunkards!'

'Really! In moderation alcohol does no harm.'

'I disagree. Even drinking in moderation from home to home, priests would be offered whisky in one, brandy in another, rum in a third, gin in a fourth, wine in a fifth and so on. Few would stop at one drink. The various drinks would take their effect. If I did this, I would be drunk by the time I returned home. It wouldn't be long before I took to drinking and I got used to it. I would not want that to happen to me.'

'Do what you think is best,' he replied. 'I'm not going to make you.'

'Thank you. I appreciate that.' He then left me in peace.

3. I asked Fr Chastagnon to take me to see the manager of the Bank of New Zealand about the church debt. He obliged but, unfortunately, because the manager did not speak French, Fr Chastagnon acted as interpreter and gave me

the same information he had given the bishop, claiming that the debt was about £300. I had to accept his explanation, but I didn't believe him because I noticed that sometimes he was uncomfortable with my questions. But how could I find out the truth and resolve my doubts with a biased interpreter? Meanwhile news spread through the valley that Fr Chastagnon was leaving and a new missionary had arrived to replace him. When the creditors heard, they pressed him for payment. I saw some of the bills and asked Chastagnon about them. He said that there was still a small amount to pay for pews and a few other things, but any other bills were to be ignored as invalid.

4. One afternoon we went by horse and trap to Ormond, a small settlement at the northern end of the valley, about sixteen kilometres from Gisborne. We reached the Ormond Hotel and were warmly greeted by the proprietor, a Protestant, but a good man and well-disposed to missionaries. His only vice was that he drank too much. Otherwise, he was very kind-hearted. His wife was a devout Catholic, without peer in the district. She practically managed the hotel because her husband was nearly always drunk. We were offered refreshments and I accepted a glass of beer. We then visited another two or three families in Ormond. Local roads were not much more than tracks and only one was well made. Throughout the district there were only dirt roads without metal or gravel. In summer they were dust-choked and in winter the mud was nearly a metre deep, making them impassable. After about an hour at Ormond, we returned to Gisborne. The following day Fr Chastagnon wanted me to have lunch with him at an Irish horse-trader's. His wife was half-caste Maori. She was a good, well-educated Catholic. They had no children, however. It's a curious fact that half-caste women are often infertile even into the third generation and frequently die quite young.

5. I was very aware of the serious difficulty of my situation due to my ignorance of English, and I urged Fr Chastagnon to stay on until after Easter to hear confessions, or at least stay a further fortnight. My pleas were of no avail. On the contrary, he was impatient to get away as soon as possible. He would have left earlier if there had been a steamer, but he was forced to wait eight days. Even before our arrival he had packed his suitcases, taking blankets, sheets, pillowslips, towels, tablecloths, serviettes, cutlery, etc. All that remained were the barest necessities and articles that he was happy to discard. He left most of the crockery simply because it would have broken during travel. He removed the only chalice from the church, four chasubles and two albs, claiming he brought them with him originally. He just left a small violet confessional stole and one for visiting the sick, and a makeshift alb made by a Gisborne lady from women's clothing. It was just as well I had brought a portable altar kit containing the necessities for the liturgy, including a chalice, etc., so that I was able to perform as a

priest. Otherwise, I would not even have been able to say Mass.

6. On Friday, about 11 a.m., the Auckland steamer entered the harbour from the south. It was to anchor for about four hours, unloading and loading mail and cargo. At midday we had a pleasant lunch together. Br Joseph cooked us a tasty Italian meal, since he was not familiar with English cooking. At 2 p.m. Fr Chastagnon left the presbytery accompanied by myself, Br Joseph and about twenty parishioners. At the jetty he embraced us warmly, shook hands and went down to board a dinghy for the steamer. Two prominent laymen were to accompany him out to the boat. As soon as they were seated, the rowers set to. The dinghy moved quickly down river into the harbour. We waved from the jetty at the departing figure of the priest. Soon the boat steered west, disappearing from sight. That was the last we saw of Fr Chastagnon. Shortly afterwards Br Joseph and I returned home. I felt bereft and distressed, finding myself in sole charge and ignorant of English.

Part 3. Alone and Aghast

Summary. – 1. Our washerwoman shops for us. – 2. Parishioners visit me; my embarrassment. – 3. On my first Sunday I say two Masses and end up fasting for forty-eight hours. – 4. The ghastly burden I face; my momentous decision! – 5. Some parishioners complain strongly about having a priest who can't speak English.

1. Br Joseph couldn't buy food because he didn't speak English. I had requested Fr Chastagnon to ask our washerwoman to do our daily shopping, for a few days at least, until Br Joseph gained some practice. She was a devout Catholic and willingly agreed. I gave her sufficient money to buy what we needed – firewood, potatoes, eggs, etc. Mrs O'Meara, an Irish woman, had cooked for Fr Chastagnon when we were there. Br Joseph helped her and thus quickly learnt where to buy groceries. The good woman was extremely helpful to us at the time and subsequently. Besides cooking, Br Joseph cleaned the church and presbytery. He also looked after the horse and trap and tended the small vegetable plot by the kitchen. The washerwoman brought us some hens so that we could have eggs, which were very expensive.

2. The day after Fr Chastagnon's departure, some parishioners visited me at the presbytery. I received them in the small drawing room. The atmosphere was strained and the situation bizarre. They spoke to me and I couldn't understand them. I said a few words in German, which they didn't understand. We then used sign language, with no better result. After a few minutes they went away sad and disappointed, and I was left feeling more crestfallen and desolate than them. For a while parishioners continued to visit me, asking after Fr Chastagnon,

to speak to me about their concerns and to pay their respects. But when they realised I didn't understand a word, they departed disheartened.

On Saturday, three or four ladies came over, including Mrs Butt, wife of the manager of the Union Bank, and Mrs O'Meara. They were some of the leading Catholic women of Gisborne, whom I had met previously. I received them in the drawing room and after the usual greetings, they indicated to me that they wished to inspect the presbytery. I had no objection. They were well used to housework and began to examine everything in the small drawing room. They chatted together in English and I didn't understand. They appeared familiar with the house. They went into every room, opening all the cupboards and drawers. Nothing escaped their attention, especially the two bedrooms and dining room. They examined the bedding, counted the sheets and tablecloths, quietly discussing as they went along. I observed them in silence. They also wanted to see my clothes and underwear. I had only one religious habit, which I wore daily inside. It was threadbare and faded. They also went through my shirts and other clothing in the drawers, taking note of everything. Not knowing where all this was leading, I was nonplussed about their examining my wretched clothing. Being a monk, my clothes were very simple, but the ladies ignored my protests. Finally, they wanted to take my measurements. I absolutely refused, but they insisted and I relented, thinking that perhaps they wanted to make me a religious habit, which I needed, and would send me an account for it. When they had done what they wanted and taken my measurements, they thanked me and left. My understanding was that the ladies wanted to see that the presbytery had everything it needed.

3. On Sundays normally the first Mass was said at six-thirty at Gisborne and the second Mass at Ormond at eleven. On the following Sunday, the first Mass was said at seven-thirty at Ormond, and the second at eleven in Gisborne. Sung vespers were always in Gisborne after sunset. Sunday arrived. Since on the preceding Sunday Mass had been said at Gisborne at eleven, the first Mass of this Sunday was said at Gisborne at six-thirty and the second at Ormond at eleven. After Mass in Gisborne, the horse and trap were made ready. I took my Mass kit and, accompanied by a parishioner acting as coachman, who knew the route well, we departed for Ormond for the second Mass. We arrived about ten-thirty. We stopped at the court-house used for Mass. The Protestant minister held his service at eleven in the local school. There were no other public buildings where Mass could be celebrated. The judge's bench was my altar. Shortly after eleven I began Mass and about sixty Catholics participated. The service finished at eleven forty-five and I put everything away in the small kit.

After thanksgiving, the owner of the Ormond hotel collected my things and invited me over. When we arrived, he and his Catholic wife took me into the dining room where others, including my coachman, were. They greeted me and lunch was served. I wanted to return to Gisborne as soon as possible, but the mistress demurred and made me understand that first I should eat. She brought me some soup, which I refused because I did not feel like food. There was plenty of meat on the table, but I had no appetite. People looked at me pointedly and muttered among themselves as they ate. I was very upset and felt like crying. My coachman ate with gusto. The hostess was annoyed that I did not eat, but with signs I made her understand that I had an upset stomach. She brought me a cup of coffee and milk, which I forced down.

Before starting off I tried to pay for lunch and their feeding the horse, but the hostess refused. They would not accept payment from the priest. They said that whenever I came to Ormond, I should regard the hotel as home. I gratefully thanked the good proprietors. With an empty stomach from the previous evening (I was fasting for Lent), I departed. When I got home I told Br Joseph everything. He immediately wanted to prepare me a meal, but I said I would eat in the evening after vespers and benediction. But even then I ate next to nothing because I felt weak, tired and most upset. Consequently, from Saturday until midday Monday I ate virtually nothing. At lunch on Monday, being even weaker and more exhausted from my exertions, I did not eat sufficiently. The same thing happened four Sundays in a row. I suffered exhaustion, general discomfort and a severe deterioration of health. Not eating for forty-eight hours and travelling thirty-two kilometres in a horse and trap every Sunday to celebrate Mass exacerbated my condition.

4. Not speaking English, being unable to make myself understood or to understand put me in a terrible position. In my room I wept like a baby over my predicament. I prayed and beseeched the Lord and Our Lady to come to my aid. How could I learn English without help? How could I learn the language if I couldn't communicate through Italian, Latin or French with someone?! How could I learn to pronounce English, which is so difficult for foreigners, without someone to teach me? I had brought an Italian/English dictionary with me from Malta, which included a pronunciation guide. But it was virtually useless without a teacher or someone to help me with pronunciation, because spoken English is very different from the written. Parishioners were unable to converse with me and left sad and disappointed. I felt like crying, and often I was on the point of bursting into tears, but I managed to control myself so they didn't notice. Mr Jennings and other members of the parish committee visited me several times and noticed my distress. With signs and gestures of support they encouraged me to be patient. But I was desolate and wept over my unhappy situation.

Three weeks went by and my affliction continued to grow. I often begged the Lord and our Heavenly Mother to come to my aid, but no miracle happened to enable me to speak English and I was left in the deepest, darkest distress. To add to my woes, I often received bills through the post. I could see the amounts owing, but I could not understand the contents. And I didn't have a penny available! My affliction troubled me so much that I couldn't eat or sleep. I was obsessed with resolving the problem, but my suffering continued, with not a glimmer of hope. My health steadily declined and I experienced a general malaise, fully feeling the seriousness of my situation. I thought that if I continued in this state of mind much longer, I would soon either be dead or go mad. Often I thought of taking a steamer and returning to Europe without saying a word to anyone. That would end my torment. I had brought sufficient money from Africa to pay for the voyage. At other times, I was tempted to return to Auckland. With God's help, however, I resisted these temptations. But my affliction grew worse.

Finally, divine assistance came. God did not perform a Pentecost miracle for me, but he sent me a good angel to help me appreciate and understand the situation. Eventually I was able to reason: I'm silly to berate myself over my ignorance of English! Did I put myself in this mess? No, I did everything in my power to prevent myself coming here! I obeyed out of a sense of duty and obedience to God's will. God put me in this mess. I had personally nothing to do with it. So, if it was God's will, He can, if He chooses, free me. He's done it for others. Now He can do it for me. I know I don't deserve it, but I am one of His flock. If He doesn't perform a miracle, maybe He doesn't want to or it's not needed. It has to be His decision. He is omniscient. He knows that I mean well and is aware of my crushing burden, sadness and distress. If He who sees and knows everything chooses to leave me in this wretched situation, it must be His will. Would God have sent me here to die from despair or go mad? Hardly. He would want to support me in doing good. Away then, melancholy! Down with depression! Pain be gone! I don't want my health ruined. I want peace and happiness and no more distress. I'll place myself in God's hands. I know I can't change things on my own! After this long soliloquy, an inner voice whispered: 'Yes, you're right. Trust in God. This is His doing. He will help you out of your difficulty. You know you can't fathom God's purpose. Leave everything to Him and your problems will disappear.' This voice greatly consoled me. I did place everything in God's hands, leaving my language problems and the rest to Him. My pain and sorrow disappeared. Peace and contentment soothed my heart, and I promised the Lord to do my best. I was singularly blessed with God's goodness. Else how could a wretch like me have survived?

5. Several parishioners complained about the bishop sending them a priest who couldn't speak English. One young Irishman, in particular, was critical of him not sending an Irish missionary. But the majority of Catholics, especially in the township, were sympathetic towards me. They supported me and hoped I would soon learn English. Those who complained were aptly rewarded later. In 1883, after my departure, Bishop Luck did send them an Irish priest who

was an habitual drunkard, causing considerable scandal. The bishop had to expel him from the diocese. In 1884 he sent another Irish priest. For several months things seemed fine. The young Irishman mentioned above arranged to marry the Irish priest's maid. Everything was organised and on a Sunday at 11 a.m. the betrothed presented themselves before the altar to be united in marriage. The missionary asked the young man if he wished to marry the young woman. He replied that he did. He then asked the woman. She emphatically replied, 'No!', and she fled the church. The congregation was shocked. But the scandal did not end there. Five days later, the Irish priest and the same young woman took the steamer for Auckland and together they embarked for the United States of America. The colony was aghast. After the unfortunate event in the church, the young man felt so ashamed he left Gisborne.

PART 4. A GLIMMER OF HOPE

SUMMARY. – 1. Regular and encouraging visits from the committee. – 2. Bills arrive, causing me to be critical of Fr Chastagnon. – 3. At last parishioners find a Frenchman to teach me English; Mr Tierry visits me. – 4. His background and personality. – 5. An explanation of the presbytery inspection visit. – 6. The ladies bring the fine things they made for me.

1. Committee members, especially Mr Jennings, often visited me even though I couldn't converse with them. They were aware of my frustration and distress. They noticed an alarming decline in my health and tried to console and encourage me as best they could. I listened, even though I couldn't understand, but from their gestures I could make some sense of things and gained comfort from their visits. I showed them the bills addressed to Fr Chastagnon or the parish priest of Gisborne which had come to the presbytery. They were meaningless to me. The gentlemen indicated that they knew nothing more than me because Fr Chastagnon dealt with the church debt. I tried to make them understand that it was vital for me to find someone who knew at least a little French to help me find out what was owing.

2. In my first two weeks the incoming bills showed the church owing debt just under £100, or 2500 francs. This did not include what the banks were owed. While not understanding the contents, I believed in my heart that the bills were genuine. Otherwise they would not have been sent. I suspected, with good reason, that Fr Chastagnon had deceived the bishop, myself and everyone else, claiming that personal bills amounted to about £20. I was very annoyed about this, realising my situation was even more critical and difficult.

3. Finally, after an extensive search, parishioners succeeded in finding a

Frenchman, Mr Tierry, who lived more than sixty kilometres from Gisborne. He was soon to come to live in Gisborne and they asked him if he would give me English lessons. He agreed, promising to come and see me when next he was in Gisborne. After a few days, Mr Tierry turned up, mentioning the parishioners' request. He said he could not start immediately, but within a week he would be leaving his home because work was not going well and he wanted to come and settle in Gisborne. I asked him if he could give me an hour's lesson three or four days a week and also go over the debt with me. He agreed and said that he could give me an hour's lesson three times a week. I asked him how much he would like to be paid for his trouble. He replied that he didn't want a penny. He would willingly provide the service gratis. I was delighted to find someone to give me some lessons. Mr Tierry was a bearded, short, stocky man, about fifty-five years old with greying hair. He spoke French and English fluently. He had an only son living with him who was about thirty, tall and thin, and more English than French.

4. Who was this Mr Tierry and where did he come from? He soon told me about himself. He was a very well-educated man who had an arts degree from Paris. He had migrated to England, intending to teach French. He there married a Protestant woman. I deduced that, although born and raised a Catholic, it didn't mean much to him and perhaps he did not get married in the Catholic church. They had a son who was christened and raised a Protestant. Perhaps Tierry was taken for a Protestant, too. He told me he had never renounced Catholicism, but did not practise it.

He obtained a well-paid position as a French teacher at a London boarding school for daughters of Protestant gentry. After teaching there for just over a year, he noticed that with the connivance of the principal and teaching staff, young males from a similar nearby school were admitted at night into the girls' school. They spent the night with the girls and in the morning stole away back to their school. This was done under the cloak of secrecy. People were unaware of this secret brothel. Mr Tierry informed the principal, who emphatically denied these goings-on. Meanwhile the evening liaisons continued. He then alerted the school board, comprising members of the London gentry. Fearing a huge scandal, they said they would have a full investigation conducted. Round this time, Mr Tierry's wife became insane and he had to admit her to an asylum, where she was still living in 1880. After a mock investigation, the school's authorities turned on Tierry, accusing him of lying and maligning the two schools. He was sacked and the scandalous behaviour was swept under the carpet. Unemployed and roughly treated, Tierry decided to migrate with his son to New Zealand.

When he arrived in Auckland he could not find employment teaching French. He left the town and rented a small holding to begin farming. He was able to survive but not save. After a few years he left the area. He had heard that Gisborne was thriving and good prices were being fetched for produce. He and his son leased land about sixty kilometres from Gisborne. In the first years things went well, but then came the crash of the Bank of Glasgow and the bottom fell out of food prices. He was ruined. He couldn't continue paying his lease and abandoned farming to live in Gisborne, renting a miserable cottage in which he had his few sticks of furniture. I simply don't know how he managed without a job. As far as I knew they just scraped by. He was really a very good man, but neither he nor his son bothered about church.

5. As I mentioned earlier, as soon as Fr Chastagnon departed, three or four leading Catholic ladies visited and examined everything in the presbytery and took my measurements. At the time I didn't know their purpose. Later I discovered that they wanted to find out if I lacked anything. They measured me to make a new habit to replace my worn and faded one. When they saw what was needed and how much it would cost, they held a meeting in one of their homes and discussed the priest's needs. Members agreed to contribute according to their means and those who could not donate money would make something. They took up a collection and bought the necessary material, which they would soon turn into fine items to present to me.

6. One morning, just over a month after the ladies' visit, Mesdames Butt, O'Meara and Jennings came to the door with the washerwoman, who was carrying a large, well-wrapped parcel. Having deposited this, she left. I welcomed the ladies into the drawing room and called for Tierry, my interpreter. They unwrapped the parcel, putting everything on the table, saying these were necessities for the presbytery. There were four pairs of sheets, four pillow slips, six towels, twelve napkins, tea towels and dishcloths. They also provided me with two linen nightshirts and a soutane to wear inside. They wanted me to try it on immediately to see that it fitted. It was perfect. I asked them how much it all cost, but they replied that there was nothing to pay. The Catholic women had provided it from their donations, not wanting their priest to go without. They wanted him to be dressed appropriately and with a dignity to match his position, which would in turn reflect well on the parishioners. I was amazed at their incredible kindness. I thanked them most sincerely and said I would pray for them. They were very pleased with their results and at my surprise, and smiled with satisfaction. They also encouraged me, saying that they were sure I would soon learn English and feel happier. Shortly afterwards they said goodbye and went home. I was edified by their devotion to their priest.

Part 5. Ascertaining the Degree of Debt on the Church

Summary. – 1. Mr Tierry accompanies me to the bank to find out the extent of the debt. – 2. I seek an answer from the manager. – 3. With Tierry's assistance I examine personal bills. – 4. Understanding the level of debt. How to repay it? – 5. I try to come to an arrangement with some creditors. Will it work? – 6. The bank refuses me a loan of £50. – 7. I ask the bishop for a loan and to go guarantor with the bank.

1. As soon as Mr Tierry came to give me a lesson, I asked him to accompany me to the Bank of New Zealand as my interpreter, so that I could ascertain the actual financial situation and how much the Church owed the bank, because I did not trust Fr Chastagnon's claim. After ten we went to the bank and asked to see the manager privately. He welcomed me courteously. After our greetings he invited us to sit down and he asked us what we wanted. I spoke in French to Tierry and he translated into English for the manager. I said that I had come to find out from him the exact extent of the debt. The manager pulled out a file, and after briefly looking through it he replied, 'The debt on the church is £550' (13,750 francs). I was astounded and said, 'It can't be that much!'

'Not a penny more, not a penny less,' was his reply.

2. I didn't know what to think. I was silent and thoughtful for a moment. Then I asked him, 'Weren't there several promissory notes parishioners signed and brought here? That would reduce the debt to £300, wouldn't it?'

'That wouldn't make any difference. No money's come from them.'

'Are they due by now?'

'No, on 30 March.'

'Won't they be honoured?'

'I don't think so. Apart from one or two, most of those who signed them don't have the money. In fact, many people told me they wrote the notes simply to please Fr Chastagnon, but they wouldn't have the means to pay them. They told Fr Chastagnon that too, but he said not to worry!'

I got a real shock, realising how much I had been deceived. After a few moments' silence, I said, 'But what was the point of getting promissory notes if they wouldn't be paid?'

'I agree. Why would he want them to sign them if they couldn't honour them?'

'Why then did the bank accept them?'

'The bank has no choice. If they are honoured, that's fine. If not, the debt stands the same.'

'But why doesn't the bank oblige signatories to pay?'

'How can you force people who have nothing? What can you get out of them? These notes' – he held them up – 'are worthless. They were signed by people without a penny to their name.'

'How could it happen?'

'Well, that's just how it is. A general depression has affected this area for more than a year. There's no work. Things have come to a standstill. Wages are only half what they were and people find it hard to find work. Most leave. And, besides, Catholics are all poor labourers. How can they pay when they have no work or savings?'

I was dumbstruck, but I gathered my wits and asked him, 'What's the interest rate on the debt?'

'On £550 at nine and a half per cent, that's £52 5s per annum.'

'Oh!'

'Don't be shocked. The normal rate in Gisborne is between ten and twelve per cent, depending on the security.'

'When is your next six-monthly interest payment due?'

'On 1 July.'

'Was the last instalment paid?'

'No, it was added to the capital.'

I realised that the debt was, in fact, £550, not £300 as Fr Chastagnon had said. We then went to the Union Bank, but the manager was out. We were, however, told that the debt was £12, as Fr Chastagnon indicated.

3. With Mr Tierry's help, I then went through the personal accounts. One was for £35 for five pews (the English pound is worth twenty-five francs). Another bill of £15 was for the building supervisor. A further bill of £10 was for timber, etc. A fourth was for £13 10s for various items sold to Fr Simpson. And there were other accounts. I wrote to Fr Chastagnon for clarification regarding the bank loans and individual accounts. He replied that my information was correct, but that parishioner promissory notes to the value of £250, when honoured, would reduce the debt to £300. He couldn't remember details concerning individual accounts, but he thought the pews cost only between £10 and £15. The supervisor was probably still owed only £5. Boyland and Company's bill for £13 10s for items sold to Fr Simpson should be disregarded. He also mentioned that £18 was still owing to an Auckland firm on the church organ. It needed urgent attention because he was being pestered by them. I wrote back that I didn't have a penny for the organ or anything else and that he had deceived me by stating that the debt was little more than £300 when it was more than £700. There was no reply. He realised that his deceit had been discovered.

4. The reader can imagine my astonishment and concern at discovering the huge extent of the debt. I was dismayed and angry with Fr Chastagnon for the trick he had played on the bishop and me. I hastened to inform the bishop. He too was startled at being deceived. He wrote me an encouraging letter, telling

me to be patient, that the parishioners would slowly repay the debt and that he would also lend his support. I, however, did not believe that the people would be able to pay it off because the impoverished Catholic population was so small. Money was needed to settle individual accounts, but neither I nor the parishioners had any. What was to be done?

5. After a long period of reflection and discussion with Mr Tierry, I decided to get rid of the private debts so I could be free to concentrate on the bank debt. Since most businesses went bankrupt because they could not pay their creditors or reach a settlement, I thought I would see if it were possible to come to an agreement with our creditors. I decided to offer them sixty per cent of what they were owed in full settlement. We went to the Union Bank and asked the teller to accept sixty per cent of the £12 owed. He emphatically refused and said there would be no point in approaching the manager. My first attempt was a failure! But I didn't lose heart. I spoke to two or three other creditors. I explained the difficulties of the situation and that some of their accounts were inflated. I couldn't say when the bills would be paid – certainly not within the next three or four years. If they accepted fifty or sixty per cent I would try to obtain a bank loan to pay them. Some accepted my proposal. Others said they would accept sixty per cent as part payment and the balance when I could pay. But I refused and was adamant that they had to accept sixty per cent as full payment. I calculated that creditors, apart from the Union Bank, would eventually agree and that with £50 or £60 I could pay them off. But where was I to find that amount? I thought it over and decided to seek a loan from the Bank of New Zealand.

6. Tierry and I went to the bank. I spoke to the manager, explaining that besides the bank loan there were private debts. I intended to pay them off and then concentrate on the bank loan, paying it off in instalments. I asked him if he would kindly lend me £50, which I would repay in a couple of months. He replied: 'What guarantee do you have? The bank won't lend without security. I've already lent the Catholic Church too much!'

'I give you my word as a Catholic priest. I always keep my word.'

'I'm sure you do, but unless you have a reputable person to go guarantor, I can't lend to you. Your parishioners can't pay back the loan and you ask me to lend you another £50!'

'Yes, make it a personal loan.'

'And what guarantee can you offer me that the £50 will be repaid?'

'My guarantee as a Catholic missionary. I'll write you a promissory note to be honoured within two months.'

'Unless someone else goes guarantor for you, I can't do it.'

I realised that the manager did not believe I could pay. I asked him: 'If you must have this guarantee, would you accept the Catholic Bishop of Auckland as guarantor?'

'Yes, certainly.'

'Good. I'll write and ask him.'

7. I was practically certain that His Lordship would go guarantor for me, having written previously that he would help me in any way he could. I wrote, providing him a detailed list of individual debtors, and including my suggestion of paying them off at sixty per cent. He replied, doubting that they would accept my proposal. But if they would, he would certainly act as guarantor for me.

Part 6. I Make A Vital Decision

Summary. – 1. Shocked at the size of the debt, I decide to hold a parish meeting. – 2. The ensuing discussion. – 3. I seek a vote of confidence. – 4. The parishioners' hesitation. – 5. Vote of confidence passed to everyone's satisfaction.

1. Shocked at the size of the debt, aware of the poverty and small number of parishioners to pay it off and upset at hearing through my interpreter that several people had complained about having a non-English speaking missionary when they would have preferred an Irish priest, I decided to hold a parish meeting and explain the financial position and seek a vote of confidence in myself to deal with it. Tierry and some prominent parishioners endorsed this idea. I wrote an announcement to be read out the following Sunday at Mass and vespers. Tierry translated it into English and prepared the final version. It went as follows: 'Parishioners are urged to attend an important meeting to be held next Sunday in Gisborne after the 11 a.m. Mass.' It would be the first time I spoke publicly in English.

2. The meeting duly took place. I asked Tierry to attend as my interpreter and explain the extent of the debt. After Mass most of the women and any Protestants left. The men and a few woman who remained totalled about forty, the majority of whom were from the township. I asked Mr Tierry to present the facts. People said they thought the debt was about that much and were satisfied with the statement. But in the same breath they added that, because of the depression and business stagnation, they could neither pay the capital nor interest due. I replied that I had not called the meeting for that purpose. I appreciated their inability to pay. It was my intention to deal with the debt in a way which would not affect them too much. I also asked them for any solutions. None were forthcoming. They simply were adamant that they had no means to pay it off, hoping it would be settled in due course. I replied that I was not talking of

paying it off, but of seeing if the interest could be decreased. They then began murmuring among themselves. I couldn't understand a word. Tierry told me they were complaining about Fr Chastagnon for building such a large church and saddling them with debt.

3. Seeing they were upset and we were getting nowhere, I told them I knew that some of them were unhappy about having a non-English speaking missionary when they would have preferred an Irish priest. I could well understand their grievance, but the bishop had no one else to send. I mentioned that I did not want to come, being fully aware of my ignorance and defects, but the bishop had no choice and he did not want to leave them without a priest. It was my duty to obey and so I came.

'I will try my best to learn English,' I said, 'I really mean it. I only want to do my best by you,' etc. They replied that they believed me, but they could not pay off the debt.

'I'm not asking you to do that right now,' I said, 'and I didn't summon you here for that reason. I know you can't. I have another purpose in mind. I realise that many of you aren't happy with me as your priest. I want a vote of confidence in me.'

4. This was something they hadn't expected. They didn't know what to say, not knowing what I was after. They began talking to each other. One stood up and said, 'We can't pay!'

'I'm not asking you to pay,' I repeated. 'I'm simply requesting you to answer whether you have confidence in me or not. That's all.'

There was no response. They just kept talking quietly. Eventually someone said, 'We don't understand why you want a vote of confidence!'

'All right, I'll explain. If you pass a vote of confidence in me, I'll stay and work with you. If you pass a vote of no-confidence, I'll take the next steamer for Auckland and that will be the last you see of me. There are many missions crying out for a priest. If you don't have confidence in me, it's pointless for me to stay in Gisborne because I won't be able to achieve anything.'

I asked Tierry to make sure they understood. But there was still no response. Eventually I said, 'I won't dissolve the meeting until you respond to my request. I'm asking for an answer, yes or no, so that I know whether to stay on or leave.' They still came to no resolution and things dragged on for an hour with no outcome. Tierry eventually restated my position.

5. After further discussion among themselves, Jennings, acting as spokesman, stood up and said, 'We all have trust and confidence in the missionary the bishop has sent us and we will continue to support you, but right now it's impossible for us to do anything about the debt.'

'That's fine,' I replied, 'but does everyone agree with Mr Jennings?'

'Yes, yes,' they exclaimed.

'You have confirmed that you have confidence in me,' I said, 'and I want you to know I have full confidence in you. I believe we can work well together.'

They applauded my comment. I then said that I knew they were unable to repay the debt and interest, but it was my intention, with the bishop's help, to sort out the debt in a way that would not be too burdensome, which the nine and a half per cent interest was at present. When I explained this, they breathed a sigh of relief, declaring they were very satisfied and would fully co-operate with me.

Part 7. Working on the Debt

Summary. – 1. I keep the original committee. – 2. I call a committee meeting. – 3. I outline a scheme for sorting out the debt. – 4. I propose weekly collections. – 5. Church expenses to be my responsibility. – 6. The ladies' committee begins its work. – 7. The bishop goes guarantor with the bank.

1. At the general meeting, I said that I was perfectly happy with the committee appointed under Fr Chastagnon. There would be no need to appoint another, not only because they had my full confidence, but because they knew the parish situation. There were six on the committee. They were keen to resign for various reasons, but the meeting and I urged them to stay on. Two of them, however, said that in fact they had resigned more than a year ago because of other commitments and the travel involved. The fortnightly meetings were too onerous. But their real reason was their unhappiness with Fr Chastagnon's autocratic decision-making. It was decided that the remaining four members would suffice. Three lived in Gisborne and one in the country. He could occasionally attend meetings, which generally were held about 7 p.m.

2. After the general meeting, I informed the committee that there would be a business meeting the following Thursday at seven in the presbytery. They all attended, with Tierry acting as my interpreter. The bank and individual debts were discussed. I explained my proposal to discharge the latter while retaining the bank debt, because private creditors were pressing for payment. The committee agreed that it would be sensible just to have the one debt, but were puzzled how it could be done considering there was no money to pay creditors and the bank would not lend us money. I confirmed that I had already approached the bank for a personal loan and been refused, because I had no guarantee.

Jennings then said, 'Since that's the case, I can't see how private debtors can be paid off right away.'

3. I said, however, that I had thought of a simple, practical way to pay them and just have the bank debt left. They asked me to explain my stratagem, which I willingly did. From what I had gleaned, I knew the identified creditors, including the Union Bank, were owed £110, and that the bank would not accept part-payment. Boyland and Company's bill of £13 10s did not require payment because, according to Fr Chastagnon, it was invalid. The others, though, were legitimate. I was almost certain I could pay them off by giving them sixty per cent of what they were owed. I mentioned that I had already approached some of them. Some were happy, others not, but I hoped they would all eventually agree. I believed that £50 or £60 would settle the accounts. I intended to get a loan from the bank through the bishop. I had written to him and he was happy to agree. The committee was very pleased with my plan, providing it was feasible. But they were dubious that individual creditors would accept my proposal. However, they gave me carte blanche to proceed.

4. I then drew the committee's attention to the necessity of collecting sufficient money for the next bank interest payment, so we would not be caught out. It amounted to £25 or £26 and was due apparently by the end of April or May. I was concerned about the high interest rate which, with God's help, I wanted to get reduced, but for the moment I couldn't do everything. Our discussion continued. Various suggestions were made for collecting money, but they were all impractical. The parishioners' poverty was the stumbling block. Finally it was agreed for the four committee members to pay weekly visits to Catholic families who could pay perhaps a shilling (1.25 francs) or even sixpence a family. This seemed the most practical suggestion and it was adopted. It was also realised that it shouldn't continue indefinitely and would probably draw in little revenue. The following Sunday I announced the scheme from the pulpit.

5. While discussing the weekly collection issue, the committee told me that the parishioners had to provide out of their own pockets for the church expenses, such as candles, wine, oil, paraffin, etc., and that this drastically affected the weekly collection, leaving little or nothing for the interest on the debt. This drain on finances had also to be taken into account. I agreed while also recognising that it was not feasible to have more than one weekly collection. I said that I would meet the church's running costs myself until the debt was paid off. From what I received on Sundays, I would pay for the candles, wine, sanctuary lamp oil and paraffin for lighting. Furthermore, I would also pay ten shillings a week (12.5 francs) to the organist who played on Sunday. They would then have only the debt to consider. They replied that the little they contributed would hardly support me, let alone meet the church expenses. I said that our needs as religious were few and we were content with the bare necessities of life, that their offerings would suffice for our upkeep and church costs.

6. The committee began work on the weekly collection, but the results were disappointing. After two months they stopped, having collected only £10 or 250 francs. I then called a meeting of the ladies' committee and selected four to continue the task. They worked on it more successfully than the men for five or six months. However, the collections dwindled, and they too decided to stop. Protestants heard about my recently appointed ladies' committee. The wife of the minister of the Anglican church asked me if she could join. I didn't know her and asked Tierry about her. He told me who she was and that she was a drinker. I thought for a moment and then replied to her that I would mention her request at the next meeting and give her a reply. The committee did not want her because it was common knowledge that she was a tippler. This confirmed what I had heard, and I certainly did not want her on the committee.

7. I wrote apprising Mons. Steins of the scheme for part-payment to creditors, which I felt would be acceptable to them. I asked him if he would kindly go guarantor for me to the bank for £50 so I could pay the accounts. The bishop immediately replied that he had put £50 at my disposal in the Auckland bank. He was happy to do me this favour and help me. The bank had already requested its Gisborne branch to give me the money. The local manager, in fact, let me know that there was £50 available for me, deposited in their Auckland main office by the bishop.

Part 8. I Pay Individual Creditors

Summary. –1. Negotiations with private creditors. – 2. My battle with the most persistent creditor. I win. – 3. Other creditors. – 4. Fr Simpson's two bills. – 5. Dealing with the creditors. – 6. The two priests from the Wellington diocese leave Auckland for America.

1. As I mentioned above, I already had discussed with creditors immediately settling their accounts if they would accept sixty per cent in payment. Both the timber merchant and building supervisor, owed £5 and £15 respectively, said they would settle for fifty per cent. I dictated a fine letter to Tierry, which he translated into English, to the trader who sold Fr Chastagnon the organ. I explained how I had settled with other creditors, the size of the debt, the poverty of our parishioners and the effect of the depression in Gisborne. Wages were not only half what they had been but work, even at a pittance, was hardly to be found. I asked him to accept sixty per cent of his £18 bill in full payment, like the other creditors. Then he could be paid immediately because I had obtained a loan for this purpose. He replied that he sold the organ to Fr Chastagnon and he would deal with him only. He had wanted cash and so far Fr Chastagnon had not paid up.

2. Armed with the bishop's credit, Tierry and I approached the creditor owed £35. I offered him sixty per cent. He said he would accept that as part-payment, but would wait for the rest.

'No,' I replied, 'that would be in full payment.'

'Well, I want the whole amount.'

'Sorry. If I pay you more than sixty per cent, I won't be able to pay the others who will accept that percentage.' He said he would discuss it with his partner. We were told to come back at 3 p.m. When we returned, they were both present. They said they wanted all the money.

'I can only give you sixty per cent. If you accept, well and good; if not, take the pews back.'

'That's no good to us. We couldn't use them.'

'Well, I'll get them independently valued and give you what they're worth. What do you think of that?'

'No, we don't want an estimate.'

'And I know why. You know they're not worth what you've charged.'

'That's not true. We're not cheats!'

'In fact, I've had them valued. They're still unused and have been valued at £2 10s each, or £3 maximum. You've charged more than £5 each.'

'But that's their value.'

'Well, take them back. I'm not paying that kind of price.'

'We won't.'

'Look, I want to be fair to you and everyone else. Why don't you get a good carpenter and I another. Let them value the pews and we'll stick to their valuation.'

'Fr Chastagon agreed to our price. We don't want another valuation.'

'Because you're in the wrong, that's why. The pews aren't worth it. If you won't accept my offer, get Fr Chastagnon to pay you. I won't give you a penny more than the sixty per cent, and that's being generous. That would more than cover their cost.' They finally accepted my offer and I gave them £21 in full payment.

3. I paid the Union Bank their £12, knowing they would not accept sixty per cent. The building supervisor's bill of £15 was erroneous. I had found a previous account for £10 in Fr Chastagnon's waste-paper basket. I called the supervisor in and showed him the two bills. He apologised, saying that the bill sent to me had been made out by his assistant and that it should have been £10. I gave him £5 and he declared he was satisfied. While busy paying the creditors, I received a letter from Fr Chastagnon. He mentioned that the organ trader was trying to get him summonsed for the £18 he was owed. He begged me to send him the money. He didn't want the embarrassment of being hauled up in court. Whatever the truth of the matter, I didn't want him treated with the same tricks and lies

that he had dealt me. I sent him a cheque for £18. Another creditor owed £5 happily settled for £2! Thus with £56 I paid off all the creditors, including the Union Bank, who were owed a total of £86.

4. Boyland and Company claimed that Fr Simpson owed them £13 10s for lamps, fishing tackle and some bottles of brandy. I said that this bill had nothing to do with the church. It hadn't used the items. Fr Simpson had. His successors hadn't recognised the bill. Neither would I. But they wanted their sixty per cent.

'No,' I replied, 'you're not getting a penny. It's Fr Simpson's own bill. He's the one who owes you, not the church or parishioners. If I went to a shop, bought a case of brandy for £10 and drank it, do you really think that if I didn't pay for it, the parishioners or church should? This is a private debt and the responsibility of the individual concerned. That's how the vendor should deal with the matter and that's what needs to be done with Simpson. If you haven't, that's up to you. It's not my obligation.'

They insisted, however, that the lamps were used in the presbytery and church. I said that Fr Chastagnon would deny this and had told me the bill was invalid. I added that I had no intention of paying and didn't want them to keep sending me monthly reminders. However, as a peace offering, I was prepared to give them £2 in full payment and I wanted no more bills! One of them, a Protestant, was prepared to accept, but Boyland, a nominal Catholic, refused the offer.

'Fine,' I said. 'That's money I've saved. If you think you have a claim, summons me to court and I'll be there. I don't owe you a penny and I won't give you anything. Stop sending me bills or I'll take action. That's all I have to say.' I departed, leaving them startled and dismayed.

5. These fine gentlemen were set on making me pay their bill for £13 10s. They thought they were dealing with a poor ignorant foreigner. They assumed they could wear me down sending me monthly bills as they had done to Fr Chastagnon. They believed I would eventually give in. I, however, was determined not to be beaten by them or anyone else. I warned them not to send me another bill. If they did I would take measures to put a stop to it. They took no notice. At the end of the month they mailed me another bill. I patiently waited to see if they would continue their game. They did the same the following month. That was the last straw. I decided to put an end to it. I wrote them a strong letter telling them to stop pestering me with Fr Simpson's bill which I had no intention of paying. I repeated that I had offered them a goodwill gesture of £2. Since they had turned it down, I would not be repeating the offer. I urged them not to keep sending me accounts. If they persisted I would have recourse to the court to stop it, because their actions were blatantly unfair and attempts at extortion.

Thinking they could use fear tactics, they engaged a lawyer. He wrote requesting me to pay up within a fortnight or he would take me to court. I was glad it had come to this. I replied, 'I don't owe your clients anything. I'm not going to pay. I'll be delighted if you go to court. Then I'll have the opportunity to let the whole of Gisborne see that their demand was totally unfair and amounts to extortion.' I never heard another word from the lawyer or the supposed creditors. They realised they were in the wrong. No more bills came my way and if they had I would have gone to court. That was the end of the matter.

6. I mentioned earlier the two priests from the Wellington diocese who went to Auckland hoping to be accepted by Mons. Steins. A few days after Easter 1880, I received a letter regarding their fate from the Jesuit lay brother residing with the bishop. He mentioned that His Lordship did not make a definite decision about them. Initially they behaved well, but this changed later. They temporarily assisted the cathedral priests. Parishioners noticed, however, that they drank a lot and had other vices. They became disgusted with them. Seeing that the bishop did not want to accept them into the diocese, the priests decided to leave Auckland for more prosperous shores. They planned their departure for San Francisco, America, on the next mail steamer from Sydney, due on Easter Sunday. Before leaving, they decided to have a last outrageous fling that would long be remembered by parishioners. What did the rogues do? On Holy Saturday they got absolutely drunk. After visiting disreputable places, they spent the night weaving along the main streets arm in arm, shouting, yelling, singing and cackling – blind drunk. The police used their discretion, trying to persuade them to get some sleep and not be a public nuisance, but they paid no heed and continued their carousing. Fortunately, most of the constabulary were Irish Catholics who knew the two drunken priests. They did not arrest them, to avoid the huge scandal of taking them to court on Tuesday for sentencing. They let them carry on carousing as a lesser evil. When the steamer for Sydney arrived on Easter Sunday morning, the two vagabonds boarded and at midday they left for America!

CHAPTER FOUR

Gisborne: A Missionary's Life
(C.1880 TO 1881)

PART 1. DAILY ROUTINE

SUMMARY. – 1. Studying English. – 2. Finding a practical way to learn. – 3. I make rapid progress. – 4. Tierry helps me with my English correspondence. – 5. My weekly timetable and routine. – 6. Timetable for Sundays and feast days.

1. As soon as I was able to engage Mr Tierry as my teacher I began studying English under his direction. Unfortunately, when passing through Malta I did not think of obtaining an Italian–English or French–English grammar, believing I would find everything I needed in New Zealand. However, when I arrived I was very upset because there was nothing. I didn't write away for one from Europe since I was told I wouldn't need a grammar book to learn English, that it would more confuse than help me. The best way was by practice. That was perhaps true about old grammar texts based on outmoded methods. But for about ten years, a new grammar by the German Oelendorf had been available. It was very practical and excellent for quickly learning a language. I didn't bring a copy from Europe, not even the one I had at Gerba to learn Maltese, because Dom Giustini Clerici took it to India. At Gisborne, I realised only too late how useful this grammar would have been. It would take about four months to get a copy sent from Europe. But Tierry said I could manage without it. Within four months I should overcome my problems with the language. Unfortunately I had a poor memory for words and pronunciation, especially the latter. Tierry gave me a lesson at nine or nine-thirty nearly every day except feast days and Thursdays. He got me to read out loud. He would correct my pronunciation and explain the meanings. The next day he had me reread the previous day's lesson, but I hardly ever remembered the correct pronunciation. It disturbed me being able to retain so little. Every day I prayed to the Lord and Our Lady to come to my aid and help me learn the language which was so necessary for me to successfully carry out my work as a missionary. But little came of my prayers.

2. After a week's tuition, I still kept forgetting the correct pronunciation, so I decided to write it down. Fr Chastagnon had an English translation of St Alfonso de Liguori's *Commentary on the Gospels*. I asked him to leave it for me so that I could use it for preaching in English. He wasn't too keen, but eventually he

agreed. The *Commentary* was in large print with generous space between lines. I decided to use the book to read from and above the print write the pronunciation of words I had difficulty remembering. Tierry approved of this idea and I immediately put it into practice. I read out a sentence and Tierry gave me the pronunciation of each word. I then pencilled it in so I wouldn't forget. A lesson lasted about forty-five minutes. When my teacher left, I went over it and previous ones several times, practising my pronunciation. This helped my memory considerably. I had learnt a little German when I was in Austria between 1866 and 1867. It helped me remember several English words, even though I had forgotten most of it. English is largely derived from the Saxon or German. Hence the English language is also called Anglo-Saxon, as are the English people.

At Easter 1880, nearly all the parishioners came to confession in Gisborne to fulfil their Easter obligation, because there was no other priest within two hundred miles. I naturally understood virtually nothing of their sins because I had been there little more than a month and had had an English tutor for only eight or ten days. I had written out the penance to give them; that is, to say five Our Fathers, Hail Marys and Glorias, which Tierry had translated into English for me. I must say, however, that really the parishioners were good, decent folk, as I was able later to verify, the men as much as the women. It was just that several men were prone to drunkenness.

3. At last, using my new method, but more particularly with the special help of our Heavenly Mother, I began to make rapid progress in English. I myself was extremely surprised. Within three months of my arrival in Gisborne and about two months' lessons, I understood what people said and I was able to reply to questions. I then began to memorise brief extracts from St Alfonso's *Commentary*, repeating them after the Sunday Gospel. My speech was not perfect, because sometimes my choice of words and pronunciation were incorrect, but I was understood. The parishioners were most impressed with my progress. They said that to understand and speak basic English normally took about six months' continuous study and practice, yet within three months I already knew enough to understand and be understood. This was true, but I must admit that it was not due to me, but through the intervention of the Lord and the Virgin Mary that this outstanding achievement occurred. I knew what a bad memory I had. My constant prayers were finally answered. I read out my first ten-minute speech to parishioners at the beginning of March, when I still was not conversant in English. I wanted to practise.

I later wrote to the bishop about it. On 10 March 1880 he replied to various issues I had raised with him. I still have his letter. He mentioned my speech. His actual words were: 'First of all, your speech. Let me congratulate you, dear Father. You'll see that things continue to improve and become easier and you will do much good. It would be rare for a holy, dedicated priest not to get on well with the Irish. I'm sure they will become very attached to you and help you all they can. Their £10 contribution towards paying off the interest proves it.'

4. I received many letters, especially in my first months, from several creditors afraid of not being paid or losing out. They had to be answered in English, which I couldn't do. Fortunately, Tierry could explain the contents. Together we then decided how to reply. I made a rough draft in French and Tierry translated it into English. I then wrote a fair copy. After two months' tuition, once we agreed on our reply, I would write in English following his dictation. He would check the spelling and then I would write the final version and send it. Thus, I was able to communicate with everyone, especially benefactors. Tierry provided this service as long as I needed it – that is, until I could write letters unaided. He helped me for about ten months to compose my most important letters in good English. I must acknowledge my grateful thanks for all the assistance he gave me at such a critical time.

5. Now let me describe my daily routine during my sojourn in Gisborne. Wherever I lived, I established a fixed routine so as not to waste precious time or be idle, a habit I shunned from first becoming a monk. Throughout the year I arose at 5 a.m. At five-thirty I went to church with Br Joseph and meditated until 6 a.m. Then I recited the office of prime and terce. At six-thirty I said Mass for the souls in purgatory, because there were hardly ever special intentions.* Br Joseph served Mass. Afterwards, he left and made coffee. I said my thanksgiving prayers and more of the office. At seven-thirty I went over and had black coffee and a piece of bread. Then I studied English or wrote letters. At nine Tierry gave me an hour's lesson. After, I returned to study. At twelve we had lunch, to which we often invited Tierry, since he would not accept payment. He ate heartily. After lunch I said vespers and compline, and at three, matins and lauds. At four or five o'clock I would visit local Catholic families. At other times I saddled the horse or took the trap to visit a family in the country. At first a parishioner acted as my guide but later I went on my own, returning home after two or three hours. Before dinner we recited the rosary. During summer we ate at eight and in the winter at six. Usually we had dinner on our own. At nine we went to bed after saying evening prayers. Between dinner and retiring, I would either read newspapers, study or write.

6. There were two Sunday Masses, one at Ormond and the other in Gisborne. In winter, however, it was usually impossible to get to Ormond because the

---

* It is a traditional Roman Catholic practice for Catholics to request that Mass be said for a special intention, e.g., for a deceased relative. A monetary offering is usually made for this purpose.

mud was fifty centimetres or so thick on the road. If the first Mass was at Ormond, in winter I left Gisborne on horseback for Ormond at six. Mass was at eight. In summer I left at five. After the Ormond Mass I left quickly so as to be back in Gisborne by ten-thirty to hear confessions. At eleven I said the second Mass. At noon I went to the hotel for a bite to eat. The lady catechists would tell me if children were coming for Sunday school, which sometimes I attended. I would then set off for Gisborne, arriving about 4 p.m. I said the rest of the office. Before sung vespers in the church, we would have dinner. Otherwise the meal would be very late. After vespers I gave a talk lasting between twenty minutes and half an hour. Benediction of the Blessed Sacrament would follow. About half an hour later I went to bed, exhausted by the strenuous day's activities.

Part 2. Regular Visits to Parishioners

Summary. – 1. The importance of regular parish visits. – 2. The great reverence Irish Catholics hold for their priests. – 3. God's special gift to the Irish. – 4. Their generosity. 5. A common vice of the Irish and Anglo-Saxons. – 6. The perils of excessive drinking. – 7. I won't accept alcohol; the opposition I encounter. – 8. Thanks to God, I gain a complete victory.

1. Regular visits to parishioners are most strongly recommended. They are useful, necessary and even vital for the faithful. A priest gets to know his flock, ascertain their needs, how they live and their good and bad habits. One can observe first hand if they are indeed practising their religion and whether they are attending church and taking the sacraments. If they are negligent, the priest realises this quickly from his first-hand knowledge. When he visits, he is able gently to recall them to their duty. He may be told why they did not attend Mass on previous Sundays. Sometimes he is presented with a thin excuse. The priest kindly chides them, encouraging them to come at least once a fortnight. If they have babies, the husband and wife can take turns caring for the children. The missionary carefully watches over their behaviour, noticing whether they teach their children prayers, the rudiments of the faith, send them for catechism, to Mass and the sacraments, etc. The priest checks that if they can't go to Mass, they still say the rosary and other daily prayers, and there is unity, peace and harmony in the home. If they indulge in alcohol, they are reproved and made to see the terrible consequences of drunkenness. If they are poor, husbands are exhorted to be temperate, to work hard, earn enough to live on, and not frequent grog shops – in short, to do their duty and seek divine assistance. Parishioners appreciate this interest in their well-being. They are motivated to practise their faith and improve their lives. At the same time, they are aware that they will be chided if they neglect their duties.

I obtained excellent results from my visits, even from people who had neglected their religion. I believe that in European Catholic countries, including Italy, if parish priests and other religious stirred themselves and went and visited their flock, encouraging, supporting and advising them, great good would be achieved. A priest might sometimes find he was not welcome, but in general he would seem like an angel from heaven. He would have marriages to celebrate, baptisms to perform, scandals to resolve and countless souls to bring back into the fold. Why are priests and curates seen in such a bad light these days? We need to recognise how much godless folk have maligned them. Catholics ensnared by socialists and sectarians fall by the wayside when there is not a benign influence to support them. The most practical way to help people keep the faith is to go to them, not just by attending groups and committees, but by pastoral visits. Otherwise the faith will disappear from the Old World and seek another home. Visits may inconvenience the priest, but they will bear eternal fruit if he carries them out carefully and zealously.

2. The persecution by the Protestant English government of Irish Catholics, especially of the clergy, was ferocious. It lasted from the first half of the sixteenth century until halfway through the nineteenth. The courageous, stalwart Irish clergy sacrificed everything to maintain the faith, support the people and follow God's will. The Irish placed their trust in their clergy's guidance, as children would in their father's. They steadfastly fought on behalf of God, sacrificing any earthly gain. Ireland's history during these three centuries is one of its finest chapters, mirroring the persecutions of the first three centuries of the Church's existence, when so many people were martyred. The persecuted clergy, hounded out of their homes and hunted down for extermination, stuck with their people, going into hiding and disguising themselves for their work. They were often discovered and mercilessly hanged. The people and clergy continued to suffer and to maintain their unity and fidelity in the face of the cruellest deaths. From this perfect union in spirit arose a great veneration by Irish Catholics for their priests, which still exists today. The Irish know that the clergy are fearless champions of their faith and rights. When they come across a priest, even a stranger, they genuflect before him. They have carried this spirit of respect and veneration into exile from their motherland, jealously guarding it and passing it on to their children. I myself often witnessed the great respect which was also shown to Catholic missionaries in New Zealand.

3. I was startled, however, to see old Catholic Irishwomen genuflect in the main street when a Catholic priest went by, whom they had never seen before and who was dressed like a Protestant minister. I was surprised at this discernment. I wanted to find out how they could pick out a Catholic priest, particularly when he was with Protestant ministers. At various times, I asked

Irish Catholics if it were true that they could discern a Catholic priest from other people, even if he was a stranger and no matter what he was wearing. They all replied positively. I then asked them what distinguished a Catholic priest when he looked like anyone in a crowd and they hadn't seen him before.

'We notice a certain something in a Catholic priest,' they replied, 'which we can't explain. But we recognise it clearly and don't see it in others, even Protestant ministers.'

I tried to find out what this particular characteristic was, but my investigations led nowhere. They just said they didn't know or couldn't say what they saw. I believe God enabled them, whether they were good or bad, to recognise the *priestly character* of his true ministers, and only God knows how they discerned it. This special gift was given by God to the Irish at the time of the English persecution. Priests were hunted down and put to death. Clergy who were in Ireland at the outbreak of the persecution were either killed or forced to flee to France and elsewhere. A few remained, disguised as labourers or farm workers, to tend to the faithful. They travelled the countryside pretending to be looking for work. Other priests were sent by Rome to Ireland to assist the persecuted people. They were complete strangers, and hence very few were known as priests. If they weren't known, the people could hardly approach them for the sacraments they desperately wanted. There was also the penalty of confiscation of all their goods and death itself for anyone supporting or receiving a priest. In this horrible situation, God came to the aid of his people, granting them the gift of recognising Catholic priests on sight through a mysterious, yet unmistakable sign. Catholics who needed a priest for marriage, sacraments, confession, communion or assisting the sick would go into towns and villages, silently searching the streets. An Irishman would notice the divine sign on a certain passerby. He would stop him, mentioning his or his family's need. The stranger would say he would come immediately or the following morning. With his labourer's or carpenter's tools he would go to the house on the pretence of doing some work. That night he would say Mass, administer the sacraments and visit other families. The priest disguised himself as well as he could. He would suffer the death penalty if he were recognised as a minister of God. And this is how civilised Britain conducted itself from 1550 to 1800!

A very good example of this power of discernment occurred in Coromandel, not far from Auckland, where I was to go later as a missionary. It happened about the end of 1885. A priest named Timothy O'Callaghan became a Protestant.* One day he went to Coromandel to preach in the Anglican church at the request of the Anglican, Presbyterian and Wesleyan ministers. He had not previously visited Coromandel and none of the local Catholics had seen

* The story of Fr Timothy O'Callaghan's apostasy was later discussed at length in the *NZ Observer and Free Lance,* 31 July, 10 August 1889.

him before. None knew he was an apostate priest. He had become so only a few months previously in Dunedin, in the South Island, about a thousand kilometres from Coromandel. One Friday the apostate and two Protestant ministers took the 4 p.m. steamer from Auckland, reaching Coromandel in three hours. Catholics noticed three ministers getting off at the jetty, the apostate in their midst. They recognised the sign of a priest and said, 'The one in the middle is a Catholic priest! What's he doing with Protestants? He must be an apostate.' None of the few Catholics there greeted him. But to make sure that he really was an apostate, two followed him at a distance, to see whether he would spend the night at the Catholic priest's or at the Anglican minister's. They saw him go to the vicarage and realised that the wretched priest was an apostate. To avoid scandalising other Catholics, they said nothing, but during the next two days several Catholics noticed him. Elderly parishioners whispered to others, 'That man who's supposed to be an Anglican minister is a Catholic priest. It's true!'

4. To force Irish Catholics to become heretics, English Protestants confiscated practically all Catholic churches, giving the properties to the few Protestants who came to Ireland from England. They confiscated other ecclesiastical properties and benefices. People who would not convert had their properties and goods confiscated and handed over to Protestants entering Ireland. Catholics were thus reduced to living by their labour to provide for their families. Once landowners themselves, they were reduced to slavery, working for their English Protestant masters, the new owners of their Irish land. You can imagine the mistreatment and squalor the poor people suffered. Misery, hunger and destitution became the daily fare of these brave Christians who would rather die than renounce their faith. They not only put up with hunger and privation for centuries, but provided for bishops, priests and religious in hiding throughout Ireland from the little food they had. When the English government eventually realised its cruel measures were ineffectual, it stayed its punishing hand. Catholics, even though poor as Job on his dung heap, went without to find money to begin building new churches and support the clergy. Even today, people in Ireland provide everything for the upkeep of the clergy and church maintenance. Irish migrants to America and the colonies in search of a basic living have continued this tradition with generous enthusiasm. The same is true of New Zealand. In Gisborne, in spite of their great poverty, the Irish never left me lacking for food or clothing. They also took responsibility for the church debt.

In New Zealand, apart from meat and bread, everything else, namely, groceries, clothing and accommodation, was exorbitantly dear. It was very difficult to live on less than thirty-five francs a week. I received an average of fifty francs a week for the upkeep of Br Joseph and myself. This was from the collections taken up after Sunday Mass and vespers. It did not include what I received for baptisms, weddings and donations made at Christmas and Easter, which amounted to between £45 and £50. We were kept in food and clothing by this money so generously given. I was also able to care for the horse, provide alms for the poor, maintain the church and pay the organist. Thanks to God and our sober way of life, we had enough to cover these costs, and I was even able to put something away. Parishioners were, however, surprised that we managed. But we made the greatest economies in food, especially with alcohol, limiting ourselves to a bottle of mediocre local beer, which cost sixty centimes for a bottle containing two-thirds of a litre. Better quality English beer was 3.13 francs a bottle. Vin ordinaire cost between ten and twelve francs a bottle.

5. Since the Irish had such great respect, affection and devotion for their priest and showed considerable generosity with his upkeep, it followed that when he visited he was made a great fuss of and offered the best of hospitality. The Irish like their drink, and are partial to spirits. They tend to offer the priest gin, whisky, brandy or rum. These are naturally served in nips, or small measures, costing not less than sixty centimes a time. A bottle of spirits would cost at least 27.5 francs. Their intention is to show respect and demonstrate their affection and devotion. Even the poorest family would keep a bottle aside for the priest's visit. If he weren't to accept a drink, it would be taken as a slight and a sign that he didn't like them. So, naturally, they insisted he accept.

6. The Irish and Anglo-Saxons share a great weakness – over-indulging in alcohol. Alcohol is very expensive in Ireland and the colonies because it is heavily taxed. Also, spirits are nearly always adulterated. Drinking spirits damages the health and, worse, it hits the pocket, impoverishing families. Workers living from their toil spend more than half their wages on alcohol. Consequently their families suffer. Getting drunk makes the situation worse. Besides losing money, they lose their jobs and their livelihood. The misery and ruin is then complete. If the Irish were to moderate their drinking, they would be the finest people in the world. They are otherwise thrifty, upright, hard-working, enterprising and extremely able in any field of knowledge and industry. Irish lawyers in England are considered better than their British counterparts. Unfortunately, drunkenness renders the Irish, in Ireland and the colonies, the poorest of the poor because they squander their hard-earned money on alcohol. The consequences for secular priests and religious who take to drink by accepting hospitality are even worse. I have known good, zealous missionaries who were excellent priests until they started accepting drinks. Pressured by Catholic families, they slowly got used to drinking, becoming habituated, to their degradation. The Irish tolerate a priest drinking as long as he doesn't get completely drunk. They won't tolerate immorality, because they deplore this in anyone.

7. About two months after my arrival, I went with a parishioner to visit as many Catholic families as I could. They all offered me a drink, as they did when I accompanied Fr Chastagnon. My guide would accept a nip, but I always firmly refused. They weren't happy about this, saying that by refusing even a single nip I showed a lack of appreciation of their hospitality and pleasure in receiving the priest in their home. I replied that I did recognise their goodness, affection and generosity, but I never imbibed between meals because of the effect of alcohol on me. That was my only reason. Parishioners, however, insisted, 'Just a drop!'

'But I've told you, it upsets me.'

'A nip can't harm you!'

'Would you want me to get sick?'

'That won't happen!'

'Well, I'd like you to let me take care of my own health, and that means abstaining.'

This kind of conversation would occur in every home I visited. I kept to my resolution, no matter how much they insisted, even when I felt thirsty. Later, when I understood English well and could make myself understood, I visited Catholic families on my own. They still persisted in offering me a drink. I kept refusing. Many people said, 'Every missionary who has visited us has accepted a drink, except you!'

'Who do you mean?'

'Fr Chastagnon, Fr Forest, Fr Simpson and others.'

'Well, I'm Fr Vaggioli, and in this respect I'm different.'

But they were not dissuaded. I also told them that if I did feel thirsty, I would ask for a drink. Finally, to end their persistence, I put it to them, 'Listen, if you insist on making me drink, I'll stop coming, because I don't want to ruin my health.'

'Oh, no, we won't keep it up. Please keep coming,' they all said.

'Well, we've agreed. That's good. If I need something, I'll ask.'

At my insistence they capitulated, but they were still unhappy, believing I drank with better-off families. They made discreet enquiries to verify this, but they found out that I accepted drinks from no one, not even the manager of the Union Bank. They were then reassured, knowing I did not favour anyone.

8. I thus averted the considerable risk and likelihood of becoming a heavy drinker, maintaining faithfully the promise I made to God and the Virgin Mary not to drink alcohol unless it was absolutely necessary, and then only the barest minimum. Initially, parishioners were puzzled by my strong, unequivocal decision not to drink with them or anyone else. Later, however, I explained to the committee my real reason for this decision; namely, so as not to expose myself to the peril of becoming habituated to alcohol. The committee explained

my reason to parishioners. They praised my strength of character. They realised I was right, having noticed that even Fr Chastagnon sometimes drank more than he should, although he never got drunk. Protestants, too, got wind of my decision and were full of admiration, holding me in higher regard than their own ministers. That I achieved this singular victory was entirely the Lord's doing.

Part 3. Marriages in New Zealand

Summary. – 1. Catholic marriages in New Zealand. – 2. I get banns established. – 3. Difficulties caused by not having them. – 4. The pestilence of mixed marriages between Catholics and Protestants. – 5. Wayward Catholic partners. – 6. Registry office marriages. – 7. Unhappy outcome of an illicit mixed marriage.

1. In New Zealand, there was a long-time practice of not announcing banns when two Catholics wished to get married. This practice had been brought from Ireland, where Irish bishops dispensed with the issuing of banns for those who paid for a dispensation. In the United Kingdom, banns were published only for those who didn't or couldn't pay. In New Zealand, dispensation was granted both to people who paid and to those who couldn't afford the fee. In Ireland, those who could not pay borrowed the amount, so they would not be identified as among the poorest. I'm not sure whether the dispensation of banns in New Zealand began under Mons. Pompallier. I suspect that it was Mons. Croke who introduced the practice. The fee was £3, or seventy-five francs, for three announcements. Bishops used the money for education. The English and even poor Irish paid the fee.

The custom of dispensation may have been feasible in Ireland where the vast majority of the population was Catholic, and people from the same or nearby areas married each other. It did not seem so suitable in British colonies, where Catholics were a very small minority, scattered over huge areas. They were migrants from the Old World, mostly on the move, seeking permanent work or casual labour. It was very difficult or well-nigh impossible to discover impediments, notwithstanding a priest's earnest efforts. The only reliable way was by using banns. Catholics in the area would then know that a couple wished to marry, and they could then reveal any impediments they knew of.

Often impediments were discovered after the marriage. Sometimes, after several years it would be revealed that a man had another wife somewhere else, even in another colony. A notorious example was reported in 1880 in Napier, in the Wellington diocese. A Catholic man who was married with children had been living for several years in Auckland. In 1879 or 1880 he went to Napier and married another woman in a Catholic church, as he had done in Auckland. After living for some months with him, the Napier woman suspected he had another wife from letters which came for him from Auckland written in a woman's hand. She secretly investigated the situation, discovering that the rogue's legitimate wife was in Auckland. She denounced him forthwith to the authorities and he was arrested. The wretch was given a lengthy sentence for polygamy. But the poor, blameless young woman could not find another husband.

2. Fearing that a similar situation might happen to souls entrusted to me, I explained to Mons. Steins the merits of publishing banns, as the Church had established them for a good reason. I deplored the present custom of dispensing with them, which was contrary to the Church's wise intention. Without banns, impediments could not be discovered. Further, Catholics knew that a marriage was valid when banns were used. When they were dispensed with, cases such as the Napier example occurred and were splashed all over the papers.

3. Many poor young Catholic women came out from Ireland to provide for their themselves and their parents at home. They were fine, devout, upright, innocent creatures. But they could easily fall prey to dissolute married men using false names, who would marry and traduce them. The very thought of it made me shudder. I wrote to the bishop to enlist his full support in getting banns published in my parish. On 5 August 1880, Bishop Steins replied in English. I kept his letter among my papers, and I quote from it: 'I have to hand your letter of 31 July. Regarding the publication of banns, please refer to the attached notice. I have included a copy of a circular of Mons. Croke, from which you will see that banns are carried out here as elsewhere. This follows the directive issued by the Council of Trent. Banns are extremely important. Before sanctioning a marriage, the Church must know whether there are any impediments or not, and often publishing banns provided the only way of knowing. I would therefore kindly ask you to impose this obligation on your parishioners. The Church can, nevertheless, dispense with banns when there are good reasons as, for example, when the betrothed cannot wait. In this situation, the bishop is obligated by canon law to impose a fee so that the precept of imposing banns is respected.'

From this letter it was apparent that, even in Mons. Croke's time, banns were published. How and when was the practice abandoned? I had no idea. The fact was, however, that it had not been used for several years and never in Gisborne, according to the parishioners. But, in fact, before 1865 there were neither Catholics, Protestants nor civilised settlers living there, just a few traders in the midst of native Maori. Following Mons. Steins's instruction, in August I announced from the altar his instruction that from henceforth banns were not to be dispensed with, except in cases of absolute necessity. I explained the reasons. Parishioners objected, saying that it would only then apply to poor

Catholics who couldn't afford a dispensation.* I tried my best to explain and in private conversations I argued strongly with opponents. Women were especially opposed. Many people complained about the bishop's instruction, but things quietened down and they acquiesced. Thus banns were issued for the two weddings which occurred between August 1880 and June 1881.

Mons. Steins became ill and resigned from the diocese. He left Auckland in May 1881 for Europe. When he reached Sydney his condition deteriorated and he could not continue his voyage. He stayed at the Jesuits' residence where he died on 7 September 1881. R.I.P.

Knowing that the Irish were opposed to banns, which weren't imposed in any other mission, and only grudgingly obeyed, I wrote to Mons. Fynes, the diocesan administrator. I asked if I could continue using banns according to Mons. Steins's instruction. He replied that I was to do what had always been done in the past; that is, publish banns for those who wanted them. He would provide dispensations for those who paid the requisite £3 fee. That would side-step canon law regarding banns. People didn't want banns published and would rather pay the fee, as in Ireland. I was most annoyed with his decision, which made me a puppet. But in spite of my displeasure, I resigned myself to the situation.

4. One of the worst evils to affect Catholicism in Britain, its colonies and the United States of America was mixed marriages, that is, marriages between Catholics and Protestants. They had ruinous effects, especially on the offspring. The Catholic Church disapproves of them and only permits them if the couple is insistent, to avoid a worse evil. It never consents, however, for a Catholic priest to officiate at such marriages unless the betrothed agree to certain conditions: (1) that the Catholic partner be freely able to practise his or her faith, and (2) any children of the marriage be baptised and raised as Catholics.

Mixed marriages usually cause harm. Young Catholic women, particularly Irish women, being the most eligible group, are the most vulnerable. These good, devout women are keen to marry and prefer marrying Protestants, hoping to better their financial and social position, and ultimately that of their children. They believe that if they were to wed poor Irish workers like themselves, they would probably stay in the same condition for the rest of their lives. It is true that sometimes their financial position does improve by marrying a Protestant, but often it is disastrous to their faith and morals. If they are not affected, their offspring certainly will be, for they are raised as Protestants or with no religion at all. In the United States of America, mixed marriages have had disastrous consequences for Catholicism. In the hundred-year period up until 1800, the

---

* Vaggioli seems to be contradicting his earlier assertion that the poor could also be exempted from payment, and thus be entitled to dispensation of banns. Perhaps he is simply rewording the parishioners' fear.

many mixed marriages produced ten million descendants. Thus, in a hundred years the Catholic Church lost ten million souls through mixed marriages! The same phenomenon, more or less, occurred among settlers in British colonies, including New Zealand, with a similar peril to the Catholic faith.

5. By 1881 in the Gisborne district there were forty-eight couples in mixed marriages, outnumbering Catholic marriages. Of the forty-eight, forty-six Catholic women and two men had Protestant spouses. Of the forty-eight Catholics married to Protestants, fifteen women practised their faith and took their children to Mass and the sacraments. Eleven others, including a male, seldomly came to church and the sacraments, and their children scarcely at all. The remaining twenty-two never put in an appearance, or rarely indeed.

A Protestant wife of a Catholic surveyor came to church regularly with her three Catholic daughters. She made sure that they participated in the sacraments on feast days. She was more Catholic than Protestant and was more attached to Catholicism than her husband. Because of his occupation he was often away from home. He rarely went to Mass. When the Catholic partner is neglectful of the faith, more often than not the children follow the Protestant parent, becoming Protestants or growing up indifferent or even hostile to religion. Catholic mothers are mainly responsible for this situation, for not being uncompromising from the outset of their marriage, serving God and providing an example to their children. Their Protestant husbands normally give little attention to their children's religious upbringing.

I tried to recall wayward Catholic partners to their responsibility and duty, but with little success. I did find, however, an example of extraordinary fortitude in one of the daughters of a Mr O'Meara, who was married to a bigoted Scottish Presbyterian. He agreed to the Church's conditions for their mixed marriage, which took place at the beginning of 1879, but he then decided to renege. He tried every means to force his wife to go to the Presbyterian church, but she staunchly resisted. Every Sunday she attended her church. She also tried to persuade her husband to accompany her, but he would not. When she had a baby at the beginning of 1880, she begged her mother to have him immediately baptised by the priest. Later she made her husband look after the baby when she went to Mass on feast days. But you don't come across many women like her these days.

6. Without a written agreement, the Church will not permit its priests to sanction mixed marriages. If the Protestant partner accepts the conditions, and the wedding is celebrated by a Catholic priest, the marriage is valid and licit. If they do not accept the conditions or have a Protestant minister officiate or are married in a registry office, the marriage is illicit but valid, because the decrees of the Council of Trent do not apply in New Zealand. Around February 1880,

I discovered there were Catholic women in Gisborne who had married Protestants in the registry office. I believed these marriages to be invalid according to the Council of Trent. I thought that its decrees were effectual in New Zealand. To make certain, I wrote to Mons. Steins for clarification. On 10 March 1880 he replied: 'The kind of marriage you describe is valid. The Council's decrees have not been promulgated here. The lack of the presence of a parish priest at the marriage does not constitute a vital impediment. The marriage, though, without a dispensation, is illicit.'

7. In 1881 a young Catholic maidservant visited me, saying she wanted to marry a Protestant. I tried in vain to dissuade her. She thought she wouldn't be able to find anyone else. I believed her because she was far from pretty.

'Well,' I said, 'let's see if we can perform the marriage according to the Church's conditions. Is the young man willing to let you freely practise your faith?'

'Yes, Father.'

'Is he willing to get married in the presence of a Catholic priest?'

'No, Father. He wants to be married in his church.'

'Will you do everything you can by subtle persuasion to convert him to Catholicism?'

'Yes, Father, but I don't think I'll succeed because he is a staunch Protestant.'

'Will he agree to having your children baptised and brought up as Catholics?'

'He's told me he wants to bring them up in his religion.'

'Really, my daughter, given what you've said, the Church can't sanction such a marriage. You cannot and must not marry him.'

She was pensive and silent. I continued, 'Tell the young man to come and see me. I'll see if I can persuade him to have the Mass celebrated according to the Church's conditions, and get him to agree to bringing up the children as Catholics.'

'He's told me,' she replied, 'that he doesn't want to come here.'

'Well, see if you can persuade him yourself to accept these three conditions: (1) absolute freedom for you to practise your faith, (2) celebrate the wedding in my presence, and (3) have your children baptised and brought up as Catholics. If you get his consent, you can get married in the Church. Otherwise, you can't, and you'll commit a mortal sin.'

'I really don't think I can. But I'll speak to him again.'

'Yes, yes, speak to him frankly, as I've told you. Otherwise, no wedding. Then come back, and let me know how you've got on.'

The young woman left. I realised she was weak-willed. She hadn't shown herself as a strong Catholic during the time I had been in Gisborne. I could not recall seeing her before, but I had thought her employers stopped her from attending church. She returned a few days later and told me the young man would not agree. I then begged her not to marry him because the Church forbade it, and she would lose her soul if she died. The poor maid was very upset by my refusal to acquiesce, but she said nothing and left. I never saw her again. A couple of months later, I learnt that she had married the man in the Wesleyan church. They went to live somewhere in Ormond. Later I decided to go in search of the poor lost soul, but the months slipped by and I forgot. She was unknown to the Ormond parishioners. One day I heard that the poor woman had died in childbirth, without Catholic neighbours or myself being told. She was given a Protestant burial by her wretched husband! Although I had no responsibility for the marriage, I was very upset by her death. If I had known she was ill, I would have hastened to her side to see if I could bring her back to the fold and hear her confession. But I only heard about her from parishioners after she was dead and buried!

PART 4. QUARREL WITH A LAWYER

SUMMARY. – 1. A Protestant lawyer's wife. – 2. I visit the lawyer's home. – 3. I speak to the woman. – 4. I receive an insulting letter from the lawyer; my reply. – 5. His explanation; his wife doesn't want anything to do with the Church. – 6. One soul is lost and another saved!

1. In the Gisborne district there were fifteen lawyers for a population of about 5000 Europeans and 2500 Maori. They were well-off, living in substantial wooden residences. Possibly the most successful of them had a Catholic wife. She very rarely practised her faith. In the eight months since my arrival in Gisborne she had come to church just twice. She was the daughter of a British soldier who had been stationed in India. She was first educated by nuns, then her father sent her to a boarding school for the children of the military to complete her education. When he retired with a pension, he and and his family went to New Zealand. The daughter married a lawyer and they settled in Gisborne. The lawyer's home was in the same street as the Catholic church, about five hundred metres away. His wife twice attended the 11 a.m. Sunday Mass. She came by carriage. Since Protestants sometimes came, I assumed she was one, and that she had come for the singing. Catholics were all poor and certainly couldn't afford a carriage. That was a further reason for my believing she was Protestant.

2. Time went by. Seeing she didn't return, I asked Jennings about her and the church she belonged to. He told me she was the Catholic wife of a certain lawyer, where she lived and that she infrequently attended church. I further enquired what kind of Catholic she was. He said she didn't bother much about her religion. She had no children and employed a maid and manservant. Hence

she had no excuse for not coming to church. I wasn't sure whether she attended at Easter, but I thought not. I determined to visit her and urge her to take her faith more seriously. One day in June or July 1880, at 4.30 p.m., I called at her home. I knocked on the front door. There was no answer. No one would have heard me, because of the size of the house. I walked round to the kitchen at the back and found the maid, who was a practising Catholic. I asked if her masters were at home. She replied that the lawyer was at his office and her mistress had gone out. I said I would return another day.

3. A week later, I returned at 11 a.m. I knocked on the front door, which was ajar. The maid appeared and told me her mistress was in, but not the master. I told her to tell her mistress I was there. She led me into a very elegant drawing room and then went to fetch her mistress. The maid quickly returned saying her mistress was attending to her *toilette*, but would soon come. She presently entered, beautifully dressed. After our greetings, she told me she regretted her husband was not home, and that he would have been pleased to meet me. I replied in the same vein. I then asked how she was and whether she had children. She had none. I went on to mention her obligations as a Catholic, not to worry about what other people thought, and to set a good example. She seemed to agree. I asked her why she did not regularly attend Sunday Mass, when it would be so easy for her. She replied that the 6.30 and 7.30 a.m. Masses were too early.

'We go to bed late, around midnight, you know, because we're often entertaining.'

I countered that even when Mass was at eleven she normally wasn't there, setting a bad example.

'But I do sometimes come,' she answered.

'True, in the three or four months I've been here, perhaps twice. Does your husband prevent you?'

'No, I'm perfectly free. I'm my own mistress. I can do as I please.'

'Well, then, you have no excuse. You should do your duty.'

I gathered that she did not like what I said. Nevertheless, she said she would come when she could. I spoke to her in English since she couldn't speak French. My English was rudimentary, because I had only been studying it for three months. However, we understood each other.

4. Two days after my visit, an insulting letter from the lawyer arrived. It was brief, blunt and blistering. I regret not keeping it or my reply. In it, he said he was angry that I had brought discord, confusion and misrepresentation into his home. He did not want me meddling in his family's affairs or upsetting his wife. As the head of the family, he did not want his wife going to the Catholic church. I was told not to set foot in his house again. I was annoyed by his letter.

I gave it to Tierry and he was startled by its contents. I decided that, as a priest, it would be opportune to teach the lawyer something about the natural law and God's will. I penned an immediate, lengthy reply, which Tierry corrected. I then copied it and sent it off. I said that I was considerably puzzled by his letter, especially coming from a lawyer, who should know right from wrong. I had only done my duty as a priest. It was not my intention to bring disharmony or disturbance to families, but rather, accord and harmony, as a messenger of God's peace. I was charged to look after Catholics entrusted to me by God, and I would never shirk my duty in this regard. I also pointed out that, he should realise, as a lawyer, that he had no right to exercise control over his wife's conscience. Only God had the right to enter this domain. Duty to God was paramount. If his wife wished to practise her faith, she had every right to do so. No law would endorse interference. I was amazed that he as a lawyer could speak in such a fashion. He should seriously consider God's judgement of his behaviour.

I got back a brief reply, in which he stated that he was master in his own home and could do as he pleased. He repeated that I was to make no further visits. I took up the matter again, explaining that while I conceded that up to a point he was master of his wife in material matters, he had no control over her soul. If at any time his wife needed my spiritual assistance, I would go to his house, whether he liked it or not.

5. The lawyer did not reply to my second letter. I thought I had finally convinced him, but that was not so. About eight or ten days later, as I was coming out of the post office, a man introduced himself. He was small, stocky, with a ruddy complexion and about thirty-five years old. He held out his hand in greeting, 'Excuse me, Father, I sent you some letters.'

'Letters?'

'Yes! Don't you know who I am?'

'No, I haven't had the pleasure.'

'I'm the lawyer you wrote to.'

'Oh! Fancy meeting you!'

'Yes, and I'm glad to have the opportunity to explain.'

Standing in the middle of the street, I said, 'Tell me, my good man, do you still entertain the strange notion that you have the right to control your wife's conscience?'

'No, no, Father. You were perfectly right. I can assure you that I leave her perfectly free to practise her religion and whatever else. I will never stop her or prevent her.'

'Then how come you wrote the opposite, and didn't want me to visit? You appear to be contradicting yourself.' ·

'To be absolutely frank,' the lawyer replied, speaking softly so he couldn't be overheard, 'it's my wife who doesn't want it. I can't explain why. She has all the time in the world and a carriage at her disposal. I can assure you, I've never said anything to stop her.'

I frowned as he spoke, indicating my incredulity. When he finished, I said, 'Excuse me, your letters say just the opposite. It's you who oppose her.'

'It's true that my letters would lead you to believe that. But she's behind it. When I returned home in the evening after your visit, she was very upset and complained about your cheek telling her to be a good Catholic. She was really angry and told me to write to you to leave her in peace. That's why I wrote to you as I did.'

'Excuse me, sir, your wife could have told me this, but she said nothing. On the contrary, she seemed to agree with me.'

'She didn't have the courage to say it to your face, but she certainly did to me. You know as well as I do that I would not only be stupid but in breach of the law to try to stop my wife practising her religion.'

I was startled and remained silent. Reflecting on what he told me, I realised that it must have been his wife who did not want to practise her faith. Even if the husband did try to stop her, a good Catholic woman would not have divulged to her husband the purpose of my visit. I replied to the lawyer, 'If it's your wife who does not want to practise her religion, have no fear, I won't set foot in your house again.' That was the end of the matter.

6. I tried to find out more about the couple from Jennings. He told me that the lawyer wasn't bigoted but keen to get rich. His wife was a nominal Catholic, who hardly ever came to church anyway. They wanted to become people of substance but didn't have the means. They were assiduously cultivating the Protestant élite, giving parties and dinners for clients, and saddling themselves with debt. I never saw her at church again. Her insult to God and reckless disregard for her salvation distressed me. Perhaps she did become a Protestant. All I can say is that she had no interest in her own faith. One soul may have been lost to God, but I had the consolation a few months later of receiving a good, straightforward Protestant forty-year-old man into the bosom of the Church. He became a devout Catholic, and a year later married a fine widow, the owner of the Ormond Hotel, mentioned above. The marriage was successful. The convert was sober, hard-working, devoted to his wife and, in short, a model husband.

PART 5. THE IRISH CATHOLIC SOCIETY

SUMMARY. – 1. The stagnant condition of the Irish Catholic Society. – 2. I try to revitalise and support its development. – 3. I become an official member. – 4. Revival in jeopardy. – 5. A Catholic member of the nobility visits Gisborne. – 7. I strongly refute his calumnies.

1. In Gisborne, as in Ireland, the United Kingdom, America and British colonies, there was a branch of the Irish Catholic Society.* It was one of many established in New Zealand, and an off-shoot of the Auckland branch whose headquarters were in Ireland. Only practising Catholics of good moral standing could become members. The aim of the organisation was to maintain the practice of religion, uphold the Catholic faith and defend the legitimate rights of the Irish which had been denied by the British Government. A condition of membership was that at least every two months members were to take Communion at Sunday Mass as a body. Subscription was a monthly fee of sixpence (62.5 centimes), for which the society provided its members several benefits: for example, medical treatment and a daily allowance in case of sickness. In cases of indigence, the society provided funeral expenses and a donation to the widow or children of a widower. It provided a fulcrum for conserving the spirit of religion in its members, uniting them in their faith and allegiance to Ireland, their motherland. But human nature shows that initial enthusiasm is often followed by lethargy. Because of the depression in Gisborne, several members left the district, while others stopped paying their fees. Some became lax about the rules. For a time only three or four members would come together for Communion. Few attended the monthly and annual meetings. The society, in short, was on the way to extinction.

2. I was apprised of the woeful situation by the society's executive. They asked me as chaplain to attend some meetings and see if I could encourage members and breathe life into the organisation. Recognising its worthy purpose I accepted their invitation. The president sent members a notice inviting them to come to an important meeting the following Thursday at 7 p.m. After dinner that day, the treasurer took me to the meeting. I was welcomed with great respect. I took my seat beside the president. I mentioned that I was amazed to find only about fifteen people present out of the fifty-strong membership. The president said that a few had sent apologies, but the others gave no reason for their absence. Finances were then discussed. The society was not in debt, but had few funds because many members hadn't paid their dues. Some hadn't contributed for at least a year, others six months, and some three months. They went on to discuss the

* Vaggioli describes the Hibernians as 'the Irish Catholic Society'. In fact, practising Catholics of any nationality were welcome as members.

attitude of members towards the society. Most had shown no interest for more than two years, neglected observing its rules regarding attendance and maintaining its reputation.

I urged those present to relay my comments to absent members, hoping to shake them out of their lethargy and indifference. I said, 'I urge you to be proud of being Irish, to defend God's honour and your motherland. Your fathers maintained a strong faith, unflagging hope and indomitable courage in defending their religion and their homeland. They suffered privation, confiscation, imprisonment and death. They endured and died for God. What about you? You have the same blood in your veins as those glorious champions and martyrs for Christ. Do you have the same steadfastness? When I consider the decaying condition of your society, I fear the same manly virtues are not manifest. Rally round your society. Keep its rules. They will help you be Irishmen not only in name, but in deed. Revive your society, not only for the honour of God, but so as not to shame yourselves before Protestants, showing yourselves incapable of supporting your own society while Masonic, anti-Catholic societies continue to flourish.' I withdrew after my speech to warm applause.

The meeting continued with the passing of the following resolutions: (1) to send an invitation to those who were behind in payment to remedy this within a month, (2) that after two months, members who were six months behind in fees would be struck off, (3) members would be similarly treated who, without a justifiable reason, did not attend meetings for more than six months, (4) the custom was reinstated of going to Communion as a body every two months. The first three resolutions were enacted, but the fourth caused some difficulty because members were widely scattered throughout the vast Gisborne district. Attending the 11 a.m. Mass would involve a lengthy fast.* The strict measures, however, forced those out of the society who were uninterested. Those who replied paid their dues promptly, but membership declined to less than half.

3. The committee continued its efforts to revive the society. I exhorted members, but with little effect. It was not so much a lack of goodwill as the effects of the depression which gripped the area, forcing the Irish to scatter through the huge district in search of work. They could only attend meetings very occasionally. In 1881 the executive were resolved to dissolve the society, or at least disband the committee. I begged them not to, but to remain in office until the expiry of their term in a year. They agreed. Seeing the risk to the society, I decided to become a member to support and, I hoped, revive it. Irish priests were members. The president was pleased with my suggestion. I formally applied at the next meeting and was unanimously accepted. This gesture seemed to have a rousing

* It was customary in this period for Catholics to fast from the previous midnight before receiving Communion.

effect because suddenly new members joined up.

Election time came for the committee. The majority proposed me as president, urging me to accept nomination. I declined, saying I could attend meetings only occasionally. They were still keen to nominate me as vice-president and urged me to attend meetings as often as I could to help revive and reorganise the society. Mr Jennings was re-elected as president. He didn't want to accept, but at my urging, he agreed. The secretary and treasurer were also re-elected. I made a brief speech encouraging members to work hard together to revive the society, for the considerable benefits this would bring them and for the good of the people and the Church.

4. The committee wished to increase the society's effectiveness. It purged the membership list and actively canvassed for new members. It did gain an injection of fresh energy and looked like growing and prospering, but the Devil had other ideas in mind. A certain young Irishman, Gallagher by name, had aspirations to the presidency. He was about twenty-seven or twenty-eight years old, ambitious, truculent and a fanatical proponent of Irish patriotism. He had been a loyal member, but when he did not gain the presidency or any other office, he had it in for the society. He stopped attending meetings but did not resign his membership. He mounted a campaign of defamation against the society, declaring the committee was failing to carry out its duties. He was instrumental in discouraging many local Irishmen from joining and persuading others to leave. I was unaware of his intentions (he was the same man who complained about having a non-Irish priest). I believed that since the society was more settled, it would flourish. I did my best to lend my support. Membership increased to forty. For a while things went well. But then inertia set in again. People living in the country said it was too difficult for them to attend meetings and go to Communion as a body. As a result, few came to meetings and only the committee made an appearance for Communion. The others came individually and then not more than twice a year, for Christmas and Easter. I kept the society alive, with a membership of about thirty, until my departure from Gisborne on 20 September 1882. After I left I don't know what became of it.

5. In January or February 1881, a tall thin 22-year-old Englishman, the son of a lord, arrived in Gisborne. (He has since inherited the title and his seat is near our Buckfast monastery.)* He had come on a tour to Australia and New Zealand. In Gisborne he lodged at the main hotel, intending to stay a week, making horse-riding trips around the district. While in the township, he attended daily Mass.

---

* Buckfast is a prominent Benedictine monastery in England, known for innovative bee-keeping methods.

Two days after his arrival, the baronet called on me and gave me his visiting card. I warmly welcomed him. As I could not speak English fluently, while understanding it well, I asked him if he spoke French. He said he had studied it but, for want of practice, he didn't speak it well. Nevertheless, he had no trouble understanding. We agreed for him to speak in English, which he spoke most elegantly, while I would reply in French. He asked me how many Catholics there were, the size of the mission, questions about the parishioners' morals, religious practice, financial condition and nationality. I answered to the best of my ability. He also wanted to know where I was from, where I had been before coming to New Zealand, and where I had learnt my excellent French, and now, English. I was happy to reply.

6. The young Englishman enjoyed chatting, and seemed in no hurry. In our lengthy discussion he asked question after question. Eventually we began discussing Ireland, the Irish and their quest for Home Rule or self-government. I had read a lot on the subject at the time, as it was a lively issue. With my usual frankness I defended the Irish, stating that they were simply seeking from England fundamental justice and the right to self-determination. What a mistake! First of all, the baronet expressed his amazement that an Italian would defend such a violent, ignorant people! He proceeded to rail against the Irish, concluding by saying the British Government had bent over backwards for them and had been repaid with the vilest ingratitude. They deserved to remain the peasants they were, and he continued his diatribe in this vein. I let the callow youth spew out his bile against the Irish, knowing full well that the English were violently opposed to them because of the prejudice fed to them from childhood and nurtured by the press.

7. When he thought he had convinced me that the Irish were a pack of rogues, expecting me to believe his lies, I dissected his statements carefully in an hour-long discussion. Here is a brief summary:
   'Tell me,' I asked, 'are you a Protestant?'
   'No, of course not. I'm a Roman Catholic.'
   'I'm surprised that you as a Catholic would speak so harshly of Irish Catholics, your co-religionists and brothers! Not even a Protestant would speak so negatively of such a brave people, who for three centuries defended God, their faith and freedom!'
   'I'm not critical of their religion, just their behaviour! You're a foreigner. You wouldn't know the facts about the Irish situation. Only we British really do.'
   'So, only the British know the true situation in Ireland? I'm sorry to tell you that speaking about the Irish as you have shows you don't know a thing. Most of the British, on principle, are against the Irish, whom they have exploited. Their version of Irish history is a pack of lies. Newspapers, journals and books

written by English Protestants are full of them too. They have a strong effect on public opinion. Even Catholics drink from this polluted spring, imbibing falsehood rather than the truth and actual facts. That is why the English Catholic aristocracy, which should know better, takes the Protestant side against the Irish. It's an English Protestant conspiracy against Catholic Ireland. It's true that as an Italian I'm a stranger to both races. But let me assure you, I have spent more than two years researching the subject from both points of view. I have read books, periodicals, British, Irish and American journals, as well as Australian and New Zealand publications. I have done everything to discover the real truth, whether it would support the Irish position or not, because, unlike you, I am not partisan. My judgement is totally impartial.

'From my studies I have to tell you that history, verified evidence and truth support the Irish, in contrast to the treachery of the Protestant British Government. For more than three centuries it has attempted to exterminate this courageous, Christian nation, after stripping it of its possessions and property. This persecuted people has every right to seek justice from England. It's sad and deplorable that English Catholics, instead of supporting their beleaguered brothers, join the Protestants and add to their torment. But let me tell you, this intrepid race, which has preserved the true faith of Christ in spite of Britain's every effort at their eradication, will not perish. In fact, I believe the day will soon come when they will wrest from the British Government the justice they have been seeking for three centuries.'

'If what you are saying were true,' he replied, 'the English clergy would support Ireland. But they take the same position as the laity.'

'My good sir, what on earth are you saying? I can see that you're not abreast of developments, even regarding events in England! Cardinals Wiseman, Manning and Newman, England's leading intellectuals, are for the Irish. Furthermore, Pope Leo XIII has publicly stated that the Irish claims and protests are just, providing they use only legal means to back their cause. Gladstone, the Protestant Prime Minister of England, is in favour of meeting the Irish claims for justice.'

The poor aristocrat, backed to the wall, didn't know how to reply, except to say, 'You're entitled to your opinion, as I am to mine. You can keep your position. I'll maintain mine.'

Having said this, he bade me farewell. Although at the beginning of the visit he told me he would come again, and certainly before leaving Gisborne, the fact is that was the last time I saw him. It really is deplorable that English Catholics side against the Irish on principle, with no justifiable reason.

Chapter Five

Sorting Out The Debt
(EARLY 1880 TO MID-1882)

PART 1. DEVELOPING A PLAN

SUMMARY. – 1. Starting to sort out the debt. – 2. The interest rate, a significant hurdle. – 3. I consider trying for an interest free loan, or one at a nominal rate. – 4. I seek the committee's opinion. – 5. Their scepticism. – 6. They eventually approve my plan.

1. I need to go back about eighteen months to take up again the thread of my adventures. As soon as I had learnt basic English, I sought not only to care for the parishioners, but to find an effective means to deal with the church debt and repay it as soon as possible. The committee, in a month, had managed to collect only £10 towards the interest which was due on 1 July, and a further £16 was required. This just added to the bank's profits, while the capital wasn't reduced one farthing. This angered me. Parishioners were depriving themselves of necessities simply to fill the bank's coffers.

2. The exorbitant nine and a half per cent interest charged made it impossible for the parishioners to pay off any capital. They were exploited by the bank and remained in debt. Thinking of the enormous amount of interest consumed me night and day. I tossed over in my mind how to resolve the complex problem. Eventually, I settled on two possibilities:
1) To try to find Catholics in Auckland willing to lend money at no interest to pay the bank, with us having to repay their loan within five years.
2) To try to set up an Auckland society of twenty-two shareholders, each of whom would contribute £25 to be paid to the bank, and we in Gisborne would undertake to pay them the capital within five years at five per cent interest.
In May 1880 I explained my proposals to Tierry and Mr Jennings, chairman of the committee. They found favour in both ideas, but foresaw serious difficulty regarding the plan of securing a free loan. They believed the second proposal had more chance of success.

3. The first proposal looked more difficult, but it appealed to me. I was sure that His Lordship and the vicar-general would lend their support in finding a few wealthy Catholics to give us a free loan rather than in trying to find twenty-two contributors to form a syndicate. It would be too burdensome to expect the

Gisborne parishioners to pay the capital and five per cent interest within five years. I clearly explained the free loan idea and consulted others about it. They poured cold water on the scheme, claiming no one would lend money without interest.

4. In June 1880 I called a meeting of the committee to discuss my preferred proposals. The debt was placed on the agenda for the 7 p.m. meeting at the presbytery. I told members about my idea of going to Auckland to see if the bishop, the vicar-general and Fr McDonald would support either proposal. I asked for their frank response. If they had any better ideas, I would be more than happy to support whatever would work best.

5. After a full discussion, it was agreed that mine were excellent suggestions, especially the first. Members were doubtful, however, that notwithstanding my good intentions, it would work, even with the bishop's support. I commented that nothing would be lost if we tried it out. One of the committee members pointed out that my return trip to Auckland would cost at least £10 (250 francs). If my living expenses for a week were included, the total cost would be £12. The committee still hadn't collected enough money to pay the interest due at the end of the month. If they deducted £12 for my trip, it would be impossible to pay the interest on 1 July. I had, however, anticipated this obstacle. I replied that I would pay for the trip and expenses out of my own funds. I added that as a missionary I had to go to weekly confession if there was another priest in the area. Since there was none, I saw it as my duty to confess at least twice a year. I had been in Gisborne five months. In this time, thanks to God's special grace, I had nothing serious to reproach myself for; but even so, I still believed I should go to confession twice a year, like any good Christian. I pointed out that I could have gone to Napier, which was closer, and would incur less expense. But I had decided to go there after Christmas, and to Auckland at the end of June, making the latter trip serve a double purpose. I had the interest of my parishioners at heart and I would do my utmost to support them. I hoped that with the help of God and the bishop I would be successful. I asked the committee to pray to the Lord to bless the project. If I were unsuccessful, they would not have to worry about money being squandered.

6. The committee were astounded and full of admiration. It was unheard of for missionaries, who are generally poor, to make a costly trip at their own expense. They praised my decision, warmly thanking me for my goodwill and promised to pray for a successful outcome to my visit.

Jennings, however, raised a concern: 'Father, how can you do it without getting into debt? I don't know how you and Br Joseph can live here on the little that is collected on Sundays for your upkeep. I collect the Mass and vespers offerings, and I know they rarely fetch more than a pound each week. It's even less at

Ormond with the one Mass. How can you manage your upkeep, church expenses and pay the organist ten shillings a week without getting into debt? I can't understand it.'

I replied that given their poverty, I was surprised that they were able to give me £2 a week, and that we were content with little. Things were expensive, but as monks we lived frugally. What they gave us was sufficient for our needs. I was able to fund special expenses, like going to Auckland, from Easter dues. Another member said, 'But, Father, even a poor labourer needs at least a pound a week for food. There are two of you, and you also have to pay the organist. How can both of you manage on only about a pound a week?'

I replied that it was sufficient because we spent little on alcohol and had no rent to pay. The committee was full of praise and left agreeably surprised and happy.

PART 2. DISCUSSION WITH THE BISHOP

SUMMARY. – 1. En route to Auckland. – 2. At the bishop's. – 3. He is pleased with my plans, giving me £50 guarantee with the bank. – 4. I outline my two proposals. – 5. They are rejected by the vicar-general. – 6. The bishop's anger at an article in the Catholic newspaper. – 7. The bishop asks why Fr Adalbert has not come; I explain, with no personal animosity.

1. On 26 June 1880 I collected my first-class ticket to Auckland, paying £10. I was concerned as to how the bishop would receive my proposals and wrestled with my hopes and fears. I was determined, however, to get out of this morass. Departure was the same day. There was a swell. I felt queasy, but I wasn't sick and I was even able to stay on deck. At about 10 a.m. on 27 June, we reached Auckland. On disembarking, I immediately went to the cathedral. The two priests were very pleased to see me again, wanting me to stay with them. I enquired whether Mons. Steins was in residence. They said he was. I thanked them for their invitation, saying I would stay at the bishop's.

2. After bidding them goodbye, I went out onto the street near the cathedral to wait for the tram. Its terminus was Ponsonby, opposite the bishop's house where it stopped for ten minutes before returning to the wharf. The tram arrived. I climbed on board and took it to Ponsonby. Mons. Steins greeted me very warmly. He was delighted to see me again. He wanted me to stay with him for the duration of my visit. That afternoon I visited the Sisters of Mercy nearby. They too were happy to see me again and to have regular daily Mass for a week. I need hardly mention the pleasure the Jesuit lay brother had at seeing me once more in Ponsonby. He was beside himself with joy. We told each other about our adventures over the past five months. When I sat down with the bishop, firstly I congratulated him for not receiving the two Wellington priests into the diocese,

recognising their unsuitability as had been revealed in their Easter antics. I then added somewhat tentatively, 'I'm sorry to hear that your compatriot is a drunkard!'*

'And how do you know that?'

'A layman told me the moment I got off the boat. Isn't Your Excellency aware?'

'Yes, unfortunately. I'm very angry about it. I have summoned him *ad audiendum verbum*.'†

In fact, he visited the bishop two days later. He would not mend his ways. Consequently he was removed from Puhoi and dismissed.

'And what about Cassidy, the Coromandel priest? Have you heard anything about him?'

'No, Excellency, I haven't.'

The bishop didn't elaborate, but some months later, he had him, too, removed from the diocese because of drunkenness and debauchery.

3. Unknown to me, Mons. Steins had maintained a secret correspondence with certain Gisborne parishioners, so he could be apprised of my conduct as well as learn how the mission was faring. I, for my part, made it my duty to keep the bishop informed about church matters, including the debt, and sought his advice over any difficulty. This correspondence had only revealed good things about me. My behaviour was even praised by Protestants. They commended the parishioners for having a *gentleman* as their missionary, far superior in every respect to their own ministers. However, I did not deserve such praise. I sought only to behave in public and private as a monk should. There was nothing extraordinary or singular about me. Because of these reports, the bishop held me in high regard. As a testimony of his affection, he told me that the £50 he had deposited as a guarantee with the bank he would now gift to the church to reduce the debt. I thanked him most sincerely for his generosity and interest. I informed him about the state of the debt, mentioning that Fr Chastagnon had left an actual debt of £645, of which about £560 was owed to the Bank of New Zealand, £12 to the Union Bank and £73 to individuals. Of the promissory notes worth £250 or £260, only one had been honoured, Mr Walsh's for £25. The total debt, held by the one bank, had been reduced to £550. Taking into account his generous gift of £50, as at 1 July 1880, the debt stood at £500, or 12,500 francs. The bishop expressed his pleasure. He praised my zeal and financial acumen. He said that, with my unrelenting tenacity, I would succeed in overcoming any difficulty.

* The reference is to the Dutch priest, mentioned earlier.
† 'for an audience' (Latin).

4. I then explained the Gisborne situation to him. 'There are about 300 Catholics in the Gisborne district. They are well-meaning but, being poor and out of work, they don't have the means to pay the interest, let alone the debt.'

'Alas, I know you're right, but what can be done?'

'At present we're paying nine and a half per cent interest, which is far too high. On £500, that's £47 10s. The parishioners can't even keep up interest payments.'

'I understand, but I don't know what to do. What do you think?'

'I've come with two proposals. The first is to find one or more Auckland Catholics prepared to lend us the money without interest to repay the bank. We would pay the lenders back within five years. The second would be to find about twenty-five well-off Catholics willing to each lend £20 at five per cent interest. We would guarantee to pay the interest six-monthly and the capital within five years.'

'Your proposals have merit, especially the first, but I don't think they're feasible. Catholics generally don't like lending to the Church, for fear of not being repaid. This is especially so in the colonies.'

'But, Excellency, I can't think of any better solutions. If you have a better idea, tell me. I'd be happy to accept it. I told the parishioners that I would be seeing Your Excellency. You must help me somehow. Otherwise, how can I face them and tell them I haven't been successful?'

The bishop was silent for a few moments. Then he replied, 'Right now, I don't have an answer. I'll get Mons. Fynes to come over. We'll talk to him and see if we can do as you suggest. He knows the Auckland situation much better than me. I would really like to support you. I admire your dedication and zeal, and I'd be so pleased if we could sort this out.'

5. The following day the vicar-general arrived. I explained my proposals as carefully as I could, hoping for a favourable response from him. He shook his head from time to time as I spoke. When I finished, he said they weren't practicable. No Catholics, even with the means, would lend money with or without interest, for fear of not being repaid. I told him we would provide written guarantees.

'Believe me, dear Father, you wouldn't be believed. They would just make excuses – like they had no money to lend.'

'Well, how's the debt going to be cleared? I can't think of any other solution. Gisborne's parishioners need an answer.'

The bishop supported me. He too was keen to find a practical solution. The vicar-general persisted that my proposals were unworkable. He regretted my situation, but said we would have to find another way of solving the problem. He would think it over and return tomorrow or the following day with an alternative solution. In the meantime we should all pray to the Lord for direction. Mons. Fynes then returned to Parnell.

6. That evening, the bishop asked me if I had read an article in the *Freeman* which discussed the future Bishop of Auckland. I replied that I had, but hadn't given it any attention. He asked me if I knew who wrote it. I replied I didn't because my Newton confrères never wrote to me and treated me as though I didn't exist. The bishop was very angry about the rash article. He said its information was supposed to be confidential between Propaganda and himself, and should never have been printed. I suspected the article had been written by one of our Newton priests, either Fr Downey or Fr O'Gara. Six months later I learnt that the latter was the author. The bishop told me that there was no certainty that Fr Sullivan would succeed him as Bishop of Auckland. He needed first to come to Auckland and demonstrate his ability. He concluded angrily, 'The writer was most imprudent. He was stupid to write such things. I alone am to decide! I'm the bishop!'

7. During my stay, I asked the bishop if he knew when Fr Adalbert Sullivan was coming to New Zealand. He had intimated to me that he hoped to arrive by February. Then he wrote that it would be Easter, then July or August. But nothing happened. The bishop said he had given him exactly the same story.

'I would insist,' continued the bishop, 'that he come straightaway. He would reply that he still had business to complete. In the meantime he kept postponing his arrival from one month to the next. You would think he would have tidied things up in nine months! Since I haven't been able to persuade him to act more urgently, I am considering writing to Propaganda to persuade him to come, one way or another.'

I said it wouldn't have taken me nine months to sort things out and get to New Zealand. Later I learnt from Fr O'Gara that Fr Sullivan used a thousand excuses for not coming, because he hoped to gain the bishopric without setting foot in New Zealand. But his plan didn't work. The bishop was silent about the matter for a couple of days. Then he said seriously, 'Your English priests are very wealthy, aren't they?'

'No, Excellency,' I replied in surprise. 'As far as I know, they're really poor and in debt.'

The bishop shook his head doubtfully. 'It doesn't appear that your Ramsgate confrères are that poor. Fr Sullivan has written that he can't come out immediately because he wants to withdraw £10,000 for the Auckland diocese. If they were in debt, they could pay off their creditors. The diocese could certainly benefit from £10,000.'

I was stunned and replied, 'Excellency, I always speak the truth. I can tell you that I don't believe for one moment Fr Sullivan is bringing that kind of money. Where would he get it from? I can assure you the Ramsgate Benedictines aren't wealthy. They have no money to give anyone. They have a debt on their school of more than £15,000 at five per cent interest. I know this as a fact, and the main culprit is Fr Sullivan himself.

The startled bishop exclaimed, 'So where would the £10,000 come from?'

'He mentioned to me some time ago that an aunt was very ill and he hoped to inherit £5000 for the missions. But even though he comes from an affluent family, I don't think she would have that much money to bequeath to Fr Sullivan, especially when there are several needy nephews to consider. I just don't believe it. It wouldn't be the first time he has concealed the truth.'

'How could the Ramsgate fathers have incurred such a huge debt? You say Fr Sullivan was to blame. I find that hard to believe.'

I then briefly told the bishop about Fr Sullivan's speculation, his well-known bankruptcy and the investigation into it by the local bishop and three cardinals in Rome. The bishop listened in amazement. When I had finished, he said, 'Did the bankruptcy follow the usual process?'

'No, the matter didn't go to court because an agreement was reached with the creditors. But I heard it was in every paper in England.'

I later learnt that the bishop wrote to Propaganda requesting them to put pressure on Fr Sullivan to come to New Zealand as soon as possible.

PART 3. A SOLUTION IS FOUND

SUMMARY. – 1. We put our thinking caps on. – 2. A further meeting at the bishop's residence; my proposals are totally rejected. – 3. Mons. Fynes's proposal is seen as the only possibility. – 4. Missionaries summoned to a meeting. – 5. They are asked to pay the interest on the Gisborne debt. My confrères' opposition! – 6. The majority accept the vicar-general's proposal.

1. After Mons. Fynes's departure, I racked my brains to find an alternative solution to paying off the debt. I prayed but no answer came. The bishop was equally unsuccessful. He said, however, that he put considerable faith in the vicar-general, who was extremely competent in such matters. We both prayed at Mass for this intention and the sisters offered up their Communion likewise. I was very anxious on behalf of my parishioners, regarding it as a matter of life or death.

2. A couple of days later the vicar-general turned up at nine-thirty, saying he had been very busy and needed more time for reflection. I was waiting for him in the front garden. I ran up to him. He was his usual happy, placid self. I asked him if he had found a solution.

'Let's hope there's a way out. I'm here anyway. Let's see.'

We went into the bishop's study. He invited us to sit down. The vicar-general asked us if we had come up with any other solutions. We had to say no. He then said that he had given further thought to the matter and still rejected my proposals as impractical. No one would lend money gratis or at five per cent. He added that trying to raise a subscription at five per cent interest would bring little relief to the Gisborne parishioners. The debt could instead be transferred to the Auckland headquarters of the bank at a reduced rate of seven per cent. The vicar-general went on, 'To really help the parishioners and your worthy self, we people are prepared to pay the interest while the parishioners are responsible only for the capital. Can you see the benefit of this?'

The bishop and I agreed that it would be a lot better than having to pay the five per cent interest.

3. 'Well, then,' continued Mons. Fynes, 'the only way I see to resolve the matter satisfactorily for Fr Vaggioli and the people of Gisborne would be for the priests of the diocese to take responsibility for paying off the interest on the debt, and you and your parishioners undertake to repay the capital within five years. What do you think, Your Excellency?' (Personally, I was very much in favour, but I was afraid the priests wouldn't agree, seeing it as too onerous for them.)

After pausing a moment, the bishop replied, 'Do you believe, Monsignor, the priests would accept your proposal?'

'I don't think, Excellency, they would refuse doing such a charitable deed for the Catholics of Gisborne and their devoted parish priest. There may be a few who are too poor, but the majority would agree. We shouldn't put pressure on those who couldn't afford it, but I don't think there would be any opposition to the idea.'

'You don't think it would be too much of a burden on them?' the bishop repeated.

'Not really, Excellency, especially if we have the debt transferred from the bank's Gisborne branch to Auckland at seven per cent. Annual interest on the £500 at seven per cent would be £35. There are sixteen of us priests. If we were to all agree to the proposal, we would each pay only £2 in the first year. As the Gisborne parishioners begin paying off the capital, interest payments would decrease each year. Surely our missionaries would be able to manage £2 a year?'

'Monsignor,' I exclaimed, 'poor though I am, I'd be the first to tell you that I would be only too happy to pay my share.'

The vicar-general ignored my outburst and continued, 'I believe, Excellency, that if you endorse my proposal, the priests will agree to this act of charity. If, however, they don't, I can't think of a more practical solution. But I feel sure you'll get their agreement.'

The bishop welcomed his proposal. I was overjoyed, but still anxious that the priests might refuse. We agreed to call a meeting of the town and district priests to see if it would be accepted.

4. Mons. Fynes immediately wrote on the bishop's behalf inviting priests out

of town to come to an important meeting at the cathedral presbytery. It was to take place, as I recall, on Thursday or Friday of the first week in July. My two Newton confrères were invited as well as the two cathedral priests. On the day the bishop, the vicar-general, the cathedral administrator, Fr McDonald and his assistant, Fr O'Dwyer, the editor of the *Freeman* newspaper, Fr Downey, Fr O'Gara and myself attended. The missionaries of Onehunga, Otahuhu, Drury and two other missions also came. Mons. Steins said a few words and then handed over to the vicar-general. He outlined the state of the Gisborne church's debt, what I had done to reduce it, the parishioners' financial hardship, the reason for my visit to Auckland, etc. He concluded, saying, 'Fr Vaggioli, who is here today, can clarify the purpose of his trip and what his parishioners want.'

I stood up to speak, but the bishop interrupted, 'You don't have to stand.'

Since they all understood French, I spoke in that language, which made it easier for me. I said that I had been sent by my parishioners to see if I could find some wealthy Auckland Catholics prepared to lend us money without interest, or at a minimal rate, so we could pay back the bank. The poverty-stricken parishioners were incapable of paying the nine and a half per cent interest as well as the capital. They hoped I would be able to obtain a loan. We would then guarantee to pay off the capital within five years. I concluded by saying that His Excellency and the vicar-general, to my consternation, believed it would be impossible to find such people. I did not have the courage to return to Gisborne without finding a solution.

5. The vicar-general then spoke. He said my proposal was not feasible. He suggested that if they were willing to make a generous sacrifice on behalf of Gisborne's parishioners, they would agree to pay the interest. Divided among them, it would be about £2 each in the first year, and decreasing from then on. He could see no other solution. The priests then began discussing the proposal. After seeking clarification from the vicar-general, the majority immediately showed they were in favour. To make sure, however, the bishop asked each of them to comment, beginning with the cathedral administrator. He willingly accepted to help, providing Gisborne's priest and parishioners agreed to pay the capital within five years. I replied that we would agree to this condition. In fact, I hoped to be able to pay it off earlier. In the meantime, I said I would pay a share of the interest. The vicar-general sought the views of the parish priests of Onehunga, Otahuhu and the other missions. They supported the proposal. He then turned to Fr Cuthbert Downey of Newton. Speaking on behalf of Fr O'Gara as well, he said, 'We can't agree to help the Gisborne mission. We're poor and we need help too. Our superior's not here. We can't make this kind of decision, especially when it involves a commitment lasting several years.'

The other missionaries were astonished at his refusal to help a colleague.

The bishop told Fr Downey that he was their superior. They could therefore in good conscience support the proposal, and all missionaries were equally poor. I was afraid that the proposal would fail because of my colleagues' opposition. I asked to speak, and said: 'I'm sure that if Fr Adalbert were here he would very willingly accept the vicar-general's proposal. However, until he comes, Your Excellency is our lawful and immediate superior. My confrères say they can't come to my aid. Well, I'll just have to accept that. Nevertheless, so as to not put an additional burden on the other, generous missionaries, I will undertake to pay for my two colleagues. I'm sure Providence will come to my aid.'

The other missionaries exclaimed, 'Bravo!' and smiled while my two colleagues flushed with embarrassment, remaining silent. Finally, Fr O'Dwyer, the youngest priest, was questioned as to whether he agreed to the vicar-general's proposal. He had been influenced by my two colleagues and replied that he could not agree, it not being fair to burden missionaries with other parish debts. I then stood up and said that I would undertake to pay for him as well, and thus be responsible for four shares.

6. The bishop, the vicar-general and the other missionaries, except Frs Downey, O'Gara and O'Dwyer, were in favour of the vicar-general's proposal. Mons. Fynes then moved (1) that the Gisborne debt be transferred to Auckland, thus reducing the interest rate to seven per cent; (2) that he and Fr McDonald undertake to arrange the collection of interest payments from the priests; (3) that they would be given a month's notice of how much they were each to pay as well as an annual report on the capital reduction by Gisborne's parishioners. The good missionaries were pleased with these proposals. I thanked everyone for their generous assistance, assuring them that with God's help we would soon pay off the capital and release them from the burden of the interest. Later, as it turned out, Providence ordained that no one would have to pay interest, as will soon be revealed. The bishop thanked the priests for their kind co-operation and dissolved the meeting.

Part 4. Bazaar or Public Auction?

Summary. – 1. My sense of satisfaction. – 2. How to raise funds. – 3. Early initiatives in Auckland for a bazaar. – 4. My return to Gisborne. – 5. I report the results of my trip. – 6. Practical suggestions for raising funds.

1. The reader can well imagine my delight at the splendid outcome of the meeting. I was delighted that my parishioners and I had only to be responsible for repaying the capital. This amazing result would have to be attributed first to God and Our Lady, and second to the vicar-general and the bishop, without

whom I would certainly have got nowhere. The sisters' prayers also had a part to play in our success.

2. Now that payment of the debt was decided, I immediately began to consider the quickest way to repay the capital. I mentioned this to the bishop, the vicar-general and the cathedral administrator. They informed me about holding concerts, bazaars and gift auctions or art unions (for which goods were donated). They did not mention, however, that organising bazaars involved up to a year's preparation. They gave the best return, but took a lot of work. They also suggested I raise money by public subscription, and take up special collections, etc. These had already been tried, however, with disappointing results because of the parishioners' poverty.

3. I considered how I could most profitably use my time in Auckland, given the cost of the trip. I decided to discuss organising a bazaar, hoping to collect handicrafts from the Catholic ladies, which I could not obtain in Gisborne. I realised from the way my Newton colleagues treated me at the meeting that it would be useless to invite their help, so I left them out. Fr McDonald was very kind. He would help anyone out whenever he could. He promised he would help me find Catholic ladies willing to make articles gratis for our forthcoming bazaar in Gisborne. He also took me to some Catholic families, promoting my cause, and gave me the names of others, telling me to write to them for help. The Sisters of Mercy at Ponsonby also promised to assist.

4. Since a solution for settling the debt had been found, and help for the bazaar promised, I decided to return to Gisborne by the steamer which was leaving on Thursday. I thanked the bishop for his kind hospitality and for all he had done for me and for Gisborne. I also went and thanked the vicar-general and Fr McDonald. Then, accompanied to the wharf by the bishop's lay brother, I embarked. The sea was calm and I was able to dine. I remained on deck until nine. When I finished reciting my office, I went to bed and slept until 5 a.m. On Friday at about 9 a.m. we entered Tauranga harbour and, after a couple of hours' stop, we departed for Gisborne. At 9 a.m. on Saturday, the steamer anchored off Gisborne. Shortly afterwards, I got into a lighter with other passengers and in half an hour we safely reached the wharf. Br Joseph and some parishioners were waiting for us.

5. The following day being Sunday, I announced at both Masses that that evening, after vespers in Gisborne, there would be a meeting at which I would tell the parishioners the outcome of my trip to Auckland. Many people came to vespers, but few remained for the meeting because it was held late, at 8 p.m., in July, the heart of winter in New Zealand. Tierry and I explained what had transpired in

Auckland. The result was that their only task was to repay the capital because the priests had agreed to pay the interest. They were extremely pleased with the unexpected outcome, thanking me for what I had done for them. They said they were fully confident that they would be able to pay off the debt within five years. They were also impressed that I was so concerned not only about their spiritual welfare but also their material well-being, having had clear proof of my solicitude.

6. I urged them to work together to achieve their goal. They promised to put every effort into clearing the debt. I had no doubt of their goodwill. A few days later, the parish committee met to discuss organising a bazaar in Gisborne, ideally for December that year. I explained my own ideas and provided information I had gained from the Auckland priests. The committee thought a bazaar couldn't be held within six months, or even eighteen months, because the Catholic ladies of the district wouldn't have sufficient time to provide the wide range of handicrafts needed. I encouraged them not to abandon the idea, mentioning I had received promises of goods from Auckland and that I would recruit other willing contributors. It was decided to have further discussion on the matter at the next committee meeting and for the ladies' committee to be consulted in the meantime, especially since they would be largely responsible for organising the bazaar.

Part 5. Working on the Debt

Summary. – 1. The ladies' committee's proposals. – 2. The parish committee's decisions. – 3. A public concert. – 4. A Presbyterian offers me a donation of £10 for the church. I refuse. – 5. The condition behind his offer; he donates the money unconditionally. – 6. I collect gifts for the auction from Auckland. – 7. The auction, a splendid success.

1. I called a meeting of the ladies' committee, explaining to them that the weekly collection they were responsible for gave poor returns and that it should now be abandoned. A better scheme needed to be found. We discussed at length the idea of a bazaar. It was decided to hold one in December 1881. Work on it would begin forthwith and help would be sought from Auckland and elsewhere. In addition, we decided to hold a public concert to be organised by our male and female singers. The committee also agreed to hold a gift auction after Christmas, especially since I had found people in Auckland willing to help.

2. I then summoned a meeting of the men's committee to discuss the ladies' committee's proposals, but they were already aware of them. The committee agreed to a public concert and for our singers to organise the programme in consultation with myself. The committee was put in charge of arranging the venue, tickets,

SORTING OUT THE DEBT 103

publicity, etc. It was also agreed to hold a gift auction after Christmas 1880, and a bazaar in December 1881, so that a substantial quantity of goods could be made.

3. We had only two male singers in Gisborne, both of whom were very good. One was Mr Butt, the Protestant manager of the Union Bank, who was an excellent tenor. The other was a Catholic. I've forgotten his name. He was an equally fine baritone. (He died at the beginning of 1882 of a stomach disorder and his death was a great loss to the parish.) The female singers comprised a married woman, four young single women and the organist, who also played the piano, was a good singer and, like the others, very versatile. They sang the Masses of Gounod and other composers. There was thus no question of their ability to give a public concert. Our singers set about finding another concert pianist and other Protestant artists since there were insufficient Catholic performers. They were willing to provide their contribution gratis for the benefit of the church.

The programme was prepared a month before the concert. It began with a march played by a Protestant pianist. A Catholic woman then sang a Rossini aria. This was followed by 'The Emerald Isle', the Irish national anthem, sung by our fine Irish baritone. The first part concluded with a piece played by the Protestant pianist and our organist. Our choir performed in the second half. They sang the 'Kyrie' and 'Gloria' from Gounod's wonderful Mass, a beautiful 'Ave Maria' and an 'O Salutaris Hostia'. The items were well received and encores were requested. Refreshments were then served for the choir. The third part opened with a piano introduction leading into a comic aria sung by three Protestants. This was followed by a march played on the piano. The concert concluded with the national anthem, 'God save the Queen'. Tickets were sold at one shilling each, or 1.25 francs. All in all, it was a great success and more than seven hundred tickets were sold. Gross takings exceeded £35. Net proceeds after expenses were £20, or 500 francs.

4. One day a Protestant visited me. I didn't know the man. He offered me a cheque for £10 and said, 'Reverend, I'm aware that the interior of your church is unfinished. I'd like to give you £10 to complete it.'

'Thank you for your offer,' I replied, 'but I can't accept it for that purpose. It would cost more than £100 to line the interior of the church. I don't have that much money. There's a debt on the church of more than £500, which I'm having serious difficulty repaying.'

'Others will help you out with that,' he said, 'and then you'll be able to finish construction. I'd love to see the interior completed.'

'I would, too, but where would I find the £100, or rather, £90? My parishioners are all poor and unable to meet the present debt on the church. I can't expect money from anyone else. So I can't accept your offer. If you could find other contributors, I would willingly accept.'

'I'm sorry, but I can't,' he replied.

'If you could make it £50 instead of £10, I'd do my best to finish the interior. Otherwise, I can't accept.'

'I can't offer any more. I'm not a wealthy man.'

'Well, I'm very sorry, but I can't accept your offer, because I can't meet your condition.'

'If I offered my minister the money, he'd take it. He would accept the condition, but not do anything about it.'

5. 'Well,' I replied, 'give it to your minister. I can't meet your condition. If you were to give me the money unconditionally, I would accept it most gratefully, recognising your kindness, and it would help reduce the debt. I'm even keener than you to see the church completed. As soon as the debt is paid off, I'll endeavour to finish it.'

'I'm not giving my Presbyterian minister any more money,' he retorted angrily. 'He is dishonest and uses church money for himself. That's why this year I've brought you my £10 donation, which I would have given to my own church if the minister were honest.'

'Good heavens! I can hardly believe my ears.'

'But it's true. Last year I and others gave more than £100 to our minister towards our church debt. He accepted the money and promised to use if for that purpose, but then spent it on himself and his family.'

'Perhaps he's not paid enough to maintain himself and his family and necessity forces him to steal?'

'No, no, he's very well paid indeed. He gets an annual cheque for £700 and is provided with a furnished house rent free.'

'If this is so, your minister has behaved very badly. I receive no such stipend from my parishioners. I accept the little they give me on Sundays for my upkeep. I get nothing from their contributions towards the debt on the church. Moreover, from the money for my upkeep I spend ten shillings a week on the organist and another six shillings for church lighting and other expenses.'

'I know and I'm glad to hear it. I've heard from your parishioners that you don't pocket any of the money you receive for the church, and that it's used for the right purpose. That's why I brought you my £10.'

'My dear sir, if I could do as you wish I would most willingly, but since I can't, I have to tell you so. Keep your money, and thanks all the same.'

The good man replied, 'Take the cheque and do with it as you think best. I will be equally happy. Just finish the church when you can.'

'You're too kind. The £10 will be used immediately to help reduce the huge debt. You can be assured of that.'

I thanked him for his offering and he remained a close friend.

6. Meanwhile, during August and September, I wrote asking the bishop, the vicar-general, Fr McDonald, the sisters at Ponsonby, and Flynn the bookseller to help us by sending articles for our gift auction, which we intended to hold immediately after Christmas. They all came to our aid, sending several articles. The committee undertook to ask Gisborne shopkeepers and merchants to contribute goods and they gave generously. Hardware items included ladles, tongs, bellows, grates, frying pans, pots, grills, etc. There were also sacks of potatoes, cabbages and other vegetables, vases, baskets, etc.

7. A large concert hall in Gisborne's main shopping area was hired for £2 a day. The goods were arranged neatly on trestle tables and benches in long rows. The ladies' committee, assisted by young women, was in charge of the stalls. On display were clothes, needlework, stationery, toiletries, baby-wear, toys, etc. Two men from the parish committee and a constable were assigned to keep peace and order, and another committee member was detailed to sell hardware, vegetables, etc. Two young ladies were in charge of a small bar on the stage which sold lemonade, soft drinks, mineral water, etc. The selling of intoxicating beverages was prohibited. The entrance fee was sixty centimes. Children under twelve were admitted free if accompanied by parents or a relative. Articles were sold at twice or three times their value. No one took exception to this, because it was for a worthy cause: to pay off the debt on the Catholic church. We thought two days would be sufficient to sell everything, but events proved otherwise.

The gift auction began at 10 a.m. on 26 December 1880. It closed at 12.30 and reopened at 3 p.m., continuing until 9 p.m. The same occurred the next day. Many people attended and were very pleased with the quantity of goods and their attractive display. There was no actual auction. A gift auction does not involve selling by auction, but displaying goods for sale. Articles are priced at at least double their value. The purchaser asks the price of an item. The lady in charge of the stall or her assistant tells him. He then takes it and pays. Only cabbages and potatoes were sold at normal retail price. The finest articles were sold in two days, but a third of the items remained unsold. It was decided to sell them on 31 December. On that day entrance was free. Selling by auction to the highest bidder began at 10 a.m. By 8 p.m. everything was sold. After paying sundry expenses, net takings were more than £200 (5000 francs). Parishioners never thought it would realise so much. The local Protestants showed considerable generosity and goodwill towards the Catholics, accounting for ninety per cent of the sales. I thanked the Lord for their kindness.

PART 6. HARD AT WORK

SUMMARY. – 1. Who will pay the interest? – 2. I suffer a bout of malaria. – 3. Preparations for the bazaar. – 4. Seeking a lottery permit. – 5. Mons. Steins's departure; his death; the Jesuit lay brother. – 6. The bazaar's outstanding success. – 7. Fr Chastagnon tries to palm his other debts onto me; I put him in his place.

1. On 2 January 1881, with the £200 from the auction, I went to the bank to lodge a payment on the debt. On 31 December, a six-monthly interest payment of about £19 was due. This was to be paid by the priests, as mentioned above. I had my share plus that of the other three priests to pay. Since I hadn't received notification from the vicar-general of the amount of interest due, I wrote asking him to let me know how much I owed altogether and I would send him the money immediately. Mons. Fynes replied in April 1881 that the proprietors of the *Freeman*, as represented by Fr O'Dwyer, had paid the interest instalment. There was nothing for me to pay. I later learnt from the vicar-general that Fr O'Dwyer, like the other priests, had been in favour of paying his share of the interest, but had refused under pressure from his two colleagues. Recognising, however, my courage, determination and willingness to shoulder the burden, he was seized with admiration for me. He felt so ashamed of his opposition that he informed the vicar-general that he would pay the interest for all three of them. I don't know who paid the other three instalments up until 30 June 1882 when the debt was finally repaid. I believe Fr O'Dwyer paid the lot. I was never asked to pay my share of the interest, even though I requested to do so. To Fr O'Dwyer's distress, however, the *Freeman* began to decline, even facing discontinuation. Towards the end of 1882, he asked the permission of the new bishop, Mons. Luck, to transfer to the Marist mission in Fiji. This was granted and Auckland suffered a serious loss by the departure of such a dedicated priest.

2. Gisborne, as mentioned previously, lies on a plain surrounded on three sides by two rivers, and its soil is composed of silt and loam. Being flat, it is frequently flooded, and water lies up to a metre deep. In summer, heat causes the stagnant water to evaporate, infecting the air. Consequently malaria was common, and many people caught it. Fortunately it produced only a mild fever. After a little rest and taking quinine, it usually lifted within a week. In January or February 1881, I got a mild dose, but it lasted only a few days. Although I got over it, I was still affected in an unusual way. It continued to affect my digestion. I couldn't eat Br Joseph's Italian cooking, and I didn't like English food. I had a huge amount of work to do. My inability to eat his excellent cooking caused me a serious inconvenience. I often had to take purges, which weakened me physically. I decided to seek the doctor's advice. He told me to eat English cooking because it was plainer than Italian food, and I would easily adapt. I

took his advice and my digestion returned to normal. From then on, I normally had English cooking, with Italian meals on days of abstinence,* this regime being foreign to the British.

3. The public auction, which concluded on 31 December 1880, had been a great success. As previously mentioned, the debt was reduced from £515 to just over £300. I then began to prepare for the bazaar, set for December 1881. Committee members began to collect items. I largely left them to it, concentrating on my missionary work in the district. I undertook, however, to seek the assistance of people outside the area, asking them to donate articles. First, I wrote to Rome, to our procurator-general, Most Rev. Dom Romarico Flugi, asking him to send a small item which would make an impression and could be auctioned at a high price. He replied that he would send me some trinkets. In fact, he sent me three pairs of gilt earrings, two of which were boxed and included brooches, as well as two or three separate brooches. They were very attractive mosaic pieces, costing him only sixteen francs. I also wrote to Fr Giustino Clerici at Dakar in India, asking him for a contribution, since I had given him a new chasuble and 300 francs for his trip to India. He replied that he would send some items in August. Nothing came. I then wrote to the manager of the P.&O. Line in Melbourne asking if a parcel had arrived for me. They wrote back that there was nothing with my name on it in their office. I again wrote to Fr Clerici asking when he had sent it so that I could track it down. He replied that he hadn't sent anything because the vicar apostolic did not want him to. I am convinced, however, that it was his decision, and the vicar apostolic had nothing to do with it. I then wrote to my superior, Fr Sullivan, the vicar-general and about ten Auckland families, enlisting their help. They all contributed items for the bazaar. I next wrote to the Sisters of the Mission in Napier for help. They sent several articles left over from their art union. I also decided to raffle the small harmonium in the presbytery. It had been used in the old church. Some of its keys didn't work and it couldn't be sold. I managed to get the keys to function, but it was still out of tune.

4. In New Zealand, as in England, raffles or lotteries were illegal. The government, however, allowed them for charitable purposes. I wrote to Hon. Mr Joseph Tole, a Catholic MHR, informing him of our decision to hold a bazaar in Gisborne on 26, 27 and 28 December that year, to reduce the debt on the church. I sought a permit to hold a raffle or lottery. I apologised for any inconvenience, not knowing whom to write to for the permit. He replied that I

---

* Such days, e.g. Fridays, would be meat-free. Other such days would include Ash Wednesday and Good Friday. This kind of regime is no longer obligatory in the Roman Catholic Church.

needed to write directly to the office of the Colonial Secretary. I hastened to do so, giving my reasons and the aim of the bazaar. I was duly granted a lottery permit for the three designated days.

5. Mons. Steins's health rapidly began to deteriorate because of a heart condition. After Easter 1881, he resigned from the Auckland diocese and left at the beginning of May for Sydney, accompanied by his Jesuit lay brother, who was suffering from tuberculosis he had contracted in Auckland due to overwork. Their intention was to return to Europe. When they reached Sydney, they stayed with the Jesuit fathers. The archbishop's health further deteriorated. He had to wait to see if it improved because he could not travel in that condition. The doctor said he would risk his life if he did. The lay brother took the next steamer and continued his journey to France, where he died about a month after his arrival. Mons. Steins hoped to recover sufficiently to be able to go to Rome and then on to France, but illness kept him with his confrères in Sydney, where he died on 7 September 1881. His treatment and funeral expenses of £800 were paid for by the Auckland diocese.

The diocese suffered a great loss through the resignation and death of Mons. Steins. He was a dedicated, magnanimous, extremely able and holy pastor, as well as an excellent administrator. The Jesuit lay brother was an exemplary religious, being charitable, good-natured and pious. I commissioned him to do a large painting for the Gisborne church. A star dominated the top part of the canvas. In the middle was Mary holding the baby Jesus. The lower section had a passenger ship battered and lashed by stormy seas. Passengers were depicted imploring the Star of the Sea to save them from peril. The good man brought me the painting in November or December 1880. I had it framed in Gisborne. I placed it over the Gothic window behind the main altar. That seemed the best place for it, since the church was dedicated to Our Lady, Star of the Sea. The painting had little artistic merit, but was a work of devotion and inspiration. The brother stayed a fortnight. He refused payment for the painting or his trip. He was happy just to have come to Gisborne. I was very sad to hear that he took ill and died eight months later. R.I.P. In 1889 Mons. Luck had the painting taken down, saying that it would be more attractive to expose the stained-glass Gothic window behind the main altar! I never knew what happened to the painting.

6. We decided to hold the bazaar in the hall where we had held the gift auction the previous year. We arranged the stalls similarly and included again a small bar to serve non-alcoholic beverages. Fr Sullivan and his relatives, Fr McDonald, the sisters and a dozen well-to-do families sent articles from Auckland. There were sofa covers, table cloths, tea cosies, embroidered aprons, baby bonnets and a large quantity of other baby-wear. The Gisborne ladies had also made

many articles during the year, and some items had been purchased. Ten days before Christmas, committee men approached Protestant shopkeepers for gifts for the bazaar. Most contributed articles. They were all beautifully laid out on the six stalls in the hall. The most beautiful, ornate, expensive items, like embroidered armchair and sofa covers, were put aside to be raffled.

The bazaar was open from 10 a.m. until 9 p.m. from 26 to 28 December. The entrance fee was one shilling for adults, and free for children accompanied by a relative. Ordinary items were not put up for auction or raffling, but were sold at the price on their ticket. Attendance was small during the day, but from 7 until 9 p.m. a crowd filled the large hall. There was considerable shouting, laughter and merriment from adults and children alike, and it really did seem like a Turkish bazaar. The small organ I had stored at home was valued at £10 (250 francs) and raffled. Two hundred tickets were sold at a shilling each. The raffle was drawn on the third day and won by a Protestant lady. The articles the abbot-procurator sent me were also raffled. The set of gilt mosaic earrings and brooch purchased in Rome for ten francs was raffled at a shilling a ticket. Two hundred tickets were sold, realising 250 francs. People said they had never seen anything more beautiful. Mosaic work was a novelty in Gisborne. The other earrings and gilt brooches, which cost five francs, fetched 125 francs. The remaining three brooches worth one franc each were sold at twenty-five francs each.

The finest articles were sold within three days. There still remained a third of the cheaper goods. These were auctioned off on 17 March 1882. Net takings from the bazaar were £240 or 6000 francs. The debt was thus reduced to £65, of which £25 was paid by the Presbyterian MHR for Gisborne, whom I will mention later. The remaining £40 was met by a special subscription of the parishioners, with myself heading the list and contributing £5. Thus by June 1882 the debt was completely repaid.

7. Fr Chastagnon learnt from a Gisborne friend that we had practically wiped out the debt he had incurred. He decided to palm off his other debts, both genuine and fictitious, God knows why. I have had the good fortune to find among my papers my reply to his strange request. On 27 March 1882, Fr Chastagnon wrote to me from Waitara in the Wellington diocese,* where he was a missionary. He mentioned that when he was parish priest in Gisborne he had borrowed £57 from the parishioners of Opotiki, issuing them with a promissory note from the Gisborne parish committee and his successor. He added that we were obligated to pay them since the money was raised for the

---

* Fr Stephen Chastagnon remained in the Pukekohe-Drury district until July 1880, when he suffered a serious fall from a horse. He went south to recuperate, ultimately transferring to the Wellington diocese. cf. E.R. Simmons, *In Cruce Salus: A History of the Diocese of Auckland 1848–1980,* Auckland 1982, p. 149.

debt and now the Opotiki parishioners had asked him for repayment. I was astounded and angry when I got his letter. He had never mentioned this loan before. I decided to investigate the matter. First, I spoke to Mr Jennings, a committee member in Fr Chastagnon's time. He said he had no knowledge of the loan. I asked him to question the other committee members and prominent parishioners, because I intended to raise the matter at the next meeting. He promised he would and to report back to the committee on 14 June. Fr Chastagnon's letter was in English and I replied in English:

Gisborne
19 June 1882

Dear Fr Chastagnon
I wish to acknowledge your letter of 27 May and am startled at its contents. You mention that you borrowed £57 for the Gisborne parish and that you issued a promissory note for that amount to the parishioners of Opotiki to be paid by our Committee and your successor. I, for my part, refuse to recognise this loan for the reasons outlined in the report of our committee, tabled 14 June 1882. The contents of the report are as follows:

Wednesday
14 June 1882

(1) Fr Vaggioli asked if any Committee members were aware of the existence of a debt the Gisborne parish owed to the parishioners of Opotiki, or whether Fr Chastagnon had been authorised to borrow money from Opotiki on behalf of the said Committee, for paying off debts on the church. None of those present had any knowledge of the loan or of having given any such authority to Fr Chastagnon. Messrs O'Ryan and Jennings, Committee members at the time, denied any such knowledge.
(2) You have never previously mentioned this loan. Only now, three years later, have you produced it, insisting I repay it. This is extraordinary!
(3) None of the Committee members or parishioners know anything about the matter. How can you then claim that they are responsible?
(4) None of the Opotiki parishioners have approached myself or the Committee for payment or even acknowledgement of the loan. If, as you say, they have written to you, then they hold you personally responsible, and certainly not our parish.
(5) There is no mention in the Bank's accounts of a promissory note for £57 owed to the parishioners of Opotiki.

For the above-mentioned reasons and several others which brevity prevents me from including, I need to say that I cannot in conscience recognise or pay this loan, because the debt was not incurred by the Gisborne parish. I trust that you will not bother writing to me again on this subject because I must tell you that any future reply will be the same.

All the debts incurred by you on the church were paid off by last May. I thank God that we are now absolutely free of debt.

With best wishes,
Yours faithfully,
Dom Felice Vaggioli OSB

Fr Chastagnon did not send a reply, because my letter did not leave room for one. However, since I wanted to be sure that he did not bother Opotiki Catholics for money, because I knew he had other debts, I wrote them the following letter, retaining a copy:

Gisborne
8 July 1882

To the Chairman of the Catholic Parish, Opotiki, Bay of Plenty

Dear Sir
I have recently received a letter from Fr Chastagnon in which he claims that the parishioners of Opotiki approached him for payment of a promissory note for £57, which he says he signed on behalf of the parishioners of Gisborne and his successor. I believe it is my duty to inform you and your parishioners that our committee never authorised Fr Chastagnon to borrow such a sum on his own behalf or that of the parishioners, who up till now knew nothing of the matter. Should this note exist, they refuse to acknowledge it.

Yours faithfully,
Dom Felice Vaggioli OSB

No complaint came from Opotiki about my letter. This confirmed my belief that perhaps Fr Chastagnon hoped that Gisborne would pay his private debts. Fortunately, he failed and nothing more was heard of the fictitious debt.

CHAPTER SIX

Final Activities in Gisborne
(EARLY 1881 TO EARLY 1883)

PART 1. MISSIONARY WORK

SUMMARY. – 1. Wairoa parishioners in the Marist Napier mission. – 2. I say the second Mass not in a state of fasting. – 3. Matters Maori. – 4. My fruitless attempt to buy land for a church in Ormond. – 5. Industrial schools in Nelson; issuing of a special indulgence. – 6. Need for a Catholic school in Gisborne.

1. The southern boundary of my mission was shared with the Wellington diocese. It contained the Wairoa district with European and Maori Catholics. Wairoa was closer to Napier, which was served by Marists of the Wellington diocese. It couldn't be reached by sea and communication by land was very difficult. There was only a rough bush track for an arduous seventy kilometres. Consequently visits were few and far between. It was easier to reach from Napier. A bullock track connected Napier and Wairoa. The Maori Catholics in the area were visited monthly by a Napier priest. An agreement was reached that he would tend to all the Wairoa Catholics within the Gisborne boundary. When Mons. Steins resigned from the diocese, the earlier agreement with Fr Reignier needed renewal. Accordingly, I wrote the following letter to the good priest:

Gisborne, 16 September 1881

Dear Fr Reignier,
During my stay in Auckland last month, I spoke to Mons. Fynes, Vicar-General and Administrator of the Diocese regarding renewal of our agreement. He agreed for me to negotiate this with you directly. He gave me permission to delegate my authority over parishioners residing in the Wairoa area. I hereby relinquish such authority regarding Maori and European parishioners living in the southern part of the Gisborne mission to yourself and Fr Soulas in all matters, e.g., preaching, baptisms, confessions, marriages, funerals, etc, until such time as a new bishop is appointed to this Diocese, when my power to delegate will cease.

Yours faithfully,
Dom Felice Vaggioli, OSB.

2. One Saturday in February 1881, I received a telegram from an Irish Marist father in Napier stating: 'Arrive Gisborne by steamer tomorrow morning.' I was delighted to receive the news. I went to the shipping company to ascertain

when the boat was due. I was told that the postal steamer would arrive in the harbour at 9 a.m. Since the priest had telegraphed that he was on his way, I assumed he would say the 11 a.m. Mass. So on Sunday I went and said Mass at Ormond. I then immediately returned to Gisborne to greet him. He reached the wharf at 9.45 to a warm welcome from myself and some parishioners. Back at the presbytery, I asked him to say the 11 a.m. Mass and address the congregation.

'I can't say Mass,' he replied. 'I felt sick last night on board and early this morning I had a cup of coffee.'

I was dumbfounded and exclaimed, 'What are we going to do now? After your telegram arrived, I said Mass fourteen miles away from here, thinking you would say the eleven o'clock Mass in Gisborne; and I had a cup of coffee too, after Mass.'

'But I didn't mention anything in my telegram about saying Mass.'

'But if you weren't going to say Mass, why would you have sent a telegram? There was no need to if you just wanted to visit here for a few hours.'

I thought it over, realising that the parishioners and many Protestants would be expecting Mass. Heaven knows what they would think if neither of us said it. So in this case I decided to ignore the Church's fasting law for the benefit of the people and to uphold our reputation as priests. In short, I decided that there would be the usual Sunday Mass. I asked the Marist father to say Mass, even though he had broken his fast, and to address the congregation, who would be delighted to hear from a compatriot of theirs, and a much abler preacher than me. But in spite of what I said, I could not persuade him to say Mass. I then agreed to say Mass, but I begged him to say at least a few words to the people. He tried to excuse himself on the pretext that he was not prepared. I insisted that he at least made this gesture, and he agreed. I began the second Mass at 11 a.m. After the Gospel, I sat down and he gave a brief sermon. It was obvious that he was no preacher. At 4 p.m. he re-embarked for Auckland.

3. There were very few Maori Catholics in the Gisborne district and they hardly ever attended church, except for an elderly couple who never missed. Unfortunately, I could not speak Maori, so I could not search them out. The Maori mission had only two priests altogether, and they couldn't attend to everything. During my sojourn in Gisborne neither of them visited the area. On 1 June 1881 a Maori girl visited me with a letter from the superior of the Sisters of the Mission in Napier, requesting me to make a good Catholic of her. I replied in French. The following is the translation of my letter:

Gisborne, 3 June 1881

Dear Rev. Mother,
Ruben Paora, a Maori girl, delivered me your kind letter of 29 May. I will do all I can to make a good Catholic of her, providing she attends church. Mr

Williamson has left the district and is now residing in Tauranga. He, however, would not be a suitable guardian for the girl because I have never seen him attend Mass or the sacraments.

I know nothing regarding Mrs Rice's daughter. I will try to get information and do what I can to prevent her being sent as a maid to that Protestant lady in Napier. I would be very pleased if she could be sent to your convent. Regarding Miss Smith, I can confirm that she attends Mass fortnightly and has once received the sacraments.

Regarding Catholic Maori and half-caste children of the district, none attend Mass or the sacraments. As long as they are at our schools they are fine, but once they leave, they nearly always revert to their old ways, or follow the religion of their parents or Sunday school teachers.

I will continue to urge those who can afford it to send their daughters to you. But the perennial excuse is that they can't afford it.

Please accept my sincerest regards,
Your faithful servant in Christ,
Dom Felice Vaggioli, OSB.

4. There were about fifty Catholics in Ormond and another thirty in the surrounding area. Since there was no church, I said Mass in the court-house. With the increase in the Catholic population, I decided to purchase half an acre of land in Ormond from the government and build a small church.

Several years previously, the colonial government had anticipated that a settlement would develop and set aside fifty hectares. A plan was drawn up with streets and lots. Half-acre sections were to be sold at a minimum price of £10 each. Prospective purchasers had to approach the government, which would auction the land to the highest bidders. The choicest central sections were sold off some years before to speculators. There were only about thirty sections left for sale, as I learnt from the Crown Land Office in Gisborne. I wrote the following letter, requesting a piece of land:

To Mr D.A. Tole
Commissioner of Crown Land, Auckland
Gisborne, 24 September 1881

Dear Sir,
Since the Catholics of Ormond wish to build a small church in the settlement, they have requested me to write to you on their behalf to obtain lot 64 or 60 at the reserve price of £10 or £12, as established at the last auction a few months ago.

Hoping to receive a favourable reply,
I remain, Yours faithfully,
D.F.V.

Mr Tole (a Catholic) replied in October that the two sections had already been sold.* I then wrote back:

Gisborne, 8 November 1881

Dear Sir,
I have consulted the Catholics of Ormond regarding the purchase of a piece of land in the settlement. We wish to purchase lots 57, 58 and 59 which are for auction. I have been informed by the Crown Land Office that the government intends holding a public sale of land, and that this will be the appropriate time to auction the above-mentioned sections.

I would like this matter to be treated with urgency since I cannot effectively carry out my missionary work until such land is purchased.

Yours, etc.

Tole did not reply to my letter, and in December the sections mentioned were not put up for auction. In January he replied that they would be auctioned at the end of January 1882. He did not keep his word and he was meant to be a Catholic!

5. The Bishop of Wellington agreed for the Marists to establish an industrial school at Nelson, in the South Island. The other two bishops were in agreement with Mons. Redwood. Needing funds for the large building project, he had notices printed asking the faithful to raise money. He sent copies to the hundred missionaries scattered throughout the colony. One arrived for me in Gisborne, sent by the Auckland vicar-general and administrator. I replied to the bishop in English:

Gisborne, 4 November 1881

Your Lordship,
One of your circulars was sent to me from Auckland regarding the Nelson Industrial School. On 30 of last month I read out your notice to my Gisborne parishioners and next Sunday I will inform the people in the country. A special collection will be taken up between 13 and 30 of this month.

Your Excellency cannot expect a great deal of us because the few parishioners here are extremely poor and saddled with a large debt on the church. Nevertheless we will do our best for this worthy charitable cause. When I have collected the money, I will send it to you.

Your most humble servant, etc.

* Daniel A. Tole, Commissioner of Crown Lands, was the brother of Joseph Augustus Tole (MHR for Eden 1876-87).

The good bishop sent me a very considerate reply. I wrote back:

Gisborne, 26 November 1881

Your Lordship,
I wish to acknowledge your kind letter of 8 of this month. I delayed replying until the collection was completed. I now have the pleasure, Your Excellency, of enclosing a postal order for £15 3s 6d (379.35 francs) together with a list of donors and the amounts they donated. (I was the first to subscribe, with £5). I would have hoped it could have been more, but this is as much as I could collect in Poverty Bay in three weeks.

Regarding the Land Company, I showed the proposal to those whom I hoped could contribute. Various people indicated a willingness to take shares, but given the present difficult economic situation, they said they would have to defer purchase until next January. About the middle of October, I wrote to Mons. Fynes, diocesan administrator, seeking permission to notify parishioners of the Jubilee Year and indulgences accorded to the faithful by His Holiness Pope Leo XIII.* He replied on 9 November stating 'having received no instruction' on the matter he had written to Your Excellency about it. Having heard nothing further from him, I am taking this opportunity to ask Your Excellency whether Mons. Fynes did actually write to you, and whether I can promulgate the Jubilee year in Gisborne without further delay.

From what parishioners have told me, no plenary indulgences have been announced here in eight years. I'm afraid to see another year pass in the same state of affairs. God have mercy on our diocese.

Your humble servant, etc.

Mons. Redwood replied that I could certainly announce a Jubilee in my mission. I mentioned it immediately and many people took advantage of its availability, especially on Christmas Day.

6. There were four government primary schools in Gisborne and the district, and a secondary school in the township to train prospective teachers. Religious education was excluded by law from the curriculum. Irreligious, Masonic teachers secretly encouraged agnosticism and hostility towards religion, especially Catholicism. Children received a completely secular, godless education and scarcely any moral instruction. Hence they grew up with little religion or morality. Protestants too complained about this type of education,

* For Catholics, a Holy Year or Jubilee Year recurs every 25 years, during which they can receive special indulgences on fulfilling certain conditions. In traditional Catholicism, the granting of indulgences ensures for the recipient the remission of part or all of the punishment that is due, especially in purgatory, for sin whose guilt has been pardoned.

especially for their daughters who, if attending a secondary school, became enamoured of liberalism, self-indulgence, hedonism and wilful independence.

Catholics did not have the means to establish and maintain Catholic schooling and were reluctantly forced to send their children to government schools, even though they were dissatisfied with this kind of education. I was even more distressed than them. I pondered this issue frequently and saw that the only solution would be to have at least four sisters as teachers. We would need to purchase a hectare of land in the township and build a convent and school at a total cost of more than 100,000 francs. Where could such a sum be obtained when more than £300 was then still owed to the bank? I decided for the moment not to do anything. But as soon as the debt on the church was repaid, I would set to work on the issue, seeking permission from the vicar-general or future bishop to raise a loan of 100,000 francs for the school. The banks would be very willing to lend to me, recognising my ability to pay off the present debt.

Part 2. Election of a Local Member of Parliament

Summary. – 1. General election. – 2. Local candidates. – 3. The three candidates approach me seeking my support for the Catholic vote. – 4. Allan McDonald, the outgoing MHR, visits me. – 5. I am also visited by Gannan, a nominal Catholic; I pull no punches. – 6. Open war. – 7. I attempt to dissuade Wairoa Catholics from voting for Gannan. – 8. I prevent his election to Ormond.

1. Parliament had completed a term. The colonial government declared a general election for October 1881. The huge Cook county extended from East Cape at 37.12 degrees latitude south to Napier at 39.3 degrees, including the southern area recognised as the Wairoa district. In the whole vast area there were only about 8000 Europeans eligible to elect a member to the colonial Parliament.

2. That year, there was a greater number of Gisborne candidates than ever before. The five candidates were unknown and lacklustre. The meritorious incumbent MHR, Allan McDonald, was completing his term. He was an honest Scots, nominally a Presbyterian, who also wanted justice for Catholics. Among the candidates was a baptised Catholic, whose parents were practising and lived in Auckland. I understand that he was non-practising. He had a wealthy land-owning Maori wife and several children. I believe he married her simply for her wealth and property. She was a Protestant.

3. A few days after their selection, the three nominees visited me separately, seeking my support for the Catholic vote. Each of them came with a Catholic supporter. They knew that I was well regarded by my parishioners and that

they took my advice. They were thus very hopeful of my support. I told each of them that as I was not a citizen and did not have the right to vote, I could not vote for them. As for my parishioners, this was a political, and not an ecclesiastical, matter. Missionaries were to keep out of it and leave Catholics to vote freely for whom they considered the most suitable. I had no idea of a candidate's suitability. I said this to all of them.

'That's true,' they would reply, 'but your advice would be enough to make them vote for the person you considered best.'

'Who knows? People like to be free to make their own decisions, and I don't intend interfering. But there are some issues for us Catholics which in conscience we cannot compromise.'

'Namely?'

'The government's injustice in not granting us subsidies for Catholic schooling. This forces us to provide it at our own expense, while the government finances godless, secular education with everyone's money, including Catholics'. This is a flagrant injustice.' I continued, 'In conscience, we Catholics cannot allow our children to attend government schools. We don't want them to grow up without religion, or lose their faith. We want the government to subsidise our schools, treating them the same as theirs.'

They replied that Catholics' demands were just, and they promised that if they were elected, they would uphold Catholics' rights.

I finished by saying to each of them: 'If I can put in a word on your behalf, I will.'

4. McDonald, the incumbent MHR, visited me and said, 'You know me and my intentions regarding Catholics' rights. I would really like to have your personal support and that of your parishioners, which I have always had in the past.'

'Rest assured,' I replied, 'you will have our full support. I will do all I can to see that they vote for you. Don't let the Protestants know. Their bigotry might make them turn against you.'

'You're right. But I'm not afraid of my Protestant friends. It's the Catholics I'm afraid of. This year, there's a Catholic candidate, Mr Gannan. It seems that his co-religionists will support him and he is assured of their votes.'

'You don't say. I don't recognise him as a Catholic. I've never see him in church. He may be nominally a Catholic, that's all. I wouldn't even recognise him if I saw him.'

'But he's telling everyone that you support him.'

'He can say what he likes, but it's not true. I am, and will continue to be, opposed to him, don't worry. Just keep me informed about what's happening. I'll see to everything else.'

He thanked me warmly for my promise of support and left.

At the next committee meeting the Parliamentary candidate issue was discussed at length. I asked them to tell me what parishioners thought and whom they supported. They replied that at least two-thirds of the faithful indicated support for Gannan, because he claimed to be Catholic. I told them that the parishioners should vote for McDonald, because in Parliament he had always voted for the Catholics regarding schooling, that he was more Catholic than Protestant, and that he helped us financially and would continue to do so.

'Gannan is only a nominal Catholic,' I said. 'I believe he's a liar. He's never come to church or the sacraments. Persuade them to reject Gannan. He brings dishonour to Catholicism. I can't openly intervene, but secretly I will do whatever I can to ensure he's not elected to Parliament.'

They promised to do what I suggested and said they would tell people confidentially to reject Gannan and continue their support for McDonald. They did just that and within a fortnight Gannan had less than a third of Gisborne Catholics supporting him.

5. On 15 September 1881, I received a telegram from the parish priest of Otahuhu, which read: 'Please support Gannan as candidate. Letter following.' I angrily threw it away. Then a long letter arrived and I tore it up. Shortly afterwards, a rather corpulent man, about forty years old, arrived in Gisborne. He came to Sunday Mass and attended Mass almost daily afterwards. I asked Jennings if he knew the identity of the gentleman. He told me that he was Gannan's brother from Auckland and that the previous Sunday he had put five shillings in the offertory plate. 'He may be able to fool dim-wits,' I said, 'but I won't be taken in!'

A fortnight later, the stranger came and visited me. I greeted him rather coolly. He told me who he was and that Gannan, his brother, had been too busy to visit me, but soon would.

'That's fine,' I replied. 'He can explain his plans when he comes.'

A few days later, the candidate and his brother turned up, the former displaying a certain patronising familiarity. I greeted Gannan frostily.

He then said, 'Don't you recognise me?'

'I can't recall meeting you.'

'You must have seen me around.'

'I meet many people on the street I don't recognise.'

He looked nonplussed, but then continued, 'As you would know, I'm a Catholic, and as such I hope to have your personal support and the Catholic vote.'

'I didn't know you were a Catholic. I'm pleased to hear it.'

'I assumed you'd have received information from the Otahuhu parish priest.'

'Indeed, I have, sir, but how can you say you're a Catholic when I've never seen you at Mass or the sacraments?'

'I would like to come but business prevents me.'

'You don't practise your religion, so you're not a true Catholic.'

'That's a fair assumption, but I often go to Wellington, and practise my religious duties there.'

Seeing he was trying to fool me, I spoke to him plainly. I exposed his lies, saying that if he didn't go to Mass in Gisborne, he wasn't likely to go in Wellington or anywhere else.

'What about Easter?'

'I went in Wellington.'

'Where was your marriage celebrated?'

'Wellington.'

'Where were your children baptised?'

'They haven't been yet, but they will be, after the elections.'

'You say you're a Catholic and you have children between five and fourteen years old still unbaptised! What am I to think of you?'

'I know it's not right, but I'll remedy the situation.'

'Bring them to be baptised straightaway. Heaven forbid they should die without being baptised!'

'It's not convenient right now. I'll see to it after the elections.'

'I personally believe that if you don't do it now, you never will!'

'No, I will, I assure you.'

I moved on to another subject, asking his views on children's education; whether he was in favour of the government's secular education policy. He said he was, but that Catholics should also get justice.

'But it's a contradiction,' I replied, 'to support the government's atheistic system and at the same time champion justice for Catholics.'

'If I'm elected, as a Catholic I will support justice for Catholics. That's why I want your support. As a Catholic, I should be backed by Catholics. I need their support.'

I replied to Gannan's peculiar demand: 'Listen, I'll tell you what I really think. I don't have a vote, so I can't give it to anyone. In spite of your claim, I don't recognise you as a Catholic. Nor do I believe in any of your promises. Therefore, I can't support your candidature to my parishioners. However, everyone is free to vote for the person they consider most suitable. Priests should not enter into politics.'

'I beg you,' he said finally, 'not to harm my chances in the election. I hope to be successful through my efforts and Catholic support.'

'Rest assured,' I replied, 'I have no intention of harming anyone. I would want to do my best by you as I would for anyone else.'

After our long discussion, he and his brother left. They didn't return and I never saw them in church again. Fine Catholics indeed! For my part, I promoted the wretch's true well-being by hindering his election to Parliament.

6. Gannan had totally lied to me. Realising that he could not deceive me, he showed his true colours: that he was a Catholic only by virtue of having been

baptised. Shortly afterwards, he made electoral speeches to the people of the Gisborne area. He stated that he was a Catholic, but that he was also for compulsory, secular, state education. He never mentioned Catholics' rights. At the same time, to win over Catholics, he had a letter published in the *Poverty Bay Herald*, urging Catholics to vote for him because he was a good Catholic and that in Parliament he would work for them. The letter was signed with the *nom-de-plume* 'A Roman Catholic'.

To ensure Catholics were not deceived, I immediately wrote a letter in English to the newspaper, stating that while Mr Gannan passed himself off as a Catholic, he was not. He never went to a Catholic church, and when he was asked by the local priest if his marriage had been celebrated in Gisborne, he acknowledged that it hadn't. When further asked if his children were baptised, he replied that their names were not in the baptismal register. Thus he was not really Catholic. I signed the letter anonymously as, 'A true Catholic'.

I gave the letter to a trustworthy parishioner who was a shoemaker. I asked him to make a copy, because my writing would be recognised by the newspaper's editor and staff. He did as I requested, and the letter was published. Gannan was furious at being exposed. He went to the editor, demanding to know who wrote the letter. The editor wouldn't tell him. Gannan took to him with a stick on the pavement, but passersby quickly intervened. The editor was not seriously injured, but nevertheless Gannan could have been charged. Friends stepped in, however, and smoothed things over. The editor eventually accepted an apology from the culprit.

7. Meanwhile, I was afraid that Gannan would try to get the Wairoa district's votes. On 16 September 1881 I wrote the following letter to Fr Reignier in Napier:

> You would be aware that Wairoa and Gisborne form a single electoral district. There are five candidates for the forthcoming election of an M.P. The best candidate is Mr A. McDonald who has done so much good for the district. The harbour works and East Coast District Land Bill are due to him. Even so, he has many enemies, namely, Masons, Orangemen and Protestant bigots, for the following reasons:
> (1) He is opposed to secular, state education.
> (2) He has always tried to get Government aid for Catholic schools.
> (3) He is opposed to large-scale land monopolies.
> (4) He is a member of the Land League.
> (5) He is a disenchanted Presbyterian who favours Roman Catholicism and attends the Catholic church.
> (6) He publicly contributed £4 in 1879 and a further £25 last February towards the debt on the Catholic church. Catholics should see the Masons' objections against him as a good reason for supporting him as much as they can in the forthcoming elections.

In the meantime, I would be grateful if you would speak privately to Wairoa parishioners and ask them to give Allan McDonald their vote in the next election. This is the way that Gisborne Catholics will be voting.

Thanking you in anticipation, etc.

8. Twelve or fifteen days before the election, a very worried McDonald visited me. He told me that he knew that most of Gisborne's Catholics were for him, but he had learnt that at Ormond they all supported Gannan, having been influenced by two or three local Catholics, especially the young Irishman, Gallagher. I replied that I knew that there were two or three Gannan supporters in Ormond, but I doubted there were more. He told me he had his information from a reliable source.

'Well, then,' I said, 'there's an 11 a.m. Mass at Ormond on Sunday. I will give some thought to how the parishioners can be brought to see their duty as voters.'

That Sunday, instead of preaching on the Gospel, I spoke about the forthcoming elections. I explained their duty as Catholics, that they were obliged to give their vote to the most suitable candidate, who in this case was McDonald. Though a Protestant, he had proven his loyalty. I mentioned that I had heard that many Ormond parishioners supported Gannan, because he was Catholic. I said that he was not a true Catholic, that he was openly opposed to Christian education, etc., and that if they voted for him, they would regret it. He should be the last person to get their vote. The congregation heard what I said. In the election, Gannan got only two Ormond votes and two or three from Gisborne parishioners. McDonald had a resounding victory over his rivals. He later came and thanked me for my support.

PART 3. BENEDICTINE AFFAIRS

SUMMARY. – 1. Fr Adalbert Sullivan in Gisborne. – 2. Local elections in Gisborne. I decide to vote, though not eligible; I justify my stand in fine style. – 3. Fr Sullivan's grandiose ideas. – 4. Laying the foundation of the new St Benedict's Church. – 5. Blessing of the church. – 6. Forced to preach a six-day retreat to the monks. – 7. Abbot Alcock's death.

1. Fr Adalbert Sullivan reached Auckland towards the end of 1880. I had written to him in Europe asking him to come via Gisborne, but he went, via Sydney, directly to Auckland. He did visit Gisborne in February 1881, arriving on a Friday morning. I hoped he would stay a few days, but he remained only about six hours, returning to the steamer and embarking for Wellington. I was happy to see him but sorry he could not stay longer. There were no fishermen in Gisborne, so there was no fresh fish. Since it was a fast day, I bought a dozen eggs for 9.5

francs. Fr Sullivan briefly inspected the church and had a short stroll through the township. He was not pleased that Mons. Steins had sent me to Gisborne. He met a few parishioners and then at 5 p.m. he returned to the steamer.

2. At the end of 1880 or possibly the beginning of 1881 local elections were held in Gisborne. As a foreigner I didn't have the right to vote, and I wasn't on the roll. Nevertheless I tried to vote. Accompanied by a parishioner I went to the polling booth in the town hall to cast my vote. I was asked for my first name and surname. They looked it up on the roll. It wasn't there. An official said to me,

'Reverend, your name's not on the roll.'

'Why not?'

'I don't know. Perhaps you're not a British subject.'

'No, I'm not.'

'That's why you're not on the roll, then.'

I was silent for a moment. Then I said, 'The council knows very well who I am and where I live because every year they come to the presbytery and collect £2 in rates for the property. But when it comes to voting, I'm not recognised. They recognise me when they want money, but not to vote. Well, from now on, don't come and ask me to pay rates, because I won't.'

People looked at each other in amazement as I walked out. I knew that church buildings were not taxed. I therefore considered that the presbytery should not be subject to tax. I researched the matter and discovered that presbyteries, etc., built on land given by the government to the Catholic Church were exempt from taxation. If the land was purchased, then the building was taxable. When the council next requested payment, I replied that I was not obliged to pay because the land had been granted by the government to the Catholic Church. The council didn't believe me. It made a formal inquiry and found I was right. I never paid rates again. Many other parish priests followed my example.

3. Fr Sullivan was almost certain he would succeed Mons. Steins as bishop. As soon as he was settled in Newton with the other priests, he decided that, since it was the most central part of town, a large church should be built there, which would eventually become the cathedral. Unfortunately, he was living with Frs Downey and O'Gara, who were his slavish followers. They would agree to anything he proposed. The disenchanted Abbot Wilfrid Alcock* had also come from Australia, and knew about Fr Adalbert's bizarre projects, having suffered their unhappy consequences. Having been burnt by them, he washed his hands of any of Sullivan's schemes, letting him to do as he wished. The other three

* Abbot Wilfrid Alcock had the distinction of being the first mitred abbot in England since the Reformation. He served in Adelaide for four years before coming to New Zealand in 1880. cf. E.R. Simmons, op. cit., p. 155 note.

missionaries – that is, Frs Luck, Fox and myself – were not consulted. We should have been but Fr Sullivan feared our opposition and so kept us in the dark. He began to look around for a suitably large building site. Instead of choosing the most sensible and attractive site, which was just under a hectare on a ridge 250 metres to the north and for sale at £800, he chose an approximately quarter-hectare plot on a hillock near the Catholic cemetery. Acting through Mons. Steins, he bought it, or rather put a deposit on it, for £1100 (27,500 francs), since he did not have enough money to pay the purchase price.

Meanwhile, he began seeking money for building the new church without bothering to pay for the land he had acquired to build it on. The church was to be wooden, but built on a lavish, grand scale. He had architectural plans prepared. It was to be a splendid English Gothic style church, with two impressive towers with side entrances flanking the façade. Fr Sullivan wanted construction to begin as soon as possible. He had already found people willing to lend the necessary money. But he needed Bishop Steins's consent. He asked the prelate's permission, while getting others to petition him also. He wanted to raise a loan of £5000 (125,000 francs). Mons. Steins was a very prudent man with considerable missionary experience. He refused permission, saying that first of all Fr Sullivan needed to pay the £1100 for the land he had bought. Then he would be allowed to incur a debt of £2000 (50,000 francs), and no more. This was confirmed in a letter Mons. Steins wrote to me on 31 March 1881. He concluded: 'I did only what my conscience would allow me. The Benedictines, I believe, don't think much of me *(je crois qu'ils m'en veulent un peu)* for not agreeing to their plan.'

In my opinion, the bishop was right but his reply did not suit Fr Sullivan or his two confrères. He hadn't paid off the land so the way was blocked to borrowing to build his church. It was just as well that the parish committee started collecting money through special subscriptions, concerts, public lectures and bazaars. Unfortunately, though, Fr Sullivan was president and treasurer of the committee. As president he made his own decisions and as treasurer he spent as he wished and paid out what he wanted because he alone kept accounts of income and expenditure, without reporting back to his committee. From what will later be revealed, I am of the opinion that he didn't in fact keep accounts. None were ever produced.

4. Fr Sullivan was very pleased when Bishop Steins resigned from the diocese and left for Australia, because he felt sure that he could then run things his way.* He immediately approached Mons. Fynes, a man of integrity but weak

* On the departure of Archbishop Steins, Mons. Fynes again took over the running of the diocese, first as administrator and then as vicar capitular after the archbishop's death. Dom Edmund Luck OSB took up his appointment as the next Bishop of Auckland in October 1882.

character. He led Fynes to believe that he (Sullivan) would be the next Bishop of Auckland. He requested his permission to take on a large debt to build the church, by borrowing £3000 from the Bank of New Zealand and £4000 from an insurance company. The pliable vicar-general was won over by Fr Sullivan's fine promise that the debt would be quickly repaid and the assurance that approximately £3000 had already been collected for this purpose. Even if this were true, that would not have affected the £7000 debt because the land still hadn't been paid for, and any other money he had collected had already been spent on the church project.

Having obtained permission to bury himself in debt, Fr Sullivan immediately set to. Excavations began for the new church. The site was levelled and volcanic rock from Mt Eden was used for the foundations. When preparations for laying the foundation stone were completed, it was decided to have the consecration of the building towards the end of summer. As I recall, Mons. Redwood, Bishop of Wellington, was invited to officiate. The priests of the diocese were also invited to attend. I tried to excuse myself but Fr Sullivan wanted me to come. The return trip cost me £10. When I arrived in Auckland, I asked to see the architect's plan. The church was to be wooden, built in the Gothic style, with three naves and able to accommodate 2000 worshippers. It was to have two wooden towers, each costing £800 (20,000 francs). I asked senior priests if they had been consulted about the church. They said they had been in a vague kind of way, but actually they were not at all in favour of building a wooden church of this nature. I plucked up courage and said to Fr Sullivan that in my and others' opinion, it would be a mistake to build such a large ornate wooden Gothic church in the middle of so many other wooden buildings and houses. He could have a brick church at only twenty per cent more cost. He agreed, but said he didn't have the money.

'A large debt's already been incurred,' I said. 'A thousand pounds more or less won't make much difference.'

'True,' he replied, 'but the contracts have already been signed.'

'Well,' I added, 'you're going to have to paint the exterior every four years. That will cost another £500 a time.'

'Well, what's done is done.'

I would have been happy with a simple, large brick church with a classical façade and a tiled roof, at a third less the price. In my humble opinion, the issue of building a new church had not been considered thoroughly enough and had been embarked on without good reason. But Fr Sullivan knew what he wanted. Many people attended the laying of the foundation stone. There were several speeches and a public subscription was called for. Fr Sullivan said building costs were already £1300.

Opposite: The first St Benedict's church, Newton, 1881–86.

5. Around February 1882, the consecration of the church took place. It was dedicated to St Benedict, our founder. The sanctuary and two side chapels were completed but the interior of the main body of the church was unfinished. The Bishop of Wellington performed the blessing before a large crowd. The same guests who had attended the foundation ceremony were invited. Another subscription was also arranged. Again, at Fr Sullivan's request, I attended the event. I incurred a similar expense of 250 francs, money I would rather have saved. I tried to ascertain from Fr Sullivan, and from priests who had his confidence, how much the church would cost, how much had been collected and the actual size of the debt, but I could get no precise information. Meanwhile I learnt that Fr Sullivan had acquired nearly a dozen houses near the church. They weren't paid for, but were all heavily mortgaged. I discovered this from Mr Brophy, a committee member, who told me that people were saying that the Benedictines were wealthy because they had bought these houses. I was surprised at the news, and said I knew nothing about it.

'I know it's true Fr Sullivan bought them,' he replied, 'but that's all I know.'

Since I knew nothing about it, he asked me to say nothing.

6. After the blessing ceremony, since all the monks were in Auckland, Fr Sullivan asked me to conduct a retreat for them from Monday to Friday evening. I gave every reason for declining, but he was insistent saying there was no one else who could. I had to obey against my will, realising that my entreaties would fall on deaf ears, because he was prejudiced against me as an Italian. I decided to do my duty, notwithstanding his attitude. I wanted to treat my confrères as I would myself. Anything I would say to them I would first make sure I applied it to myself. One day I was speaking about the virtue of humility for monks, as prescribed in St Benedict's Rule. I said that instead of living in a simple state of humility, a spirit of pride and ambition, unworthy of monks, polluted many of them.

'How many religious,' I said, 'aspire to ecclesiastical offices and bishoprics! But the Holy Spirit is discerning with His gifts. If such offices are seized upon, the recipient is bound to be harmed! Therefore, let us always humble ourselves if we wish to receive divine favours. Perhaps one of us aspires to the bishopric of Auckland? God will not serve such ambition,' etc.

My frank comments did not please everyone. Some were astounded at my audacity, others said I was right to speak plainly. After the retreat, three or four priests left on Saturday morning for their missions. I had to wait until the following Thursday to return to Gisborne. The Monday morning paper had the following telegram notice: 'Rome. The Pope has appointed as Bishop of Auckland Rev. Fr Edmund Luck, an English Benedictine, who is presently in Malta.' The news came like a bolt of lightning!

7. Abbot Wilfrid Alcock's family lived in Auckland. He and Fr Anselm Fox had

come from the Adelaide diocese in Australia the previous year. The abbot suffered from heart disease and a stomach ulcer. He was very ill and had to remain in bed when the church was blessed. He was a fine, eloquent preacher, and also gave public lectures. On feast days, he was asked to preach in the cathedral. If he hadn't been ill, I'm sure that Fr Sullivan would have asked him to take the monks' retreat. But because of his illness he couldn't even attend. Dr Lee, a Catholic, was his physician and took good care of him. When he began to deteriorate, Fr Sullivan wanted to bring in a consultant, to which Dr Lee agreed. The town's most eminent physician was engaged. I can't recall his name. He was a prominent Mason and his reputation was garnered from this rather than from his medical knowledge. When he visited his patient, he said, 'There's nothing to worry about. He just needs fresh air.' He ordered the windows and door to be flung open.

'He'll be completely cured in a few days,' were his parting words. Dr Lee, who didn't enjoy the same standing but had intelligence, was startled by his casual pronouncement. But he followed instructions and left the doors and windows open. Less than an hour later, however, the sick man became weaker and started to gasp. He begged the doctor to close things up so that he could manage to breathe. He did so and soon his patient felt more comfortable. On Thursday I left for Gisborne. His condition then was serious but not hopeless. Dr Lee continued caring for him, but about a week later he passed away. R.I.P.

PART 4. BENEDICTINE AFFAIRS (CONTINUED)
1882

SUMMARY. – 1. The abbot-general asks my financial assistance for the Italian province's novitiate. – 2. The procurator-general asks me for information regarding native Maori customs. – 3. The Bishop of Auckland elect. – 4. Claimants' consternation. – 5. Attempts to block the appointment; fruitless in effect! – 6. My opinion. – 7. Fr Sullivan leaves for Sydney. – 8. He suffers a fall in Sydney, breaking his hip.

1. Our abbot-general had learnt in 1881 that I still had 1860 francs in gold napoleons, which was the money I had left from my sojourn in Africa. It was money I did not personally need. He wrote to me mentioning that I would do our Italian province a great kindness if I could send him the money for the struggling new novitiate in Malta. I wanted to support this worthy cause. I tried to change the coins but there was no currency exchange facility in Gisborne. To send them by registered mail to Italy would be expensive and difficult because there was no international postal convention with New Zealand. I was told at the bank that the coins could be accepted and melted down. If the silver content in the alloy was the same as for the sovereign, I would be paid 16

shillings or 20 francs a napoleon. If it was higher, I would be paid less. But the manager said the operation would have to be done in Auckland. Knowing I was to go to Auckland for the consecration of St Benedict's, I decided to take the money there myself. The coins were found to be worth 20 francs each when melted down. Altogether they fetched £74 10s or 1862.5 francs. I sent this sum by registered mail to Dom Nicola Canevello and he duly thanked me for my kindness.

2. The procurator-general had also written to me from Rome at the beginning of 1881. He commented that Italians knew nothing about the life and customs of the natives of New Zealand, and he asked me for a brief description. He also promised me, as mentioned earlier, to send me gifts for the bazaar held after Christmas 1881. I was keen to oblige and collected and studied accounts of New Zealand history. I then wrote my own brief history of New Zealand describing Maori customs and warfare and European involvement. In all, I wrote more than two hundred pages. I sent the bound manuscript to the procurator in April 1882, not being able to complete it earlier. This brief history was the embryo, so to speak, of the history* I wrote and later published from notes taken in Auckland and Coromandel between 1883 and 1887. He thanked me for my humble work, saying that I had far exceeded his expectation, and that it was no small achievement. I later regained possession of the manuscript, which I destroyed when the *Storia della Nuova Zelanda* was published.

3. I did not personally know Mons. John Edmund Luck, the newly appointed Bishop of Auckland, but I had often heard him spoken of as a good, holy, zealous monk who strictly observed the Rule. He was a member of the Ramsgate community and came from an affluent family. He had two brothers, one of whom was a secular priest and the other a Benedictine friar and missionary at Kihikihi in the Waikato, in New Zealand.† Their exemplary, devout father, after his wife's death, studied theology and was ordained a priest. He became a Benedictine oblate of Ramsgate and bequeathed his mansion to the order. After his death they converted it to a secondary boarding school for one hundred students, which it still is today. His cash assets were divided among his children, each receiving £5000 or 25,000 francs. When the Malta novitiate was established in 1881, I understand that Fr Edmund Luck was sent there as bursar. While waiting for a transfer, he was summoned to Rome and told that he was to become Bishop of Auckland. He tried to refuse the office, but obedience compelled him to accept.

---

* *Storia della Nuova Zelanda e dei Suoi Abitatori*, Parma, 2 vols, 1891 and 1896. The second volume was translated into English and published by University of Otago Press, 2000.
† The second reference is to Fr Augustine Luck OSB.

4. News of his appointment threw the two or three aspirants to the bishopric into consternation and confusion. They were acquainted with Fr Edmund and knew that he was a very devout monk. They were dismayed at his appointment, however, realising he would be opposed to Fr Sullivan's reckless schemes. They also regarded his appointment as a deliberate affront to them, especially to Fr Sullivan. They immediately set about plotting and scheming. In the presbytery they were openly hostile, but were careful to mask their feelings in public, except to insinuate that he was unsuitable and would not succeed, etc. I said to them, 'I wouldn't claim to be a prophet or the son of one, but I did get it right this time. Remember when I said that it is the Holy Spirit who chooses bishops?'

'Yes, indeed, we do. He has selected someone no one would have dreamt of.'

5. News of the appointment appeared in the papers, catching local Catholics by surprise. They were delighted to have a new pastor. Many visited St Benedict's, hoping for more information. The losers were disconcerted and embarrassed. They gathered their wits, however, and said the appointment hadn't been confirmed, they didn't believe it was true and that there was no definite news. 'One shouldn't take too much notice of newspaper reports', etc.

The same day the news came out, Fr Sullivan consulted his two Benedictine cronies and then rushed over to Parnell to see the vicar-general with whom he had a long discussion. On his return, he called Frs Downey and O'Gara into his room. They talked confidentially for some time and had further meetings in the afternoon, the evening and the following morning. Fr Sullivan then went to the vicar-general's. On his return, he looked much brighter. He said that the vicar-general had sent a telegram to Propaganda asking them to suspend the appointment, pending the arrival of a vital letter. I never learnt the contents, but I considered any opposition pointless, believing that Rome would not back down.

6. With all the futile machinations going on, I was desperately keen to be on the steamer, on my way back to Gisborne. I thanked God that Fr Sullivan was not appointed, believing him to be unsuitable. He would only accumulate debts and reduce the diocese to ruin. His deeds, so far, were a portent of financial disaster. He was an autocrat, who did exactly what he wanted, listening to no one. I was pleased indeed to return to Gisborne, resolving to distance myself from the goings-on at St Benedict's. I wasn't happy with the way they were ignoring our Rule. But this was wishful thinking. As it transpired, I had to get involved in their intrigues. It was just a miracle that I didn't go under.

7. Fr Sullivan may have been waiting in Auckland for letters from Rome or the general of our order regarding the new appointment. I think, though, that he received confirmation that the new bishop was Fr Edmund Luck. About a month

after the announcement of the appointment, Fr Sullivan took a steamer for Sydney. I'm not sure of the purpose of the trip. From what I later learnt from our Auckland priests, it seems that he went to meet with the Benedictine archbishop and his fellow monks, to see if it would be possible to join their community or have his own mission, and quit Auckland. The archbishop was a much revered, scholarly and distinguished preacher. Fr Sullivan stayed at his residence while also visiting the Benedictines' boarding school and other religious houses to meet the members.

8. Back in Gisborne, towards the end of May or beginning of June, I received a letter for Fr Downey mentioning the sad news that while Fr Sullivan was at the Benedictines' boarding school in Sydney, he had tripped down the stairs, falling four or five metres. His hip was broken and he was laid up in the hospital. The doctors hoped not only to save his life, but to ensure that the accident didn't leave him with a withered leg. They said treatment would take at least two years. I was upset at the news, because things in the mission were not going well. In fact, the situation was steadily deteriorating. Fr Downey, the senior priest, would have to manage Benedictine affairs, but he was incompetent. Fr Sullivan was still in charge, but managing from such a distance would try even the most capable person. Things just couldn't work out. We had fallen from the frying pan into the fire! Who would take charge of the enormous debt the Newton parish was saddled with?

I wrote to the abbot-general requesting that the new bishop come as soon as possible, and that he be made the monks' superior. He replied that the bishop would be sent at the earliest convenience but it was not considered appropriate for him to assume the role of superior. Fr Sullivan was to retain this role.

PART 5. PRESSING ON
1881–1882

SUMMARY. – 1. A Catholic couple's strange betrothal. – 2. They apply for marriage; the young woman's vacillation; her partner's sangfroid. – 3. A happy outcome for them. – 4. I write to the procurator-general about the situation in the Newton parish. – 5. The Gisborne parish is freed of its debt. – 6. Summary of parish finances from February 1880 to July 1882.

1. About October 1881, an Irish labourer by the name of Sullivan, from a big holding at Warenga-ikaika, between Ormond and Gisborne, visited me. He was a fine, reserved, upright Catholic, about thirty-five years old. He was accompanied by a young Irish Catholic woman, who was also a good type, employed as a maid. They told me they were wished to be married, and that

they were betrothed. I enquired if they had parents or relatives in Gisborne. Sullivan told me that he was on his own, producing documents confirming that his relations were in Ireland. The young woman said she had parents and relations in Ireland, and a sister who was a maid to a lawyer. He was the man I had cause to write to regarding his wife, as already mentioned. She too produced her papers. I questioned them each separately to be sure of their intentions. I found that they both wanted to be married. I told Sullivan to go to the registrar of marriages, to tell him that they wanted to get married in the Catholic church and to get the certificate authorising me to celebrate the marriage and bring it to me. We would then arrange the wedding date. I gave them some further advice before they departed. Two days later the young woman returned on her own. She was about thirty and I knew her to be a very good Catholic. She told me she was very hesitant to marry Sullivan, fearing the marriage would not work out.

'What reasons do you have for your fears?' I asked her.

'None,' she replied.

'Is he a drinker?'

'No, no,' she said, 'he's a fine man, but I'm still afraid.'

'I certainly have always known him to be a fine, upstanding Catholic. Does he have any other vices?'

'No, none at all.'

'Well, I can't see any basis for your fears. Maybe he doesn't love you?'

'No, he loves me and tells me he loves me.'

'Are you in love with him?'

'Yes, I think so, but I'm not too sure.'

'Perhaps you love another?'

'Oh, no, Father!'

'Maybe he's betrayed you and broken his promise of betrothal?'

'No, he's always treated me with the utmost respect.'

'Have you been courting long?'

'Only a couple of months.'

'Well, my child,' I concluded, 'if you've told me the truth, don't be afraid to marry him. The marriage will work out well.'

'If you say everything will be fine, I will marry him.'

After our long discussion, she departed.

2. When the wedding day arrived, at eight-fifteen the betrothed came for confession. Nuptial Mass was to begin at 9 a.m. I went to the side door of the church, but I was stopped by the young woman in an agitated state. She whispered, 'Father, I can't go through with this. I'm afraid for the future.' Then she blurted out, 'I'm afraid to get married!'

Her unperturbed partner turned to her and said, 'Don't you want to get married now? Please yourself.'

'I do and I don't,' she replied. 'I can't make up my mind.'

I was startled by her ambivalence and said to her, 'Don't be ridiculous! You must decide now, before going in. If you don't want to marry him, go home, and let that be the end of it.'

'What's your advice, Father?'

'I'm not giving you any advice,' I replied. 'Do what you want, but I do think your fears are unfounded.'

But the young woman was still confused. Sullivan stood silent, waiting for her to make up her mind. Frustrated by her indecision, I sternly said, 'The witnesses and your sister have arrived. Make up your mind. Don't make a fool of yourself. If you can't decide, I'll lock up the church and go home.'

When I said this, the young woman replied, 'Very well, I will marry him.'

'Watch out,' I said, 'I don't want any nonsense in church.'

'No, Father, I've made up my mind.'

We entered the church and I heard their confessions. They were indeed good Catholics. Before the celebration of the Mass, I united them in matrimony. Mass then proceeded and they received Communion.

This story may seem like a fabrication, but I assure the reader that it is absolutely true in every detail.

3. After Mass, I entered their names in the marriage register. They and their witnesses then signed it. The couple were pleased and satisfied. While the witnesses were signing, I asked the bride in her husband's presence, 'Are you happy now? Do you have any doubts?'

'No, none, Father. I'm quite certain my fears are over. I'm very happy.'

'Rest assured,' I told them, 'your marriage has been blessed by God. You will be very happy together.'

Their marriage was one of the happiest I have ever known. They loved each other with a deep, holy love and they enjoyed complete harmony. I visited them several times at Warenga-ikaika and always found them happy and content. Ten months after their marriage, the wife produced a beautiful baby. This fruit of their love served to unite them even more with mutual affection. During my sojourn in Gisborne I never found them other than content with each other.

4. When I returned from Auckland towards the end of October 1881, after the laying of the foundation stone at St Benedict's, I wrote to the abbot-general that Fr Sullivan had bought several houses around the church, with what money I had no idea. I asked him if he had authorised the purchases. I also wrote to Abbot Flugi, the procurator, about the matter. The general replied that he had no knowledge, and he would write to Fr Sullivan for an explanation. Four months later, he wrote to me that Fr Sullivan had received the money from friends for

investment in New Zealand. He used it for those purchases. He had thus used capital which was neither his, nor the Church's, but that of Irish friends. When I returned to Auckland in the spring of 1882, I went to the mortgage office for information regarding the eight houses and sections bought by Fr Sullivan. I discovered that he had purchased them in his own name, but paid only a ten per cent deposit. They were heavily mortgaged. Thus it was not true that he had money to invest, because the properties hadn't been paid for. I couldn't understand why he bought them. It was a silly speculation which would result in loss. I wrote in the same vein to our general when I returned to Gisborne. He replied that he had written to Fr Sullivan requesting him not to get involved in purchases and business transactions which had nothing to do with the mission. Fr Sullivan immediately transferred the titles to Dignan, the lawyer, but he still maintained his financial involvement in the properties.

5. By March 1882 the debt on the Gisborne church was no more than £40. I had in hand £25, and thus needed only £15 to clear the debt. I hoped that the manager of the Bank of New Zealand would donate the money in recognition of my speed in repaying the debt. I wrote to him on 28 March 1882 and delivered the letter to him personally. He told me he did not have the authority and would have to refer the matter to his head office in Auckland.

'Well,' I replied, 'you may as well not bother. The gentlemen there are either Jews or Masons and scorn religion.'

'There are some fine men among them. They would certainly recognise your sterling efforts.'

'If you lend your strong support, perhaps they might make some contribution, but I'm rather sceptical.'

'I will support you. Let's hope for the best.' He sent off my petition with his endorsement. A fortnight later a negative reply came back from the Mason grandees, saying they couldn't donate any money to the church.

In June I paid off the last farthing owed to the bank. I was enormously relieved to have freed the church from debt. The Catholic Church never defaults! When I made this final payment, the manager said, 'Father, you have performed a miracle! With a tiny, impoverished Catholic congregation, you have succeeded in two years in paying off a debt of more than £600.'

'Why are you so amazed?'

The manager, ignoring my interruption, continued, 'Not only I but our general managers considered the money lost. We could not take possession and auction your church because it was built on land given by the government to the Catholic Church. You have done what no Protestant minister with a much larger and wealthier congregation could have done. In fact, they've increased their debts rather than paid them off!'

'But, my dear sir, I replied, 'don't you realise that the Catholic Church always honours its commitments and will never default on them?'

'Well, it's an absolute mystery to me! I don't know how you can live without a fixed income and still pay the debt! Our ministers are well paid and even so can't manage, let alone pay off the debts on their churches. How can you explain it?'

'Easily,' I replied. 'We receive special help from God and He never fails us. We have neither wife nor family to maintain and provide for. We live simply without luxuries or making demands, and we adapt to circumstances.'

The Anglican was silent for a moment, and then said, 'Your Church demands sacrifices, but it's well run.'

'Now that the debt is cleared,' I said, 'it's very likely that I'll need to raise another loan of £4000 (100,000 francs). I want nuns to come here and provide a good Christian education for the children.'

'That's a good idea. Many non-Catholic parents would want this for their children too. If you need money, come and see me. Just ask, and I will lend you up to £5000 (125,000 francs).'

'No, my dear sir. I'll never approach your bank again. In 1880 when I came here, you wouldn't even give me £50 credit.'

'True, but I didn't know you then. Now that I do, I'll lend you as much as you want.'

'Another reason why I won't return is because last April your bank's Jewish managers in Auckland refused me a miserable donation of £10 or £15. That was an utter insult to my Church. That's why I won't come back. There are other banks willing to lend me as much as I need.'

The poor man didn't know what to say and I left.

6. Gisborne had four churches: one Catholic and three Protestant. As I mentioned previously, in March 1880 they were all in debt. The Catholic church, being the most recently built, was the most indebted, to the tune of £750. Next was the Anglican church, owing £650. The Presbyterian church owed £400 and the Wesley an £390. By July 1882, or two years three months later, their financial state was as follows: the Catholic church was debt free, the Anglican church owed £1300 or £1400, the Presbyterian £615 and the Wesleyan had reduced its debt to about £190. Being free of debt was a special favour from God and Mary. I cannot express in words my delight, which the reader can well imagine. I conveyed the good news to the vicar-general, Fr Sullivan in Sydney, the abbot-general and the procurator-general. I also mentioned my proposal to provide schooling by bringing nuns to Gisborne.

Part 6. The Anglican Minister's Downfall

Summary. − 1. The Anglican minister's wife's drunkenness. − 2. She elopes with her lover. − 3. The poor man visits me for advice; I try to dissuade him from divorce. − 4. He is adamant, but lacks the means. − 5. I speak to the Catholic maid. − 6. I advise the minister against divorce, but to go to Australia. − 7. He can't afford the trip. I speak to the chairman of the Anglican vestry and achieve my purpose. − 8. The minister and his family leave. − 9. Disgusting condition of his home!

1. The Anglican minister was a tall, thin, bearded man with greying hair, about fifty-five years old. His wife was a small, stout woman, about forty-five or fifty, and given to drinking. They had five sons, the eldest being about fifteen years old. Often the woman was found sprawling on the roadside dead drunk, incapable of getting up, let alone finding her way home, and someone would take her back. Her disreputable behaviour gave frequent cause for people to criticise the minister for not dealing with the situation. Many Anglicans, because of this, no longer went to church. The poor minister begged his wife not to disgrace him publicly. She promised to behave, but didn't keep her word. The minister would not have alcohol in the home, but she visited grog shops and drank as much as she wanted. She charged the bill to her husband and he had to pay up. The minister was provided a rent-free house by his Church and a salary of £400 plus more than £200 from the Church Missionary Society. Even so, his wife's thirst left the unfortunate man penniless.

2. As well as drinking, his wife sinned against the sixth commandment. But she covered her tracks so well that the public was unaware of her illicit relationship with the editor of a weekly paper, who was a married man. Their trysts occurred when the minister was away. The man went to the woman's home, taking alcohol for her. He would stay several hours and sometimes overnight. The minister believed his wife was faithful and was unaware of anything untoward. Sometimes the man visited when the minister was at home, but the visits were brief and he showed no sign of affection towards the woman.

One day, at the beginning of January 1882, as I recall, while the minister was on a long trip away, the wife left her home and children and departed with her lover by steamer for the South Island. They went to Invercargill, a small town, to quietly continue their affair. The news got out in Gisborne the same day. Tongues began to wag about their affair, their flight and the simpleton of a minister. It caused a major scandal. That evening the minister returned, to find that his wife had abandoned the marital home and her family to elope with her lover. Words could not describe the wretched man's reaction. The Anglicans were outraged. The majority vowed they would never again set foot inside the church of a minister who had such a wife, and they wanted him, too, to leave as soon as possible. Up to three months previously, the minister had employed an

Irish Catholic maid. He asked her if she had witnessed any goings-on between his wife and her lover. She confirmed that she had seen the man visit the house on several occasions when he was absent, remaining in the mistress's room for quite a while, but she had never seen anything untoward.

3. One morning the minister came to my presbytery, approaching me hesitantly. We sat at a table and I asked him, 'How can I help you? I would like to do anything I can. Please talk freely. Anything you say will be treated confidentially.'

'Thank you, Father,' he replied, 'I have come for your support and advice.' Tears came to his eyes. Then he continued, 'You will be aware of what my wife has done!'

'Yes, I know all about it, and I'm very upset about the scandal and shame it has brought on you and your position.'

'Thank you for your sympathy. I want to divorce her.'

'Why would you want to spend your money on that wicked woman?'

'Because she has disgraced me. I want to disown her and never let her set foot again in my house.'

'Good for you. If she ever comes back, which I very much doubt, shut the door in her face. That's what you should do.'

'Yes, but if I don't get a legal divorce, she has the right to return home!'

'What a strange law!'

'But it's true!'

I was silent for a moment and then said, 'Do you have clear proof that your wife was with the man, or committed adultery?'

'Not personally, but the Catholic maid would have found them in bed in my home. I did question her, but she gave me only vague answers. Would you please see her and get the truth out of her? She would be a key witness in divorce proceedings.'

'I wouldn't mind doing that.'

'I'm sure she would tell you everything.'

'It would have been difficult for the maid to have seen them openly committing adultery.'

'But I believe she would have, because the affair had been going on for some time, and it always happened when I was away.'

4. I listened in silence, frowning, then said, 'Are you sure you want a divorce?'

'I certainly do, to free me forever from the woman.'

'Are you aware of the considerable legal fees involved?'

'Yes. I've been told it would cost at least £1000 (25,000 francs).'

'Do you have that kind of money?'

'No. I have nothing. My salary is hardly enough to support my family. My wife has also left me with a number of debts for the alcohol she bought secretly.

I have to pay them, but I don't have the means.'

'And you're considering divorce!'

'Yes, I am.'

'Are you thinking of remarrying?'

'Not for the present, but I do have a young family and I need a woman to look after them. I can't.'

'I believe divorce to be against God's law. You can separate from your wife for adultery, but you can't remarry. This is the Catholic Church's teaching and the Word of God.'

'But British law permits divorce as does the Anglican Church.'

I still wanted to do all I could for the poor man. I replied, 'Let's leave aside the divorce issue for the moment. Wait until you have the thousand pounds. The most important thing now is to consider your family and how you are going to provide for them. I've heard that your parishioners don't want you as their minister any more, that they intend giving you three months' pay and sending you packing!'

'Yes, you're right. Here I am, penniless and debt-ridden, and they want to get rid of me immediately.'

'I believe you have the right to six months' pay, because you're not the one to blame.'

'But vestry wants to give me only three months' pay. What can I do with £100? It wouldn't even pay my trip.'

'True. Why don't you stand your ground and request a year's pay and say otherwise you won't leave.'

'They wouldn't agree to that.'

'Listen here. Don't back down. I'll tell your vestry chairman to give you a year's salary. I hope I can persuade him. Don't you give in.'

'Thank you for your kindness. Don't worry, I won't budge, but I don't think you'll win.'

'I'll do better than you and plead your case very well, you'll see.'

The poor minister thanked me for my assistance. He then asked me to interview the Catholic maid and get the truth out of her. I told him I would happily oblige. He was to get her to come over the following day when she was free. I would let him know the result of my interview. He agreed and, somewhat reassured, he departed.

5. The next day, the maid arrived and the following conversation took place:

'I've come, Father, at your summons. What do you want?'

'I called you,' I replied, 'to get information from you about the Anglican minister's wife.'

'He's already questioned me closely because he wants a divorce.'

'Tell me now, when did you leave his service?'

'Only just over six weeks ago.* I left him because I had to work too hard and was paid only twelve shillings a week.'

'How long were you employed by him?'

'About a year.'

'Did Mr — often visit the house to see your mistress?'

'Yes, he came when the minister was away from Gisborne.'

'Did you open the door to him?'

'Sometimes. I ushered him into the drawing room and would advise my mistress, who then took him to her room. But usually she let him in.'

'Tell me, did he stay long with her?'

'Yes, several hours. Often he had alcohol with him.'

'She drank?'

'Did she ever! She was often drunk.'

'Did you ever suspect they were up to something together?'

'Yes, sometimes. But since they were both old and married, I assumed they were just chatting.'

'Did you know that Mr — stayed overnight with your mistress?'

'I believe I did, because I twice noticed him leaving the house early in the morning, on occasions when the master was away.'

I exhorted her to tell me the whole truth because she would be compelled to do so in court. I went on, 'Did you ever catch them in bed together, or compromised in any other way?'

'No, Father. She kept the door locked. She wouldn't even open it to her children when Mr — was there. If anyone came wanting to speak to her, she would ask me what was the matter. I would say that so and so wanted to talk to her. From inside her room she would reply, 'Tell them I'm sick in bed. If anyone else calls, tell them I'm out.'

'It still seems strange to me that in all that time you never caught them out!'

'Well, I was usually in the kitchen or out the back. I had so much to do. I never approached the mistress except to call out to her or advise her of visitors.'

'Did you ever take letters from her to Mr —?'

'Yes, often, especially when the minister was away in the district.'

'He always came to your mistress's?'

'Yes, Father.'

'Can you swear that you never caught them in a shameful act?'

'I couldn't have, Father, because the door was always locked. They opened it to no one.'

I was somewhat sceptical and said, 'What about when the children wanted to see their mother? Didn't she open the door to them?'

---

* There is a discrepancy here. She was meant to have left the minister's employment three months previously (p. 137).

'Not really, Father. If she really had to, she would, but only after a long time, and I wasn't present. I'd be in the kitchen.'

'But you saw her dishevelled and half-dressed many times, didn't you?'

'Yes, Father, but she'd be in her night-gown, and would call me to help her with her make-up, saying she'd been in bed unwell. If she had had a lot to drink she was even more unkempt.'

After my interrogation, I dismissed the young woman. I realised she had no proof of adultery, but it could be established from circumstantial evidence.

6. Two days later, the Anglican minister returned. I said to him, 'I've heard the maid's story. She told me she never saw them committing any indecency or adultery. They were behind closed doors. Naturally they wouldn't call her or let her in. So she can't testify against them. It's quite evident, however, that Mr — would stay overnight, not to mention the lovers' flight. This would be grounds enough for divorce. But tell me, what would you gain by incurring a debt of £1000 to gain a divorce? I can't see the point. Surely you have other preoccupations right now. The wretched woman has left Gisborne with her lover. She won't be thinking of returning right now. Let her get on with her life. Think of your children. If you must leave Gisborne, don't stay in New Zealand. Go to Australia. Don't tell anyone here your whereabouts in Australia. It's a big country. Eventually you'll find a parish which will accept you as their minister. Your wife won't know your whereabouts. She wouldn't go looking for you over there, so you and your children will be able to settle down.'

'But how can I go to Australia without money and all my debts here? Vestry will only give me £100. This might pay off my actual debts, but it wouldn't be sufficient to cover the cost of the trip which would be at least £250. I've already asked for a year's salary but they've refused me outright.'

'Stand your ground and tell them you'll only leave if they give you a year's salary. If they refuse, you'll stay in Gisborne, because you have the right to stay till the end of the year. Don't budge on this point. I'll plead your cause to the vestry chairman, on the grounds that if they give you the money, you'll leave immediately. If they gave you £400, would you?'

'Yes, certainly, but you won't succeed. Believe me, the chairman is absolutely furious with me.'

'Never mind. I hope I can make him see reason. I know him very well through his position as manager of the Bank of New Zealand. I have no hesitation in approaching him. I can speak frankly because he respects me enormously. He'd certainly listen to what I have to say, even more so if the financial interests of the Anglican Church are involved.'

'You'd do me a great favour if you did. He's the one who makes the decisions. I'd be eternally grateful to you. I'll leave the divorce matter till later, since I don't have the money for it. I won't tell anyone where I'll be living in Australia if I get the money from the vestry.'

'Rest assured, I'll speak to the bank manager within the next two or three days. Come and see me towards the end of the week, and I'll tell you the outcome.'

7. Two days later, I spoke to the manager at the bank. I came straight to the point. I told him that I had an urgent matter to discuss with him, namely, the situation regarding the minister's wife. He flushed, and was clearly angry not only with the woman but also the minister. I asked him if it was true that he wanted to get rid of him.

'I certainly do. He has to leave as soon as possible, but he doesn't want to go. We'll have to force him to leave.'

'I, too, believe he has to go and can't stay in Gisborne after what his wife did. But what reason does he give you for refusing to go?'

'He's claiming a year's salary. The vestry has given him three months' pay and will provide an additional three months'. The wretched man is not content with this.'

I let him vent his anger and then said, 'My dear sir, listen to me. You're quite right wanting the minister to leave Gisborne because of his wife. But he's not to blame. You should be more understanding.'

'We have been understanding, too much so. He'll have to go.'

'Let's take things slowly. Look at the size of his family. How could he leave without money and so many debts to pay? How could he go with only £200? That wouldn't even cover the debts. Think about it!'

I calmly continued, 'You say it's impossible for him to remain, but he has a year's contract with you. Six months before its expiry you want to cancel it and get rid of him. If you want to send him packing, you'll have to give him a year's salary.'

The chairman replied, 'Vestry intends to give him only another three months' pay, up till the end of June. Then he'll have to go.'

'Well, he won't. If you want to get rid of him, you'll have to give him a year's salary. Anglicans are well off. Just make this sacrifice and he'll leave. It's to your advantage to have him gone as soon as possible.'

'I'd be willing, but the other members wouldn't.'

'Well, there's no other way of getting him to leave, because the poor man is penniless. You as chairman are the most influential member. If you agreed, the others would fall into line.'

He was silent for a moment and then asked me, 'Do you really believe he'd leave if we pay him a year's salary?'

'Certainly. That's what he told me. And it would be to your advantage if he left because, as you are well aware, people aren't going to your church any more.'

'That's true. I don't even go because of the scandal.'

'So, make a settlement, and he'll be off.'

'We're having a vestry meeting the day after tomorrow. I'll try and persuade the others to grant him a year's salary, so he can leave as soon as possible. I can see you're right. Without the necessary means he can't leave. It's up to us to get him out as soon as possible. It would be good for him and our congregation. After what his wife did, no one wants to go near him. Rest assured, I'll do my best. In the meantime, thanks for your wise advice. It seems to offer the best solution.'

I wanted the best for everyone concerned, and thanked him for listening to me sympathetically. I then left.

8. The following day I met the minister on the street. I told him not to worry because I had convinced the vestry chairman to give him a year's salary so he could leave. He thanked me for all I had done for him. A few days later, I saw him again. He told me that the vestry had granted him his full stipend. He was packing his bags for Australia, as I had advised. He hoped to obtain a minister's position, which he was already negotiating. I asked him if he was still thinking of a divorce.

'Yes,' he replied, 'but not at this moment, for lack of money. I'll reconsider it when I have a position in Australia.'

'Forget about divorce and that woman. Don't tell anyone where you'll be living. Then she won't be able to find you.'

'All right. I'll think it over.' He thanked me for my kind support. A few days later he left for Melbourne. I never saw or heard of him again.

9. The Gisborne vicarage was a large, beautiful two-storey dwelling standing on half a hectare. The house alone had cost £1300. Vestry decided to sell it, however, because it was full of borer. The newly appointed minister from Auckland did not want to live in it for this reason. If borer get into a house, it is impossible to eradicate them. Because the mansion was infested, the vestry decided to sell the whole property. It was put up for auction with a reserve of £400, which would not even have covered the cost of the land. Vestry would stand to lose £1300 on the house. The property was bought by a private individual. The house was demolished and the land left vacant for a few years to get rid of the insects.

Part 7. Dreams for a Rosy Future Dashed!

Summary. – 1. The parishioners are pleased. Some would be even happier if I were Irish. – 2. The Protestants' admiration and approval of me. – 3. My ambitious plans for Gisborne's future. – 4. A bolt of lightning dashes my plans. – 5. Catholic and Protestant dismay about my departure. – 6. I leave everything behind in Gisborne, including my Mass kit and sacramental vessels. – 7. A sad farewell to my parishioners. – 8. Gisborne from 1882 to 1886 with Irish missionaries in charge.

1. I don't like to blow my own trumpet, but I do need to tell the truth. I do this not out of a sense of personal vainglory but to praise God. I am simply His humble instrument and cannot claim personal responsibility. If I have achieved anything, it is a result of God's doing. My parishioners realised the effort it cost me to learn English so quickly and at the same time provide the church's running costs from my personal funds. Their amazement turned to admiration. Apart from the one Irishman, Gallagher, they grew really fond of me, struck by how quickly I achieved my intention. There were, however, a few rabid Irishmen who would have preferred I was Irish, an expectation I couldn't realise! They muttered among themselves, 'He's not familiar with English but he preaches well enough. Imagine what he'd be like in Italian?' 'He hasn't mastered English but he's managed to produce miracles, earning universal admiration and esteem. What a pity he's not Irish!'

The parishioners in general spoke very highly of me to their Protestant neighbours.

2. When I first arrived in Gisborne, the Protestants ignored me. Hardly anyone greeted me, and naturally, I didn't greet them if they didn't acknowledge me. I simply went about my business. The Protestant ministers were disdainful of me, but I took no notice. The Protestants took note, however, of everything I did, so as to have something to talk about. I was polite to everyone, intent on my role as a priest and religious. I never went out at night, nor to dinner, concerts or shows of any kind. I only went out to attend to the sick. When they realised I was frank, honest, trustworthy and courteous to everyone, and that I was working constantly for the good of my parishioners and the church, and assiduously paying off the debt, many, especially the most influential, came to hold me in high regard. When they met me, they would greet me respectfully. Several of them frequently invited me to their homes and would have been very pleased had I accepted their invitations. I knew that they really wanted to know more about me, and so I refused, saying I didn't have even enough time to visit my own parishioners. This got me out of it. Their esteem for me continued to grow, and many gave me money for the debt on the church. More of them than the Catholics attended our concert, auction, bazaar and lotteries because they had a lot more money and were much better off. They said among

themselves and to my parishioners that I was a real gentleman, cultured, intelligent and superior to their ignorant, uneducated, venal ministers. They praised me generously and many attended the Catholic church on feast days.

3. As soon as the debt was paid off, I moved on to new projects promoting the parish. I had sent to me from Genoa six large brass candlesticks and four smaller ones. I bought some beeswax and made six candles for the large candlesticks and a dozen candles for the others. I had also, as mentioned previously, been working for more than a year on trying to buy a piece of land at Ormond for a small church and presbytery. In addition, I had decided to purchase at least half a hectare in Gisborne to build Catholic schools and a convent, so children would not have to attend secular government schools. Several Protestant gentlemen supported this project. They, too, wanted their children to have a good convent education.

4. I engrossed myself in these projects, urgently considering the best way to buy cheap land, build a convent and schools, raise the 100,000 francs needed at a favourable interest rate, and repay it. Suddenly, out of the blue, came a tremendous bolt of lightning, shattering all my plans for Gisborne. What was it that sent everything flying? I received the following letter from Dom Adalbert Sullivan in Sydney.

> Peace.
> Sydney, 9 August 1882
>
> Dear Fr Felice,
> I regret to inform you of your recall from Gisborne. The Vicar Capitular* deems it necessary to have you recalled given the present needs of the diocese which is still without a new bishop. My personal serious illness, and the return to Europe of one of our priests, force us to take this regrettable measure. Doubtlessly, the new Bishop will appreciate the necessity of quickly providing for the needs of the good people of Gisborne. Please ensure, therefore, that you make the necessary plans for preparing for your departure at your earliest convenience. The lay brother is to return with you. Please remember me to my friends in Gisborne, exhorting them to bear their forthcoming trial with patience.
>
> Your devoted brother in St Benedict,
> Adalbert Maria Sullivan OSB.

I was not only personally terribly upset by this letter, but also on behalf of my poor parishioners, who were so callously to be left without a parish priest. The 'present needs of the diocese' did not necessitate such an action at all. The

* The reference is to Mons. Fynes.

real issue was Auckland's embarrassment with Fr Sullivan's stupidity in incurring such an enormous debt. I must frankly admit that after I received this letter I regretted somewhat paying off Fr Chastagnon's debt on the Gisborne church so quickly when I had five years to pay it. I replied that I was willing to obey, but I begged Fr Sullivan not to leave the mission without a priest. I wrote a similar letter to the vicar-capitular. They both replied that they had no other priest to send to Gisborne and that I had to take over the debt on St Benedict's Church in Newton.

I had always acted out of strict obedience to God's will. God used me, his most unworthy instrument, to carry out His designs. Perhaps my new plans for Gisborne were not what He wanted. By remaining, I would not continue to be an unquestioning instrument of His will. God, through my superior, was calling me elsewhere to do good, even though I could only see things differently. I was upset that my parishioners, who had worked alongside me with such self-denial and selflessness, would be left without a priest. However, I had to obey.

5. I read out Fr Sullivan's letter at the next committee meeting. They were astonished and dismayed, and begged me to do everything I could to stay in Gisborne. I told them that there was nothing I could do about it personally. My duty was to obey. I was most upset about having to leave, but was even more distressed that they would be without a priest. I continued, 'If you so choose, you could write to the vicar-general, but I can't do anything myself. I'd most certainly stay if I was allowed to.'

They immediately wrote at length to Mons. Fynes, begging him to permit me to remain in Gisborne, and that they were very happy with me; that the parishioners as well as many Protestants were upset and distressed at my news, etc. He replied that I was needed in Auckland and that he was sorry to take from them a priest who was so loved and who had done so much for them. They were not to worry, however. As soon as the new bishop arrived, he would see that they had another priest.

Meanwhile, news of my recall spread quickly among the parishioners of the town and district. Many were incredulous, but when the committee confirmed it, they unanimously denounced my superior's decision. Several people asked me if I had applied for a transfer. I replied that I would prefer to stay in Gisborne and that I had never considered moving. I tried to calm them, but with little success, because they were too upset. I added, 'By my going, I hope that your wish to have an Irish priest will be accepted. Then you'll be happy.'

'No, no,' they replied, 'we're really pleased with you. We wouldn't want anyone else.' Many Protestants told me that they were upset that I was leaving because I was a real gentleman: upright, frank and trustworthy in every regard.

6. Although I knew that neither I nor any of our priests* would return to Gisborne, I decided nevertheless to leave behind everything I had brought with me three years previously, or had had sent to me at my own expense. I left the candlesticks and beeswax and the portable altar kit, excluding the monastic missal not used by secular priests, and a large ciborium,† too big for Gisborne's needs. These I would take to Newton. I took few household items, leaving behind sheets, blankets, rugs, serviettes, cutlery and towels. I handed them over to the committee for the new priest. I took only £119 personal savings with me.

7. When a priest left his parish on transfer or to return to Europe because of illness or some other reason, it was customary for the parishioners to present him with an illuminated address of appreciation. The artwork alone could cost between 400 and 700 francs according to its intricacy. They would also take up a collection for his trip. The Gisborne parishioners wanted to do the same for me. I begged the committee not to go to this unnecessary expense, saying that I was sure a mutual bond of affection would remain forever. I asked them not to take up a collection, knowing their poverty and the sacrifices it would cause. Moreover, it would only be a short trip, and I had sufficient money for it. They reluctantly acquiesced. Several people, however, visited me personally with tokens of their appreciation, saying I would need them in my new post. I didn't want to accept, but to avoid giving offence, I took their offerings, which amounted to 625 francs. Before my farewell address in church, I visited as many parishioners as I could, exhorting them to remain faithful to God, on Sundays and feast days to say the rosary since they couldn't attend Mass without a priest, and to act as devout Catholics, etc.

At the Ormond Mass, the Sunday before my departure, I made my farewell to the parishioners of the district. It was a very sad occasion for all of us. Many wept quietly, others had tears in their eyes. Everyone was very moved. I tried to console them, but I too needed consoling because I loved them very much indeed. Instead of preaching from the Gospel, I urged them to remain strong in the faith and loyal to God like their forebears, and never to be ashamed of being Catholic. I told them that when the new bishop arrived, I would plead their cause to ensure they were sent a new priest.

It was the same in Gisborne in the evening after vespers when I began to make my farewell speech. It broke my heart to see how distraught the parishioners were about my departure. When the time came for me to leave Gisborne, nearly all the Catholics of the town and several Protestants accompanied me from the church to the wharf. They all looked very sad. Many

* That is, Benedictine priests.
† Container for Communion wafers.

had tears in their eyes. I said a few consoling words, but I too was very moved. They kissed my hand for the last time and, after shaking hands with the Protestants, we embarked with three parishioners who accompanied us to the steamer. They returned to shore when the boat was due to cast anchor. My departure occurred towards the end of September 1882.

8. After my departure, the Gisborne parishioners sent another petition to Mons. Fynes, begging him to send me back to Gisborne. They praised me and my work to the skies. He replied that he regretted recalling me, but had a more onerous task he needed me for. He urged them to be patient and that the new bishop would attend to their needs. When Mons. Luck arrived in Auckland, they exhorted him to return me to Gisborne. He said that he was sorry that Fr Sullivan had removed me, but the decision about my return was not his to make. He too counselled patience, and promised that he would eventually send them a replacement. In April 1883 he sent down an Irish priest called Boyle, whom the bishop had only recently accepted into the diocese. His behaviour was far from good. He got drunk every day and wandered around the township in this state. He was denounced to the bishop, who asked me to gather information about his conduct. I wrote to Jennings to tell me what was going on. He sent me a lengthy reply on 21 April with evidence to support the accusations. Mons. Luck recalled Boyle and expelled him from the diocese. Gisborne was once more without a priest.

Towards the end of 1883 or beginning of 1884, the bishop sent another Irish priest, recently arrived from Australia, to Gisborne. As his housekeeper he took the sister-in-law of Sullivan, mentioned previously [page 133]. He too was a drinker, but he drank secretly in the evening. The maid was a tippler also, and a loose woman to boot. Illicit relations occurred between master and maid as subsequent events revealed. She became pregnant and a way had to be found to avoid a scandal. The young woman, probably at the behest of her master, agreed to marry Gallagher, the young Irishman. Marriage arrangements were made. At the altar, when she was asked whether she wished to take Gallagher as her husband, she replied 'no' and fled the church. But that wasn't the end of the matter. When the next steamer for Auckland arrived, the Irish priest and his maid left on it, and thence to the United States of America. This was reported in all the colonial newspapers, causing an enormous scandal.

CHAPTER SEVEN

Auckland: I Pay Off Others' Debts!
(OCTOBER 1882 TO JANUARY 1884)

PART 1. AN INEXTRICABLE DEBT

SUMMARY. – 1. Benedictine list of membership, Auckland diocese, October 1882.
– 2. My critical view of affairs in Newton. – 3. The insurance company demands
payment. – 4. The financial mess; the company manager threatens to auction off the
church. – 5. I ask Fr Sullivan for the church accounts; he says they are at Newton but
they can't be found. – 6. I summon the committee to ascertain the extent of the debt;
they know nothing. – 7. Parishioners' speculation about the extent of the debt.

1. As at October 1882, we had twelve religious in the Auckland diocese: eight
priests and four lay brothers. Fr Adalbert Sullivan, still recovering from his
accident in Sydney, was attached to Newton. Frs Cuthbert Downey and
Ethelwald O'Gara were in charge of the Auckland mission. Newton also housed
an Irish lay brother, Br Adalbert, and Br Samuele Nannini from Subiaco, Italy.
Br Joseph Ricci and I also joined this community. Fr Swithbert Breikan, a
German from our French province, was parish priest to the German settlers.*
Fr Augustine Luck, the new bishop's brother, was stationed at Kihikihi in the
Waikato. Fr Anselm Fox was in charge of the Hamilton and Cambridge parishes
in the Waikato, and he was assisted by Br Isaiah, an Italian. Finally, Fr Noboa,
born in Puerto Rico in the Americas, had the Coromandel parish.

2. I had stayed in Auckland for nearly two months after my arrival from Africa.
At that time I was of no practical use, and stayed at Mons. Steins's residence.
By the time I returned, I had a reasonable knowledge of English and no need of
an interpreter. My position at Newton, however, was not easy. In Fr Sullivan's
absence, the interim superior was Fr Downey. He and Fr O'Gara did not like
me. They would have preferred that I was nowhere near them, so they could
feel free to follow their own inclinations. But they had to accept the situation
because Fr Sullivan had assigned me to resolve the debt problem. It was vital
for me to remain. I too would have been very pleased not to have to live with
them, but I had to resign myself to it.

The reason for their opposition was they were used to leading an unrestricted
life, particularly in the evening. They were afraid I would discover their goings

* Actually Bohemian, not German.

on. They had a secret arrangement with the Irish lay brother who provided them with alcohol and drank with them. The three tipplers were not only wary of me, but of the two Italian lay brothers. But since the Irish lay brother was their provider, and they drank late at night when we Italians had retired, they thought they could keep their secret. For a long time I was unaware of their reprehensible behaviour, but the two lay brothers noticed that they were drinking excessively and they alerted me to it. I, however, did not really believe them, because I had never seen them drinking, let alone drunk. They also did not like me because they claimed that we Italian religious wrote to our superiors, unjustly criticising our British confrères. This was absolutely untrue. I ignored their negative attitude and took no action regarding the Italian brothers' complaints. I treated them impartially as colleagues, even though they believed I was a spy. Their suspicions were unwarranted. It is true, however, that if I discovered anything seriously wrong, I would write to my superiors so that the matter could be rectified. That was my charitable duty.

3. Fr Sullivan and the committee borrowed £4000 (100,000 francs) from a fire insurance company at about seven per cent interest, conditional on paying £250 capital annually and interest six-monthly. The loan had already run for eighteen months and Fr Sullivan had paid only a year's interest and not a penny of the capital. The company manager wrote to him requesting the previous year's instalment of £250 when the next six-monthly interest payment was due. Fr Sullivan paid the next interest instalment, but begged the manager to be patient until after the consecration of the church, when he would pay the £250 capital. The manager trusted his word, and agreed to wait, but insisted on prompt payment, which he was assured he would get. When the church was blessed, several hundred pounds were collected which Fr Sullivan used to pay off pressing debts. He hoped the company would continue waiting and paid them nothing. Shortly afterwards he had his accident in Australia. When the manager did not get his promised money, he wrote to Fr Sullivan requesting payment. Not knowing he was in Australia, he sent his letters to Newton. Fr Downey neglected sending them on promptly to Fr Sullivan, causing a considerable delay. Fr Sullivan didn't bother to reply. Instead, he wrote to the committee secretary asking him to attend to the matter. This he could not do, because he had no money either. He wrote back to Fr Sullivan requesting funds. When the insurance company manager got no response, he became very concerned and threatened legal proceedings to recover his £4000, since the conditions of the contract had not been observed.

4. This was a terrible state of affairs. There were debts everywhere and no money for them. Fr Sullivan realised that if he did not find a solution within six months the new church would be put up for auction. He needed to find a

Fr Cuthbert Downey, OSB, parish priest of St Benedict's, Newton.

Simon of Cyrene to take up the burden of the debt.* And he found him in me. When the Newton parish committee was advised that I was to be put in charge of sorting out the debt, they washed their hands of the matter. I wrote to them that pending my arrival in Auckland they were to crave the manager's patience. But what a predicament this placed me in! Did I have the money? No. How then was I to pay the debt? All I could think of was, 'Where there's a will there's a way.'

The angry manager, being apprised of the situation, declared that if the £250 was not paid soon, he would initiate legal proceedings and that the church would be auctioned off. The poor secretary begged him to be patient, and that things would work out. As soon as I arrived in Auckland, he urged me to speak to the manager and placate him. Knowing how angry he was with Fr Sullivan, I said that before I went I needed to see the accounts and know the exact extent of the debt.

5. Fr Downey was meant to have the accounts, but he said that Fr Sullivan had kept them and now they should be with the secretary. The secretary denied all

* Simon of Cyrene is mentioned in the Gospels as having been enlisted to carry Jesus's cross. (Matthew 27:32).

Ethelwald O'Gara, OSB. Downey's accomplice at St Benedict's.

knowledge, except that he had a few receipts for bills paid after Fr Sullivan's departure. I immediately wrote requesting Fr Sullivan send me the church ledgers. He replied that he had left them with Fr Downey and I should get them from him. I questioned him and every member of the Newton community. They all said that Fr Sullivan must still have them. I wrote to Fr Sullivan again and he simply repeated the same story. 'They must be there,' he said. 'Look for them. I'm certain they're there. That's where I left them.'

We all searched the place without success. One thought I had was that the other priests had hidden the ledgers to put me in a jam. My other thought was that Fr Sullivan still had them, but, not being a true record, he didn't want to hand them over to me. However, after reading the committee's minutes, I came to the most likely conclusion that he kept no accounts at all and it was therefore useless looking for them.

6. While engaged in this search, I notified the committee of a meeting the following Thursday at 7 p.m. to deal with important church matters which required them all to be present. This was my first meeting with them as chairman. They all turned up. I opened the meeting, mentioning the difficult burden placed on me, which was beyond my capacity to resolve. Only out of obedience had I accepted the task. I would do my utmost to sort it out, but it was vital to have their support to achieve the goal. They unanimously agreed and promised to co-operate. The previous meeting's minutes were read out and passed. I then said, 'I have no idea of the extent of the debt on the church. I'm new here and need the income and expenditure records of the past three years. Who has them?' I imagined that the secretary and treasurer would have had this responsibility. The secretary said that Fr Sullivan kept the accounts and also acted as treasurer.

'But, my dear sir, you must have kept some records of income and expenditure?'

'No. Fr Sullivan never gave me a single account to enter.'

I was very upset hearing this and said, ' You're a fine kind of committee. No one knows anything. The accounts are supposed to be in the presbytery. Fr Sullivan wrote that he left the ledgers here. But they can't be found, and you don't have them. What's to be done now?'

They were all surprised that there was no trace of the accounts. There was silence for a few moments. Then the secretary said, 'Father, for more than a year, we badgered Fr Sullivan for financial statements, but for one reason or another, he never provided them. He would promise to present them at the next meeting and then would make the excuse of not having had enough time to prepare them, and would keep postponing. So we never saw them!' He read some minutes out confirming this.

The reader can imagine my consternation at these revelations! I now had to believe that there were no accounts because he hadn't kept any and that his St Benedict's building project was to be another fiasco, like his previous ones! But I kept this to myself. A heavy gloom descended on the meeting. After a few moments silence, I said, 'Gentlemen, we are in a serious predicament! Without records, we can't know the extent of the debt! We're really in a hole, and we can't dig our way out! People will think we have acted irresponsibly and this will greatly discredit me, yourselves, Fr Sullivan and the Benedictines in general! You must try and see if you can find at least some accounts so we can get an idea of the size of the debt! The parishioners have the right to know how much money has been collected in the past three years, and what has happened to it. We can't prepare a report without the right information.'

They agreed. They also mentioned that a considerable amount of money had been collected in this period, but they didn't know how much or how it had been spent. They could only say that Fr Sullivan had written to them a month previously telling them he had no more money for the church and that they shouldn't send him any more accounts for payment! I stipulated that, since things were in such a mess, the committee needed to meet every Thursday at the same time. I asked them for their ideas about extricating ourselves from our plight, to avoid a huge scandal caused by bad management, and salvage our reputation. They promised to do so, but were pessimistic. I also asked the secretary and Mr Patrick Brophy, if possible, to meet with me daily to gather more details.

They agreed. The meeting was then closed.

7. I arrived in Auckland to a rumour among the Catholics that St Benedict's debt was nearly paid off, because of the large amounts of money collected in the past three years. Subsequently, collections had decreased significantly. Some committee members, equally ignorant of the extent of the debt, also believed

there was little to pay off. Others, however, thought there was still a large debt outstanding. In fact, a considerable amount of money had been collected through several public subscriptions. There had also been a public lecture, a bazaar and other events. But no one knew anything about the expenses incurred because Fr Sullivan had presented no financial reports. The parishioners wanted to know how things stood. The committee shared their concern and had asked Fr Sullivan to be accountable and provide a report, but to no avail.

Part 2. I Manage to Put Together a Statement

Summary. – 1. I visit the insurance company manager; his anger towards Fr Sullivan. – 2. Frequent meetings with two committee members. – 3. Need to notify the parishioners of the extent of the debt. – 4. The committee can't see how a public report can be made. – 5. My proposal for clarifying the situation and reducing expenses. – 6. We have to avoid being discredited. – 7. I undertake to prepare a statement covering the past three years. – 8. Achieving this without actual accounts! – 9. Success! Doing the books without records!

1. I delayed visiting the insurance company manager until the end of October 1882. However, having learnt from a committee member that the director was now available, he wrote a stinging memorandum again threatening legal action if the money owed to the company was not paid immediately. After receiving the letter, I went to see him accompanied by our secretary, because I didn't know where the office was. The secretary didn't want to go in. He was afraid of an ugly scene with the manager and so I entered alone. The manager received me coolly and began insisting on payment. I let him go on for a couple of minutes, remaining calm and collected. I then said, 'Excuse me, sir, do you know who I am?'

'Yes, you're the chairman of the Newton parish committee.'

'Yes, sir, that's right. I've been a week in the position. Your memorandum here is addressed to my predecessor, Fr Sullivan.' I handed it to him and continued, 'I find your threatening tone offensive. I'd rather I didn't have any business dealings with you at all.'

'I've written several times and never had an response!'

'I can't answer for that. I was in another mission. I had no responsibility for the Newton parish. Rest assured, however, the Catholic Church never fails to meet its obligations. I don't warm to threats, though. I don't deserve them and you have no reason to blame me because I wasn't responsible.'

'I'm sorry. I didn't know you were new. I thought you were the priest who originally borrowed the money.'

'Have you ever seen me before?'

'No, I don't believe so.'

'Well, let me assure you that I am completely new to this position. Take note of my name – Rev. Dom Felice Vaggioli, OSB, of St Benedict's, Newton. If you have any queries, write to me. In the meantime, I crave your patience until 15 November for payment of the next interest and the £250 capital. I have to find out our financial situation. I hope to be able to pay you what you are owed. I don't think I can do it any earlier. That's why I'm asking you to wait until 15 November.'

'Will you really pay up?'

'Yes, I promise you'll be paid by 15 November. I'm a man of my word. If I say I will, I will; but I accept no responsibility for the past.'

The manager accepted my proposition with good grace. I kept my promise, paying him what he was owed on that date. From then on we became good friends.

2. I met nearly every day with the secretary and Mr Brophy, principal members of the committee, to get information on the debt. I asked them if they remembered how much the construction of the church cost. They said several contracts were involved because changes were made to the original contract.

'Who would have the contracts?' I asked.

'I have copies,' the secretary replied.

'Thank goodness for that! That way we can know how much the church cost. Bring them to me as soon as possible.'

'But they're practically useless as accounts. Besides, some of the contracts were altered verbally.'

'Never mind. They'll still be useful to provide some light on the debt.'

I next asked how much the land cost. The original piece of land and title cost £1200, I was told. Later, a second lot was bought for the church sanctuary for an unknown sum. It was estimated that the total cost of the land and certificates would have been about £2000. I asked them to give me a rough estimate of income over the past three years. They said they had no idea. Fr Sullivan took the takings himself and didn't tell them. They knew that a lot of money was involved but they didn't have the least idea how much. I asked them how much was taken in the church collections. They said there were the pew takings – sixty centimes for front seats and thirty for rear seats per person. There were also special collections for the debt, as well as special donations from individuals.

'I heard there was a bazaar a year or two ago.'

'Yes, that's right,' said Brophy. 'And there was also a concert and a public lecture given by Abbot Alcock, but I don't know how much was collected.'

The secretary suddenly remembered that about seven months previously, Fr Sullivan had been challenged to provide a statement of accounts to the parishioners. He did prepare a brief statement for publication in the Catholic paper, but it was incomplete. It contained no mention of the cost of the church or land, or receipts for the public subscription. There were only figures for a few donations, the bazaar and the public lecture. The paper provided draft copies, but Fr Sullivan decided not to have a statement printed, saying it was still incomplete and he would give a full account for publication later.

The secretary then told me that he had these copies, but they didn't amount to a real account. I asked him for the statement, explaining that it could be useful. He brought it to me the next day.

3. At our next meeting, I said that it was obvious that we could not keep the extent of the debt concealed from the parishioners. They had a right to know how their money had been spent, and how much more was needed to settle the debt. They committee agreed, saying that people had been very frustrated waiting for a report, wanting everything put on the table. The person who had all the information, however, always found excuses for avoidance. Now a report couldn't be given because the accounts were lost. I replied that we were indeed in a parlous situation with no accounts, ledgers or income and expenditure details. This might have been how business was conducted in the past, but I had no intention of acting like this in the future. It was vital to get out of this mess. We needed a coherent, credible financial statement. Then things would be fine.

4. I asked the committee if they had any ideas for formulating a public statement. They said they had deeply considered the matter but, without accounts of income and expenditure, it would be impossible to prepare a statement, especially for the three-year period. Someone proposed holding a general meeting to inform the parishioners that it was impossible to give them a report on the debt. I told them that if they made a public statement to this effect, it would reveal their incompetence. They would be condemning themselves. Another suggestion was that we forget the past and start afresh, faithfully keeping accounts of income and expenditure, and that we forego providing an annual report for the current year but do so at the end of the following year. I also rejected this proposal for two reasons: (1) a public subscription needed to be organised urgently to pay arrears, and (2) at the meeting proposed for the following year, people would still want the previous three years' reports. The sorry business would come back to haunt us.

5. I then gave a report about my visit to the manager of the insurance company and the promise I had made regarding capital and interest payments by 15 November. To honour it, another loan would have to be taken out. I told them I was a man of my word, and I wanted to keep my promise. I asked the secretary and Brophy, acting treasurer, how much cash they had in hand. They had £90 between them. I commented, 'We need to find the £300 we're short of within a fortnight.' I asked them to see if there were people who still hadn't paid their

subscription. I asked the secretary to record all takings in the minutes and hand them over to me for itemising in the records. I would take on the role of treasurer and keep an accurate record of income and expenditure. We immediately began to use this system. I enquired what happened to the pew rental money after Fr Sullivan left. Brophy told me it had been used for individual debts and to pay for gas, cleaning and other minor church expenses. I said the gas bill was too high. There was a lot of wastage on Sunday evenings, the lamps being lit often an hour too early and kept going too long after worship. It was the same on Saturday evenings for confession. The servant responsible had been lax. I ordered strict economising, and that only necessary expenses be incurred in the interests of avoiding future financial embarrassment.

6. I then said that we would need to give the parishioners a financial report as soon as possible. They wanted one and had a right to it.

'You're right,' they answered, 'but we can't without accounts.'

'I'll come to that later,' I said. 'In the meantime, we need to call a general meeting and give parishioners a report covering the past three years. We have two months to get it ready. I'll give you two good reasons for the report:

1) To avoid a major scandal, the blame for which would fall on Fr Sullivan and this committee. I can't allow this to happen, even though he was negligent in keeping records. The reputation of the clergy is at stake. We would all be seen as incompetent.

2) To avoid people criticising you for not having supervised the accounts. You should have insisted from the outset that Fr Sullivan regularly produce his accounts, instead of leaving him with a free hand. The meeting would pass a vote of no confidence in Fr Sullivan and yourselves, and appoint others to replace you –'

'We would be more than happy to resign,' interrupted a committee member. 'We're really upset the way things have turned out.'

'Their censure,' I continued, 'would bring bring dishonour to you and the others. Simply resigning would seriously damage the Church, because, as things stand, critics might replace you, but they would be incompetent. That's why we need a public report.'

7. The committee was now convinced that, to maintain their good reputation, there needed to be a financial report, but the question was how could it be prepared without the necessary information? The secretary insisted it would be impossible for him to prepare anything without the figures and the others backed him up.

'I can understand your point of view,' I replied. 'But let me work on it. I hope I'll be able to convince the parishioners that the accounts are perfectly in order.'

They were very surprised at my statement, saying they would be delighted if I were successful, but they were indeed sceptical of my chances. I assured them that things would be fine and they would eventually share my optimism. I then asked the vice-chairman, Mr Brophy, and Mr Mahon, the secretary, to visit those who had done work on the church (excluding the contractors) and provided goods, to ascertain any monies owing and get their accounts. If they had already been paid, Brophy and Mahon were to get copies of receipts and bring them back so I could use them in preparing my report. They agreed and we decided to hold another meeting the following Thursday.

8. When I had the accounts I requested, and copies of the contracts, I immediately set to work. First, there was the land purchases for about £2000, then twelve contracts for excavating under the church for a large Sunday school; reinforcing the subsoil; construction of the main body of the church, the belfry, sanctuary and two chapels. The costs related to building the new church and buying the land had risen to about £10,500. Some individual bills had been paid, and others not. They included accounts for laying the foundation stone and consecrating the church, amounting to £1500. I went to the Bank of New Zealand, asking them to give me an exact statement of how much they had been paid in the last three years, and how much was still owing on the church. I didn't go to the insurance company because I knew £4000 had been borrowed and the interest due at six per cent for the last six months was £120.

9. From this information, I drew up the following statement:

	£	s
Cost of construction and purchase of land	12,000	
Total income for three years	6,484	10
Debt remaining	5,515	10
Debt owing to the bank	1,200	
Debt owing to the insurance company,		
including interest	4,120	
Individual debts	195	10
Total	5,515	10

Three months later, further bills arrived: for the three-day hire of a carriage for the Bishop of Wellington for the consecration of the church – £15, and payment for the choir and orchestra for the ceremony – £35. The final debt at 1 November 1882 stood at £5565 10s. In my public statement, however, I used the former figure of £5,515 10s. I had thus roughly calculated the church's income and expenditure, but my task was still not complete. Expenditure was stated as £12,000 and income, £6484 10s. I had to account for where these figures came from. I had a second task to perform. This is how I made up the accounts:

	£	s
Pew takings for three years	2,652	5
Bazaar	800	
Public concert	50	
Public lecture	70	
Special collections over three years	2,912	5
Total income	6,484	10
Balance Expenditure	12,000	
Income	6,484	10
Remaining Debt	5,515	10

At the next committee meeting, I produced the balance sheet and said, 'Here is an exact statement of income and expenditure over the past three years, and the debt remaining. It is an exact account of what is still owing, unless there are other creditors we don't know about.' I handed the statement to the secretary and asked him to read it out. The other members listened in rapt silence. In their eyes I had become a financial wizard who had produced a convincing report out of thin air. They said that people would think the figures came from accurate accounts. They were amazed at how I did it. I explained my procedure because many of them thought Fr Sullivan had sent me the accounts and I had concealed the fact. But the executive members knew that this was not true. I was pleased indeed to have got us out of the morass, but we still needed to sort out the urgent debts. *Vexatio dat intellectum.** I thanked God for his help.

PART 3. MONS. LUCK OSB

SUMMARY. – 1. Arrival of the new bishop in Auckland. – 2. Official reception at the cathedral. – 3. The bishop's critics. – 4. His opposition to Irish political agitation. – 5. An angry response from the Irish. – 6. I make a few polite observations. The bishop rebuffs me. – 7. His change of mind.

1. Mons. John Edmund Luck OSB arrived in Auckland, as I recall, towards the end of October 1882. He was accompanied by Fr Lenihan, an Irish secular priest, who was a strong, fit young man, approximately twenty-eight years old. After Bishop Luck's death, Fr Lenihan succeeded him as Bishop of Auckland.

Mons. Luck also brought with him from Ramsgate as his secretary Fr Osmund Egan, an Irishman and accomplished organist, as well as another Benedictine, whose name I have forgotten.[†] A priests' and laymen's committee

---

* 'Necessity is the mother of invention' (Latin).

† This was Dom Gregory de Groote, a Belgian. (cf. *St. Augustine's Abbey, Ramsgate; an informal history*, unpublished, probable author Abbot David Parry, p. 180)

was set up to organise a suitable reception to welcome the bishop to the diocese. A telegram was received informing us of his departure from Australia and approximate time of arrival in Auckland. Nearly all the priests of the diocese, the special committee and leading parishioners were at the wharf to greet him. Fr Cuthbert, who was well-known to the bishop, and the vicar-general boarded the steamer as soon as it berthed. Fr Cuthbert introduced the vicar-general to the bishop and they disembarked. Mons. Fynes then introduced the bishop to the priests, the committee, a member of the Legislative Council, an MHR, and some prominent laymen. People took their seats in the waiting carriages, which then proceeded to the bishop's residence in Ponsonby. The official reception was postponed for two days, as I recall, because of the bishop's tiredness after his fifty-day voyage.

2. Mons. Luck's reception was not as grand as Mons. Steins's. Only twelve carriages were used in the procession following the same route from the bishop's residence to the cathedral. Many parishioners spilled into nearby streets because the cathedral was packed. When the bishop entered the sanctuary, the vicar-general said the opening prayers. Mons. Fynes then read out an address on behalf of the clergy. Fr McDonald, the cathedral administrator, made another speech on behalf of the parishioners. Mr Tole, MHR, followed with an address on behalf of the laity. The president of the Irish Society made the final speech. I expected Fr Downey to deliver an address on behalf of our Benedictine community, especially since the bishop was a confrère. Moreover, Fr Downey represented our superior, who was recovering in Sydney. He didn't say a word, however. If I had known, I would have made a speech myself. People noted what happened, especially the secular clergy. The bishop made a brief appreciative reply, but was very circumspect when he mentioned the Irish. Benediction of the Blessed Sacrament followed the speeches.

3. The bishop had made enemies even before reaching the diocese. The first was our superior, Fr Sullivan, who was disappointed at not being appointed Bishop of Auckland, and because the bishop was opposed to his risky business undertakings, which had already ended badly. Frs Downey and O'Gara were also opposed to him because they had hoped Fr Sullivan would be the new bishop. They realised, too, that Mons. Luck wanted reliable, devout religious in the mission, and he had a reputation for strictness. That's why no speech was made by them. The Catholics of the diocese were mostly Irish. They were not favourably inclined to English bishops who were critical of Irish aspirations. They would have preferred an Irish bishop. They would not have known, however, that their bishop was anti-Irish were it not for the three above-mentioned monks. They rashly said to an Irish friend that the new bishop was anti-Irish and against their protests.

Naturally the rumour spread quickly among the faithful. Hence the prelate's welcome was frosty and almost hostile. The parishioners would have preferred Fr Sullivan because he was Irish and in his speeches he presented himself as a true patriot. But he was not a committed Irishman, as I discovered through my various discussions with him. Many parishioners asked me if I knew the new bishop and whether he was anti-Irish. I said I didn't know him personally and couldn't answer their question. I believed that he would seek justice for all.

4. Just a few weeks after his arrival, the bishop called a secular priests' meeting, forbidding them to participate in meetings with their Irish compatriots which promoted freedom and autonomy for Ireland, or Home Rule. He should never have done that! The priests were incensed. Most, however, confined themselves to muttering about the bishop, but the more rabid told people about the bishop's ban and that he was rigidly anti-Irish. They protested that they would not obey the ban and wrote to friends in Ireland and America about the bishop's hostility. The news was publicised in their patriotic newspapers. The prelate believed he was in the right giving such an order, but it was a stupid act. Perhaps he thought that secular priests were the same as monks in having to strictly obey their superior's orders without demur, but that was not the case. His actions were based on inexperience more than anything else. I have to say that the bishop was foolish to give such an order without consulting experienced, competent people, or at least seeking Rome's opinion on the Irish question. I say this, because there could be serious consequences. If the faithful cannot rely on the clergy for guidance in all things, including political matters, their faith can be adversely affected. Even worse, if they lose respect for their pastor, Catholicism is sure to suffer, to the cost of the faithful. One of the most fiercely nationalistic priests tried to convince the bishop of his error and make him realise that the church did not condemn protesting as long as it was within the limits of the law. The bishop, unfortunately, did not have an adequate understanding of the Irish question and the extent of the upheaval in Ireland. He had gained his distorted view from English newspapers. Consequently, he would not budge and continued to prohibit priests from any involvement.

5. The priests were so patriotic that they would not be restrained in commenting on the prelate's ban. The news that the bishop was anti-Irish and against their rights quickly spread. People began to criticise him and his anglophile prejudices against Catholic Ireland. They contrasted him to the Bishop of Wellington, who, although a Marist and English, supported justice for Ireland and its heroic people, while their Benedictine bishop opposed the very parishioners who generously supported him and the rest of the clergy. The Irish were so angry that they made him feel the pinch by discontinuing their contributions to the Sunday collection. Offerings decreased to such an extent that the bishop had to

impose a five per cent tax on the takings of the missionaries of the diocese. One secular priest in particular was, I believe, the ringleader who probably wrote overseas criticising the bishop. Several American and Irish newspapers, widely read throughout the colony, criticised his anti-Irish position.

I was dismayed at the situation, damaging as it was to episcopal authority and Catholics' duty of obedience. Many Irishmen complained directly to me about the bishop's attitude, knowing I supported Ireland's seeking justice from the British Government. Several members of the Newton parish committee also criticised the bishop. In their view, if he did not support the Irish cause, he should at least say nothing and keep his opinions to himself. I tried to make excuses for him, saying he was new and not conversant with the situation. When he really considered the matter, he would change his mind. They suggested that one of the clergy speak to him and tell him not to enter into Irish politics, particularly if he didn't want to give the Church a bad name. I promised that when the occasion arose I would act.

6. Wanting what was best for the bishop and the faithful, I visited him one day, mentioning the general dissatisfaction the Irish felt. I told him about their comments, including their threats. I asked him if he had any inkling of what was going on. He replied somewhat brusquely that he had heard of some grumbling, but he had no intention of acting differently. The following conversation then occurred:

'Your Excellency,' I replied, 'as an Englishman, you would naturally be regarded as an enemy by the Irish. Hence it would have been better if you hadn't even mentioned this subject.'

'I did so out of a sense of duty. Irish protests have been prohibited by the Holy See, as stated in a brief sent to the British bishops.'

'It's true that illegal protesting is prohibited, but lawful protests, within the definition of British law, are legitimate, and approved by Pope Leo XIII.'

'You're absolutely wrong!'

'On the contrary, Excellency. If you want proof, I'll send you tomorrow the latest copy of *Civiltà Cattolica*, the Jesuit periodical published in Rome, which I subscribe to even from New Zealand. In it you'll find confirmation of what I've said. The Irish bishops submitted the matter to the Church's supreme authority, and this was the Pope's response. But putting the pontiff aside, logic alone would suffice. If the British Government acts unfairly towards the Irish, why shouldn't they be entitled to seek justice by legitimate means?'

'They're nothing but revolutionaries!'

'Spoken like a true Englishman. I would acknowledge that the Fenians are a radical party. But Catholics in general are only seeking legitimate ways of getting fair treatment from an oppressive government. Irish Catholics are neither Fenians nor revolutionaries.'

'What would you, as an Italian, know about the Irish question? Leave it to the English. We know what it's really about.'

'Excuse me, Excellency, but I need to say that I know more about the matter than you realise. I've studied it thoroughly for two years. I'm now convinced that the Irish have not been treated the same as other British subjects. Moreover, if the clergy take a divergent political view to the faithful, the parishioners will become disaffected. I must mention that I myself became a member of Gisborne's Irish Catholic Society.'

'Really! You, an Italian! I don't believe it! That's incredible!'

'Yes, me, Excellency, because I saw the society as an excellent means of providing support for the people.'

'I'm simply amazed.'

'It seems perfectly natural to me. We missionaries have to be all things to all men, to serve the common good. That doesn't mean getting involved in wrong-doing or illegal activities. In normal events, I would say it's best to let parishioners make their own decisions. No good comes from meddling. I believe you would have done better, Your Excellency, to have kept right out of the Irish question. It's a shame that English Catholics are mostly against the Irish quest for justice.'

'And every Catholic bishop!'

'Not all of them, Excellency. The most renowned, like Cardinals Manning and Newman, support justice. Here in New Zealand, Mons. Redwood, Bishop of Wellington, supports the Irish too. However, Your Excellency, do what you believe is right. You're in charge. I have expressed my own humble opinion with your goodwill and well-being at heart, and our mutual calling as monks allows me the liberty I have taken.'

'I very much doubt that their protests are legitimate and would be endorsed by the Pope.'

'Why don't you write to Rome for official clarification? You'll find that I'm right.'

I then left, realising that the bishop had not taken too kindly to my remarks. I, however, had no regrets because I was acting for the common good. I also wrote about the matter to our abbot-procurator in Rome.

7. For nearly a year, the bishop continued to be critical of the Irish protesting supported by Parnell in the British Parliament. He then began to refrain from negative comments, even attending public addresses given by Redmond, an Irish Member of Parliament.* He had come to New Zealand to explain the

---

* Vaggioli claims Luck attended public addresses given by Redmond, but Davis (*Irish Issues in NZ Politics*, p. 102) disagrees. *New Zealand Herald* (20 Nov 1883) said that Luck 'refused to appear on the platform with him, and generally gave it to be understood that he discountenanced the mission of these agitators to the colony.'

reasons for Irish grievances and the general unrest. Mons. Luck certainly remained unsympathetic to Irish demands, but at least he had the prudence not to enter debate about this controversial issue. Our abbot-procurator wrote to him, giving him similar advice to mine. Two years later, Irish Catholics in Auckland were no longer complaining about their bishop.

PART 4. SORTING OUT THE DEBT

SUMMARY. – 1. Determining the size of the debt. Annual running costs. – 2. Decision to call a general meeting of Auckland's Catholics. – 3. The bishop is invited to preside. – 4. His visit to inspect the accounts. – 5. The general meeting. – 6. Proposal for a special subscription to decrease the debt. – 7. Vote of thanks.

1. As I mentioned previously, the debt on the church as at November 1882 was approximately £5560. A summary of the situation was:

		£
1.	Owing to the Bank of New Zealand, Auckland	1300
2.	” to the Insurance Company	4000
3.	” to individuals	260

Expenditure from November 1882 to 31 October 1883:

1.	Outstanding capital owed to Insurance Company	250
2.	Capital due for payment by April 1883	250
3.	Interest owing to the Bank and Company (7 %)	371
4.	Fire insurance premium (on £4000)	75
5.	Cost of gas for church lighting at an avg. of £4 weekly	208
6.	Candles, altar wine, paraffin, annually	45
Total		1199

Excluding the capital owed to the insurance company between 1882 and 1883, the usual running costs on the church and interest payments amounted to £699, or 17,475 francs per annum. There was no regular income to cover running costs. Everything had to come out of personal offerings.

2. Before presenting a financial report to the public, we decided to submit it to the bishop for his approval, and then have it printed and distributed. We also decided to ask the bishop to chair the meeting to be held on the second Sunday in January 1883. The clergy were to advise their parishioners and the newspapers would also be notified. The secretary and two other committee members were appointed to prepare a succinct financial report covering the past three years. We

decided that there needed to be a general subscription, not leaving the debt as the Newton parish's responsibility, since the new church would be an asset to the whole town. We agreed to propose a motion for a special subscription for the arrears from those who could afford to contribute. We also decided to present the annual financial report in January, regarding income, expenditure and progress on the debt.

3. I visited Mons. Luck and told him about the forthcoming general meeting which I invited him to chair. I then presented him with my financial report for the past three years. He examined it carefully and then said: 'You've done an excellent job. It's very clear. I'm very pleased. Did you bring the receipts as well?'

'No, Excellency, because I don't have them. No one has any accounts, not even Fr Sullivan.'

'That's impossible! I don't believe it! Your report is so exact. You couldn't have done it without receipts. You just couldn't.'

'Nevertheless, that's just what I've done. My Newton confrères and the parish committee can confirm it. Just ask them.'

'I still can't believe it. The accounts have been itemised to the last penny!'

'Very true, and just how they should be.' I explained the situation I had inherited and how I had made up the accounts. The bishop didn't believe a word of it. He held the report up and said, 'You couldn't have prepared this without receipts or ledgers. No one would believe you.'

'But that's exactly what I have done. Why would I choose to lie? If I had the actual figures, I wouldn't hesitate to show them to you. Your Excellency is entitled to see everything. But, I repeat, no one gave me any. I simply don't have them.'

The bishop, flustered with my explanation, said, 'I'll come to Newton tomorrow or the following day and do a thorough investigation.'

'Excellency, come whenever you like. You'll see that I'm telling the truth.'

I returned to Newton with the realisation that the bishop still thought I had prepared the accounts from ledgers and receipts which I didn't want him to see, which was absolutely untrue.

4. Mons. Luck visited as he promised. He came to my room and I showed him my new ledger. Our conversation went as follows:

'This is a new ledger. You've shown me these accounts. I want to see the ledger Fr Sullivan kept.'

'I've never had it. I can show you the letters claiming it was left here.'

He read them.

Then I continued: 'My colleagues told me he left no accounts here. No one's been able to find any.'

'You must have ledgers and receipts. You just don't want me to see them.'

'I can swear I've never had any. I believe Fr Sullivan simply didn't keep accounts. Hence he couldn't furnish them for me. So that he wouldn't look incompetent, he said he'd left everything here, but couldn't remember with whom.'

'So, it's all a mystery! Well, who does have the accounts?'

'Who knows? Certainly not me! I've been searching high and low for more than a month and got nowhere!'

'But if what you say is true, you'd have no records for preparing the report. The accounts must be here. That's the only way you'd be able to.'

'Well, let me tell you how I did it.' I then explained exactly how I had gathered information, made estimations and eventually prepared my report.

The bishop listened in silence and then said: 'Well, you've given me your explanation. I still can't believe that Fr Sullivan didn't keep records, and even less that you could have made this report without proper receipts.'

'You can believe what you like, Excellency, but it's exactly as I've said. I had to rack my brains to sort it out. And I did it in this way not only to save Fr Sullivan's reputation, but, more particularly, the Benedictines'. If I'd told the parishioners no accounts were kept, it would have caused a scandal.'

'There's too much detail here for me to believe you.'

'Excellency, why don't you ask Fr Downey, Fr O'Gara, Br Adalbert or the committee if what I'm saying is true? They're reliable witnesses.'

'Surely that's not necessary. I need to trust you. Don't get upset!'

Nevertheless, the bishop was still unconvinced. He still believed I didn't want him to see the accounts in case he found out exactly how much money St Benedict's had. He never forgave me for what he perceived as a lack of respect and sense of duty towards him. My conscience was clear. I took no notice, knowing that God is our judge and I was telling the truth.

5. One Sunday in December or January, the general meeting took place at St Benedict's. At 2 p.m. the Blessed Sacrament was removed from the tabernacle and taken to the sacristy. The church doors were opened and committee members distributed copies of my financial report for the past three years. The church could accommodate about 2000, but only the heads of families, mostly men, came. About 300 people attended altogether. At exactly 3 p.m. the bishop, vicar-general, local clergy, Benedictines and Mr Mahon, the committee secretary, took their seats in the sanctuary. The secretary sat at a table with his papers, etc. Mons. Luck acted as chairman. He briefly explained the purpose of the meeting and congratulated the audience on such a large turnout. He then asked the secretary to read out the financial report in detail. It included favourable mention of the parishioners' generous efforts in reducing the large debt of £12,000 to £5515 10s within three years. He then read out details of income and carefully explained how the money had been spent. The conclusion mentioned that the debt was still significant and needed to be further reduced and ultimately paid off as soon as possible. This was the real purpose of the meeting.

The bishop, clergy and laity expressed their satisfaction with the committee's report, praising their painstaking efforts. They also expressed a desire to have annual financial reports. I replied on behalf of the committee that we had already decided to do this because people had a right to know how their money was spent. I thanked the laity for their invaluable support and begged them to continue their generous assistance. Within a month we had to pay £500, £250 of which had been owing to the insurance company since the previous April, and a further £250 of accrued interest. The cathedral administrator and vicar-general mentioned their satisfaction with the report, adding that further sacrifices were needed to reduce the loan and repay the most pressing debts.

6. A leading layman stood up and proposed a special subscription for settling urgent debts. The bishop, as chairman, put the proposal to the meeting. It was passed by a majority. A list of subscribers was immediately drawn up. The bishop pledged £100. The vicar-general put his name down for £50, and the administrator for £25. Several people pledged amounts varying between £25 and £10. In all there were subscriptions for about £400 (10,000 francs). It was then agreed that committee members would visit every family deemed able to contribute, and collect their subscription. The names of subscribers and the amounts of their donations would later be read out at Sunday High Mass. The committee was also requested to devise plans for further fundraising.

7. Before closure, a vote of thanks was proposed to His Lordship for chairing the meeting and to the clergy for their generous support. A vote of confidence was also passed in myself as the new chairman, and in the committee for their dedicated involvement. I thanked the gathering for their trust in our selfless committee. A vote of sympathy was also passed regarding Fr Sullivan, convalescing in Sydney. It was hoped that he would soon get well and return to Newton. The administrator proposed a vote of thanks to all who had attended. The meeting was then closed.

PART 5. A YEAR OF INTENSE TOIL

SUMMARY. – 1. Regular committee meetings. – 2. The committee's hard work. – 3. My own efforts to find money. – 4. I have a nasty fall off my horse; miraculously saved! – 5. I insure the church for £5000 against fire. – 6. 1883 financial report.

1. When Fr Sullivan ran the committee, the members realised that he was not dealing openly with the church debt and some of them made various excuses for not attending meetings. After the public meeting mentioned above, I asked the members to attend regularly or resign. One member asked to be excused

because he worked until 9 p.m. It was then decided that if a member could not explain his absence, after three absences his membership would be cancelled and he would be replaced. A couple of members who had withdrawn under Fr Sullivan returned as active members. Regular fortnightly meetings were held and this continued while I was responsible for the debt.

2. Following the decision at the general meeting, four committee members were appointed to visit all but the very poor Auckland Catholic families, and collect subscriptions. They immediately set to work. It was also decided to have a public concert, monthly if possible, to raise money. Three other members were appointed to find pianists, violinists, singers and other artists among the Catholics and Protestants who would be willing to offer their services gratis. There was an old disused wooden Presbyterian church near St Benedict's which was for sale. It was occasionally used for concerts. The committee decided to hire it because it could seat 500 people. Hire was only £2 per concert. Our concerts would be on a small scale and expenses would be modest. They began at Easter 1883, starting at 8 p.m. and ending at 10 p.m. Although I was fully occupied as a priest, I undertook getting tickets printed and distributed to sellers. After the second concert I had 6000 tickets printed, visiting-card size, leaving blank the date of the concert. I would then write in the time of the next concert and send off 700 at a time to the ticket sellers. Most would be sold, although many purchasers would not actually turn up. The average takings were about £12, once the costs of hiring the venue, lighting and refreshments for the entertainers were deducted.

3. It was not my responsibility to visit families for subscriptions because I wasn't familiar with the area and I had too much to do. However, I did call on a few the committee deemed it more appropriate for me to visit. What I did undertake to do myself was to periodically visit the vicar-general, the Parnell convent and the sisters at Ponsonby to get the names and addresses of rural subscribers and hand them on to the committee. Yet I still had to carry on my duties as a priest. By the evening I would be exhausted and anxiety about meeting church expenses and the interest on the debt would prey on my mind. Day and night I was preoccupied with this burden, trying to think of the best way through.

4. The town was more than six kilometres across. To travel about, one had to go either on foot, which was tiring in summer, by tram, coach or on horseback. I often walked. The tram fare cost between sixty centimes and 1.25 francs. A single coach fare to the outskirts was at least five shillings (6.25 francs). To avoid the expense, I usually walked or rode. We had a horse at Newton which we used around town to visit the asylum, etc., as well as around the presbytery.

The servant used it for errands. Fr Sullivan would also ride it over to his relatives. He bought a second horse for £28. It was ten years old and seemed gentle enough but it turned out to be skittish and a bad mount. No one thought to mention its bad habits to me. In fact I was told it was as gentle as a lamb. It was hardly used, however, people preferring the other horse. I knew nothing about its nastiness, and the first time I rode it without incident. The second time I was nearly killed.

One morning, about 10 a.m., I saddled the horse and rode it to the cathedral. I then went along Parnell Road for about three kilometres, to the vicar-general's (the return trip to Newton was four kilometres). Continuing on my way, I left the main thoroughfare and took the shore road which went straight for 500 metres and then skirted a hill to the left. I had to ride to the side because the road was congested with carts and carriages going in both directions. At the beginning of the straight, the horse went over a grating. It reared up at the sound and began to hurtle along the road. I tried to rein it in, but with no effect!

Pedestrians and vehicles were in front of me. They yelled out in fright: 'Stop! stop!' I pulled on the reins with all my might, but got nowhere. I really thought I would hit a vehicle or run into people. I prayed fervently to God and Our Lady, thinking this was the end. Fortunately, I did not lose my presence of mind. I tried to steer it away from the road, but it still wouldn't respond. Through grace or good luck, the wild, careering horse turned sharply into the hill, stopping dead in its tracks. It was amazing that I wasn't catapulted to the ground like a sack of potatoes. But I avoided a nasty fall by keeping my hands firmly on the mane.

The terror I suffered caused my heart to race wildly, and brought on the palpitations which continued to afflict me over the years. I dismounted, trembling from head to foot. My heart was beating furiously. I took the horse by the reins and continued on foot to the bottom of Parnell rise. I then remounted and rode on to Mons. Fynes's. He noticed I was pale as a ghost and asked me what was wrong. I told him about the incident. I rode the horse back very gingerly and only on rises would I let it trot. That was my last ride on the beast. My confrères weren't surprised when I told them what had happened, mentioning that our servant had had two or three similar experiences. A few months later it was sold for £7. Six months previously, it had been bought for £28!

5. In 1881, before the construction of the church was completed, it was insured, I believe, for between £3500 and £4000. This policy expired in March 1883. When it was due for renewal, I decided to try to reduce the premium while increasing the sum insured to £5000. The committee welcomed my proposal. The secretary was appointed to find an insurance company willing to co-operate. He found one which would insure the church for an annual premium of one pound, ten shillings, instead of the £2 5s required by the previous company. He then handed it over to me. I visited the tendering company and was pleased to

confirm his report. One major obstacle, however, stood in the way. The original company, which lent £4000, had a clause in the contract that the insurance was to be provided by them at their price. I approached this company and told them that I wanted to raise the insurance to £5000 and lower the premium, explaining that other companies were willing to provide a lower premium. The director angrily refused. I was determined to win and calmly persevered. The following conversation took place:

'You might not believe it, my good man, but the final building costs were more than £7000.'

'The church is not worth that much. It wouldn't be worth more than £4000.'

'You're wrong there. In 1881, you yourself insured it for nearly £4000. That was before the sanctuary, choir stalls and the two chapels were completed. Isn't that right?'

'Yes.'

'Well, they're completed now. Then Fr Luck had the beautiful main wooden altar built for £500. Four confessionals were added at £100 each, then 105 pews, and an organ which cost nearly £100. And all that shouldn't be included? If you want to continue the policy, they have to be.'

'But I don't want to increase the amount, in case your Irish parishioners burn the church down!'

I erupted at this scurrilous insinuation and said, 'It's obvious you don't know Irish Catholics, but I shouldn't be surprised at a Protestant maligning the Irish. They don't burn down houses or churches, least of all their own church. Your comment is unfair and unjustified.'

He apologised for his remark and went on, 'If you're prepared to include the organ, pews and main altar in the policy, you can increase the insurance to £5000.'

'That's what I intend doing anyway,' I said.

The manager then pointed out to me that according to the contract, the church had to be insured with his firm.

'Very true,' I replied, 'as long as the annual premium is not more than what other reputable firms would charge. Another company has quoted us a figure a lot less than yours.' I mentioned its name.

'That's impossible. Besides, it's a disreputable firm.'

'Well, I can assure you that I've spoken to the manager, and don't tell me that it's unreliable or disreputable. That's simply not true. It's just as reputable as yours. The fact is that it's competitive.'

'But we can't reduce our premiums to that extent.'

'Then you'll agree for us to insure the church with a company that offers more favourable terms.'

He was startled at my suggestion, exclaiming we had to insure the church with his firm.

'True, on condition that you offer similar terms. Otherwise I deem myself freed of the contract and able to choose another company. The conditions of the contract allow for this.'

'I don't believe you can make that interpretation.'

'If you need convincing, consult your lawyer. I've already sought expert legal advice, and they've confirmed my interpretation.'

'I'm still not convinced that the firm you mentioned could offer such favourable conditions.'

'Well, go and find out. I'll come back in a week.' I then shook his hand and left.

When I returned, I found him much more accommodating. He agreed to insure the church, including the additions, for £5000, under the same terms as proposed by the other company. The contract was extended for six years, and the annual premium reduced to one and a half per cent instead of the original two and a quarter per cent. The annual premium was thus reduced to £75, while previously, when the church was insured for £3500, the premium was £87 10s. It was a stroke of good fortune to get this deal, as will be revealed, because of the fire which occurred about two years later.

6. On the first Sunday in January 1884, a general parishioners' meeting, chaired by the bishop, was held to present the 1883 financial report. The clergy and most of the faithful attended, numbering some 500 people. The secretary read out the report:

	£	s
Income: subscriptions, pews, revenue	2,685	10
Expenditure: capital paid to bank and		
insurance firm	1,965	10
interest on loan	320	
fire insurance premium	75	
lighting, wine, candles, paraffin	325	
Total expenditure	2,685	10

In January 1883 the debt was £5565 10s. During the year, payments amounting to £1965 10s had been paid off the capital, reducing the debt to £3600. The Bank of New Zealand had been completely paid off, with only the debt to the insurance firm of £3600 outstanding. The public applauded the substantial reduction and the committee's dedication. The secretary said that the splendid result was mainly due to the indefatigable selfless efforts of their chairman, Fr Vaggioli. Further applause followed. I thanked them on behalf of the committee, acknowledging the widespread support we had enjoyed. I had indeed laboured tirelessly to reduce the debt and had consequently ruined my health, overtaxing my mind and body. My constitution had suffered enormously.

Part 6. Laxity at St Benedict's

Summary. – 1. Burying the dead added to my duties. – 2. Observance of the monastic Rule at St Benedict's. – 3. Questions about Fr Sullivan's property purchases. – 4. An unexpected knock at my door; false alarm! – 5. Secret tippling. – 6. Estimating the presbytery income. – 7. What happened to the money? – 8. Fr Sullivan and his cronies let our mission down. – 9. I advise my superiors about the situation. The general doesn't believe me. The procurator-general decides to abandon the mission.

1. The Catholic cemetery was on a hillside next to the new St Benedict's church. In 1850 the land reserved for this purpose was more than a kilometre outside the planned town perimeter. But by 1883 it was almost in the centre of the sprawling township. Frs Downey and O'Gara were in charge of the Newton parish, while I was to deal with the debt. They were also responsible for Catholic burials. They were often away all day, however, and not available to officiate. I went out on business, from 9 a.m. until 11 a.m. I would return at the latest by eleven-thirty, and I wouldn't go out again except in rare circumstances. As acting superior, Fr Downey begged me to take over burying the dead who were not Newton parishioners. I told him I was already burdened with a tremendous amount of work. I would do it as a favour, but only if there was no one else.

At that time the Catholic population was about 10,000 souls. Hardly a day went by without a death, and sometimes there were four or five in a single day. It was common, especially among the Irish, to have an evening vigil, which extended to the next day, in the room in which the deceased lay. Relatives and close friends would attend. After a few prayers, they would begin drinking and smoking until they were drunk! They would often accompany the body to the cemetery in this state, staggering along the way! I would often find myself castigating people for this outrageous behaviour and for causing a serious public scandal.

2. From 1881 Fr Sullivan had decreed that there would be communal morning meditation. But none of the priests, including himself, took part. In October 1882, when I arrived in Auckland, I discovered that our Rule was not being observed. A brother rang the bell at 5 a.m. and the other lay brothers joined him, but there was no priest to read out the text for meditation, so they could not begin. When I arrived the bell was rung at five or five-thirty. The Italian lay brothers and I meditated together, and sometimes the Irish brother joined us. The two Irish priests never came because they never retired at the proper time, but about midnight. There were no communal spiritual readings, recitation of the rosary or visits to the Blessed Sacrament. In short, there was nothing to indicate monastic life. The only thing that was fixed and settled was lunch at midday and dinner in the evening!

I never went out at night, except to visit the sick. But when the other two priests knew that I had retired to my room after dinner, they went out to spend the evening with women friends until very late. The two Italian lay brothers often told me that the servant, the Irish lay brother and the two fathers secretly drank alcohol together, and sometimes got drunk. I didn't believe this criticism because I had never seen them drinking or inebriated. I couldn't have, since I retired to my room after dinner to read or study, and I didn't go out again. At ten, I went to bed.

The others then went out, returning about eleven for drinks in Fr Downey's room. Br Adalbert claimed that he didn't drink alcohol. In fact, at lunch he didn't even drink beer, like the others. But in the evening, he secretly drank whisky, rum, wine, etc., because he had the key to the cellar. The other brothers often saw him tipsy. In reality, our Newton presbytery was more like an ordinary household than a monastery because there was no observance of the Rule or even normal priestly conduct. The two lay brothers set a much better example than the priests. I am saddened to have to make these criticisms of my confrères, but the truth must be told. It must be acknowledged that if a person does not serve God as he should, his works will not find favour with Him. This will be evidenced in due course.

3. I mentioned earlier, that shortly after Fr Sullivan's arrival in Auckland, he set about buying houses and sections near St Benedict's. Naturally, the parishioners got to know about the purchases. A rumour spread that the Benedictines were wealthy because they could buy properties. I minded my own business in Gisborne and Auckland, and was thus unaware of the secret purchases. Mr Patrick Brophy, however, as mentioned elsewhere, apprised me of the situation. One day I went to the Deeds Office and asked to examine titles on Newton properties. The fee was a shilling a search. One property, I found, had cost £600, for which he paid £100 and had taken out a £500 mortgage. He bought another for £450, paid £50, leaving a mortgage of £400. The other titles I examined were similarly mortgaged. I had never come across anything so bizarre in my life. No one in his right mind would buy a house and section without paying most of the purchase price! I wrote to the general about it. He replied that Fr Sullivan made the purchase on behalf of investors. I replied that it seemed odd to me that his name still appeared on the titles. Nor could I see that he had the money because he had paid hardly any capital. Apparently, the general wrote to Fr Sullivan instructing him not to make purchases in his own name, to avoid scandal.

4. One evening, about midnight, there was a knock at my door. I woke up, exclaiming, 'What's the matter?'

The Irish brother replied, 'Fr O'Gara is very ill. Come and help him!'

I immediately got up, threw my robes on and rushed to his room. I was puzzled why he had called for me and not Fr Downey, his confessor and close friend. He had very little time for me and I knew from others that he made critical comments about me. The explanation could be that he would have asked for Fr Downey, but he probably thought he was too drunk to come. Because he was so ill, he had called for me instead. When I entered his room, I found Fr O'Gara sprawled on the floor. He had vomited into a basin and on the floor. The lay brother had tried to clean it up. There was a nauseous stench of brandy in the room and the drunkard was as white as a sheet. He was moaning about a sore stomach from something he'd eaten, but that was a lie. However, the vomiting had helped him. My sense of smell was never sharp, but the horrible stench of alcohol fouled the room, nearly making me retch.

'What's this horrible smell of brandy?' I exclaimed. 'You've been drinking, haven't you?'

The lay brother immediately replied, 'No, the poor man felt sick and I gave him a tot of brandy to settle his stomach, but he threw that up, too!'

'One tot wouldn't cause this stench!'

Noticing that having vomited up what he had drunk he was now reasonably comfortable, I said, 'He's got rid of the alcohol and doesn't need my help any more. He'll be more careful next time.' I said goodnight and went back to bed.

5. I had been in Auckland about a year when one day the good Mr Brophy asked me in confidence, 'Father, nearly every week at St Benedict's they get a case of brandy, whisky, rum and expensive imported wine from me. How do they manage to drink it all?'

'My dear Brophy,' I replied in astonishment, 'this is the first time I've heard of these goings-on in our presbytery. That's not how monks normally behave. Only on major feast days like Christmas or Easter would those partial to it imbibe a small glassful with their post-prandial coffee. Outside these occasions, wine or spirits of any kind are not drunk in the community. The only alcoholic beverage consumed is half a litre of local beer each with meals.'

Brophy then went on, 'So what happens to all this liquor, then?'

'I've never seen any crates or bottles, and I haven't been shown any accounts, so I can't explain it. I suppose they drink it secretly at night.'

'They couldn't possibly drink so much. In three months they've bought eighty pounds' worth, which I gave them at cost price. They still said they couldn't afford it!'

When Brophy, who was a fine, reputable man who cared about us, told me the horrible news, I was shocked and disgusted with my confrères. I didn't say anything to them, however, because I knew they would deny it. I asked the Italian lay brothers for confirmation if they drank secretly.

'Indeed they do, and how! They're often drunk! You just wouldn't believe us!'

'I certainly do now.' I mentioned what Brophy had told me, which was no news to them. Br Samuele told me that a few months previously he found two bottles in the stables which had been hidden by the servant. This proved there was secret drinking going on. I angrily realised that my confrères were drinking to excess. I could see that if things continued like this, the Benedictine mission in New Zealand would collapse amid scandal. The blame lay with Fr Sullivan, who had neither observed nor enforced the Rule, and he now had drunken, incompetent advisers. Furthermore, he had placed his trust in Br Adalbert, who was a real rogue, completely duping him. And he gave him a free hand because he thought he was a real saint!

6. St Benedict's had four main sources of income:
1) Collections at Sunday Mass and vespers. They averaged £20 (500 francs) a week;
2) Christmas and Easter dues. At these times it is customary for British Catholics to have special collections for the clergy. A committee member was appointed to collect the offerings at the church door. He would write down each contributor's name with the amount donated. The list would then be read out from the altar at the end of the service. At St Benedict's, between £1200 and £1500 were collected at Christmas, and between £800 and £1000 at Easter, a total of between £2000 and £2700.
3) Special Mass requests. Very few came from Europe. Auckland parishioners averaged two or three a day at about five shillings a request. The annual return based on an average of two a day at five shillings each would be £182 10s.
4) Baptisms, marriages and funerals. There were between two and three baptisms a week. Parishioners, though generally poor, seldom gave less than ten shillings. The well-off, however, gave £1, £2 or even £3. Allowing for 100 baptisms a year, the average income would be £100 or 2500 francs. On average there were never fewer than forty marriages a year. Offerings varied between £2 and £5, according to people's means. At an average of £2 per wedding, income was £80 or 2000 francs per annum. Burials, including children's, for a population of 10,000 Catholics averaged at least one a day. Usually a simple Mass, rather than a solemn Requiem Mass, was celebrated. The offering for children of poor parents was five shillings, and ten shillings for the others. For adults it varied from ten shillings to a pound, according to the family's circumstances. At an average of a funeral a day at seven shillings per burial, annual income from this source was £122, or 3050 francs.

Summary of income:	£	s
1. Sunday collections	1040	
2. Christmas and Easter dues	2000	
3. Masses for special intentions	182	10
4. Baptisms per annum	100	
5. Marriages per annum	80	
6. Burials per annum	122	
Total income	3524	

or 88,112 francs*

These figures are only approximate because our priests never showed me the accounts of income and expenditure, which they kept secret between themselves and Fr Sullivan. However, I was able to get verbal confirmation of the Sunday collection, dues and special intention figures from them. The other figures I gleaned partly from the priests, lay brothers and the committee. The reader may well be astonished at the large amount of income, a figure I have not exaggerated. Two factors, however, need to be mentioned. The New Zealand currency was practically valueless. A pound, which had a value of twenty-five francs, would be worth only five francs in Italy. Second, Catholics held us in very high regard and hence were exceedingly generous.

7. Our usual expenses were for food, clothing, laundry, etc. These were not too high because local produce was reasonably priced. I couldn't get exact costs from the priests, having to resort to the lay brothers for information. Our meals consisted of coffee, milk, bread and butter for breakfast. At lunch we had soup, meat and vegetables, dessert, cheese or fruit, bread and half a litre of local beer. Supper consisted of a meat dish, fruit or cheese, bread and half a litre of beer. This was our normal fare except for Fridays and other fast days. There were very few days when we didn't eat meat. Prime quality meat cost sixteen Italian soldi or eighty centimes a kilogram. Lower grade cost sixty centimes. Butter, lard and cheese cost three francs a kilo each. Coal and coke were abundant and cheap. Beer cost just under four francs a gallon (the equivalent of five litres). There were seven of us, comprising three priests, three lay brothers and a servant. I wouldn't have thought that food and fuel together would have cost, on average, more than four francs a head per day, but to be generous, let me allow five francs a day, or thirty-five francs in total.

* Expenditure and savings total 86,112 francs not 88,112 francs.

Total annual expenditure:

provisions	12,775 francs
servant's wages, 25 francs per day	1,300 francs
upkeep of horses, 6 francs a day	2,190 francs
clerical suits	2,500 francs
personal and presbytery laundry at 40 francs per week	2,080 francs
household goods and kitchen equipment	10,000 francs
sundries	12,000 francs
Total expenditure	42,845 francs

This was an enormous amount for a small community, even in New Zealand, with only one member paid an income. In Gisborne, Br Ricci and I didn't spend more than 4000 francs altogether for food, clothing, laundry, etc. Even so, we ate better than at Newton, and on major feast days we enjoyed a bottle of good wine costing between six and ten francs.

Balance:

annual income	88,112 francs
annual expenditure	42,845 francs
net savings	43,267 francs *
(cash or deposits)	

Were the savings in a safe or at the bank? Frankly, neither. I tried to get the truth out of Frs Downey and O'Gara, who were in charge in Fr Sullivan's absence, but got nowhere. They told me they didn't even have enough money to pay the monthly bills! One day Fr O'Gara admitted they made a lot of money every month, but Fr Sullivan had collected it and its whereabouts was unknown. The lay brothers confirmed his report. At any rate, all my investigations proved fruitless. God only knows what happened to the money. Even if the four tipplers, including the servant, drank every day of the year, they couldn't have used up the 43,000 francs savings. It must have disappeared into other holes. I'll only know on Judgement Day what happened to it all. I believe that the generous donations were simply frittered away,* or even worse. They were certainly squandered, as will be revealed.

8. When Fr Sullivan, our superior, was in Auckland, he neither observed the Rule nor insisted on its observance by others. The situation was made worse by his absence. I am not just referring to the monastic life, but the daily running of the presbytery. Fr Sullivan's confidants were Fr Downey, and to a lesser extent, Fr O'Gara, who was deemed less discreet. The other monks were disregarded. They weren't sycophants and would not hesitate to speak their

---

* In the original text *'andava in sacculum pertusum'* (Latin), which would have a more literal meaning of 'slipping through the net'.

mind, even if Fr Sullivan wouldn't like it. But this was the spirit our Rule required. Fr Sullivan confided fully only in Fr Downey, knowing he would agree to everything he said. I regarded it as a matter of conscience to inform the general and procurator-general about what was happening in Newton. Dom Nicola Canevello, our general, however, trusted Fr Sullivan implicitly and regarded our English fathers as saints. He simply did not believe my reports! If we had had a good superior, the Rule would have been observed and suitably adapted to missionary conditions as elsewhere. There would not have been presbytery parties or nocturnal visits, dinner engagements, soirées and carousing. The Rule would have been observed and our superior would have provided an example. Instead, the monks did as they pleased. When Fr Sullivan was in Auckland, he was the first to go out at night, and when he returned from Sydney, he continued his old tricks. With a good superior, the mission would have prospered to the parishioners' edification. It would have had God's blessing and the support of the faithful. But when they saw how lax things were, they lost their respect for the monks.

Under a competent superior, the finances would have been healthy. There would have been sufficient money to buy a large piece of land and build a presbytery. With 40,000 francs per annum and the contributions of other missions, about 60,000 francs per annum could have been put aside. Instead, in four years (with Fr Sullivan in charge for three), not a penny was saved! Frs Fox and Augustine Luck, both devout monks and able missionaries, were appalled how St Benedict's was run. They kept well away and didn't show up at Newton unless summoned, to avoid censure. Personally, I was most distressed to find myself in the middle of such a nightmare. I also had to suffer the disapproval of three of my confrères, including the Irish lay brother. How often I rued not being in Gisborne, in the midst of such wonderful people who cherished me and whom I had worked devotedly for, or that I couldn't simply get away from Auckland!

9. Even though our general paid little heed to my letters, I diligently continued to inform him of my discoveries. He placed more faith in Fr Sullivan and the excuses and denials of others. In our correspondence around 1883–1884, he wrote that my reports were 'very exaggerated, with little foundation'. I denied this, replying that I never lied, and time would prove me right. I concluded, saying: 'I have written about these matters to relieve my conscience and for no other reason. From henceforth I will not mention or write another word about the mission's affairs. I have already said too much, and the time has come now for me to be silent. Rest assured, Your Reverence, that I will mention nothing more.'

The procurator-general, however, believed my reports and deplored the deterioration that had occurred. In a letter dated 29 October 1883, he wrote: 'Our Order cannot accept responsibility for the diocese or the mission.'

This decision was a vindication of the collapse I had described, and a portent of the Benedictines' eventual abandonment of the Auckland mission.

CHAPTER EIGHT

Missionary Life
(1882 TO 1885)

PART 1. ITALIANS IN NEW ZEALAND

SUMMARY. – 1. Italians abroad; shameful characteristics. – 2. Italians in New Zealand and Auckland. – 3. Mostly fishermen from Southern Italy. – 4. Marriage of two Tyrolean Italians in Gisborne. – 5. I search out Italians in Auckland. – 6. Summoned to attend a seriously ill Italian woman. – 7. Why I didn't want to be identified as an Italian in Africa or New Zealand.

1. People who migrate to America or the colonies do so to better their financial position, and, ideally, make their fortune. Italians do this in their own special way. While they do very well and earn good money, they generally cry poor. To save money, they scrimp on food and education, dress shoddily and live rough. Generosity is not a typical trait of Italians abroad. They rarely contribute a penny to the Church or the priest's upkeep. But they're not shy to seek his help. Many indulge in gambling and drinking and squander considerable amounts of money in pubs. Italians, in general, are disliked and even despised by the British, who consider them an inferior race, only slightly better than the Chinese, because they lack education and manners and are too brash. But a worse feature is their moral and religious torpor. In Italy most people carry out their religious duties, but Italian migrants cease attending church after a few months. Most then abandon their religion and obligations. Their faith slowly erodes. After anything between six and fifteen years, they return home with plenty of money in their pockets, but leaving behind them in their adopted country the last vestiges of their faith. The majority then scandalise the good local folk with their scorn for religion and ridicule for churchgoers. They are a thousand times worse than Protestants! It disturbs me to be so critical of my compatriots, but I have to speak the truth. Some do remain virtuous practitioners and return home the good Catholics they were when they left, but they are few and far between.

2. There were not many Italians in New Zealand when I was there. According to the 1876 census, there were 300 throughout the colony, including those from the Italian Tyrol, Trieste and Istria. According to mine and other priests' reckoning, there were about sixty Italians in the Auckland area. There was a certain Amodeo from Trieste, who had an Irish wife and several children. He was captain of a New Zealand shipping company steamer. He and his family

were excellent Catholics. There was also a Genoan who had been living in the colony for several years. He had a well-known, very successful bakery. Eventually he retired to live off his savings. He had one daughter, and his wife had died some years previously. They too were fine, generous Catholics.* Most of the other Italians were Southerners. Some had changed their names, perhaps because they had been in trouble with the Italian authorities and wished to avoid discovery. They never, or hardly ever, came to church or the sacraments. In general, apart from the two families mentioned above, they were extremely negligent of their religion, some even becoming Protestants. They mostly lived in the poorest, most disreputable areas. They frequently changed home, never telling the priest their address. In a town of 65,000 people, scattered far and wide, it was practically impossible to find them.

3. The great majority of Neapolitans and Calabrians were fishermen. They were employed by a company which supplied fresh and smoked fish to city shops and exported smoked and dried fish. The company provided its own boating and fishing equipment. Fishermen were paid £4 a week, regardless of the catch. But they had to provide their own food and clothing. They also had to transport the fish to smokehouses late at night or in the morning. The men, however, made their wives and children do the job. They would go to the nearest pub to drink and gamble away most of their money, leaving their family in misery. Poorly clad wives and children toiled and sweated, particularly on winter nights, to get the fish in. They often contracted bronchitis, while the menfolk were wasting their money in dockside pubs. Their homes were rude, squalid and spartan, with no comforts. Because of the men's drunkenness and gambling, misery reigned supreme. If it wasn't for their vices, with the good wages they earned they could have lived comfortably and been able to save half their income. Food was cheap and second-grade beef cost only twenty centimes a kilogram.

4. Two Italian workers from Trent in the Tyrol came to Gisborne in May or June 1882. After a couple of weeks they visited me, saying they wanted to marry their young fiancées, whom they introduced me to. They told me that they had previously worked in Gisborne from 1877 to 1879, but because of the shortage of work they went to Napier. They returned to Gisborne because there was now little work in Napier. They showed me their papers, which were in order, proving they were free to marry. I told them that if they wished to have a dispensation from the banns they would have to pay the church office in Auckland a fee of £3 each. They said they were poor and had been unemployed for a long time and didn't even have enough money to rent a house. I told them

* Vaggioli, a northern Italian, born in Tuscany, may be here betraying a prejudice against his southern compatriots!

that if they didn't pay, they would have to wait for the publication of the banns. They kept on making excuses.

To be quite frank, I didn't believe the story about their so-called poverty. I knew that even labourers like themselves were paid at least ten francs a day. I also was aware that they were not gamblers or drinkers. Hence they must have had the money. I told them that if they didn't pay the fee, they would not be given a dispensation and I wouldn't be able to marry them. They repeated their story and begged for a free dispensation, adding that if this was refused them, they would be forced to marry in a registry office. I understood they had told the Napier parish priest the same story. He knew them well, was unsympathetic, and stood his ground. Hence they came to Gisborne to try their luck on me, thinking that being an Austrian subject* I would be sympathetic to their situation. I took a similar stand, however. Nevertheless, I also took into consideration that they had brought their fiancées with them. They claimed that they were lodging separately in an hotel, but perhaps they were already cohabiting. I wanted to prevent sinning, so the sooner they were wed the better. I said to them, 'I'll write to the vicar-general for a dispensation. I'm not too hopeful, but I'll do my best.'

I farewelled the two young men, telling them to return the following week for a reply. I then questioned the women on their own, confirming they were happy to marry them. They were sisters. I asked them how they could marry poor men, without a penny to their names. They said that they weren't poor at all, but had had many expenses setting up house because they hadn't brought anything from Napier. I wrote to the vicar-general explaining the situation, and asking for a free dispensation of banns since they were poor labourers. He agreed to my request. I celebrated the marriages. Not only did they not give me a penny, but they had the cheek to ask me for assistance! I did no such thing, knowing they were not as poor as they claimed. About a week afterwards, they left Gisborne, and I never saw them again. I imagine they returned to Napier and to the certainty of work there!

5. In my frequent visits around Auckland, I tried to find out where there were Italians and encourage them to come to church and the sacraments. I managed to find several. They promised to come, but didn't keep their word. The few I made contact with in the Newton area acted in the same way. When I spoke to these wretched Italians, I realised that they didn't want to be pestered about their religious obligations. It was patently clear they had no interest in religion whatsoever. I also often visited impoverished Irish families, who were enormously pleased to see me. The Irish rarely neglected their religious duties.

* cf. Introduction, p. ix.

6. One morning in 1884, about 9 a.m., a twelve-year-old boy came to St Benedict's. He said that his Italian mother was ill and was asking for the Italian priest. I got the lad to accompany me since I didn't know the address. I took holy oil* and the Blessed Sacrament with me and hurried to the sick woman's home, which was on a hillside near the harbour. I found her in bed with a high fever caused by bronchitis. No one else was there. The boy soon left and did not return. Poverty and squalor were apparent everywhere. Her husband was away fishing. An English woman neighbour was kindly tending to the poor woman. She was Neapolitan, as I ascertained during our conversation. She was about thirty years old and was thin and exhausted. She looked as if she did not have long for this world. Even though she was so ill, her despicable husband forced her to keep working while he was in the pub! She said she could not go to church because of her poor clothing and not having decent shoes. Though poverty was so apparent, her husband earned 100 francs a week. She said they had enough for food but not for anything else. I comforted her as best I could. Because she was so ill I gave her Communion. I asked her to let me know, through her son, how her health was. She promised to do so, but he didn't turn up. After seven or eight days, I returned but the house was shut up. A neighbour told me she was better and out working. Another time, I was told that the family had shifted. No one knew where they were. I never saw the woman or boy again!

7. I had been considered a deserter by the newly established Italian Government because in 1865 I did not present myself for military service. This was owing to the fact that I was then a monk living in the Veneto region, which was still under Austrian rule.† This unjust law, contrary to canon law and previous governments' legislation, angered me so much that I decided to migrate rather than live under an injustice. Moreover, my fellow monks and I were very attached to Francis V, Duke of Modena, who governed his small state like a real father. The Masons and their ilk detested him, however, because he ruled in accordance with human and divine justice. I was also aware that the new Italian state was the work of Masons and similar societies which hated God, the Catholic Church and God-fearing citizens. It had been established through murder, robbery and plunder. Its main aim was to strip the Papal States, churches and religious houses of their goods in order to satisfy its grasping, revolutionary members. How could I, as a true Italian and monk, embrace a godless government, the persecutor and despoiler of everything I held sacred and precious? It was, and continues to be, unthinkable. I thus migrated to Austrian territory and sought Austrian citizenship, without renouncing my native land. As a missionary, however, I never mentioned that I was Italian because generally the Italian

* For the anointing of the sick, a ritual practice.
† cf. Introduction, p. xi.

consuls were prominent Masons. They would have given me no support and, in fact, would have made my life difficult, even though I had citizenship through Cittanova in Istria, which geographically is part of Italy. Besides, Italians abroad did not enjoy a good reputation, as I have mentioned above. Quite frankly, I would have been ashamed to say I was Italian. I would rather have said I was a subject of the Sultan of Turkey. I thus declared I was an Austrian subject. I must admit that up to the present, I have had no reason to regret my decision. I am still ashamed of the new Italy, my fatherland, because the government hates, despises and despoils the Catholic Church and the Papacy through its creation of detestable, secular education. It rules 35 million people, two-thirds of whom have been raised to curse God, the Virgin and the most sacred aspects of life. Every day it wrenches young people from their ancestors' faith. Through its more than 5000 socialist teachers, it sows impiety, immorality, theft, murder of innocent people and other horrible crimes. I weep for my fatherland as it heads towards ruin, anarchy, earthly and eternal destruction, mainly because of its Masonic, godless government.

PART 2. THE MASONIC MOVEMENT IN NEW ZEALAND

SUMMARY. – 1. Origins of Masonry. – 2. Masonry in New Zealand. – 3. English, American and colonial Masons' deceit. – 4. Masonry as an international conspiracy. – 5. Mason-biased articles in the New Zealand press, including the Catholic newspapers. – 6. My rejoinder; debating the issue!

1. Masons claim that their sect had its origins at the time of Solomon and was developed by the Templars. Its antecedent spirit, however, can be traced to Lucifer's rebellion against God and the sin of Cain; that is, to the beginning of time. Its actual foundation as a society dates from 1717, and it was first practised in London about 1722. Its founders were English Jews who, like Jews everywhere, loathe Christ the Redeemer, whom they wanted to restore the kingdom of Israel. Instead, He came into the world to establish a kingdom of divine love. They equally hated the Church He founded. They established their satanic society with its vile rites and evil oaths to wage ruthless war against the Church and to exterminate it if possible. They called their new anti-Christian sect the *Freemasons*, in contrast to the Masons in Europe who had formed a society building churches and oratories. The Italian name for *Freemasons* was *Framassoni or Massoni*. They are now known simply as *Massoni*. The Jewish founders removed God's name from their society. They did not use the Hebrew expression *Jehovah*, or the Christian word *Trinity*, but the pantheistic title *Great Architect of Nature,* which is not a valid representation of God. The new society adopted rites, symbols, ceremonies and abominable oaths abusing and deriding

dogma and the Bible as well as supporting its wicked aim of destroying Catholicism. This was done covertly through formulae and arcane rituals designed to dupe ingenuous recruits. Thus those admitted to the junior levels of the society were unaware of its true aims.

A few years later, it was divided into three main branches, the largest being the Scottish. But they still constituted a single society with the same purpose: namely, war on Christ and His Church. The numerous influential Jews infiltrated English Protestant society. Through promises of material reward, they recruited a large number of Protestants, while reassuring them that Masons were free to follow their individual beliefs. The sect soon spread throughout England and crossed the Channel. Rationalist French philosophers were among the first to join up. Masonry quickly penetrated every country in Europe. The British then planted the society in America, India and their other colonies. Eventually it reached New Zealand and other areas in the Pacific the British had contact with.

2. By the first half of the nineteenth century Masonry was very powerful in England and the British Government was under its control, with its Prime Minister, Lord Palmerston, a grand master. By 1845, although there were only about 3000 British and Americans in New Zealand, it appears that a Masonic lodge was already established in the Bay of Islands. By 1880 Masons were well represented at every level, from the Governor to the lowest level of Protestant society. The four main towns of Auckland, Wellington, Christchurch and Dunedin had several lodges, each with a chapter and grand council. Every township, district and settlement had well-supported lodges. There were Masons even among the natives! By 1880 there were more than one hundred lodges throughout the colony, with a European population of still only about 550,000. They were branches of the original English society, while following the Scottish rite. There were also a few women's lodges. I could not ascertain the number of Masons in the colony, because they did not publish their figures. I believe there would not have been fewer than 70,000. The majority were Protestants, but the ringleaders were mostly Jews. The few Catholic Masons were mostly French or Italian. Many Protestant ministers were also in their ranks. Every lodge had as chaplain a Protestant minister. None of the hundred Catholic priests in New Zealand were members.

3. English, American and colonial Masons claim that theirs is simply a benevolent society, unconcerned about religion. This is a smoke-screen to fool new recruits and disguise satanic aims. Around 1884 or 1885 a clear example surfaced in Auckland, showing that English Masons did not recognise religions other than their own. Their leaders asked the city council for a block of land for their own cemetery. The public was informed prior to the council meeting. The request generated much discussion throughout the town because it was a

demonstration that Masons did have their own religion. It also provoked correspondence in the local papers as to why Masons no longer wanted to be buried in the Protestant cemetery. Because of the controversy, the Masons decided to withdraw their request and not alienate the majority of their irate members.

4. In New Zealand, as elsewhere, Masonry was not simply a benevolent society but a politically inspired movement, clandestinely forming a ruling body within the government, even exercising absolute control. While its agenda was the annihilation of religion, particularly Catholicism, it subtly exercised its power over MHRs and members of the Legislative Council through the promulgation of despicable laws aimed at the destruction of the place of religion in family life and society. Masons wanted to impose secular state education and they approved of divorce. They occupied the best positions in the colonial government, councils and boroughs, wanting both wealth and control. No one in New Zealand, including Protestants, could gain a well-paid government or local body position unless they became a Mason. Bosses would openly say this to applicants and it was common knowledge.

One incident in Auckland in 1885 will suffice to illustrate this point. I had the story from a Protestant applicant for a position. The twenty-six-year-old man applied for a position at the agricultural inspector's office. Applicants had to present their qualifications and sit an examination. He met with Masons who promised him the position if he joined up. He replied that he did not want to be bound to any society, that he loved his freedom and had no intention of compromising it. If he was not the best applicant, he would be happy not to be accepted, but if he was the most suitable, he should in all fairness be appointed. The Masons told him that they knew he was the best applicant. In fact he was the only one qualified for the position, but he would not get it unless he joined. The young man steadfastly refused. More than two months previously he had submitted documentation pertaining to the completion of diplomas in agricultural theory from English universities as well as suitable diplomas from other institutes. The Masons were well aware of this. He then waited for the examination day. The other applicants had no such qualifications and everyone recognised that the young man should get the position. In the examination he gave splendid evidence of his theoretical and practical knowledge, even to the amazement of the examiners. The others' results showed their complete ignorance and inability. The Masons made a final attempt to get the upright young man to enter their detestable society, assuring him he would be appointed if he accepted. He replied that the examiners had to appoint the best applicant in accordance with the regulations, that being a Mason would not equip him better for the position, and that he was bound to no one. The upshot was that the Masons, who were behind the committee, rejected him and appointed an ignorant fellow-Mason to the position! The poor man did not deserve such treatment. He was a luckless young victim, unaware of the fact that Masons controlled the government and everything else to their own advantage.

5. In 1884 the French Masons officially decided in their great council not to recognise the existence of God. English and colonial Masons were startled and dismayed at their decision and wrote lengthy articles criticising it. They went so far as to say that British Masons should separate themselves from their French confrères, and that the Masonic Order had until then upheld belief in a supreme being (who was, however, according to their description the Great Architect of Nature, not God as we would recognise Him). It was curious to see the Masons' agitation and their espousal of God when it was patently obvious to those who knew even little about them, that they did not believe in a personal God. Masonic leaders stirred up their ignorant colleagues' agitation against the French Order because they were afraid that ingenuous members' eyes would be opened and they would abandon the society en masse.

Someone even wrote an article in the *New Zealand Freeman's Journal,* the Catholic newspaper, that English Masonry believed in God and admitted Christians as members, leaving them free to follow their own beliefs. The article concluded that it was different from the French and other continental versions. I couldn't find out the author, but I imagine it was a Mason, determined to set a decoy for guileless Catholics. I asked the editor of the paper why he had published the article. He said he could see no harm in it. I informed him that it was a tissue of lies intended to dupe the public and Catholics, and encourage them to enter the society. He told me that he knew nothing about the Masons and had published it in good faith. After my comments he regretted doing so. I asked him to allow me to reply and set things right, which he agreed to.

6. I then wrote an article which took up a column and a half in the paper. I warned Catholics not to believe in the Anglo-Saxons' claims that their society was different from that of their continental brothers. I then demonstrated that all Masonic lodges were offshoots of English Masonry, their parent body. I pointed out that its leaders were mostly Jews who hated all religions, especially Christianity. I further proved that English lodges were in league with all others, sharing the same secrets, symbols, ceremonies, oaths and aims. French Masons simply had expressed the logical intentions of English Masonry's principles. I also said that the Great Architect of Nature was nothing more for Masons than the force of nature, expressed as the 'generative force' by one of its leaders! That's how the Masons see God! What a horrible blasphemy and shameful insult to humanity.

My article struck a raw nerve among Auckland's Masons. One of them wrote a brief reply, which was printed. He did not have the courage to sign it. It had only his initials and Masonic rank, which simply revealed that he was a master Mason, and therefore belonging to the fourth grade. He maintained that Masonry was a benevolent society, insisting that it admitted members of any religion and that they were free to hold and practise their own beliefs, while Masonry in Europe was the opposite, etc.

I replied to his article, stating that I felt sorry for him because he too had been duped, that a Mason of the fourth grade could not know the society's true aims and intentions, that he would need to ascend much higher to learn the truth, and that should he climb even another thirty grades he would still have only a glimmering of understanding. It was true that Masonry was a benevolent society. Since its members controlled government and attained the best positions, their subscriptions enriched their lodges. They then used their secret funds for political ends, to gain worldwide dominion and carry out their underhand, clandestine intention of destroying religion. English Masonry, it is true, showed a greater tolerance towards its members' religious beliefs than its continental colleagues did. But it did so simply to increase its membership and deter members from leaving. Masonry, in fact, did not respect religion. This could clearly be seen by its assiduous efforts to break up families by imposing divorce and secular education, denying religious instruction to children in government schools in order to raise up generations without faith or morality, to promote promiscuity and encourage men and women to mate like animals. The master Mason realised that this Italian monk had more than a sniff of what was in the Masons' pot. He decided it would be prudent not to ply his pen again in case even worse things about his society were revealed.

PART 3. A TRACT IN SUPPORT OF THE CONGREGATION FOR THE PROPAGATION OF THE FAITH

SUMMARY. – 1. The Italian Government's decision to despoil the Sacred Congregation. – 2. The Congregation petitions bishops and missionaries throughout the world to protest against the injustice. – 3. At the bishop's request, I write about thirty lengthy articles in the *Freeman*. – 4. I publish them as a single tract, to sell on behalf of the Congregation. – 5. I send copies to the cardinal prefect; his reply. – 6. I send the profits of 825 francs to the Cardinal of Sydney; his reply.

1. As soon as the Italian revolution swept through Rome, the Eternal City was proclaimed the capital of the new Italian Government and the Pope was deprived of this last remnant of his states. It was also decided to strip the Church and religious congregations of their wealth. Even the Emperor Napoleon, the great plunderer of church property in Italy and everywhere else he gained dominion, respected the property of the Sacred Congregation for the Propagation of the Faith, recognising it as a benefactor of foreign missions which it maintained through its own revenue. The new Italian Government was more grasping. It

decided to appropriate all the Congregation's fixed assets as it had done to bishop-rics and cathedral benefices throughout Italy. The Congregation opposed this move with good reason. The Holy See petitioned other governments to maintain the Congregation's autonomy, since all countries benefited from the institution. But they declared they could not interfere in the internal politics of another country.

The real reason, however, was that the major powers were linked to the Italian Masonic government and allowed international Masonry to work towards the destruction of the Catholic Church. The Congregation had developed its internationalism for religious reasons, especially for the good of heathen countries. This Napoleon had recognised. When it realised that the thieving Italian Government would not listen, the Congregation took the matter to the supreme court, but it concurred with the government, ordering the Congregation to turn over its assets.

2. The Congregation issued a circular, which it distributed to Catholic bishops throughout the world, describing the injustice it had suffered and asking them to protest to their respective governments and to their parishioners about the terrible harm the depredation would cause the Church and particularly foreign missions. Mons. Luck, Bishop of Auckland, duly received a copy. At the same time, our procurator-general sent us a copy saying that we Benedictines too should protest to Catholics about the injustice perpetrated by the Italian Government. The circular reached New Zealand during the first half of 1883, as I recall. I asked the bishop what he intended doing about the matter. He said that he would ask the two Irish fathers in Newton to write articles for the *Freeman* against the injustice. He told me that he would do it himself, but he didn't have the time. Frs Downey and O'Gara, however, declined the request on the pretext of business.

3. The bishop then turned to me, asking me to write in support of the Congregation. I pointed out to him that I didn't have a good command of English. He said that the editor of the paper would revise my articles and correct any mistakes. I accepted the task and immediately set to work. This was towards the end of 1883. I proposed to write a number of articles and collect them in booklet form to sell on behalf of the Congregation. I can't recall exactly how many articles I wrote for the *Freeman*. There would have been at least twenty or so. I began with the court's decision and showed how the usurping government's injustice not only violated the congregation's rights, but that of the Holy See, causing havoc to our missions, especially those in heathen lands. I then described the robberies and unfair treatment suffered by the Holy See, especially in regard to the Pope's missionary endeavours. The government described itself as Catholic, but it was actually Masonic, and intent on persecuting the Church. I alluded to the confiscation of religious orders' properties and benefices. I described how an infamous law despoiled religious

orders and cast out their members, male and female, into squalor and penury.* This was done because of the government's hatred of Catholicism. Thus, hundreds of thousands of consecrated men and women were stripped of everything and forced to fend for themselves.

4. My articles were published in 1884 in a booklet. I included Pope Leo XIII's encyclical condemning Masonry. The work ran to over a hundred pages. I gave the tract the pointed title of *Plunder No Robbery!*† The enclosed encyclical was translated into English so that English-speaking readers could learn the Catholic Church's teachings on Masonry. The bishop wrote a short preface praising the work and its subject. Two thousand copies were printed. I myself paid for the printing costs, so that the Congregation would get the maximum profit from sales. I retained one hundred copies, which I sent to various parts of Europe, including the Congregation in Rome, our monasteries and missions in India and America. I endeavoured to sell the remainder at sixpence each from the church porch at Sunday Mass. All the profits were for the Congregation for the Propagation of the Faith.

5. I sent three or four copies of the work to His Eminence, the Cardinal Prefect of the Congregation. He sent me the following reply:

Secretariat
Congregation for the Propagation of the Faith
Ref. No. 4686
Rome, 25 October 1884

Dear Father,
I wish to sincerely thank you for your kind consideration in not only defending the cause of our Sacred Congregation in the press, but also for taking the time to collect and publish your articles as a work, and for sending the money from sales to help the Congregation. I have not yet had the opportunity to peruse the booklet, but I certainly wish to acknowledge the goodwill behind it. I trust the Lord will give you the rewards you so richly deserve.

Yours etc.,
p.p.
Cardinal Giovanni Simeoni
Prefect

* The reference is to a law of 1866 which declared that almost all the religious orders and congregations should have their houses dissolved and their goods confiscated. Seminarists were also made liable to military service, as mentioned earlier by Vaggioli. cf. Denis Mack Smith, *Italy: A Modern History*, Ann Arbor 1969, p. 91.
† The Italian title is *La spogliazione non è ruberia*! which gives a clearer idea of the ironic nature of the title, literally, 'Despoiling is not theft!' The deletion of the verb in English renders the title ambiguous.

6. I tried to sell as many copies as I could while in Newton, but it took a lot of time. In January 1885, I gathered the proceeds, and from Coromandel I wrote the following letter to Cardinal Moran in Sydney:

14 February 1885

Please find enclosed an order made out to the Bank of New Zealand in Sydney for £15, to Your Eminence as a contribution to the Congregation for the Propagation of the Faith. I hope to send you the rest of the money from sales before the end of the year. Regrettably, however, seven or eight hundred copies will probably remain unsold.

Your humble servant in Christ, etc.

The cardinal's reply went as follows:

St Mary's Presbytery
Sydney
18 February

Dear Father,
I wish to thank you for the bank cheque of 15 pounds which you sent as a contribution to the Congregation. It will be a great consolation to the Holy Father to know that your work has been so efficacious, providing also material support for the missions' administration in Rome.

With every blessing,
I remain
Yours faithfully
Patrick F. Moran
Archbishop of Sydney

In November 1885 I sent Cardinal Moran a final donation of £18 from sales. Altogether I had made £33. On 20 November the cardinal replied, acknowledging receipt of the money and thanking me.

PART 4. DISCUSSION WITH A MASON

SUMMARY. – 1. I am requested to give an impromptu sermon. – 2. I preach on Masonry. – 3. I notice a strange reaction from two men in the congregation; I disregard it. – 4. Who were they? – 5. They approach a Catholic friend for information.– 6. The master Mason's manual is inaccurate; I identify the omissions. – 7. The Mason's surprise; they want a discussion. – 8. The Mason's defeat. His friend declares he will not join them.

1. One Sunday in 1884, Fr Cuthbert Downey was to preach at the 11 a.m. High Mass. Since he hadn't prepared a sermon, he asked Fr O'Gara to do it, but he refused, saying he would be preaching at vespers. While he was vesting in the sacristy, he had me called in and asked me to preach in his place, saying he wasn't feeling well. I told him he should have given me notice, not asking me at the last moment. He replied that earlier in the morning he hoped he would be able to, but now he felt ill. He added, 'You don't need to have a sermon prepared. Please just do it for me.' I reluctantly agreed.

2. While he was vesting, I opened the missal and read the Sunday Gospel, searching for a topic. Unfortunately, I couldn't find a suitable theme. I was still undecided when Mass began. Finally, it occurred to me that no one had preached in Auckland about Masonry. Not even Pope Leo XIII's recent encyclical had been read out and commented on. I therefore decided to make this the subject. I said intercessory prayers, which I always did before preaching, especially when I was unprepared, and climbed into the pulpit. The papal encyclical condemned international Masonry, and I used this in my introduction. I then elaborated on two points. The first was that Masonry throughout the world is one movement, and that there is no difference between the English and Continental versions, nor between any others. They share the same spirit. Only a few lodges openly adhered to the principles on which Masonry is based. Anglo-Saxon lodges actually recognised them, but refused to endorse them overtly so as not to cause scandal to new recruits or enquirers. Catholics were forbidden by the Pope to join the evil sect. My second point was that Masonry was not, in spite of its members' protestations, a benevolent, philanthropic society. On the contrary, I demonstrated that it was an anti-Christian, anti-religious and anti-social movement which disguised its sinister purposes by distributing offices to the benefit of its members. Its real aim was the destruction of all traces of religion in people and society at large. To achieve this it had instituted divorce, set up secular education and liberalism and encouraged hedonism. I mentioned that its evil intentions were known to only a very few high-ranking Masons who took awful oaths. If a person did not keep them, he would be spirited away or put to death. I exhorted them to steer well clear of such a pestilential organisation.

3. The 11 a.m. Sunday Mass and vespers were sung by our excellent choir, using the works of famous composers. Many Protestants also attended the services, attracted by the beautiful music. They behaved very respectfully in church and I swear they could have been taken for Catholics in their following of the service. During my sermon, on the right side of the central nave, I noticed a thick-set man about forty years old who every so often tugged the elbow of his neighbour and pointed his finger at me, drawing his attention to my words. The other man was lean and bearded, and about thirty-five years of age. He seemed annoyed and uncomfortable. At first he stared at me, then lowered his gaze and didn't look up again. No one noticed and I disregarded them. I assumed that, being Protestants, they hadn't heard Masonry being commented on, and weren't too happy about it. That didn't stop me continuing my exposition. My sermon lasted about forty-five minutes, an unusual length for me. Normally I didn't preach for more than thirty minutes.

4. I learnt later from an Irish Catholic who was an acquaintance of theirs that one was a master Mason, and the other his close friend. The Mason, though married, was a filthy, dissolute libertine. I did know him because some good young Catholic women told me he had tried to seduce them on several occasions, but they had bravely rebutted the Mason pig's lascivious advances. Some Protestant women, however, acquiesced, but made him pay handsomely for their favours and the dissolute man was always in debt.

He had borrowed £24,000 (600,000 francs) from his Protestant friend, telling him he would be repaid when he sold land he owned on the North Shore. He said it was worth twice the amount of the debt, whereas it wouldn't match a third of the amount owed. For some time the Mason had badgered his friend to join up, but he hesitated, needing to know the society's aims. Under continuing pressure, he eventually agreed, on condition he got some of his money back. The Mason, in fact, had no money, but urged his friend to become a Mason immediately, saying that he would then be repaid. The Mason was motivated by self-interest. He believed that if he succeeded in getting his friend into the society, he could avoid repaying him. This was because if his creditor joined, he could not have recourse to legal remedies for the payment of a debt from a fellow Mason. He could only approach the society, which would protect a master Mason. The creditor was unaware of this factor.

5. When they came out of church, the non-Mason told his companion that he wanted to talk to the preacher, whom he saw as being very knowledgeable about Masonry. His friend protested, declaring I knew nothing and that anything I said about them was untrue. He insisted, however, stating that I couldn't have said what I did without knowing something about the subject. The Mason took his friend to an Irish Catholic who lived two hundred metres from the church.

They asked him my name and who I was, etc. He mentioned my name and that I was Italian. The Mason then said, 'These foreigners are very shrewd, but they don't know anything about Masonry and the fact that it is a benevolent, philanthropic society.'

The Catholic replied that he didn't know anything about the organisation himself, but if I had spoken against it, I would know what I was talking about, and he would believe me. The Mason's friend was determined to hear my explanation. The Mason tried to dissuade him, but he became more insistent, saying, 'The preacher must know something about Masonry, and I won't become one until I've heard what he thinks about them.'

The Mason told the Catholic that to convince him of Masonry's benevolent aims he would bring him their manual.

'You can read it yourself. You'll find nothing objectionable in it.' He then added, 'I'll return for it tomorrow. Make sure you don't give it to anyone else. My friend here is familiar with the contents. Judge for yourself. You'll see there's nothing wrong with Masonry.'

The Mason brought the manual to the Catholic about 6 p.m. He said he would collect it about ten the next day.

6. The Irish Catholic leafed through the roughly fifty-page booklet, not making a lot of its description of ceremonies, oaths, warnings to secrecy and sentences with parts missing. The good man, not knowing what to think about it, came to me and told me what had happened. He asked me for an explanation. I picked it up and leafed through it. Then I said, 'It only describes the first four grades of the Masonic ritual, because the man who gave it to you has only reached the fourth grade, that is, he is just a master Mason, able to preside over a lodge. The manual would have been given to him when he was initiated into this rank. However, it has gaps and is incomplete. There are many sentences and many words missing, especially regarding the taking of oaths, which is a vital part of the ritual. In this booklet, they are only indicated by dots.' I showed him.

'In the meantime, leave the manual with me. This evening I'll complete some of the missing sentences. Come back about 8 a.m. tomorrow and I'll return it to you with my additions.' The Irishman was very pleased with the idea. He thanked me and left. That evening I copied out the missing sentences from a complete manual I had purchased a month before. Or rather, just about half a dozen, as there were more than fifteen uncompleted sentences in the booklet. I filled out those especially regarding oath-taking, indicating the correct page and line in the manual. I wrote, 'After phrase such and such the following words are missing,' and I would supply the complete text. The following morning the Irishman returned. I handed him the booklet and my piece of paper with additions, saying, 'When the Mason comes to collect the booklet, tell him that because you couldn't understand the contents, you brought it to me. As soon as

I glanced at it, I told you it was a manual which covered only up to the fourth grade, and that he was only a master Mason of this grade, who would know little about the true nature of Masonry. Even worse, the rituals and oaths are often uncompleted. Although he says I know nothing about Masonry, I know more than him even though I've never been one. To prove it I've written on this sheet of paper five additions missing in the manual. When he reads them he'll see that they are the actual words he swore on his initiation. Give it to him and tell him once and for all that I'm not the ignoramus and liar he has made me out to be.' The Irishman happily said he would do as I suggested.

7. At 10 a.m. the Mason and his Protestant friend arrived at the Irish Catholic's home. The Mason asked him if he had read the booklet. He replied in the way I had suggested to him. He then gave him my piece of paper with the missing words of the ritual. The Mason was stunned and speechless. When he read what I had added, his face went white. 'What a cunning foreigner!' he exclaimed. His friend, though, was now even more determined to meet me. The Mason said he did not want a debate or discussion with me, but the other man said he wanted to hear my views before making a decision about joining. The Mason had to give in. They sent the Irishman to ask me if we could all meet. I agree to do this for the friend's sake and said they could come to the presbytery the following Thursday between 7 and 10 p.m. My invitation was accepted. Towards evening, the Mason sent me a message through the Irishman requesting a meeting with me on his own the same day. I replied that I would only see him with his friend. Consequently, the meeting did not eventuate. The reader may well be wondering why essential details are omitted from Masonic manuals. The reason is that Masons are afraid that a profane person – that is, a non-Mason – would get their hands on the rituals and publicise the secret rites, or that when a Mason died the secret rituals might fall into non-Mason hands and be revealed. That is why the manuals contain deliberate omissions.

8. At 7 p.m. on Thursday, the Irishman and the two other men came to the presbytery. After an exchange of greetings and pleasantries the parishioner departed and we three sat in the parlour for a discussion. The Mason wanted to show that Masonry was a well-intentioned, benevolent society with no sinister motives. He began by praising Catholicism, saying that he supported it, that he was a churchgoer himself, etc. When I realised that he was evading the question, I interrupted him, saying, 'Leave Catholicism out of this. That's not the point at issue. Prove that Masonry is the good organisation you say it is. I'll then disprove it.'

Brought up sharp, he said that Masonry helped its members with money and employment, and supported its members' orphans and widows.

'Yes,' I replied, 'you're right, but they hate non-Masons and certainly don't help them. This is contrary to the will of God. He commands that everyone is loved and that people help one another as best they can. Masons don't help non-members, whom they regard as profane, even if they are their own relatives.'

I cited various examples of Masons helping their brother Masons, even at the risk of their own lives, while they excluded non-members, even when it would have been easy for them to lend a hand. He had no answer.

'An authentic society,' I continued, 'would want people to know its aims, intentions, methods, rules and every detail. Masonry, however, keeps things secret even from its members, which is a sign that it is afraid of the light, and that its aims are evil and antisocial. If its intentions were good, it would let people know them so as to gain members. Not doing this is proof that its aims are actually evil, anti-social and anti-Christian.'

I then proved in detail how Masons helped one another through deceit and injustice, bribing judges, government officials, magistrates and clerks, to get off offences and obtain positions and offices even though the applicants were incompetent. Non-members were passed over, demonstrating a continual flagrant social injustice. I further proved that Masons, through their abhorrent oaths, were compelled to conceal colleagues' skulduggery, even if it ran to murder, treason, etc. The Mason vehemently denied this. I replied, 'I'm sorry if you haven't been enlightened by your colleagues. You haven't attained the fourteenth grade in which this oath is taken. Here's a practically complete manual. Look for yourself.'

I handed it to him to read the oath. I then continued, 'Here's the proof. You're still just a fledgling as far as Masonry is concerned.'

The scoundrel was stunned and dismayed. He could only ask me how I had come into possession of the manual.

'I bought it here in Auckland,' I replied, 'for seven shillings, and sixpence. Anyone can buy a copy.'*

Our discussion continued a little longer, but eventually the master Mason had nothing more to say. He concluded by admitting that not even he knew everything about Masonry, and he was in no position to disprove my accusations, including the alleged intention of destroying family life through divorce, secular state education, etc. Our discussion lasted from seven until nine, and the Mason had to admit his defeat. His friend had listened carefully to our conversation, without comment. When he saw we had concluded, he said to his companion, 'You've been trounced.' He then turned to me: 'Thank you, Father, for agreeing to this meeting. I promise I'll never become a Mason because I realise how evil the organisation is.' They then left. I met the man again a few days later and he said the same thing, but he was afraid that he would lose the

---

* There seems to be a contradiction in Vaggioli's statement here that comparatively full knowledge of Masonry is readily available, while stating earlier that the master Mason's own manual was deliberately rendered incomplete by the society.

£24,000 he had lent. I told him why the other man wanted him to join. Then I suggested that he get everything out of the Mason he could, and take him to court for the rest. That was the last I heard of the matter.

Part 5. Trying to Save the Catholic Paper

Summary. – 1. British journalism's bias. – 2. Catholic journalism. The Auckland paper is running at a loss. – 3. Negotiations to prevent its demise. – 4. Auckland Catholics meet to salvage the situation; a fruitless discussion. – 5. I put my finger on the problem and speak my mind. – 6. My practical solution; rejected by the bishop. – 7. Forming a syndicate with £5000 capital. It is unsuccessful and the paper collapses.

1. Before starting a journal or newspaper, the British make sure they have advertising guaranteed for at least half the journal and two-thirds of a daily newspaper, ensuring that advertisements meet the newspaper or journal's costs and provide a net surplus. They are also keen to ensure that advertisements are taken out for the whole year. They canvass companies for regular advertising. When they have these contracts they begin publication. The income from newspaper sales is hardly taken into account in their reckoning. It is of small consequence because sales are uncertain and many papers are unsold. The English believe that if advertisements can't pay costs and provide a profit, their journals or newspapers are doomed to fail. In this, the British have more acumen than they are credited for in Italy and elsewhere. Traders patronise newspapers because they know that the public blindly believes anything in print. Thus publicity for them is a major way of making money and deceiving their readers. Most British newspapers are Protestant and sectarian. They are usually hostile to Catholicism, and Irish Catholics in particular, for their tenacious adherence to the faith. However, their hostility is less virulent than that of continental Europe, the Latin variety being particularly nasty.

2. Catholic journalism in English-speaking countries is relatively rare, and apart from a total of about fifty daily newspapers, there are only periodicals for a population of about thirty million people throughout England, Ireland, the United States of America and the colonies. The expansion of Catholicism among the British is almost entirely due to the Irish, who have upheld it wherever English is spoken. The Irish have a great affection for their Catholic faith and their homeland. Ireland has been denigrated, reviled and plundered by the British Government, which since 1540 has used all the means within its power to make it Protestant, but without success.

In New Zealand in 1884, out of a European population of about 600,000, unfortunately only 100,000, mostly Irish, would have been Catholic. They had only two weekly papers, the *Tablet* in Dunedin in the South Island and the

Freeman in Auckland. There were two reasons why the *Freeman* could not cover its costs. First, it carried little advertising. Its twelve pages comprised mostly articles and notices, which entailed significant costs in typesetting and wages. The lack of advertising was partly due to the fact that few Catholics were involved in commerce or industry as owners and hence they could provide few advertisements for the Catholic paper. In addition, Protestants' bigotry ensured an unwillingness to provide patronage for a Catholic paper. The second reason was the paper's limited circulation of about 1500 copies, as many non-subscribers read the paper.

The editor was Mr Dignan, a lawyer. He saw that costs were soaring above the income received from advertising and subscriptions. Profits were disappearing.The typesetting equipment was deteriorating, without money to maintain it. Within three years there was a loss of about 50,000 francs. Mr Dignan spoke to some priests, myself included, about the financial predicament of the paper, declaring that in the present circumstances he could not keep printing it. It was suggested that he first approach the bishop, Mons. Luck. This was the only Catholic paper in the diocese and the bishop would need to investigate the matter and find a solution. Pope Leo XIII also placed considerable importance on the Catholic press. I told Mr Dignan that while the bishop was not sympathetic to the aspirations of the Irish, he could not deny that the *Freeman* defended Catholicism. Thus his personal opinions needed to defer to the common good, and he needed to involve himself in helping the paper survive and flourish. Mr Dignan conferred with the bishop on several occasions. The latter urged him to continue publishing while efforts were made to find a solution. They both spoke to prominent local parishioners, who were all adamantly opposed to letting the paper die. After several weeks' deliberation, it was decided that the best way to keep going was to create a syndicate with shares and unsecured capital of at least £5000 (125,000 francs). I told the bishop and the editor that this was impractical. The bishop and clergy believed the scheme would work, but the editor was sceptical, and said that if it failed he could not continue publication. He said he would leave it to the bishop and laity to determine the *Freeman*'s fate.

4. One Sunday it was announced from the altar in every church in Auckland that there would be a meeting of the laity at 3 p.m. the following Thursday in the Catholic secondary school hall to discuss the continuation of the paper. The bishop chaired the meeting, which was attended by the clergy and about 150 parishioners. He opened proceedings, explaining the purpose, and his desire for the *Freeman* to continue to be published. He said that it would be dishonourable to let it die for lack of support. He then called on the editor to explain the actual situation. Mr Dignan pointed out that the newspaper had never met its running costs, that it had few subscribers, and not all had paid

their subscription. He mentioned that Fr O'Dwyer, the previous editor and manager, lost £6000, and that in three years he (Dignan) had lost more than £3000, including non-recovery of printing and equipment costs. He could not continue publication at this rate and was handing the paper's future over to the people. The prelate suggested that the best way to ensure the paper's survival would be to form a syndicate so as to have a fund to meet costs. Several people spoke in support of keeping the paper going. The meeting agreed that it would be a terrible shame to let it die. The majority decided in favour of a syndicate with shares to the value of £5000. Some said the proposal was impractical, that it would not be easy to find that sum, but the majority considered there was no other way to keep the paper going. The bishop and others urged people to sign up, beginning with the clergy.

5. I listened in silence to the discussion, considering the merits of the proposal. I came to the conclusion that it would be impossible to set up a syndicate. Although the majority were in favour of forming a syndicate, I was not afraid to vigorously oppose them for the good of the paper, and fearlessly face the assembly's anger if necessary. I asked the chairman if I could speak, and he immediately agreed.

'Your Excellency, gentlemen,' I began. 'After a long discussion you have agreed to form a syndicate with £5000 capital. It's a great idea, but who is going to subscribe this amount? Where's the money to come from? I would say you'd be lucky to get £500, let alone £5000! It's easy to say: "Let's form a syndicate with £5000 capital", but who is going to provide it? I'd like to hear your answer, gentlemen. What I do know is that there are several people here who are subscribers to the *Freeman*, but haven't paid their subscription for three years!'

'Hear! hear!'

'Gentlemen, would the same people take out shares? [*Silence and general consternation.*] Mr Dignan, a lawyer and editor of the paper, is here today. He can tell you that he is owed over £800 by subscribers, most of whom are from the Auckland diocese, who have not paid for the last three years! Surely, the first thing to do would be to get debtors to pay up, and then decide not to send the paper to anyone who has not paid his subscription in advance, so as not to place the editor in this situation.'

'Yes! Well said!'

Someone then stood up and said, 'If you make people pay in advance, there'll be few subscribers.'

'In that case, it needs to be acknowledged that the majority of parishioners get the paper for nothing, and that's ridiculous! Or should it be said that Irish talk of upholding the faith is simply a farce and humbug?'

'Absolutely; right again!'

'But, to continue. I am convinced that the proposal won't work for two reasons. First, there's no profit to be made and hence investors will stay shy. Second, people will only consider subscribing on secured shares; from the proposal it's plain that there not only will be no profit, but the capital will disappear. [*Cries of consternation.*] And finally, even if the proposal were to go ahead and £5000 were subscribed, if the paper continues as it is, the deficit would increase over the next five or six years, and we'd have exactly the same predicament. Then what? Gentlemen, I leave you to draw your own conclusions.'

6. My diatribe upset the plan. People were muttering among themselves, but I couldn't understand. After a short while the cathedral administrator asked me, 'But if the syndicate's not set up, how will the paper keep going? Do you have a better solution?'

I replied, 'Look, the proposal's not going to work. People won't want to throw their money away. We need to find a simpler, more practical way. In my opinion, the advertisers and subscribers should meet the running costs.'

'Yes, indeed,' people exclaimed.

'There won't be a significant increase in advertising. Protestant bigots aren't keen on advertising in Catholic papers. But the number of subscribers could be increased dramatically. The *Freeman* has a circulation of about 1500 copies. It has 1000 subscribers, most of whom are from the Wellington diocese and the South Island. Only 500 are subscribers from this diocese. That's a small number, and many of them don't even pay. However, we have about 25,000 European Catholics here, a good number of whom are young, single workers. I propose that His Excellency the bishop co-opt a dedicated, enthusiastic priest for six months to travel throughout the diocese, visiting parish priests and preaching the value and importance of parishioners' supporting the Catholic press which defends their faith and rights, and urging them to subscribe to the *Freeman*. He would collect the subscriptions and, where he thought it appropriate, arrange meetings to discuss the importance of this cause. This man would need the support and encouragement of the rest of the clergy, which I believe would be forthcoming.'

'Hear! Hear!'

'What Catholic could refuse to pay a pound a year, or ten shillings every six months, in advance? I'm sure no Irishman would not subscribe to the *Freeman*, which defends his faith and his homeland, so insulted and reviled by Protestants. [*Much applause and shouting: 'Absolutely true! You're right! Yes! Yes!'*]

'Look at how much money is squandered on alcohol. Who wouldn't spend a pound on one's dignity, faith and homeland? Surely I'm right! [*Thunderous applause.*] I realise that there are few priests, but if His Excellency were to make a sacrifice, entrusting the apostolate of the press to one of us, the

200 A Deserter's Adventures

newspaper's financial difficulties would be easily resolved. It couldn't be done by a layman. It needs a priest's authority. Gentlemen, I'm convinced that if His Excellency were so disposed, within six months the paper would meets its costs, and begin to flourish and have a future. If it's not done, let me tell you frankly, the *Freeman* will die, because I can't see any other way of keeping it alive.'

The assembly recognised that my proposal was practical and could work. All eyes turned to the bishop for his decision. The bishop agreed that mine was the best and most practical solution, but he had to refuse it because of the scarcity of priests. He went on, 'To put into effect Fr Vaggioli's proposal, I have only a couple of priests capable of the role, but they have other onerous duties which can't be shed. I'm sorry I can't agree to his proposal which, indeed, would have every chance of working. I simply can't release anyone.'

7. The bishop suggested a return to the first proposal. Shares would be £5 each, and the capital £5000. It was put to the vote and passed by a considerable majority. He declared the meeting closed, and asked those who were willing to give their names to Mr Mahon, the secretary, indicating the number of shares they wanted. Further subscriptions could be taken out at the secretary's or the editor's office. Three laymen took out two shares each and one took one share, a total of £25, but £5000 were needed! Other subscriptions were taken out later by two laymen, some priests and the bishop. But the total was still less than £500! I had hit the nail on the head! It was all talk. The paper continued to stagger on at great cost to the owners. Eventually it folded at the end of 1887 or the beginning of 1888.*

Part 6. I Stagger on, up to My Neck in Work

Summary. – 1. Fr Swithbert, disillusioned and confused! I seek him out and arrange his return to the monastery. – 2. A dissolute Irish priest tricks the bishop and disappears without trace. – 3. We eventually learn his whereabouts and exploits! – 4. The wretched apostate fetches up in Auckland with his degenerate partner. – 5. Visiting the sick and insane. – 6. Tussle with a drunkard! – 7. Serious deterioration of my health. – 8. Making little headway on the debt. – 9. Financial report, January 1885.

1. Fr Swithbert Breikan was a German, but belonged to the monastery of Pierre-qui-vire in France. Towards the end of 1880 he had come out with Fr Sullivan and had spent about two years in Newton, working on clearing the section for the presbytery and church. Fr Breikan was a good, simple, holy man, but uncultured and of limited intelligence. Though his mother tongue was German, he was not fluent, and although he had spent more than fifteen years in France, his

---

* The last issue of the *New Zealand Freeman's Journal* was published in February 1887.

knowledge of French was rudimentary. When in 1881 the Dutch priest was removed from the German settlement,* Fr Breikan was sent there because he understood German. He said Sunday Mass and returned to Newton on Monday. Frs Downey and O'Gara teased him, however, showing him little charity or sympathy.

One evening about the beginning of 1882, the poor priest decided on a kind gesture for parishioners attending benediction in the cemetery chapel. He decided to give them a brief sermon in English, but, in fact, it was a garbled hotchpotch of German, French and English. His listeners couldn't understand a word, or work out which language he was speaking. The other priests had a great time mocking him. Fr Sullivan forbade him ever to preach again. Fr Breikan was so upset by his Newton confrères that he decided to leave and stay with the German settlers. Fr Sullivan tried to recall him several times, but he refused. The superior tried to enlist the vicar-general's support, in the bishop's absence. But he was equally unsuccessful. Fr Breikan was also temporarily suspended from hearing confessions, and keeping well out of the way, he let it be known that he would never return to the malicious monks at Newton.

Meanwhile, the poor man had no change of clothes or religious habit. The German settlers were very poor and could hardly even provide him with the barest necessities of life. The wretch suffered hunger, thirst and all kinds of hardships. He was unkempt, emaciated, and dishevelled because he had nothing else to wear. I gained this description from parishioners who attended his Sunday Mass. Fr Sullivan and his confrères did not know what to do. Fr Breikan ignored their summons and letters. A priest was sent to invite him to return to Newton, without success. So they simply left him to his own devices.

When I arrived in Newton towards the end of 1882 and heard about his wretched situation, I was moved with pity, particularly since we had been together at Pierre-qui-vire from 1867 to 1869. I was determined to try to win him over with compassion. I heard one Sunday that he would be saying the 10 a.m. Mass at the North Shore boarding school. I boarded the ferry from Auckland and then transferred to the tram for the school, keeping an eye out for him. About halfway, I spotted him walking along. He was sweating profusely. I got the tram to stop and alighted. I hadn't seen him for nearly two years. I greeted and embraced him, asking where he was going. He said he was on his way to visit a friend in Auckland, and would return to the German settlement the following day. He wasn't wearing his clerical collar. I asked him where it was. He replied that he had discarded it because it was too dirty and worn. He was wearing a rough pair of shoes. His clothes were reasonable, but they were stained and covered in dust. I asked him if he had had breakfast. He replied that he had had some coffee.

* The reference is to Puhoi, a Bohemian settlement established in 1863. The Dutch priest mentioned was Fr J.L. Adelaar.

'Me, too,' I said, 'that's all I've had.' I asked him to come and join me for lunch at Newton, and we could greet his colleagues. He exclaimed that he had no intention of ever setting foot in Newton again. As we continued along, I gently tried to placate him. Eventually, I succeeded in persuading him to come, but only on one condition: 'I'll come with you willingly, because you're kind to me, but I refuse to see the others,' he said.

He then told me how they had treated him. I asked him if he needed anything, including money. He said he only needed a collar, and that he had enough money for necessities, and that the Germans, though poor, helped him as much as they could. I told him I had several clerical collars and would give him some. I paid the fares to get us to town and to Newton. When we arrived, there was no sign of the two priests or the Irish lay brother, because I had told Br Joseph to warn them not to show themselves and frighten him away. We ate together. The poor man was starving. Every so often he cast a furtive glance at the door, afraid that the monks would appear. I reassured him that they were out, but he didn't believe me. After our meal, I urged him to stay until the following day, but he said he couldn't and he didn't want to see his colleagues. He trembled at the thought of it.

Seeing him reduced to such a state, I decided that the best thing for him would be to return to the cloisters. After lunch, he wanted to leave immediately. I accompanied him through the town for about a kilometre. He didn't want to show me where he was going to sleep. He would only say that he was staying at a friend's. I asked him if he would like to return to France. He told me that he would be very pleased to accompany French priests of our order to work in the Indian missions in the United States of America, but that he didn't have the money to pay for the trip.

'If you really want to go,' I replied, 'tell me clearly, and I'll arrange everything necessary.'

'I'd be delighted if you would and I could get away from this lot, but I don't think you can.'

'Leave it to me,' I replied. 'I'll see that you get to the Indian missions and the money is provided for it. Trust me. I'll give the matter the utmost urgency.'

He warmly thanked me and we bade each other farewell. I never saw him again. I wrote to Fr Sullivan in Sydney describing his situation in detail. He replied that he would send him to America as soon as possible because he feared for Fr Breikan's sanity. The money for his voyage duly arrived and he left for the Indian missions, without farewelling his fellow monks.* There he found peace and serenity, dying in 1906 at the age of eighty-six. R.I.P.

* Fr Breikan left New Zealand on 5 December, 1882. cf. Simmons, op. cit., p. 156 note.

2. In 1883, Timothy O'Callaghan, an Irish secular priest about forty years old, arrived in Auckland from Australia.* He presented his credentials, which were in order, to Mons. Luck. He asked to be accepted into the diocese. The bishop, who was very short of priests, agreed. He placed him temporarily at the cathedral with the other two priests. Noticing he was well educated and eloquent, after two weeks the bishop appointed him inspector of Catholic schools. He was invited to reside with the bishop and eat with him. The clergy secretly complained about this decision. One of them commented directly to the bishop, but he made a real fuss of the newcomer, saying he was fortunate to have such an intelligent, well-educated, holy, dedicated priest.

Quite frankly, I didn't have much faith in the bishop's new acquisition, because I knew from previous experience that good, upright priests didn't wander the world. Only shiftless degenerates kept changing location. One Sunday, the Thames parish priest had to go to Te Aroha. Beforehand, he wrote to the bishop asking him to send a priest down on Saturday for the Sunday Mass and other duties. The bishop gave him permission to go and said he would provide a priest for Thames. He assigned Fr O'Callaghan the task. He accepted and left for Thames on Saturday. When Fr O'Reilly returned to Thames on Monday evening and discovered that the priest had not shown up, he wrote to the bishop complaining of this. The bishop was stunned. He replied that Fr O'Callaghan had left for Thames on the Saturday. Perhaps he had taken the wrong boat. The bishop visited us and told us the news. He asked if we knew his whereabouts. He was afraid that he had got lost. I replied that I suspected an ulterior motive and that he was a rogue like many others of his ilk. I reassured the bishop that O'Callaghan would eventually surface.

'Don't be so critical,' the bishop said.

3. At St Benedict's, I was the first to get up, at 5 a.m. Before going to the church for meditation, I fetched the *Herald* from the porch where it was thrown at 4.45 a.m. every morning. I would glance at the latest news from Europe and in the colony, put the paper on the table and then go to church. This was my routine except for Sunday, when there was no paper. I was on the lookout for news about Rev. Timothy O'Callaghan. I hoped he would surface somewhere and the mystery of his whereabouts would be solved. Some three weeks later, the *Herald* did provide the answer. There was a news item from Dunedin: 'Yesterday in the cathedral the former Catholic priest, Rev. T. O'Callaghan, was received into the Anglican Church.' What a scoundrel! Angrily I put the newspaper in my pocket and went to meditation. At breakfast I read out the news to my confrères. They were astounded and couldn't believe it was the same person. I then hurried to the bishop's and asked him if he had heard the

* See p. 72.

news about O'Callaghan.

'No,' he replied, 'I haven't heard anything.'

'Well, Your Excellency, I have! Here!' I showed him the paper, pointing out the item.

'Oh!' exclaimed the bishop. 'It can't be true!'

'But it is, Your Excellency. It's him, all right. Isn't his Christian name Timothy? How could it be anyone else? And the surname's the same. There can be no mistake.'

'I can't believe it's him.'

'But it is. If you look at the government *Gazette*'s list of Catholic priests, which is reliable and published annually, you'll see there's no priest with that name. That's why I'm certain it's him.'

'I can't believe that he would stoop to that!'

'Why don't you write to the Catholic Bishop of Dunedin. He'll clarify the matter.' The bishop remained silent and upset. I bade him farewell.

4. The wretched apostate was indeed Timothy O'Callaghan. From enquiries made, it was revealed that when he was in Australia he converted to Protestantism, and then reverted to Catholicism. No one knew the reason, but perhaps the sixth commandment had something to do with it.* A few months after his apostasy, the wretch left Dunedin and came to Auckland, seeking a position as an Anglican minister. Protestant papers lavishly praised him, while he sought a comfortable, lucrative post. The Anglicans were building a church in Surrey Crescent, between St Benedict's and the bishop's house. They chose him as their minister because he was cohabiting with the foreman's daughter. The wooden church was soon completed and Rev. T. O'Callaghan was made vicar of Surrey Crescent with great solemnity by the Anglican bishop. Naturally, a woman was at the bottom of the scandal. A few months later, O'Callaghan married the young daughter of the chairman of the vestry with great celebration in the Anglican church. It was described as a fine ceremony, when, in fact, it was just dressing up fornication, and sealing his fate.

Priests who abandon their sacred duties and succumb to lust fall into serious sin. First, they deny their vocation because their hearts are corrupted. Second, they fall into the prey of passion and marry a concubine! I pitied him his fate. Alas, he had closed the door to divine mercy. Woe to us priests if we are not vigilant and faithful to our holy vocation!

5. I was fully involved in clearing the debt and my priestly duties of hearing confessions, preaching and conducting funerals. One day, however, Fr Downey told me that he and Fr O'Gara had too much parish work and could not take

* The reference is to adultery.

care of the hospital, prison and asylum. They wanted me to. The hospital was three kilometres south-west of Newton, and the asylum more than four kilometres north-east. To keep the peace, I accepted, recognising I was the presbytery donkey. My work, instead of decreasing, kept growing, even though my health was deteriorating. I accepted this additional burden *pro bono pacis.* *
I actually believed the priests wanted to get rid of the hospital because several patients had typhus and they were afraid of contracting it! Once the outbreak was over, they had no hesitation returning. Fortunately the presbytery had a telephone and we could keep in touch with the hospital and the asylum. I visited the asylum on horseback, but sometimes walked to the hospital.

6. One evening about 8 p.m., a poor woman sent her ten-year-old son to St Benedict's to fetch a priest urgently. I was the only priest at home. The sobbing, terrified boy said that his father had come home blind drunk and was beating his mother and destroying everything. The priest was desperately needed. I got changed immediately and hurried to the boy's home. The dishevelled, sobbing woman was waiting for me on the doorstep. The husband had broken chairs, smashed plates and bowls and anything he could get his hands on. The wife rushed to her husband and cried, 'The priest's here!'

At that moment I entered, and sternly exclaimed, 'Hey, you! What are you doing?'

He turned around. Seeing the priest, although I didn't think he would recognise me in the state he was in, his eyes nearly popped out of his head. He stammered, 'Fa – fa – fa – Father!'

He was dumbfounded. He wanted to say more, but he couldn't because he was so drunk. The children were crying.

I cast a stern glance at him and said, 'You rotten drunk! What's going on here? What a fine example you are to your family and the neighbours! Sit down and be quiet! Otherwise, you'll have me to deal with!'

But there was nowhere to sit because he had smashed all the chairs. His wife found him a box to sit on. He hid his face in his hands and began weeping.

I gave him a fatherly warning, threatening to get him arrested. I told him it was time for him to come to his senses and stop getting drunk, upsetting his family with his shameful behaviour and disgracing his religion and Ireland, his homeland, etc. I then turned to his wife and children and said, 'If he ever creates a disturbance again, or dares to beat up anyone, call me immediately. I'll make sure that he's put in gaol. There'll be no mercy. In the meantime, I'll get the police to keep an eye on him.'

The motionless, weeping drunk murmured, 'For – for – for – forgive me – fa – fa – Father! For – for – forgive me!' He looked confused and humiliated.

* 'to keep the peace' (Latin).

He was ashamed of upsetting me. The respect of the Irish for the priest is so great that even when drunk they show this deference. I stepped outside and said to his wife, 'I hope he'll stay calm, but if he starts up anything again, call me and I'll sort him out.' I then left. I wasn't called again that evening. The following morning, about 9 a.m., I passed by their home. The oldest daughter told me that the previous evening after I left, he had gone peacefully to bed and to work the next morning.

'Praise the Lord,' I replied. 'Let's hope he will show better judgement in the future!'

'Normally he's fine and drinks only occasionally,' she said, 'but when he gets drunk he becomes a real devil. He doesn't recognise anyone!'

7. From the end of 1883, I began to feel debilitated. I was disturbed by a general lassitude which defied diagnosis. Although I ate regularly and never outside meal times, and retired no later than sunset so as not to aggravate my susceptibility to rheumatism from humidity, I continued to feel unwell. This was not a serious condition, but I did not have my former stamina. I found it particularly difficult walking uphill and would get out of breath. This upset me considerably because it affected my ability to work on the debt. Sometimes, even at night, I would suddenly become breathless, but after a few minutes it would pass. Pain in my feet also distressed me, but fortunately it would last only a few seconds. Otherwise it would have been unbearable. I attributed my indisposition to the concern I felt at seeing St Benedict's affairs going from bad to worse. I tried to ignore the evidence staring me in the face by becoming busier than ever, but I didn't have sufficient energy. It was impossible to ignore things when I was in the midst of them. Nevertheless, I tried to forge ahead without worrying about my health.

8. By 1883 I had reduced the debt from £5556 10s, to £3600. During 1884 I tried to raise more money for the church's expenses, pay the interest and reduce the debt. I had hoped at the beginning of 1884 to collect sufficient money not only for running costs, but also to reduce the debt by £1000. I did not succeed. Two or three committee members assisted me as much as they could, but they had their own affairs to attend to, and thus we collected much less than the previous year.

9. In January 1885, a general meeting was called to hear the report on work carried out in 1884 and how the annual revenue had been spent. It was chaired by the bishop. The secretary, Mr Mahon, read out the financial report, including the payment of £500 capital. The report concluded that as at 31 December 1884, the debt had been reduced to £3100 or 77,500 francs. It was explained that because of my poor health, I had not been as involved as much as I wanted, and that I needed a few months to recuperate. The meeting voiced its satisfaction

with the report and passed a vote of confidence in the committee and chairman, whose energetic work had exceeded expectations. The meeting then passed a motion expressing the hope that, following my holiday and recuperation, I would return to the task of debt reduction with my customary enthusiasm. I thanked the gathering on behalf of the committee for their faith in us, and I assured them that if my health were restored, I would continue working on the debt.

PART 7. FORCED TO ABANDON WORKING ON THE DEBT

SUMMARY. – 1. Circular from the Congregation of the Propagation of the Faith sent in 1884 to missionary bishops and religious superiors regarding the collation of native customs and practices. – 2. An incorrigible drunk. – 3. My serious heart disease. – 4. I inform my superiors about my condition; their reply. – 5. Loose living in Auckland. – 6. Dangers to missionaries. – 7. A woman imperils my salvation!

1. On behalf of Pope Leo XIII, in 1884 the Sacred Congregation of the Propagation of the Faith sent a circular to missionary bishops and superiors throughout the world requesting them to have missionaries (1) send to Rome native artifacts illustrating their arts and knowledge, and (2) collate their ancient customs, beliefs, laws and practices so that a lasting record could be maintained. On receiving the circular, Mons. Luck asked the Marist Fr Lemenant* of the Wellington diocese to visit Maori and collect ancient artifacts on behalf of the Auckland diocese, which would then be sent to Rome for Pope Leo XIII's 1888 jubilee exhibition. The bishop also commissioned a European to make a wooden kauri desk to be sent. I don't know, however, if the Marist father did acquire any artifacts for Mons. Luck, or what was sent to Rome. The bishop asked me to collate information regarding Maori beliefs, laws, customs, etc. Our procurator-general had apprised him of my 100-page work on this subject. I accepted the task because from 1880 I had been collating this information.

2. One day an Irishman came to me for confession. He had a very large family but had been drinking for years. He said he wanted to stop and he asked my help. His wife came with him, begging me to do whatever I could to prevent him getting drunk and causing shame and harm to his family. I welcomed him warmly and heard his confession. I told him that if he wanted to rid himself of the vice, he would have to follow my recommendations. I was aware of his goodwill and gave him absolution, telling him to return to confession in two weeks. He duly did so, but in the meantime had got drunk three or four times. I refused him

* The reference is to the Marist Fr Theophilus Le Menant des Chenais (1836–1910), author of *The Church and the World* (NZ Tablet Printing and Publishing Co, Dunedin, 1905).

208 A Deserter's Adventures

absolution and told him to come back in a further two weeks. He returned and had not got drunk in that period. I gave him absolution and the following morning, being Sunday, he received Communion. But the same evening he got even drunker than usual. This I learnt from his distressed wife. He returned for confession, but, in the circumstances, I denied him absolution. I was determined to get him to mend his ways. He begged for absolution, but I steadfastly refused.

After a month's trial I gave him absolution, but on the Sunday he got up to his old tricks. He returned for confession and once again I denied him absolution, telling him to return in a fortnight. When he returned, I denied him absolution for two or three months so as to rid him of the vice, and he remained sober throughout the period. At this stage, I believed he had changed. He promised me he would never drink again. I gave him absolution and he left delighted. The following morning, after receiving Communion, he immediately began drinking again and said to his wife, 'Father got me to stop drinking for three months. Now I'm going to make up for lost time!' He got drunker than he had ever been before! His desolate, desperate wife told me this following day. Never believe the promises of those who are in the grip of the vice of drunkenness! Reality has told me they don't change. He never returned to see me or for confession.

3. Realising that my health was deteriorating, I decided to visit a reputable doctor for his diagnosis. Since 1883, I had written to our procurator-general that I was not well and that if I did not improve it would be advisable for me to return to the cloisters and prepare myself for death. In October 1884, I visited Dr Richardson, a fine doctor. He asked about my symptoms and listened closely to my heart. After a thorough examination, he said, 'You shouldn't have come here on your own. I would rather have talked to your confrère. It's difficult to tell you directly.'

'Doctor,' I replied, 'tell me frankly what's the matter. I'm not afraid of dying at any time. I have to die sooner or later.'

'If that's the case, and it won't upset you, I'll tell you.'

'Go ahead. I prefer the truth.'

'You have heart disease, and it's more advanced than you probably think. Let's hope nothing serious happens in the meantime.'

'God's will be done. That's all I can say.'

The doctor asked me to describe my routine. I described my work, preoccupations and concerns. He urged me to stop working and have a complete rest. My anxiety and the burden of work were affecting my health and would continue to do so. He went on, 'You could die at any moment unless you have a complete rest. I'm telling you this for your own good.'

'Thank you, doctor,' I replied, 'but how can I if there's no one else to take over.'

'Life is more precious than work or duties.'

'I'll take every precaution, and do what I can.'

'I urge you to have a complete rest. In meantime, take the medicine I prescribe for you. When it's finished, come back. But when you do, walk over, so I can check your heart and see whether the medicine is working.'

About a week later, I returned. He gave me a thorough examination and detected a slight improvement.

'I recommend that you give up any stressful work and take as much rest as you can.'

I asked him if my condition was curable. 'I don't think so,' he replied, 'but it could improve.'

'How much longer do you think I'll live?'

'If you continue at your present rate, maybe three or four months. If you give up work and rest, you could live another seven or eight months, perhaps longer. I also believe that if you returned to your own country and environment, you could live for several years.'

I told him that I would be out of town for two or three weeks for a break. In the meantime, I would try to lighten my duties. The doctor urged me to do this as soon as possible.

4. I immediately wrote to my superior, Fr Sullivan, to the procurator-general and our general telling them the news, and not mincing my words. I mentioned that if my health did not improve, I would seek permission to return to the cloisters in Europe. Fr Sullivan replied telling me to take a rest, but he begged me not to consider returning to Europe. He also mentioned that he would soon be returning to Newton, since he had nearly recovered. I went to the Waikato and then came back to Auckland. I was a little better, but I still needed to be freed of work on the debt. Fr Sullivan agreed and handed it over temporarily to Fr O'Gara for the last couple of months of 1884. Dom Romarico Flugi, the procurator-general, wrote to me on 17 December, as follows:

> Having informed our general of your state of health, he wrote to me that he would not be opposed to your return, since the bishop will soon have reinforcements. (The bishop had gone to Europe in the first half of 1884.) You can discuss your return with your superior. I will be pleased to greet you personally and welcome you in the Spring.

On 30 December, he wrote another letter:

> As soon as I received your letter of 8 November from Hamilton (Waikato), I wrote to the Most Rev. Abbot General that, given the seriousness of your condition, it is vital that you return to Europe forthwith. He replied that he too had received correspondence from you and that he would write to Fr Sullivan in the same vein as myself. After speaking to me in November, he had written to Dom Adalbert to discuss your return, or whether you would prefer to stay in

Auckland, or go to Mons. Ballsieper's mission. But the latter options appeared unsuitable, given the deterioration of your health. I would like you to know that should you wish to return to Europe, there will be no opposition on my part or by His Eminence, the Prefect of the Congregation for the Propagation of the Faith.

I remain, etc.

Fr Sullivan returned to Auckland at the beginning of 1885. He was adamantly opposed to my leaving because he considered me indispensable for clearing the debt. I had received the letter from the procurator-general dated 17 December 1884 which, as I have mentioned, permitted my return to Europe. I gave Fr Sullivan the choice of either allowing me to go to a lighter mission where I could recuperate or letting me return immediately to Europe. He said I could choose any mission I liked, so long as I abandoned the idea of returning to Italy.

5. Among the Nordic races, including the English, the inclination towards fornication is far less strong than among Mediterranean people. The former are sanguine, less hot-blooded or passionate. My observation is based upon experiences of living in Austria, Italy, France, Gerba in Tunisia, and New Zealand. But this was not so in Auckland, with a population of more than 60,000, mostly Anglo-Saxons. The town displayed every appearance of decorum and decency. To the casual observer, it seemed a model of propriety. But behind the façade of righteousness, vice and immorality were a contagion.

The main causes were the prevalence of drunkenness in men, but also in women. A surprising freedom allowed single women and girls to wander around town on their own up until 2 a.m. The young women were easy-going and I would even say provocative as well as impressionable. They readily took up with men, sometimes complete strangers, and would often end up in places of ill-repute.

Another cause of immorality among Protestants was their belief that affairs were not sinful, but perfectly permissible. The only precaution was around avoiding pregnancy. Even among married Protestant women, there was considerable philandering, and even more so by husbands. In short, brazen affairs were aplenty. Widows were most inclined to indulge in fornication because a solitary life was intolerable. They were easily seduced by the promise of financial security and marriage. There were brothels, but it was rare for artisans and workers to frequent them during the day. Gentlemen, however, would fornicate in carriages, their homes or in hotels. Immorality was rife through all classes of society. It was carried out secretly at night. Syphilis and other venereal diseases were on the increase, claiming more and more victims. By 1883, doctors were so concerned that they wrote articles for newspapers, deploring the spread of syphilis. They claimed that if nothing were done, it would become endemic. They urged the government to take action against the prevailing evil. They proposed that men, as well as prostitutes, should be checked by the doctor. The matter was discussed, but nothing came of it.

Young Protestant women who had the misfortune to fall pregnant would not blame themselves. It might prompt them, however, to abandon their loose living. Catholic women, on the other hand, realising the seriousness of their fall, would often take to drinking and be lost forever. There were about a hundred women in Auckland's women's prison. They were mostly there for drunkenness and prostitution. Nearly half of them were Catholic, even though Catholics accounted for only a sixth of the population. When the wretches were freed, their disgusting companions would be waiting to pick them up and continue their evil behaviour! And the government and citizens just let it happen!

6. For more than fifty years, priests in British towns who had to go out at night to tend the sick and dying were urged to wear a clerical collar for recognition. They could thus avoid being drawn into the homes of women of ill-repute when they visited seedy, run-down areas. Catholics priests in Auckland needed to exercise great caution. Although there were comparatively few known brothels, there were several private ones. The practice of visiting the priest by married women, widows, and especially young women is another danger he faces. Long conversations can lead to confidences and familiarity. The Devil intrigues in a myriad ways to cast souls into hell! Visits are well meant and intended to be about religion and moral behaviour. There is no sinister intention, but if one is not extremely vigilant, the Devil leads the unwary from spirituality to sensuality. The local clergy were generally exemplary and faithful to their vocation, even though they were in the midst of corruption. But if they gave in to the vice of drunkenness, their ruin was inevitable.

7. I was always wary about visits, and usually kept them to just a few minutes, whether I went out or people came to me. I never went out at night nor would I receive late calls. I considered myself naïve regarding the Devil's ability to conceal himself under a cloak of charity, virtue and piety, even though I had studied such matters! I needed my wits about me and God and Mary's help to save me from disaster.

In 1883, a 35-year-old widow and her two nephews came to live near our parish church. She was well known to the clergy as a very devout, regular communicant who attended daily Mass and voluntarily worked for the Church. Frs Downey and O'Gara were delighted that she had come to Newton because they could continue to get her to work on the church's drapes and vestments. Often they would remain in church to speak to her, but I very rarely did. For more than a year, I never set foot in her house, unlike the other priests. She often invited me. I said I had little free time, but that I would come when I could; but I never did. One day in 1884, about 4 p.m., as I was returning, I passed by her house. She came out and begged me to come in and tell off one of her nephews for staying out late at night. I went in and did as she asked. The widow then told me about her circumstances, seeking my advice. She knew that I had some knowledge of medicine and finances which could be useful to her. She mentioned that she had rheumatism in the back and other ailments causing her considerable pain. I suggested suitable remedies and advised her to consult her doctor, since I was not qualified. She owned a house near the port which she rented out cheaply because it was old. She supported herself and her nephews from the rent. But it was not enough and she had to borrow £100 from a Protestant money-lender at sixteen per cent interest. She was hardly managing to pay this, let alone the capital. She was being pressed for payment. He was prepared to lower the debt if she would sleep with him. Horrified, she had refused and now her creditor was threatening to have her house seized.

I was deeply moved by her story, particularly so since our priests had her constantly working for nothing. I said I would try to extricate her from her awful situation. In fact, I lent her £100 on the understanding that she would pay it back a little at a time. It was to free her of the money-lender and his loan. In my naïvete, I had no idea of her true motive. She first paid me £10, then £40 and a further £20. In all, she repaid me £70 in six months. She wove such a careful plot as to seduce the wariest man. The wretched woman partially succeeded in tricking me, but not snaring me. Thanks to God and Our Lady's mercy, I was able to extricate myself, forsaking the thirty pounds to get out of her clutches. I eventually realised that the evil woman had for some time harboured an impure love for me without revealing the least indication right up to the end. Only at the last moment did she show her true colours. As I recall the peril I was in, now as I am writing, my hand is trembling. This was to be my payment for my kindness towards the unhappy woman! I hope that God has forgiven her!

PART 8. ENDING MY WORK IN AUCKLAND

SUMMARY. – 1. While negotiating to be released from working on the debt, I visit the Waikato. – 2. Some Sisters of Mercy deceive the bishop. – 3. The vicar-general requests me to take the nuns' retreat. – 4. I accept on condition that I have a free hand; eventually he agrees. – 5. Mother Superior carries out my orders. – 6. I speak frankly to the nuns. – 7. The vicar-general listens in on my preaching; his evaluation. – 8. I put things right in the end.

1. I negotiated with Fr Sullivan, as mentioned above, to be released from working on the debt because of the deterioration of my health. I could only get about two months' leave. I went to Hamilton in the Waikato to stay with Fr Anselm Fox. I found it hard to relax, however, because the incompetent Fr O'Gara had been appointed to replace me. Fr Fox often took me for excursions through the Waikato, showing me the various villages in his mission and that of Fr Luck, his neighbour. I also had several days' holiday in the spectacular thermal areas of Rotorua, Wakarewarewa and the central North Island. I took notes of my observations and was enormously pleased to see such marvels. The scenery corresponded to our Dante Alighieri's vivid descriptions of hell in *The Inferno*. The time eventually came for my departure. I thanked Fr Fox for his kind hospitality and returned somewhat recovered to Auckland. But my improvement was short-lived. In September my health deteriorated and in October I visited Dr Richardson, as already mentioned. Fr Sullivan, in agreement with the bishop, sent me back to the Waikato in January 1885 to replace Fr Fox for a month, since he was needed to visit the Maori of the diocese.

2. The Sisters of Mercy had five convents and their mother house in Ponsonby. Three-quarters of them were Irish, and the rest English. Nationalism caused a rift between them. In 1883, elections took place for a new superior. An Irish woman was elected and the English superior lost her position. She was able and shrewd, but arrogant. Two of her associates were also demoted. The aggrieved threesome plotted revenge, even though the new superior had sent them and another sister to Coromandel. The deposed superior had Fr Downey's backing. He hoped she would be reappointed, but this did not happen. The three malcontents, with Fr Downey's connivance, pestered the bishop to have the Coromandel convent made independent so they could keep control. Even though the rebel sisters painted a pious picture, the bishop was aware of the tactics. He agreed, however, to two of their requests. The first was that on his return from Europe towards the end of 1884, he would grant them their much coveted autonomy. The second was that they would not be required to attend the Ponsonby retreat in August 1884. Fr Downey would conduct their retreat in Coromandel. The ambitious women were very pleased with the bishop's agreement. After Easter 1884, he left for Europe.

3. On 31 July 1884, the vicar-general visited me and asked me to take the nuns'
retreat in Ponsonby. It was to begin on 6 August and end on the morning of the
15th. I commented that my health was poor, that I had a lot to do and my
English was not adequate to the task, recommending that Fr Downey officiate.
He said that Fr Downey had refused, mentioning that he was taking the four
sisters' retreat in Coromandel. Up till then I had not been privy to what had
been winkled out of the bishop with Fr Downey's connivance. I replied, 'Why
can't the Coromandel sisters come to Auckland for their retreat?' He mentioned
the agreement with the bishop. I went on, 'They all have to make a retreat and
belong to the same order, so why can't they come up here?'

'It was decided not to make them come to avoid disagreement and trouble
between the two factions.'

I remonstrated with the vicar-general about the bishop's decision. I said
that the bishop, acting in ignorance, had messed things up. His decision would
cause unfortunate gossip and snide remarks in town. I pointed out that the
arrogant nuns could not and should not be independent, etc.

'You're right,' he replied, 'but I have to obey the bishop.'

'Quite right, Monsignor, but if I have to take the sisters' retreat, I want to
do what's best for them. I'll take the retreat on one condition.'

'Namely?'

'That you give me a free hand to do or undo what I am guided by the Lord
to do, without being held to an episcopal decision, which, in my opinion, was
ill-judged and should never have been made.'

'But I can't go against the bishop's orders.'

'I'll be accountable to the bishop.'

'But I can't see how I can give you this authority.'

'Well, then, Monsignor, get someone else to take the retreat. I certainly
won't.'

'I can't assume this responsibility!'

'Let me. I'd be doing everyone a favour.'

4. The vicar-general shook his head, perplexed. He was afraid of the bishop's
rebuke on his return, but also anxious that friction between the nuns would increase
if the Coromandel sisters came up. I, however, was convinced that the bishop
would approve of my intervention, which would prevent an awkward situation,
and I was also certain that discord would not only be controlled, but even
extinguished. Mons. Fynes asked me for two or three days to think it over. I
thought he'd probably go looking for another preacher, but I didn't like his chances.

'Yes,' I said, 'think it over, but not for too long. The retreat's due to start on
6 August.' He agreed, and departed. At 2 p.m. on 5 August, the vicar-general
returned and told me he would give me a free hand. I was sure he had consulted
Fr Downey and delayed his reply so that the Coromandel sisters would not

have enough notice to get to Auckland in time. God, however, had other designs, and the plan was thwarted.

5. As soon as I had the vicar-general's permission, I rushed off to Ponsonby in the tram. When I reached the convent, I called for Mother Superior and told her to immediately send a telegram to the Coromandel sisters, requesting them to leave by boat the following morning for the retreat that evening. She had no idea about the negotiations between the vicar-general and myself, and was taken by surprise. She began to say, 'But the sisters in Coromandel ...'

'Silence!' I said. 'I'll explain everything later. I'm in charge now. Do as I say. Sit down and write the telegram.'

She composed the following message: 'Sister – , Sister – , Sister – , and Sister – are to leave by steamer tomorrow to attend the retreat with the other sisters. Signed, Mother Superior.'

I told her to get the gardener to take the message to the Central Post Office immediately, so it could be sent straightaway, and the sisters would have time to prepare for their departure the following morning. I then told her what had transpired between the vicar-general and myself. I explained why the Coromandel sisters also needed to attend the retreat. I said that, in my opinion, the bishop had been deceived by the sisters, and their seeking autonomy was against their Rule. The superior recognised that my comments were accurate and she was happy with my actions. She added, 'They'll be hostile to me for summoning them.'

'I'll take full responsibility, and I'll publicly state that I called for them, and that if anyone's to be blamed it's me and not Mother Superior. She simply obeyed instructions.'

'Actually, I'm pleased, because now there won't be any gossip in town. But tell me, do you really think they'll turn up tomorrow?'

'I believe so. When they get the telegram, they'll think the bishop changed his mind at the last minute before leaving, and decided to order them to join the others on retreat.'

'I'd be really glad to see them come and avoid a scandal.'

On the afternoon of 6 August, I went over to set myself up at the bishop's residence in Ponsonby. I had learnt that the Coromandel sisters had arrived about 10 a.m. and had not asked for an explanation for their summons.

6. August in New Zealand is in the heart of winter. I arranged with Mother Superior to hold the first meditation at 5.30 a.m. I would say Mass at six-thirty, which local parishioners could also attend. At ten there would be instruction for the nuns, and at 5 p.m. there would be a second meditation. At 5 p.m. on 6 August, I opened the retreat and preached for just over half an hour. There were sixty-three or sixty-four nuns present. Before my sermon, I made an

announcement:

'Some sisters didn't think they had to come on retreat. Who summoned them, then? I did, and I had full authority to do so. Mother Superior didn't do it. I did. She simply carried out my instruction. I did this for the good of your community, so that you wouldn't be gossiped about. There's already been enough of that. If they hadn't come, people would be saying, "Why didn't the Coromandel sisters come? What's going on? There's something fishy. The sisters aren't getting on! There's real trouble!" etc. I didn't want public gossiping, bringing disrepute to Catholicism, especially by Protestants. That's why I summoned them and I take full responsibility.'

Another day, as I was speaking about observation of the Rule, I said that perhaps there were some sisters who wished to set up an independent convent. I added that this was prohibited. The Rule stipulated certain procedures. First, the sisters would need to discuss if it was necessary, and if so, the general chapter would determine which nuns would form an independent community. It was contrary to the Rule for religious to act independently. This would smack of self-love, false pride and wilful independence of spirit. Such motives were not sanctioned by God. ('Heed and observe the Rule, and all will go well,' etc.) In my preaching and talks I spoke very clearly about the duties of religious. I was agreeably surprised to experience the Lord's assistance in easily and clearly expounding the sisters' duties in a foreign language.

7. When I was preaching, only the nuns were present. The church doors were closed. The vicar-general was keen to hear my preaching and what I was saying to the sisters. Without my being aware, he sat in on my 10 a.m. instruction. Once or twice, he also attended the evening meditation. To avoid being noticed, he came by the convent passage and concealed himself in a corner. Only Mother Superior knew, because before the sermon he talked with her, asking how things were going and assessing the nuns' reaction to my preaching. I spoke *ex tempore* from notes in a notebook I had brought with me from Africa.

On the third or fourth day of the retreat, the vicar-general came about 11 a.m. to the bishop's residence and asked how I was. I replied that I was a little tired, but quite well otherwise. I told him that my preaching had been frank and I put my finger on common faults in the religious life. I had no idea what the sisters thought of my directness. Mother Superior had indicated that, apart from two or three, the rest were happy, and the community was in harmony. The vicar-general commented that the sisters were very pleased. He said that I was doing very well and that I should continue just as I was. The Lord would bless the retreat and the sisters would reap the benefits. I replied, 'Don't put too much store by what the nuns say. They're inclined to exaggerate.'

'No, no, it's just as I say.'

'How can you know, Monsignor? You haven't heard me preaching.'

'I actually do know. I've come several times without your knowledge to listen to your sermons. I can tell you that you've done very well. I'm delighted with you. Continue as you are. Things are going very well. God will be pleased, as will the sisters. Much good will come of it.'

8. At the end of the retreat, the sisters confirmed they were happy. There were only two malcontents: the Coromandel superior and a faithful companion of hers, who had no real vocation but became a nun to please her mother. The superior didn't reveal her displeasure, but her companion certainly did. The older sisters declared they had never heard preaching like mine. They thanked me for all I had done, saying they would treasure my words. I'm sure they had heard finer and more eloquent preaching than mine, but they would not have heard the truth spoken so frankly and plainly. Of the four Coromandel sisters, two completely abandoned the idea of independence, while the other two retained their original position. The latter pair, with one of the former, returned to Coromandel, and did not mention independence again. When the bishop returned from Europe in December, he fully approved my actions. He was pleased to be freed of his embarrassing position with the Coromandel nuns and thanked me. I suggested that the best thing he could do for them was to make sure they observed their Rule and otherwise leave them to their own devices.

Dom Felice Vaggioli, OSB, happily wearing his Benedictine robes, c. 1885.

CHAPTER NINE

A Missionary in Coromandel
(LATE 1884 TO MID-1887)

PART 1. I CHOOSE TO GO TO COROMANDEL

SUMMARY. – 1. Fr Sullivan's reluctance to grant me a rest. – 2. I insist, on my doctor's orders. – 3. My superior gives in; I choose Coromandel. – 4. My reply to Fr Sullivan's letter; the general's letter. – 5. I publish articles opposed to state education. – 6. A dissolute coachman. – 7. I speak frankly to him and he heeds me.

1. I told Fr Sullivan, as mentioned elsewhere, that I needed to be relieved of debt-collecting. Worrying about it had ruined my health. Now it could ruin someone else's, because I was half-dead. He prevaricated and made excuses.

2. Because of his indecision, I visited Dr Richardson again, asking him to put in writing his request for me to be relieved of responsibility for recovering the debt, to have a change of air and requisite rest. He was only too keen, and wrote down what he had urged on me in October. I sent a letter enclosing his note to my superior in Sydney. I told him it was about time he released me of the burden and allowed me to resume missionary work. These negotiations occurred in December 1884. I couldn't get a definite decision from our general and procurator-general to the questions I had put to them in October because it took about four months to get a reply from Italy. Dr Richardson's message was plain. Either I be relieved of my present position or I would soon be in the grave. On receiving this information, Fr Sullivan replied that he would release me from the role until I was completely recovered. He gave me permission to select any mission in the diocese. I simply needed to let him know my choice and I could go when I was ready.

3. I have never been averse to work, even when unwell. I loathe sloth and idleness. I had no intention of resting up in a mission. I would do the best I could within my capabilities. I considered the various missions in the diocese. Coromandel had been without a priest for nearly six months. Fr Noboa, my confrère, was sent there, but he was a young, inexperienced twenty-six-year-old and found he could not manage. After about a year he asked to return to the cloisters and eventually he left for Puerto Rico, in America. With him gone, the bishop sent a priest down weekly or fortnightly to celebrate Sunday Mass. The mission was so impoverished the clergy wouldn't consider going there when it could not even provide them with the necessities of life. Parishioners

were poorer than elsewhere and were not particularly devout. On the other hand, Coromandel was in an elevated position and had a healthy climate. It was surrounded by hills and mountains on three sides and the sea on the other. The mission area was not extensive. Besides Coromandel township, there were small settlements scattered over a forty-mile radius, the most substantial being at Mercury Bay. The missionary's work, therefore, was not excessive. For these reasons I decided to choose Coromandel and take Br Joseph with me. I advised Fr Sullivan of my choice. He replied that he was very happy for me to go there and commended my missionary zeal while urging me not to work too hard and take every precaution over my health. The vicar-general was also very pleased, because he was freed of having to find temporary priests for the mission.

When all the preparations had been made, I remembered that the sisters who wanted their independence were at Coromandel. I suddenly realised that since I had brought their plans to ruin, they would not be happy to have me there, and would oppose me. I was amazed that I hadn't thought of this before. If I had, I probably would not have made this choice; even more so since I would be the only priest and they would have to have me as their confessor. Without their trust, serious trouble could develop because of their aversion towards me. For some days I remained undecided whether to cancel my departure or stick to my original decision. I realised that my superiors would take a dim view of me if I went back on my word, so I decided to go, trusting in Divine Providence. Some years later, I realised that my going was a grace God gave the two malcontent sisters, even if its effects evaporated after my sojourn ended.

4. I was already settled in Coromandel when the general's and procurator-general's replies came to my letter and Dr Richardson's note. I have already mentioned the procurator's letters. Fr Sullivan wrote to me from Newton, on 4 February 1885:

> In the penultimate post I received a letter sent to Sydney for me from Very Rev. Abbot General. In it he briefly mentioned your request to be allowed to return to Europe. He mentioned that if this is still your wish and you would like to be transferred to the vicariate of Mons. Ballsieper in East Bengal, he grants his permission. I would be displeased if you are still intent on this course. It does not reflect well the spirit of obedience, but a concession to a personal request. I believe that now that you have the opportunity for more rest and are less burdened, you will recover in health. By remaining in Coromandel you will demonstrate your obedience to the Rule. The same cannot be said if you were to go to India. You will be aware that your departure from Auckland would seriously inconvenience me.

> With every blessing and good wishes, etc.

On 7 February 1885, I replied to my superior's letter as follows:

The procurator-general's letter, which I include and ask you to return, makes no mention of India. Nor did I make any request to be sent to another mission. On the contrary, I expressly did not want this. My request was for a recall, not because I wanted or desired to wander from mission to mission, nor because I'm unhappy here, but because of poor health, which would apply equally whether I was in Bengal or New Zealand. If I'm not fit enough to work here as a missionary, I won't be any better in India. Hence, if my superiors do remove from here, I'll return to the cloisters. This has always been my intention and what I asked for.

However, I promised you that I would wait three or four months before making a final decision, depending on my health, and I'll keep my word. If I don't improve, I intend to accept the permission to return to Europe. The general didn't mention where I would be sent, should I return to Europe. There's time enough for that. I can't go to Italy because of my avoidance of conscription. As far as I know there's been no amnesty for deserters of my period.

You urge me not to take up this permission for the reason you gave. The general would be the best judge of the matter of obedience. I am certainly very clear about my motives. In the meantime, let's wait and see about my health. I regret that my departure from New Zealand would inconvenience you, but where else should an infirm, unwell monk go except the monastery? At the moment my health is *sicut erat.** Some days I'm fine, other days I'm not. At present I have a cold. Let's see how things develop. You are very welcome to mention the above when next you write to the general.

Coromandel is going from bad to worse. Anyone who can is leaving. What is worse, those who remain are poor, drunkards and non-practising Catholics. Only a third of the parishioners go to church, even though more now come than when Fr Donatus Noboa was here.

The general wrote to me from Subiaco on 16 January 1885:

I wish to acknowledge receipt of your welcome letters of 16 September, 13 October and 9 November last year. I can't tell you how upset I was to receive the bad news about your health. I made sure that I wrote to Dom Adalbert Sullivan to urgently take steps to attend to your health, which is so important to me. If you consider that your return to Europe is imperative and you don't believe you can stay any longer, I have absolutely no objection to your return.

Mons. Ballsieper wanted you for his Bengal mission. I told him I wasn't opposed to the idea if you were to leave New Zealand. However, I thought that if you needed to return from New Zealand, you wouldn't want to go to Bengal. Enough said.

Be of good cheer, dear friend. Trust in the Lord. As for myself, rest assured that should you return to Europe, you will be welcomed with open arms and the

---

* 'much the same'. Literally, 'as it was' (Latin).

fatherly affection you deserve.

With blessing, etc.,
Dom Nicola Canevello.

I replied to the general that, following Fr Sullivan's plea, I would see if my health improved in Coromandel. If it did, I would continue working in the Lord's vineyard. But if not, I would return to Europe.

5. While I was in Auckland, I became aware of the ruinous effects of government secular education on children, both Protestant and Catholic (since many Catholic children attended government schools). I eventually decided that a priest should lift his voice not only from the pulpit, but also in Catholic papers against the pernicious doctrines promulgated by the Masons at the cost of Christian youth. I mentioned this to several priests, urging them to write articles denouncing state education. I recognised the value of bringing to public awareness, especially among Catholics, its deleterious effects. My plea was ignored, however. They said they didn't have the time. I decided to write myself, even though I wasn't well. I also thought that such an onerous task would distract me from my preoccupation with my health. About halfway through 1884 I undertook to write a series of articles against state education for the *Freeman*, which were usually published fortnightly. When I went to Coromandel, I continued sending articles to the paper until my departure for Europe, on 25 July 1887. No other priest continued my battle.

6. Among my Newton penitents was a coachman with a landau. Like many others, at night he drove women of ill-repute to married Protestant gentlemen for a rendezvous. The men made sure reliable, discreet coachmen were hired. Their predilection was a weekly liaison, sometimes even in a separate part of their own home. Our coachman, when he reached the destination, would wait until the man appeared to open the door for the woman, making it seem like nothing out of the ordinary. I should also add that the same coachman indulged in such immorality. I warned him not to have courtesans as passengers, that he would be sinning by association. It would also tempt him into an occasion of sin, threatening his faith and marriage. He promised to stop and was remorseful and contrite. I absolved him and requested him to return in two or three weeks. He kept his word, but mentioned that he was still taking women for their secret trysts and that he himself had indulged with a couple of them in lewd behaviour. I sharply but compassionately rebuked him. He swore that he would never touch any of them again. However, I even forbade him to take them as passengers, telling him it was a mortal sin. He pointed out that the women and gentlemen asked specifically for him. If he didn't take them, other coachmen would and he wouldn't be able to survive.

'That may be,' I replied, 'but you must not continue. You can't be an accomplice to sinful behaviour.'

He said that the majority of night coachmen did this kind of well-paid work. 'If I refuse to take the women where they want to go, I won't earn a penny.'

'Just work as a coachman during the day and you won't be involved in sin.'

'But you don't earn much.'

'Well, get another job.'

Eventually he promised to stop. I deferred absolution, telling him to return in a fortnight. He later returned, and had kept his word. I exhorted him to keep to his resolve. When I gave him absolution, I asked him to return in a month, which he promised to do.

7. He continued to vacillate for two or three months. I realised that he did not have the determination and resolve to remove himself from temptation and desist from wrongdoing. He would wring his hands and promise to mend his ways, but in reality nothing changed. I was determined to use every means I could to get him to stop. One day I rebuked him: 'Listen, my son, I can't give you absolution. I don't want you to end up in hell, but I have to tell you frankly that if I were to give you absolution, I'd be committing a sin because you haven't met the conditions, and you would be committing a sacrilege. I don't want you leaving with a further sin on your soul.'

'But I really do want to change!' he replied.

'That's what you say, but you do the complete opposite. You've been promising for months, but nothing changes! What's the use of hearing your confession when you make no effort? This is just mocking God! I can see you want to end up in hell! I weep for your poor soul.'

'So you won't give me absolution?'

'No, my son, I can't, because I don't want to join you in hell! And I need to add that if you don't mend your ways as I've told you to do so often, go and find another priest. Don't come back here, because if you won't change, I won't absolve you.'

He started to cry. Eventually he said, 'Won't you really give me absolution?'

'No, no, I can't. I can see you want to perish and you'd like to take me down with you. If that's your wish, well then, "Go to hell!" Don't expect me to join you!'

The English expression, 'Go to hell!' is an oath or curse. It's not normally meant to be taken literally. I realised this. But at the time I really wanted to get him to change his ways. When I said this, he got up and left without a word, and I didn't see him again. About four months later, I left Auckland for Coromandel and gave no further thought to the coachman. About halfway through 1885, I was on a business trip to Auckland. As I was walking along the main street on my way to Newton, a man came up to me and greeted me warmly.

I shook his hand and he asked how I was, etc. I looked at him and was taken aback. He realised that I didn't recognise him and exclaimed, 'So, don't you recognise me any more?'

'No, I'm afraid not.'

'I'm the coachman you told to "go to hell!"'

'Oh! Now I remember. Well, what have you got to say for yourself?'

'Ah! Dear Father. After what you said that day I was really shocked. I thought seriously about my situation and about changing my life. With God's help, that is exactly what I have done. I've followed your advice. I want to thank you. I'm really happy.'

'I am so pleased about your change of heart. Thank God. Are you still a coachman?'

'Yes, Father, but from the day you uttered those words, no woman of ill-repute has entered my carriage. Thanks to God, I'm still doing fine.'

This was a real triumph of God's grace.

Part 2. Coromandel

SUMMARY. – 1. My arrival in Coromandel at night. – 2. The sisters take their revenge; we retire hungry to bed! – 3. I visit the sisters; a frosty reception. – 4. The difficulty of my situation. With God's help I am able to speak frankly to them. – 5. My negative impressions of Coromandel. – 6. Coromandel's brief period of prosperity from goldmining. – 7. Coromandel in dire straits.

1. As I was preparing to leave with Br Joseph Ricci for Coromandel, the bishop's servant, an Italian from the monastery of Subiaco, asked if he could accompany us on a first visit to the township. I agreed. A few days previously, I had written to the superior of the Coromandel sisters advising her that the three of us would arrive by steamer on the evening of the following Friday. I can't recall the exact date. It was probably about the end of January. I said that we would arrive about eight-thirty, and asked her to prepare three rooms in the mission house and a fire to warm us on our arrival. I didn't give any further details, because I presumed that being familiar with the trip, she would know that leaving Auckland at three-thirty we would need a meal on our arrival.

Moreover, since none of us had been to Coromandel before, I presumed she would send someone to the wharf to collect our luggage and accompany us to the presbytery. I assumed that she would have notified the parishioners, or at least some of them, of the priest's arrival, as was customary, ensuring that we would be met and welcomed at the wharf and taken to the mission. But the wretched woman never said a word to anyone. She had plenty of time to reply to my letter, which I had written a week previously, but she didn't. I was well-disposed towards her and assumed that she shared this spirit. I thought she would act kindly, but I was proved wrong. It was a rough trip and we reached Coromandel late, at 9 p.m. There was no one waiting to collect our luggage. Being late, there were only two or three men on the wharf awaiting the arrival of their friends. Only about seven or eight passengers were on board. We disembarked and looked unsuccessfully for a porter. We took our own cases and, following the others, we reached the township in ten or fifteen minutes, but we couldn't see much of it. Not knowing where to go, I turned to one of the locals, asking him to kindly tell me where the Catholic presbytery was. He told me to follow him since he would be passing it on his way. He pointed it out to us and wished us goodnight.

2. The house was unlocked with a light on in the drawing room. The bedrooms were prepared. There was a good fire burning in the kitchen and water was boiling on the stove, but not a soul was to be seen! We warmed ourselves, and feeling hungry, we searched for something to eat. Eventually we found two pieces of stale bread and a couple of eggs! We looked at each other and burst out laughing. It would hardly feed one, let alone three! What could we do? We had no lantern to go out and find the convent and ask for food. And we didn't know where the shops were or if any were open. I knew the sisters had a maid, but there was no sign of her. It was 10 p.m. by now. We were really stuck, with nowhere to turn.

It suddenly dawned on me that there was a purpose behind this. The sisters had gleefully seized their opportunity for revenge. Fortunately, we were all in good humour, despite our predicament. We chuckled over our rather unpleasant adventure. We didn't mind not having a proper welcome and joked about the fast imposed upon us by the sisters, which was somewhat more rigorous than the usual Friday one.* To appease our hunger, I asked Br Joseph to boil the eggs. That would have to be the limit of God's bounty that evening. I would sort things out the next morning. I wasn't really hungry and just had a quarter of an egg and a crust of bread. The others' supper was still very meagre. We washed it down with a glass of water! Finally I said, 'We'll just have to put up with things tonight. At any rate, we'll sleep better on light stomachs! It's nearly eleven. Let's turn in. Things will be better tomorrow.' We then retired to our rooms.

3. I rose at five and dressed to go to church, which was only about ten metres from the presbytery. The others had also risen. I found the church unlocked. We meditated, and about six I rang the bell for Mass. The sisters came. After thanksgiving I went back and had breakfast of coffee and milk with bread. After nine we went to the convent. The nuns welcomed us at the door. They showed us the children's school rooms and their own accommodation area.

* The reference is to the traditional meatless Friday fast.

Their welcome was rather restrained, although they tried to make out otherwise. I acted in a cool, kind and courteous manner towards them, hiding any other feelings. I didn't mention their failure to leave us dinner or send over the maid to attend to us. Their hostility and resentment was more an issue for them than myself because I took no notice. Since there was no other priest available, they were obliged to go to me for confession. But how could they make a good confession to a priest they harboured ill-feeling towards? This was a serious matter and I didn't have an answer. They strongly believed that I was against them and that I didn't like them, which was completely wrong. I had to disabuse them of this idea, but how should I go about it? Would I be able to change their minds? I couldn't see how. I decided for my part to exercise considerable charity, and do as much as I could for their well-being. I also prayed to the Lord and the Virgin Mary to inspire me to treat them in the way I would like to be treated. I then left it in God's hands to direct matters for His honour and glory and the good of their souls.

4. About 4 p.m. that same day, the superior sent over the maid to ask me when I could hear their confessions.

'Whenever you like,' I replied. 'It's all the same to me. Tell me when it suits you and I'll be ready.'

The maid departed and reported what I had said. Shortly afterwards she returned, saying that the sisters usually went to confession at 6 p.m. on Saturdays. They would like to continue, if that wouldn't inconvenience me.

'Very good,' I replied, 'that's what I'll do.'

In the meantime I thought a good deal about the delicate issue. I prayed again for divine guidance and for God to put the right words in my mouth, and He came to my aid. At the arranged time, I entered the confessional and the sisters, beginning with their superior, came to confession. Before each began, I made the same speech: 'Listen, sister, before you make your confession, I have to tell you something that concerns me. You think that I'm against you. That's not true. I am neither for nor against you. If you carry out your duty as a nun and don't get involved in my affairs, I will always be on your side and support you. If you do the opposite, I will have to oppose you. I'm telling you this as the plain and simple truth.'

The sisters were sour for a few days, but then became more amenable. I continued to be courteous and affable towards them and I went to great lengths to attend to their spiritual and material well-being. Realising this, they began to behave suitably and in a short while they began to show me considerable affection. I had only praise for them during the rest of my sojourn in Coromandel and I continued to look after them in every way I could.

General view of Coromandel township, c. 1880.

5. Coromandel is an extensive peninsula, more than 100 kilometres long and averaging 30 kilometres wide. It is extremely hilly and is dotted with bays. It contains two counties with two representatives in the colonial Parliament. It has the two Catholic missions of Thames and Coromandel. The township of Coromandel is near the sea. By 1885 it had a population of about 600 inhabitants. About one and a half kilometres away was the settlement of Kapanga with about 300 inhabitants. A further 100 people lived on a hill overlooking Kapanga.

The houses were wooden, small and simply constructed. Many were dilapidated or uninhabited. The whole area had the stamp of poverty and misery. The soil was boggy and infertile. Nor were the plains very fertile and the few animals grazing them were emaciated. The district had a small branch bank. There were two Catholic churches. The one in Coromandel was attractive and pleasant. It could seat 400 worshippers. The other at Kapanga was small and looked more like a house than a church. It could hold sixty or seventy people. There were also three Protestant churches in Coromandel. The Anglican church had a resident minister. The Presbyterian church was usually locked and the Methodist church was without a resident minister. Coromandel also had the convent and a government school. There was a state school at Kapanga. Coromandel had five hotels and Kapanga two. Several others were scattered through the district. The government primary school was also used as a concert hall. Most of the Coromandel population were extremely poor. There were a few small shops. The Coromandel road went as far as Kapanga. It was called a carriage-way, but was suitable only for ox-carts. Moreover, carriages were not to be had. When I considered Coromandel from a religious, moral, social and financial point of view, I was left with a bleak impression. There were no real businesses and the goldmines which had been in operation for some years had ceased yielding. But people still stayed on in the hope of striking gold.

6. Coromandel had been almost exclusively inhabited by Maori when, suddenly, twenty-five years ago, it had erupted into new activity and in little more than a year it became a flourishing town with more than 15,000 fortune hunters. How did such a wild, deserted area undergo such a transformation? News spread like wildfire through the colony of the discovery of rich deposits of gold in Kapanga and the surrounding hills. Eager, greedy European settlers rushed to Coromandel. Speculators were the first on the scene, buying land near the claims, hoping they could make money out of the tailings. Some Aucklanders dismantled houses and shipped them down on large boats. They were reassembled as shops. Others appeared with tents as shelters for miners and other people flocking in. Still other speculators came with carpenters and labourers and built hotels, banks and houses. Since food was scarce, everything was imported from Auckland and elsewhere.

Within a few months, the population soared to about 7000 inhabitants. Streams, hillsides and ridges were soon swarming with men feverishly digging for gold. Workers earned up to £2 (50 francs) a day and the cost of foodstuffs increased enormously. Everyone was making money. A simple two-roomed cottage cost at least £2 a week to rent. And everything else was just as dear. Within a few months, about thirty high-yielding goldmines had been opened. Several companies were established with considerable British and colonial capital to develop them. In the meantime miners swarmed all over the peninsula in search of gold. They clambered over ridges, gorges, gullies, streams and creeks in a fruitless quest. The rich pickings at Kapanga and its environs lasted two or three years. Then the precious ore became scarce and what was extracted barely managed to cover the costs. Companies made no headway and spent their capital. Many went under, while others started a new venture, hoping to strike gold by mining deeper into the bowels of the earth.

In 1856 and 1859 news spread of the discovery of gold in the Nelson district, in the South Island. There was a great exodus from Coromandel. In less than a year, half the population left, taking their tents and houses with them. In 1861 large deposits of gold were discovered in the Dunedin province. This dealt the death blow to Coromandel, since about 6000 people left for Dunedin within a few months. Thus, Coromandel, which in 1854 had a population of 15,000 inhabitants, by 1862 had less than 2000! And they would have left too if they had had the means.

7. All the goldmining companies of Coromandel were liquidated except Kapanga's. But it folded several times, only managing to revive through

receiving new partners. Its shareholders were in London and had an Auckland agent. The company was still in existence in 1885 and it continues to operate now. It had about sixty poorly paid workers, and for several years it paid out no dividends. There were small quantities of gold in all the mines. One could say that the peninsula was full of gold, but it was too expensive to refine. A ton of metal yielded only a third of an ounce of gold. Because of the exorbitant cost, all the goldmines, except for Kapanga, were abandoned. Those people who stayed on in Coromandel, if they were not publicans, shopkeepers, farm labourers or workers at Kapanga, were individual miners who worked for themselves or were paid a small weekly amount to prospect for others. But they had meagre rewards. I often explored the dark tunnels dug into the hillsides in the goldrush days. The shafts were the height of a man and there was only passage way for one person. They reminded me of the Roman catacombs.

PART 3. MISSIONARY ACTIVITY IN COROMANDEL

SUMMARY. – 1. Laxity of Coromandel Catholics. I try unsuccessfully to coax them back. – 2. Stern reprimands the next step; I threaten to leave. – 3. The other Catholic settlement. – 4. The Anglican minister, a Catholic sympathiser. 5. – My health improves. – 6. The terrible road conditions. – 7. The enchanting beauty of the forests.

1. There were about two hundred Catholics in Coromandel, Kapanga and the neighbouring district. I said two Masses on Sunday, if I didn't have to travel elsewhere. The first was at 8 a.m. at Kapanga, which had about sixty parishioners, who were rather neglectful of their religious duties and too partial to alcohol. I heard confessions and then said Mass. After the Gospel I would preach for about twenty minutes on the scriptures or some other theme. At ten I returned to Coromandel. There was Low Mass at 11 a.m. Only on solemn feast days would there be a sung Mass. The women's choir sang the 'Kyrie' and 'Gloria', accompanied by the organ. I preached after the Gospel. Then the choir sang a motet and 'O Salutaris Hostia' after the consecration, and finally the 'Agnus Dei'. In the evening at the Angelus time,* we had sung vespers. I would then preach and finally there was the benediction of the Blessed Sacrament.

Coromandel Catholics were no better off than their Kapanga neighbours. They were nearly all extremely poor. Some were so indigent they needed charity, but they were too ashamed to ask. There were three prosperous Catholic families

* This is a traditional prayer to the Virgin Mary recited at midday and at 6 p.m. In religious communities it is announced by a tolling of bells. Angelus refers to the first word of the invocation, *Angelus domini annunciavit Mariae*, the Angel of the Lord announced to Mary (that she would be the Mother of God).

who owned hotels. In general, the parishioners were very casual about their faith and very few attended church. When I first arrived, only about fifteen parishioners attended the Coromandel Sunday Mass, and hardly more at vespers. I exhorted people to come and asked those present to tell their absent brethren to honour their faith and attend. I preached with fervour and eloquence, but my entreaty was couched with gentleness and patience. However, my words fell on barren ground. I patiently persisted for a few months in this vein, hoping more parishioners would come to church, but I realised to my chagrin that they were deaf to my entreaties. It was true that not everyone could attend, but at least sixty, if not more, could have come to Sunday Mass in Coromandel and about thirty to Kapanga. But I was a long way from attaining these figures.

2. Seeing that my subtle, gentle pleas had no effect in arousing them from torpor and indifference, I determined to use stronger language to make them comply. One day I preached as follows: 'You are proud of being Irish. That's fine. But do you know what being Irish really means? It means people who are proud to show by their actions that they are good Catholics. It means a people who cherish their faith. Are you Irishmen of this calibre? You who come to church are; but not those who hardly ever attend. They aren't true Irishmen! They are Catholics in name only. And what a fine example these insipid characters give to Protestants! What must they think of our faith when they see it treated so casually? It would hardly make a good impression. They would have to believe that we're no better than them! If your ancestors were to return to Earth and see their descendants' laxity, they would be furious and revile you as unworthy of the name of Irishmen and traitors of your Catholic homeland!'

My tirade was noised abroad and much discussed. Most agreed with me, but still nothing happened and I continued waiting. A few weeks passed by, and seeing that the Mass attendance did not increase, I made another attempt to get the malingerers to church. I suggested that I put brandy instead of holy water in the font by the church entrance and give everyone a nip attending. That could be an incentive. The congregation laughed. I went on, 'But I can't do this for three reasons: first, I couldn't afford it. Second, it would be an insult to God to get people into church in this way. Third, it would cause a scandal to good Catholics and Protestants alike.'

At length, since they remained deaf to my appeals, I threatened to go elsewhere, where there were more devout Catholics. I said, 'Please realise that I came here for no other reason than your spiritual good, and because you were without a priest. Other Catholics, better than those of Coromandel, are still without a priest, because of the great shortage. They are really upset and the bishop can't help them. You, on the other hand, have your own priest to assist you in practising your faith. I have been here some months now, but you do not seem to want to take advantage of my presence, which really upsets me.'

Seeing that still only a few people were attending church, I gave the parishioners two months to mend their ways or I would go to a more suitable mission. I told them to think it over and that I would keep my word. After my supplications, entreaties and threats, the parishioners roused themselves. The majority began to attend church regularly and I was indeed gratified.

3. The biggest settlement in the peninsula, after Coromandel, was at Mercury Bay, about forty kilometres away, with about two hundred inhabitants, thirty-five of whom were Catholics. It had two hotels. About halfway between Coromandel and Mercury Bay was the settlement of St Andrew's with about a hundred people, but only roughly a dozen Catholics. The two settlements had large sawmills for milling kauri. Mercury Bay's was larger and powered by electricity. The other used coal. The tree trunks were milled into planks of various sizes and sent to settlements and towns for housing. At Cabbage Bay there were only three or four Catholics, who came to Coromandel for the sacraments. When the weather was fine and the roads passable, I went to Mercury Bay once a month to say Mass. I would stay on Sunday and return to Coromandel the following day. I went to St Andrew's twice a year, on feast days. The Catholics scattered throughout the peninsula were lax and I had little success in changing them.

4. The Anglican minister at Coromandel was a small thin man, aged about thirty-five, who had a liking for ritual. He believed that the Catholic Church was the true Church. He was well read and had a good knowledge of the history of the English Reformation. He also believed in Christ's real presence in the Blessed Sacrament. He was married with four or five daughters. Every Friday he worshipped the Real Presence in the Catholic Church for at least a quarter of an hour. He enjoyed detaining me to discuss religion and would ask me for explanations about Catholic ceremonies and practices. He complained that his parishioners were lax, some even agnostic, and given to drink. I hoped that he and his family would become Catholics. He told me that he would convert if he had the means to support himself and his family without being a minister. But since he did not have sufficient money to survive, he couldn't see how he could. Unfortunately, this is the stumbling block for many Protestant ministers. They know that Catholicism is the one, true Church of Jesus Christ, but they won't change their allegiance because they want to keep their fat stipends. The minister's two eldest daughters were sent to the convent because he said that he knew they would receive a good moral and scholastic education from the nuns, which would not be provided by government schooling. Local Anglican bigots, however, did not take kindly to his sympathy towards Catholicism, and his refusal to run down the Papist religion, as they called it. Hardly any of them had any tolerance for ritual. Hence they loathed their minister and any ritual in his service. They were so opposed to him that he was forced to seek another post.

5. The Coromandel climate was very healthy. There were large stands of pine trees around the presbytery, church and convent. The presbytery had a front flower garden, thirty-five metres long and fifteen wide. There were very few other houses and I felt as though I was breathing the fresh air of the countryside. The closest house was fifty metres away. Moreover, I didn't have to fret over church debts and the worry of paying them off. I wasn't too taxed on Sundays. I just had three sermons to deliver at Mass and vespers. Kapanga was only about two kilometres away and I could walk there within thirty minutes. Usually, however, I rode over. It was an easy fifteen-minute trip. Here I was, breathing the pure, fresh air, untroubled by debt collection or any of my Auckland stresses, and not having to make long journeys on an empty stomach. After about two months of this regime, my health began to improve considerably. I suffered shortness of breath and palpitations much less and could sleep well at night. Only rarely did I experience a sense of suffocation. It certainly happened less often than in Auckland. I described my improvement to Fr Sullivan, the abbot-general and the procurator-general. They were very pleased with the news. With new vigour, I was able to become more involved in tending to my parishioners, schooling, etc. I wondered if the improvement would last. I had to leave the answer in God's hands. I decided to remain in Coromandel as long as I was physically able. If ill-health returned, I would leave forthwith for Europe. I had some anxiety about my health because of the extreme humidity which beset the whole colony, but I resigned myself to God's will.

6. The road – or track, rather – from Coromandel to Mercury Bay was horrible for about two-thirds the distance. It crossed ridges and mountains and was extremely muddy not only on the flat, but through the rugged, dense bush. The track was generally no more than fifty centimetres wide. We were forced to ride single file, the horses' hooves digging up the ground and torrential downpours turning it into thick mud. Constant traffic trampled the soil and even across ridges the mud was up to fifty centimetres deep. Sunlight could not penetrate the density of the bush, so sometimes the track would be muddy for more than nine months of the year. On the flat it was almost always muddy. The worst stretch was at St Andrew's Bay, twenty kilometres from Coromandel. At high tide the sea spread into the valley. For more than two kilometres there was a swamp which had be traversed. The track through it couldn't be seen, even in summer. It was indicated by stakes, planted on both sides, to guide people through and prevent them drowning in the bog. The slush was as high as a horse's stomach.

Another danger was on ridges and hills. Small flat boggy areas concealed roots and deep holes. They had to be crossed, but the rider was well advised to let his horse lead, leaving the reins loose on its neck. Horses seemed to have a sixth sense. They would test the ground with their front hooves. If they couldn't feel solid ground underneath, they quickly withdrew them and moved a little to the side. The rider would watch, leaving the horse to find a way out of the difficulty. Generally this worked well. If, however, the horse got bogged down, the rider would immediately leap from the saddle into the mud, so the horse could extricate itself. He could then remount and continue his journey. I never suffered this misfortune, because the horse lent to me by a Coromandel parishioner was a very intelligent beast, even though blind in one eye.

When I made the trip I usually ended up covered in mud from head to foot from the horse's hooves. To avoid dirtying my clothes and to protect myself from frequent downpours, I wore oilskin leggings and cloak and a hat. The forty-kilometre trip took me up to three and a half hours. The chestnut horse would arrive in a lather and need a day to recuperate. Once when I was trotting along a mountain ridge with a 400-metre drop, its back legs stumbled. We nearly toppled down the slope, but my guardian angel protected me, and the horse quickly regained its footing. My heart was thumping and I slowed the horse to a walking pace, so that I could regain my breath.

7. The virgin forests, which covered many of the mountains and hills not only in Coromandel but also throughout New Zealand, were truly magnificent, breathtaking and enchanting. Europeans who haven't visited this country can have no idea of what I mean. The forest belongs to what naturalists call the fossil period. The forests that I saw would be coalfields in Europe and long since non-existent as forests. They have three layers of growth, impenetrably entwined with myriad-shaped vines. The undergrowth reaches a height of eight to ten metres. It consists of small tree ferns, some between fifty centimetres and a metre high and others up to eight and ten metres, and other vegetation. The ground is completely covered in bush choked with thick vines. The second layer is of tall ferns, palms with inedible berries and trees up fifteen metres high, towering over the bush. Above these two layers, colossal trees raise their two to four-metre thick trunks up to a height of twenty to twenty-five metres. Their lofty, enormous branches overshadow the forest and bush beneath. Some specimens would even reach a height of forty to fifty metres, cloaking the forest with their mantle. Sunlight fails to penetrate the undergrowth and the bush is undisturbed by storms. Only the tops of the great colossi of the forest sway under the fury of tempests. The bush remains evergreen throughout the year. A twenty square metre area would contain at least forty different species of shrubs and plants.*

The forests are a real delight to European visitors and those who enjoy

---

* Vaggioli gives a detailed study of the flora and fauna in his *Storia della Nuova Zelanda*, vol. 1, including personally classifying the 'Prince of Wales feather' tree fern as *Cyathea penniformis* (p. 118).

sightseeing, but they lost their first allure for this poor missionary, breathless, exhausted and mud-spattered after stumbling through them. Under the destructive hand of British colonists, the mighty forests were decimated daily. The most handsome and largest trees, such as the kauri and puriri, were chopped down, sawn into blocks and floated downstream to sawmills. The timber was used for the construction of houses and furniture. The forest was then put to the torch, and for months in the summer millions of hectares were burnt. One Saturday on my way to Mercury Bay, I found that both sides of the track I was passing through were on fire. To avoid being burnt alive I had to get my horse to gallop, but the intense heat nearly suffocated me. Fortunately I had only to cover about 500 metres to get through, and it took only a few moments. Otherwise I would have perished. Once the forest was burnt down, the bush would not regenerate. Only bracken, similar to that in Europe, sprang up. After the burning, colonists sowed grass seed for grazing.

PART 4. THE WOODCUTTERS OF COROMANDEL

SUMMARY. – 1. The woodcutters and their primitive life in the bush. – 2. Publicans exploit them. – 3. Woodcutters' stupidity in squandering their wages and savings. – 4. A Protestant family's hospitality. – 5. The new Anglican minister in Coromandel. – 6. I tell him to go ahead with his lies. The Catholic Church has nothing to fear. – 7. Conversion en masse; I'm not really serious.

1. There were many men in New Zealand, especially in the North Island, who led very harsh lives, spending most of the year in virgin forests cutting down huge trees for housing. The trees were sawn into blocks and floated downstream from the hills and mountains and transported to mills where they were sawn into planks and boards. The men lived in the bush in huts and tents from between 10 and 15 January until Holy Week, and from the Wednesday or Sunday after Easter until 15 or 20 December. They worked in gangs of six to eight men with a foreman, living in cabins made from branches covered with boards. They had regular hours of work, with fixed rest and meal breaks, six days a week. On Sundays and during the long evenings they spent hours playing cards, chatting and smoking.

In the Coromandel mission area there were about 160 woodcutters, of whom about 20 were Irish Catholics, the rest being Protestants. They could not attend church because of the distance and had no horses available. The majority, however, said their morning prayers and the rosary in the evening. On Sundays, in the absence of Mass, they said the rosary at 11 a.m. I could not visit them because of the inaccessibility, but they came to church for Christmas and Easter. The timber company provided them with the basic provisions of meat, flour and potatoes, which were transported to their camps by horse once a fortnight. Weekly wages varied from £1 10s to £2, and even higher, depending on a man's skills and stamina. It was strictly prohibited to take alcohol into the camps because men would get drunk and not work. To ensure that they didn't drink, the company paid the bushmen only twice a year with bank cheques, at Christmas and Easter.

2. The Coromandel woodcutters nearly all went to Auckland to spend their holidays and their wages, which amounted to at least 800 francs and even 1500 francs for many. Many publicans went themselves or sent their servants to wait for the woodcutters at bush exits, inviting them to their hotels to squander their earnings. The woodcutters were tired, thirsty and very hungry after trekking through the bush. They would eagerly accept and later enjoy a good lunch or dinner, and drink so much whisky or brandy they would get drunk. Publicans would take their cheques for safekeeping while the fools kept drinking. They were charged whatever the publican liked. Catholic publicans were generally honest, but the Protestants really robbed them blind. There were Protestant publicans in the Gisborne area, too, where I resided from 1880 until October 1882, and in other districts in the colony. I am told on good authority that they would make sure the wretched woodcutters who fell into their hands were kept drunk in their hotels for up to six days at a time. To succeed in their ruse, they would put a large number of empty bottles (up to twenty or thirty) in a man's room. When they thought he was sufficiently drunk, they would stop plying him with alcohol. When the man was sober the publican would present the bill, saying something along these lines: food and lodging for five days at £1 a day, £5; supply of alcohol with four meals a day, two bottles of whisky at 16 shillings a bottle, 32 shillings; additional alcohol consumed at meals, £8. For twenty bottles of whisky, brandy and rum consumed in the evening, at 16 shillings a bottle, £16; total £29 (725 francs).

Our poor befuddled man would exclaim, 'But I couldn't have drunk that much. It's impossible!'

'You were drunk all the time,' would be the reply, 'so you wouldn't remember. See the empty bottles on the floor? You drank all that. There's the proof!'

The woodcutter wouldn't know what to say. He had no memory of how much he'd drunk. He knew the prices were correct. He was simply dumbfounded.

The publican would continue, 'You gave me your cheque for £35 to look after. You owe me £29. Here's £6. Now get out.'

If the exploited man protested, he would be forcibly evicted from the hotel at that late hour, and not allowed back. Some publicans fiddled their accounts even more. Wretched woodcutters would be robbed of their last farthing, and even told that they owed several pounds. Some would take the coat off their back and throw them out like dogs! I was told this by witnesses.

3. The least intelligent woodcutters, who were in the majority, were exploited in this way. But it was their own fault. They themselves allocated some money for clothes, and the rest of their earnings was for food, alcohol and entertainment. Nothing was put aside for sickness or family needs. Their conduct was stupid. Married men generally behaved similarly. By the time they reached home, about half their earnings were gone. They hadn't given a thought to their family. The wife would have to try to keep the family alive because her husband would still spend a lot of what was left on drink.

The few sensible men, when they got out of the bush and reached Coromandel, would have lunch and take the next boat to Auckland. They went home, paid the bills and put the rest of the money in the bank, withdrawing it only as needed. These families never lacked for anything. Similarly, prudent single men deposited their money in the bank and took a room in a nearby hotel. They would buy what they wanted to drink, ask for the bill and pay the account daily, spending nothing more.

Heavy drinkers, however, moved from family to relatives to hotels, spending their savings in theatres and on amusements, drinking in dives and places of ill-repute, until their holidays were over. When their money ran out, they returned to work in the bush! If the fools had any sense, they could have saved about 2000 francs a year, but instead they saved nothing. Unfortunately, most Catholics behaved the same as Protestants, squandering their savings. Some Catholic woodcutters visited me occasionally in my two-year sojourn, proffering me ten shillings or a pound, saying: 'Father, here's some money to help you along. I've just come out of the bush, and I need to think of my priest.'

'Give it to me tomorrow. In the meantime, get ready for your confession tomorrow morning.'

'No, Father, I'm leaving for Auckland this evening. Take it now. In a few days I won't have a penny left! I'll go to confession in Auckland.'

When they spoke to me, they would still be half drunk! I told them in no uncertain terms not to get drunk and throw their money away. I might have saved my breath. A wolf can disguise his appearance, but not his habits. It was the same for them. They drank too much and couldn't give it up!

4. On the way from Coromandel to Mercury Bay there were two Protestant families who owned farms. They employed farm hands and ran a good deal of stock. I was often invited to stop by for a day or two and they would be delighted to offer me hospitality. I would thank them but excuse myself, saying I couldn't delay, but in an emergency I would willingly accept their generous offer. One Monday afternoon after I left Mercury Bay, I was caught in a downpour which lasted more than an hour. The track became a quagmire and my horse would

only go at a walking pace. Nightfall was approaching and I was still an hour and a half from Coromandel. The track was too dangerous for travelling in the dark. I decided to stop and spend the night at the first Protestant farm. It was nearly 6 p.m. when I reached the farmhouse. I rode up to the front door and called from the saddle. A maid immediately came out followed by a manservant. They begged me to dismount and come inside. I didn't budge, asking if the master was in.

'No,' they replied, 'he went to Auckland several days ago and is returning the day after tomorrow. But the mistress is at home.'

'I'm the Catholic priest of Coromandel. I'm soaked and it's dark. But if your master's not here, I won't stay. I'll carry on. Please let your mistress know.'

The mistress was listening at the half-closed door. She came out and approached me. She shook my hand and said, 'I'd be very pleased for you to stay. My husband's not here, but he would be very happy if you honoured us with your presence. Don't go on. It's pitch-black. The track's terrible. You could get lost and fall down a ravine. I won't let you leave.' She insisted that I dismount, but I didn't budge.

I said, 'I didn't realise your husband wasn't here, dear Madame, I'm sorry for disturbing you.'

'Not at all. On the contrary, it's no trouble at all. My home is at your disposal. I insist that you stay, and you're absolutely soaking!'

In fact, I didn't want to dismount because her husband wasn't there. I knew that he wouldn't, in his absence, have a Protestant minister stay the night. But eventually I gave in to the good lady's entreaties. I dismounted. She ordered the manservant to stable and feed my horse. We went inside. In spite of my oilskins I was soaked. She fetched a pair of her husband's trousers and a jacket for me to change into and got a good fire going in the drawing room. She also brought me a large shawl of hers, telling me to put it around my shoulders. She gave me a pair of her husband's socks and slippers as well. A maid took my clothing away to get washed in the kitchen. Dressed in this fashion, I accompanied her into the drawing room to dry out by the fire and avoid catching a nasty cold. Then we began chatting. Our conversation lasted about two hours. She told me that when her husband was away she would not receive men to stay overnight, not even her own minister. But she welcomed me willingly, knowing that her husband would be very pleased. She concluded, 'Father, no matter what time it is, if you feel like stopping by, please do so. My husband and I would be greatly honoured.'

The mistress had dinner ready an hour earlier than usual, saying that I must be tired and need to sleep. It was a fine meal. Later all my nicely dried clothes were put in my room. She wished me goodnight and had the maid show me to the room prepared for me. I got up the following morning at 6 a.m. The mistress was already up and wanted me to have breakfast, but I said I was to say Mass in Coromandel and needed to fast. I thanked the good lady for her hospitality and left.

Dear reader, you may well ask why wasn't their own Protestant minister able to spend a night if the husband was away. The reason was that the ministers often tried to take advantage of hospitable ladies (and some had actually done so), excluding the lady I have referred to. This was common knowledge. Catholic priests, on the other hand, were welcomed because they had no such heinous reputation.

5. One day in the spring of 1886, as I was returning by steamer from Auckland to Coromandel, I noticed a small, weather-beaten man about forty years old. He had the rough physical appearance of a woodcutter or farm hand. He came over and greeted me, saying he had just been appointed as the new Coromandel Anglican minister. He asked me for information about his parishioners and Coromandel. When he pressed me for more details, I decided to ask him for more information about himself. I learnt that only six months earlier, he was still a farmer cultivating a small holding. He had a young family and was scarcely making a living. Thus he decided to change his career. First, he changed from being a Presbyterian to an Anglican. He then applied to train for the ministry. After six months studying Protestant theology, he was ordained by the Anglican Bishop of Auckland and appointed to Coromandel. He added, 'I leased out my farm. With the rent and income as a minister, I'll do very well indeed.'

There's surely something wrong with a Church which makes ministers within six months! Christ took three years to make ministers of the Gospel out of poor, simple fishermen. Even then, three years' teaching by the divine Master was insufficient. The gifts of the Holy Spirit needed to be added. This, compared to the hasty steps I have described! What a sad state of affairs for the Anglican Church.

6. Two days later, being Sunday, the minister preached for the first time to the large congregation who had come to see and hear their new pastor. He railed against the idolatrous papist Church of Rome, saying some wicked things. But being a country yokel, his preaching was dismal. His parishioners, apart from a few dyed-in-the-wool bigots, were not at all happy with him. The vestry members shared their displeasure. They found him coarse and ignorant, and complained equally to Catholics about him. The following Sunday, as I was returning from Kapanga, I came across the Anglican minister walking over for his service. He held out his hand and greeted me. I enquired about how he was finding his parishioners. He replied that they were cold and indifferent. I then said, 'They told me that last Sunday you made quite a speech against my Church.' He flushed and didn't reply. I went on, 'Well, good on you! Bravo! The bigots in your flock will be very pleased with you! That's how to get their approval! Rail

against the Catholic Church as much as you like. It has no concern about the lies, big or small, that Protestant ministers peddle to their parishioners. For eighteen centuries, pagans, heretics, schismatics and Protestants have vilified the Church. But she is fearless and has always triumphed and surged forward, continuing her universal mission of good. Your brand of Protestantism is the creature of Queen Elizabeth, not Christ's religion. Within three centuries it has split into 200 denominations in America, 140 in England and 90 so far in New Zealand. Trumpet against Romanism as much as you like. It'll make your fame and fortune!'

The poor man was dumbstruck by my outburst. I didn't stop there: 'Say what you like against my Church. I'm not afraid, and such bizarre, false accusations only make me laugh. I explain to my parishioners the true history of the Reformation recorded not only by Catholics, but by Protestant writers such as Cobbett.* There is only one truth, my dear sir, and the truth sooner or later triumphs over lies.'

After a moment he replied, 'It's true, Father, I have spoken against your Church, but I promise not to do it again.'

'Well, your flock won't thank you for that.'

'Nevertheless, I won't do it again.'

Although an uneducated yokel, he realised that lying about Romanism was not to his advantage. From that day on he kept his word and never again criticised the Catholic Church, at least during my sojourn in Coromandel. His parishioners, however, were disgruntled, not attending church or supporting him. They wanted him gone.

7. A few months later, as I was returning home, I passed a vestry member's shop. He beckoned me to come in and talk to him. I found another two or three Protestants inside. The owner criticised his minister for being coarse and ignorant. He added that Protestant ministers were neither as cultured nor as well educated as Catholic priests, who were gentlemen and superior to Protestant ministers. I replied, 'How could your minister be well educated and cultured if he was a Presbyterian farmer a year ago and six months later, God only knows how, he becomes an Anglican and is made a minister? In the Catholic Church, it takes twelve years' strenuous training and education to become a priest.'

'Catholic priests are an honour to their Church. Ours are a disgrace. Their whole intention is to make money. They're always complaining they're poor, even with their £400 annual stipend.'

'It's just a job for them, my dear friend, and they want to make the most out of it!'

'How much do your parishioners pay you?'

* The reference is to William Cobbett, also cited in Vaggioli's *History of New Zealand and Its Inhabitants*.

'I don't receive a salary. If they can manage something, that's fine. If not, never mind. I'm content with what they put in the plate on Sunday. That's enough.'

'How is that possible? There are very few Catholics, and they're poorer than us! How can you survive?'

'Well, I manage, and I have enough to live on. Besides, I don't have a wife and children to support and dowries to find, like your minister.'

'That's true. But I'm still amazed at how you manage to survive. Perhaps you get money from your missionary society in Rome or your bishop, like our ministers?'

'No, I don't receive a penny that way. I provide the lay brother and myself with food and clothing from what my parishioners give me. That's sufficient.'

They were amazed and said they had a real struggle providing their minister's salary. I had things to attend to at home, so I said goodbye. The shopkeeper asked me to wait, mentioning that he had something important to tell me.

'I can't right now, but I'll return later.'

'All right,' he replied, 'but when?'

'I'll return at 2 p.m. Is that convenient?'

'Yes, that's fine. I'll expect you at two.'

I then departed. I returned at the agreed time and asked him what it was he wanted to tell me. He then said, 'I'm a vestry member. We have discussed that the people of Coromandel cannot maintain three ministers: the Anglican, Wesleyan (Methodist) and Catholic.'

'Excuse me, I've never heard Catholics saying they can't support me. And I've never asked them for money or a salary.'

'That's true,' he replied. 'I'm not talking about your parishioners, but us Protestants. We're considering supporting just one minister, and the others can go elsewhere. We thought of you. You're an educated gentleman and you're upright, dedicated and frank. We'll come to your church and be Catholics.'

I replied that to actually be Catholics required more than just going to a Catholic church. If they attended, they would still remain Protestants. To become Catholics they would have to believe everything the Catholic Church teaches, and have to observe its laws.

He then said, 'What do you have to believe and do to be a Catholic?'

'You have to believe that the Pope is Christ's Vicar and the visible head of God's Church.'

'That's fine; we can agree to that. Anything else?'

'Recognise that there are seven sacraments, not just two as you maintain; that divorce is unlawful, etc.'

'That's fine by us. What else?'

'You have to confess your sins to a priest, who is God's minister, at least once a year, plus abstain from meat on Fridays and other days the Church decrees and fast on certain days.'

Hearing all these conditions, their faces dropped and they exclaimed, 'That would be difficult!'

The shopkeeper added, 'We couldn't do all those things! I'm sorry, we can't take them on.'

'Well, you can come to the Catholic church as often as you like, but to be accepted into the Catholic Church without believing and practising what the Church requires is absolutely impossible.'

'So, it can't be done.'

'That's right; it's impossible. You would be Catholics in name only. In fact you would be just the same as you are now.'

'We thought we could.'

'Well, no, you can't – unless you accept the Church's conditions.'

After a long discussion, they realised they couldn't do anything about it. I left. They never mentioned the subject again, but they still retained an enormous respect for and deference towards me.

PART 5. SINGULAR EVENTS

SUMMARY. – 1. Coromandel Masons and their monopoly. – 2. Old Testament Maori. – 3. The secretary of the local education board makes accusations against the nuns. I defend them. – 4. I nearly get drowned. – 5. Huge earthquake and fresh eruptions. – 6. Divine premonition of my mother's death; I dismiss it. – 7. I take out British citizenship.

1. By 1886 there was one Masonic lodge in Coromandel with about fifty members and another at Mercury Bay. The MHR was also a Mason.* He was dim-witted and not capable of making even a short speech. But being a Mason gave him licence. The Masons controlled everything. They were on the education board, teachers in government schools, managers of the banks and the Kapanga Company. The few public offices and small businesses were in their hands. In short, they ruled the roost. The government schools in Coromandel left much to be desired. Immoral behaviour was rife. The teachers not only took no notice, but joined in it themselves. Fortunately there were good Catholic schools, where strict morality was maintained by the nuns.

Protestants who weren't Masons, seeing this travesty of an education system, were irate and discussed what they could do about it. New elections to the education board were due in 1886. They decided to voice their concerns and prevent the same members being re-elected, thus removing the Masons and particularly the arrogant secretary. They wanted them replaced with competent members who would promote a sound moral education. This was easier said

* The reference is to Alfred Jerome Cadman (MHR for Coromandel 1881–90).

than done because the Masons were powerful and influential. Nevertheless things were put in motion by the establishment of a committee. They asked me to come to their meeting to force opposition against the education board. I told them that since we had our own schools, I had no particular interest in being involved. They begged me to come for everyone's benefit, and said that Catholics should attend to vote for sounder representation. They mentioned that the Anglican minister was coming and that I should come to speak about moral education. I agreed. I made a bold closing speech at the meeting attacking the board. They had suspected something would happen and only the secretary had the courage to attend. He tried to exonerate the board, but his justifications did not satisfy the majority. I exhorted Catholics to vote against the Masons and for the reputable candidates. They did so and none of the old members were re-elected.

2. One afternoon I decided to visit a Maori village on the coast about three kilometres west of Coromandel to find out about the customs and religious practices. There were about two hundred natives living on the coast in scattered huts, or hovels, with meagre vegetable plots and scraps of lands. When I arrived I found only a few old men and women squatting on the ground near the church, smoking pipes. I asked an old man if the church was open. He said it was and got up to show me in. Native churches are not like European ones. They are built in the style of their traditional homes, but on a larger scale, with a covered entrance. They have a single nave. Roofs in large churches are supported by a single beam in the middle, or by two either side. They are steep-pitched, with guttering two metres from the ground, and timber-built. Their church could hold four hundred people. It was clean inside. I asked my guide to show me the Protestant Bible, which was in Maori. I found to my astonishment that the New Testament had been removed. The Maori, or native, who accompanied me, and whom I believe was their minister, told me that some years before (about 1865) the Maori had forsaken the Gospel of the British, because the latter, while making the Maori observe it, didn't do the same themselves. They decided to invent their own religion and renounce that of the pakeha (Europeans).

This was nothing new to me since I had heard the same thing from other natives and read about it in books and newspapers. They were neither Jews nor Christians, but Hau-Hau, or members of a new religion which was a concoction of Judaism, Christianity and paganism. (For further information, refer to my *Storia della Nuova Zelanda e dei Suoi Abitatori*, especially Volume 2.) The Maori were rapidly declining in numbers every year, because they had adopted European vices and contracted their diseases, especially drunkenness and venereal diseases through relationships between European men and Maori women. In 1886 there were 44,000 throughout the colony, of whom 5000 were Catholic. I couldn't say how many were Protestants, but the great majority of them were Hau-Hau. The Maori population was decreasing by a thousand every year. The people, who were deserving of a better fate, were dying off and would eventually face extinction.

3. The new secretary of the education board was a fervent Methodist. He was my neighbour and I got on very well with him. He was trying to sort out the mess created by his Mason predecessor. When he checked the accounts, he found that the sisters had not paid for renting the school hall for their concert in 1884. He mentioned it to the ex-secretary, seeking an explanation. He brusquely replied that if there was no record, they couldn't have paid. The secretary asked me if the sisters had paid the £2 for the concert, and if they hadn't they needed to do so immediately. I replied that I didn't know because I wasn't in Coromandel at the time, but I would enquire and let him know.

The sisters said they had paid the fee about a month after the concert, just as they had done in previous years. I then said, 'Give me the receipt, so I can show it to the new secretary.'

'We don't have it. We didn't ask for one. We trusted the secretary's honesty.'

'That was a mistake. Do you have any witnesses of the payment?'

'No, we don't, but we certainly paid it.'

I told the secretary what I had been told. He was very annoyed that they hadn't requested a receipt. The ex-secretary could not then be charged with embezzlement because there was no evidence. The secretary was convinced that the sisters had paid and the Mason had pocketed the money, because he had discovered that Protestants had given the Mason about £15 for the school, but there was no record and no receipts. The Mason could not deny it, but made the excuse that the money had been spent on a holiday for the pupils, because there was insufficient money for that purpose. But that was untrue. That year the Mason would have pocketed about £50. The man pestered the nuns for the receipt, knowing full well they couldn't produce it. The sisters, however, stood their ground, refusing to pay twice. The ex-secretary was angry at being placed in such an embarrassing situation and let it be widely known that the sisters had not paid and had no intention of doing so. He published a letter in the *Herald* exonerating himself and blaming the nuns.

At this point, I turned to the new secretary and begged him to expose the Mason's financial machinations and deceit. He said he would approach the school donors and get their names. But they had been intimidated by Coromandel's chief Mason, who was a wealthy and influential man, and told to keep their mouths shut about it and say things were fine. They complied and the secretary declined to proceed further, since he too was frightened of reprisals by the Masons. I asked him to intervene at least on behalf of the sisters, but he said that unfortunately he could not do so since he had no legal proof of payment.

I could not remain silent regarding the accusation against the nuns, which would discredit them in the eyes of the Protestant community. I decided to go to their defence publicly. I could have replied to the calumny in the *Herald*, a

Masonic paper, but I decided to send my letter to the *Evening Star*, which was non-Mason. I didn't mince my words. Consequently a paper war began between the Masonic liar and myself. I went to Auckland to speak to the editor and owner of the *Evening Star*. He was an honest man and a former Presbyterian minister. He was loathed by Masons because his paper took much revenue away from the *Herald*. He welcomed me warmly. I told him everything and asked him for his paper's support. He replied, 'Unfortunately, I know what the Masons are like. They're waging a secret war against me too, but I forge ahead and take no notice of them. Send me your letters and I'll publish them. It's a good job you're unmasking them and their schemes. I'll lend you all the support I can.'

The ex-secretary, realising he was being put on the spot, used the *Herald*, and I rebutted him in the *Evening Star*. The Mason then threatened to take the matter to court. I urged him not to hesitate. Then he would be publicly exposed not only for the falseness of his accusations against the sisters, but for misappropriating other money. I was determined to completely expose his wicked deeds. Fearing a major scandal, the Coromandel Masons warned their colleague to silence. I didn't say another word. That put an end to the matter. Coromandel's non-Masons were convinced that the sisters had paid, and that theirs and others' money had been squandered by the deceitful secretary.

4. There was a very difficult two-kilometre stretch of road approaching the settlement and sawmill at St Andrew's. At high tide the sea covered much of the valley, causing a quagmire. At low tide this was not a problem. But at high tide, after 500 metres you had to veer left and find high ground, skirting the hillside to reach the settlement. There were no marker-posts.

On my first trip, a guide came with me. The second time, I met people on the way whom I joined. The third time, which was after Easter 1886, I was all alone. I searched in vain for the track. I thought it was low tide and that if I moved quickly I would make it to the hillside before high tide. I could see there was only a little water in a low-lying 200-metre stretch. I prodded my horse into a gallop. I was about 300 metres from the hillside when I noticed the water rising at an alarming rate. It was already halfway to its peak. There was a five-metre difference between high and low tide. Seeing the danger ahead, I stopped in my tracks. I heard a man calling from the hillside and gesturing for me to turn back. I did so, but the water had cut off my retreat and I couldn't see the track. I didn't want to return home, but to press on to the settlement. So I decided to traverse the ford. I turned round on dry ground and pressed forward. If my horse bucked, I would be thrown into the water and would have to swim to the bank. My heart was thumping with anxiety, but I had no time to lose. The horse neighed, reluctant to enter the channel. I prodded it into action, and it moved slowly forward. To avoid getting my legs wet, I swung them round its neck and the horse started to swim. I urged it on. Familiar with such situations, it swam straight ahead against the current for the landing. I prayed to the Lord and the Holy Virgin to save me from disaster. The water rose to the top of the saddle, but only my bottom got wet. My Mass kit remained perfectly dry. My horse just managed to float under my weight. It neighed, holding its head high to keep its muzzle out of the water. I was ready to jump off if it couldn't manage. There was about 300 metres to cover. The horse was hesitant until about halfway because he couldn't see the bank, but once he saw it he got his second wind and swam on. With God's help, he brought me safe and sound to high ground.

When I reached terra firma I dismounted, shaking from head to foot and my heart pounding frantically. I couldn't carry on. After about a quarter of an hour's rest, I remounted and travelled at a walking pace the nearly three kilometres that separated me from St Andrew's settlement.

5. In a few moments about 2 a.m. on 10 June 1886, a huge volcanic eruption destroyed the thermal area of Rotomahana and surrounding district for about thirty miles. Craters suddenly appeared from which were hurled rocks, boiling mud and ash for more than fifteen kilometres. All the 102 inhabitants of a native village were instantly buried under five metres of scalding mud, even though they were actually four or five kilometres from the eruptions. Fifteen kilometres away, two Europeans and two Maori perished, and three hundred others just managed to save themselves in headlong flight. (I describe this disaster in my history of New Zealand.* The reader may care to peruse my account in that work. I had visited the area seven or eight months previously and described what I saw.) In 1886 Rotomahana changed completely. Although I was eager to revisit the devastated region, I could not because it was too dangerous.

6. On the evening of 12 June I went to bed at eight-thirty, because the following day, Pentecost Sunday, I was to rise at four-thirty to hear confessions before Mass, which I was to say at Kapanga. I was in a deep sleep when I was disturbed by a feeling of my left shoulder being shaken. I was sleeping on my right side. I woke with a start, thinking that Br Joseph Ricci had come to call me out to someone who was ill.

'What's the matter?' I exclaimed. He wasn't there. But immediately I heard an unfamiliar voice in my ear saying, and these were the exact words, 'Your mother has died right at this moment. Pray for her!' These words sounded clearly and distinctly in my ear, as though I was listening on the telephone. Then I heard the voice saying, 'Your mother is now in heaven', and an ineffable, indescribable joy filled my being. My heart was indeed consoled that my mother had gone to heaven. But at the same time, realising that she was no longer present on earth caused me great sorrow and tears came to my eyes; but I

* cf. *Storia della Nuova Zelanda e dei Suoi Abitatori*, vol. 1, pp. 60-63.

couldn't cry because of the contrasting feeling of happiness in my heart. I called her name several times and said three Hail Marys. The thought of not having been able to see her before she died, when she would have wanted so much to see me again, brought me tears of regret. My brother Don Giuseppe had written to me a year earlier, telling me how keen my dear mother was to see me again, but I was 30,000 kilometres away. I immediately lit a candle. I looked around the room to see if anyone was there, but not a soul was present. The door was shut and the house was wrapped in silence. I looked at the clock. I noted the time and decided to write to my brother the next day for news of mother. Then I thought perhaps the whole thing was a dream or fantasy, and I shouldn't believe it. On the other hand, I had heard the words clearly when I was awake and it was impossible that I had dreamt or imagined it. It had been a real experience, both hearing the voice and being shaken.

My mother had always been a devout Christian from her childhood. She took the sacraments weekly or fortnightly. She gave her children an excellent education and provided a wonderful example. She fasted regularly and was extremely devoted to the Blessed Virgin. She was charitable, especially to the poor, whom she helped as much as she could, following the example of her own fine parents. The whole village lamented her death and accompanied her to her final resting place. The poor were particularly bereft, saying they had lost their good mother. Being so humble, patient, repentant, charitable and compassionate during her life, she certainly had no need of my prayers to help her reach heaven.

On Pentecost Sunday, I said Mass for my mother, which I often did. If she was in fact dead, for her dear soul, although I was sure she didn't need it. And if she was alive, that the Lord would continue to protect her. I immediately wrote to my brother, asking him to let me know how she was, and I described my experience of the previous evening. The letter reached him fifty days later. Out of a sense of false duty, he deceived me by concealing the truth from me. He replied that she was well, although not completely cured, and that she was eager to see me again. I believed him and thus I did not bother to exactly record my experience, which remained a puzzle to me until I returned to Europe.

7. At the beginning of 1886 Catholics and Protestants invited me to take part in local body elections, since they wanted to get rid of the oppressive yoke of the Masons. They urged me to take out British citizenship because of the local body elections that year and national elections the next. Realising that by taking this step, I could benefit the community and the public in general, I agreed to seek citizenship from the colonial governor. Although it was rarely granted, I was assured that I would have no trouble. I sent the government the necessary information regarding my application. After about three months, I was informed that I would be granted citizenship and that I was to appear before a magistrate and swear an oath of allegiance to Queen Victoria and her heirs. In June or July

I swore the oath on a Catholic Bible before the Coromandel magistrate.

At the beginning of September my certificate of citizenship was sent to me. It stated:

William F. Drummond Jervois, Governor   86/2642
To whomsoever it may concern.
Greetings.

Domenico Felice Vaggioli, Roman Catholic Priest of Coromandel, in the Colony of New Zealand, being a person of good character, having applied for naturalization and a certificate to this effect, as required by law, and having already taken the oath as prescribed by the Aliens Act.

Let it be known that I, William Francis Drummond Jervois, Governor of the Colony of New Zealand, in conformity with the power invested in me by the said Act, confer on the said D. F. Vaggioli, this Certificate of Naturalization, and declare that the said D. F. Vaggioli will from henceforth enjoy all the rights and privileges of anyone born in the United Kingdom, these privileges being equally applicable in the Colony of New Zealand.

Given by authority of His Excellency Sir William Francis Drummond Jervois, Lieutenant-General of Her Majesty's Armed Forces, etc.

Issued under the seal of the said Colony, in the Governor's Residence, Wellington, 30 August 1886.

Seal and signatures of the Governor and the Colonial Secretary.

Part 6. Ill Again

Summary. – 1. No change to the debt on St Benedict's. – 2. My health deteriorates again and I decide to return to Europe. – 3. Militiamen at Mass. – 4. Their commander is annoyed at my speech and refuses to allow the Protestants to return. – 5. The abbot-general's odd reply. – 6. I answer, clarifying ambiguities. – 7. General dissatisfaction with the lacklustre Coromandel MHR. – 8. A Protestant deputation asks me to accept nomination as their MHR. I have to refuse.

1. Before I left Auckland, as I mentioned elsewhere, responsibility for sorting out the debt on the church was given to Fr O'Gara. He, however, was both unsuited to the task and uninterested. Without an energetic, active person in charge, the committee could make little headway on the debt. Consequently, they wrote to Fr Sullivan requesting him to return to Auckland now that he had recovered. He returned in January 1885 and assisted Fr O'Gara with the debt, but he was even less able to make a difference. The good Fr Sullivan always had wonderful, grandiose but impractical ideas. In addition, he kept no records and wasted money. He made no financial reports for 1886 and 1887. Nor did he hold any public meetings, perhaps fearing he would appear in a poor light

for failing to reduce the debt by even a farthing in that period. Fortunately he was able to pay the running costs of the church, but I couldn't ascertain whether he managed to pay the interest on the debt.

2. In Coromandel, the pleasant climate, less onerous responsibilities and greater peace and harmony improved my health considerably. Even if I did not make a complete recovery, I hoped to make further progress. But I was deceived. The gains did not last. The setback was caused by the shock I got when I nearly drowned on my way to St Andrew's after Easter in 1886, as mentioned above. For more than a year my heart had given me no trouble. But after this perilous incident, there was a deterioration and I found it difficult to travel by horse, because galloping affected my condition and I had to slow down to a walking pace, which then meant it took me an inordinate time to reach Mercury Bay. Storms, wretched roads and tracks and the hilly terrain also strained my heart on long journeys and were certainly not likely to improve my health. I realised that my missionary days were over because I was not fit enough to carry on.

Since my health was deteriorating, I visited the Coromandel doctor, who was an elderly, experienced man. After giving me a thorough examination, he said I had heart disease. He prescribed digitalis, no disturbance and rest, and recommended a change of air as soon as possible because of the extreme humidity in New Zealand. I could only agree with him. This visit occurred in October 1886. I mentioned the state of my health to Fr Sullivan, saying that since it had not improved, I wished to take up our general's permission to return to Europe the following spring. He replied that he hoped my indisposition would be temporary and I would abandon the idea of returning to Europe. I wrote to the abbot-general that since my health had deteriorated, I had decided to take up his permission to return. I also asked him if I could travel via Genoa and Marseilles on my way to Rome, so that I could spend a few days at Sarzana and visit my aged mother, who was longing to see me again. I had left home in 1863 to become a monk, and the poor woman had not seen me since.

3. In Coromandel there were about a hundred members of the militia under the command of a captain. They didn't enter military service except in the case of war. Hence they weren't paid by the government, but it did provide them with mounts and arms. Only six or seven of the volunteers were Catholics. Every two or three weeks from November, according to the captain's whim, there was a Sunday parade which began at 10 a.m. and lasted an hour. It was attended by about sixty or seventy militiamen. The captain, a bigoted Anglican, wanted the Protestant members at least to go to Sunday service in their church. None were obliged to do so, but he tried to make them. So as not to upset the Catholics, he arranged that the militia alternated attendance between the Anglican and Catholic churches. On Saturday evening, the captain would send a notice to either the

Anglican minister or the Catholic priest stating: 'Weather permitting, the volunteers will attend your church at eleven. Please expect them for the service.'

The parade finished just before eleven. The volunteers would then march in pairs to church. When they reached the porch, the captain dismissed them and they were free to enter or go elsewhere, including to their own church. When it was the day for the Anglican service, the captain was the first to enter, but few Protestant volunteers followed him. The Catholics always went to their own church. When the militiamen were directed to the Catholic church and dismissed, the captain went away, but nearly all the Protestant volunteers entered and sat in seats reserved for them. They came particularly for the beautiful music and to hear the sermon and explanation of the Gospel. This had been the routine for four or five years.

4. One Saturday in December 1886 or January 1887, I received the usual notice that the following morning at eleven, the militia would be attending our church. I requested that a dozen pews be reserved for them. At five past eleven the volunteers entered the church, leaving their rifles in the porch. The captain also came, for the first time. I started saying Mass and the choir sang the 'Kyrie' and 'Gloria'. I had my sermon prepared. My subject was 'The Origin of Protestantism'. At this last moment, I could not change it, since I didn't have time to prepare another sermon. After the Gospel, I expounded on the topic, demonstrating that the English, up to the time of Henry VIII, or 1540, had had the same faith as other Roman Catholics, the faith that followers of Jesus Christ had maintained for nearly fifteen centuries. I explained why Henry VIII cut himself off from Rome, the centre of Catholic unity, out of lust, wanting to divorce his lawful wife and marry a young courtesan; that the Pope had refused his consent to this evil and how Queen Elizabeth, a lover of novelty, planted Protestantism in England and Scotland. I further explained how Protestantism was established in England through violence and war, vile persecution and pillage, and through nefarious laws; that only the heroic Irish people had preserved their original faith, despite three centuries of horrible persecution and carnage. I concluded my sermon, exhorting them to read Protestant writers' accounts of the Reformation, such as Cobbett. They would there find confirmation of what I said.

A few days later, I bumped into the captain. I asked him if he had enjoyed attending the Catholic church. He said that he had quite liked the service and the singing, but that my sermon had attacked the foundations of his belief, casting doubts on his religion. He was angry that he had come and said it was not an experience he would repeat. Nor would he conduct his volunteers again to either church. I replied that what I had said was the historical truth and since there can be only one truth, it is imperative to seek it, find it and follow it. But he said that was not his concern. From then on, the captain dismissed the corps on the parade ground. They then went their own way.

5. I was keenly aware of Fr Sullivan's intention to keep me as a missionary at all costs. I should not have been so naïve as to make it evident to him that I was set on returning to Europe. I should have written only to the general about my intention. However, since it was my sacred duty to observe obedience, I believed that my immediate superior needed to be informed of my state of health and my decision; even more so, since I went to Coromandel on trial and on condition that only if I kept in good health would I remain. Otherwise, I would have no hesitation in leaving for Europe. If he wanted to twist things, that had nothing to do with me.

On receiving my letter, Fr Sullivan would certainly have written to our general to see if he could persuade me to stay. Although I had no evidence, the general's reply, retracting his permission of the previous year, was proof enough. Whether he didn't believe I was ill, or had simply changed his mind, here is the general's reply:

Subiaco. S. Scolastica
26 December 1886

Rev. and Dear Fr Dom. Felice,
I wish to acknowledge receipt of your letter of 6 November. *In primis,** many thanks for your kind wishes. I regret receiving news of your desire to return to Europe. You may recall that I did not express willingness for you to return unless it was explicitly stated as necessary by doctors because of your health. Your present state of health does not warrant your return.
Furthermore, it is hardly more than ten years that you have been a missionary. I do not see the necessity of an urgent return. And as for your wish to visit your mother, you must be patient. It is, in fact, most unusual, and, I would even venture to say, unheard of, for a monk to leave his post and undertake a journey of thousands of miles to see his mother! I would urge you to think about this and I am sure that as a sensible and thoughtful monk you will recognise the inconvenience that this would cause.

For religious, there is nothing more alluring and deceptive than love of one's relatives. Nor should you be swayed by information from home about your mother's health. I know of good monks in our community who receive news that a parent is dying. The trip to see them would only be a few hours, but they decide to make a supreme sacrifice and renounce the opportunity, thus bringing credit on themselves, and, I am sure, spiritual benefit to the parent concerned. Nor should you impose such a large expenditure, which such a long journey would entail, on your Mission, where you have been scarcely six years, even taking cognizance, as I do, of your hard work and efficacious results. My dear Dom. Felice, I urge you to reconsider your proposed course of action, and to make a decision worthy of a monk of your steadfast faith, more appropriate to the circumstances and more likely to set an example to your confrères. On the other hand, were you to return to Europe, you would create an unfortunate precedent and set a bad example. I am sure that you will, as you have in the

* 'First of all' (Latin).

past, heed my advice and agree to what I have said, and send me the kind of reply I would expect from you.

With every blessing and wishing you a happy and holy New Year,
Yours affectionately
Dom Nicola Canevello OSB, Abbot General

P.S. This letter will be forwarded to you by Rev. Superior Fr Dom Adalbert, who is aware of its contents.

6. The general's letter came as a shock. I couldn't account for his dramatic change of attitude and the misrepresentation of my request to return to Europe and spend a few days with my mother. I decided that Fr Sullivan was to blame because he was determined to keep me and he must have written to the general in such a way as to get an agreement from him for me to stay in the mission field. This could be the only explanation. I replied calmly and carefully to the general, retaining a copy of my letter:

Coromandel
26 February 1887
Most Rev. Fr. Abbot-General.

Your Reverence,
I wish to thank you for your kind letter of 26 December. You are absolutely right to seek medical reports, and I herewith include Dr Hovell of Coromandel's certificate, which I asked him to provide so that I could send it on to you.
I am indeed aware that Your Reverence desires only my well-being. If I were not convinced that, given the precarious state of my health, it would be advisable for me to retire to the cloisters, I would not have requested your permission to do so. I cannot see anything wrong with my request.

Regarding visiting my mother, I certainly agree with everything you say. However, I have not wanted to leave my post simply to see my mother. My intention was and is, that having obtained your permission to return to Europe because of my health, I would visit my village on my way to the monastery. I simply sought your permission to spend a few days with my mother, given that many other monks have been allowed to do so. You do not have to concern yourself regarding the cost of my trip. Apart from paying for it myself, I will be able to leave £150 (3750 francs) with the Auckland mission, which I have saved for the benefit of the monks. Hence I will be no burden to them, nor will I incur any debt for my return. Having clearly explained my reasons, I hope that there will be no further obstacles and you will accede to my request.

Please accept my humblest respects, and begging your blessing.

I remain your most obedient servant, etc.

Dr Hovell's certificate reads as follows:

The Rev. Fr Vaggioli of Coromandel is, and has been, for some time past, suffering from heart disease. Exertion or excitement, however trifling, is positively harmful. He requires perfect rest of mind and body. Change is, for his health's sake, imperatively necessary. This climate does not appear to suit him. I would advise his speedy return to his native land.

Coromandel
February 1887
Dr Charles H. J. Hovell.

I was indeed ill, but not half-dead, as intimated by Dr Hovell's certificate, because I was still able to work as a missionary. But the doctor was, according to a rumour, a Mason, or at least had allegiance to them, and would have been pleased to see the back of me and the Masons left alone. Hence he wrote this somewhat exaggerated diagnosis, which I sent to the general.

7. The local Member of the House Representatives was coarse, dim-witted and incapable of holding a conversation or making a decent speech. He did nothing for his electorate, simply backing the government and feathering his own nest. But he was a Mason and that was all that mattered, since the colonial government was riddled with them and they had absolute control. For two terms, or six years, he had promised to do wonders for his Coromandel electorate, but he never did a thing for the general public. All he did was help the Masons as much as possible. Protestants and Catholics alike were sick and tired of him, wanting to replace him with a more suitable candidate in the general elections due to take place in August or September 1887. They wanted someone who was eloquent, able and energetic and who had the interests of the electorate at heart. In March an electoral committee was established. They announced a public meeting to be held in the Kapanga hall. The MHR was invited to speak and give an account of his activities to the voters. I was also invited by the committee to address the meeting and represent the interests of the electorate. I decided to agree. By the time I arrived the meeting had been in progress for half an hour. The hall was crowded. Very few women were present. The MHR was making excuses, saying he was not to blame, that he had done everything possible. But people didn't accept this. Various speakers demonstrated that he had given no thought to the good of the electorate. He made fine promises, but did nothing. The two Protestant ministers were invited onto the stage to speak, but said nothing of consequence.

I was then invited to express my opinion. As I mounted the stage, I was greeted with general applause. My speech went as follows: 'Any MHR who takes his duty seriously, before promising to meet people's wishes, needs to examine whether such requests are fair and practicable, as one would hope them to be. Once he gives his word, he needs to carry out his promises. If he doesn't, he is failing in his duty, and people have the right to elect another candidate to Parliament who will. I was not in Coromandel three years ago when the Honourable Member here present made certain promises. But you can say whether he has fulfilled the mandate entrusted in him by yourselves. [*Exclamations of: "No, no; he hasn't carried out his promises!"*]

'If that is the case, you have every right to remove his mandate and entrust it to a more competent, reliable candidate. Such a man would need to work vigorously for the good of his district and the public. He would need to remove any injustices he comes across. He would need to raise his voice in Parliament and represent the district's parlous state to his colleagues. His word must be sacred and kept faithfully. Otherwise he commits betrayal and deceit. An MHR who does not keep his word is unworthy of consideration and deserves only contempt!' [*Applause*]

The Member did not reply to my speech. Among the many Masons present, two spoke in his defence, excusing him and blaming the government, etc. But the vast majority weren't at all satisfied with the excuses.

8. Among the people of Coromandel, none was readily suited to becoming an MHR because they weren't well educated, being mostly workers and shopkeepers. To seek an unknown candidate outside the district was risky. People wouldn't readily vote for him, and the Masons would scare him off. Several Protestants discussed their dilemma with their friends, who suggested that I would be a suitable candidate. They held some secret meetings and the idea found general support. They also mentioned the idea to some Catholics, swearing them to secrecy, until I was approached. They too were very happy with the idea, but doubted that I would accept. It was agreed that two Protestants on the election committee would approach me, together with a Catholic, and ask me to accept candidacy as their MHR I knew nothing about this.

One evening, about 8 p.m., the Protestant delegation visited me and were introduced by the Catholic. I greeted them courteously, asking how I could help them. They explained the reason for their visit. They said they were considering me because they knew from experience that I spoke the plain, unvarnished truth at all times and that I had the good of the district at heart, etc. They concluded saying that if I accepted the candidature, they were confident I would be elected, that I was the only person in the county capable of effectively representing their interests in Parliament, and that the Catholics warmly supported their request.

I thanked them for their faith in me and agreed that I was frank, fair and keen to do good for all. But it was not possible for me to accept the candidature because I had heart disease for which my doctor had ordered me rest and complete peace. I also mentioned that I had decided to return to Europe in a few months, to recuperate if possible, following Dr Hovell's strong recommendation. Not only was I unable to become an MHR, but I would not be remaining in the colony. I also told them even if I were to stay, and my health was fine, I could not accept being an MHR in Wellington because the bishop would have to replace me in Coromandel when Parliament was in session. They said they were very sad about my illness and disappointed that I could not accept the candidature, and even sadder to lose me. They departed, deeply upset. I later learned that in September the Member was re-elected. By that time I was already in Europe.

Part 7. My Final Months in Coromandel
February to June 1887

Summary. – 1. Newton's financial shambles! What's Fr Adalbert's game? – 2. St Benedict's church is burnt down! A fortunate accident. – 3. The Benedictines discuss buying land and building a presbytery. – 4. The abbot-general's favourable reply regarding my return to Europe. – 5. Catholics upset with the news. – 6. Address and offering made by Coromandel's Protestants. – 7. Catholics' address and collection on my behalf. – 8. My farewell and departure from Coromandel.

1. By the beginning of 1887, it appeared that my Newton confrères did not have sufficient money to pay their running costs, even though they received more than 600 francs in the weekly collections. Why this was so was a complete mystery. And yet Fr Sullivan himself kept the accounts and paid the bills! He knew that when I was in Gisborne, in two years I saved £216, which I deposited in the bank for the needs of the Benedictine mission. He did not know that I had to withdraw just under £10 for my trip to the Waikato and for Br Joseph and I to go to Coromandel. The acting superior, Fr Downey, didn't give me a penny, saying he had no reserves for these expenses. Other priests didn't want to go there because there wasn't enough money to support them. Br Joseph and I, however, managed and we had no debts. In fact, we even managed to save a few pounds by making the most stringent economies. In Auckland, which had huge resources to support six people, they were in debt! I simply couldn't understand.

During the second half of 1887, Fr Sullivan wrote me an obsequious letter mentioning the wretched financial state of the Newton presbytery. He said that he had to pay several pressing bills and he didn't have a penny. He begged me to send him all the money I had in the bank, promising that he would pay for my trip to Europe if I decided to go. I believed that he had seen the general's letter denying me permission and that he wanted to get the money off me, thus preventing my departure by later refusing to pay for my trip on the pretext of not having any money. In fact, this was his game, as I will explain later. Being an obedient monk, I replied saying I would send him the money which amounted to £206 11s 7d (5164.45 francs). I sent him a bank cheque by registered post. His telegram followed:

> To Fr Vaggioli, Coromandel (2 February 1887)
> Received cheque and letter, everything in order, many thanks, Fr Sullivan.

2. One morning, probably about the beginning of March 1887, a member of the Newton committee sent me the following telegram: 'St Benedict's Church and presbytery and surrounding buildings burnt down.' At this incredible news I raised my eyes to heaven, exclaiming: 'Thank you, Lord, for Your gracious mercy! May Your Name be ever praised! You have truly blessed us!' I was not only not upset by the disaster, but I was ecstatic with the news, and I will explain why. The brief dispatch said nothing about how the fire occurred or whether everything was destroyed. I waited until the next day for the details, knowing that it would be widely reported in the papers. This is how the fire occurred. A wooden house about 150 metres north of the church caught fire. A strong wind carried sparks onto the church roof. Cinders fell on a sparrow's nest setting it alight. Soon the wooden roof was ablaze. There was hardly time to remove the Blessed Sacrament and the vestments from the sacristy.

Firemen rushed to the scene to put out the fire, but because of the height of the church, pressure from the reservoir on the hill was insufficient to pump water up to the roof. The firemen couldn't do a thing, and within eighteen minutes the church was completely destroyed, as were the Protestant church I had used for concerts, the house next door and three other houses behind the church. The presbytery behind the church was also burnt down and a nearby house. Since the church was destroyed, services had to be carried out in the small chapel in the cemetery. But this was inadequate, and a temporary wooden building was erected where the Protestant church had stood. It was built in three weeks and all the services were performed there until a new church was built on the site of the original church. The reader may well be surprised at my pleasure about the destruction of St Benedict's. My pleasure was justifiable for the following reasons:

1) There was an outstanding debt of £3100 on the church which neither I nor the other monks had been able to pay off. And it was a long way off being repaid. I had taken out insurance for £5000 on the church. Because of the fire, this had not only cleared the debt, but left a surplus of £1900 to build a new church.

2) Fr Sullivan would now abandon the silly idea of building a wooden Gothic-style church, and content himself with a large, modest, much cheaper brick building.

3) Mons. Luck, the bishop, was a very shrewd man. He would not permit Fr Sullivan and the committee to undertake such an enormous debt again. He would hold them to a restricted budget. After I left the colony, this is exactly what he did.

3. A few weeks after the fire, Fr Sullivan summoned a chapter of our missionaries. I was included, and saw the damage with my own eyes. He explained that we did not own the house we had lived in, etc. He said that nearly all the furniture had been destroyed in the fire, and that we would need a new presbytery, beginning with the purchase of land for it. He also mentioned that the Newton community had no money for this or for running costs. He therefore needed our assistance. At this, Frs Augustine Luck, Anselm Fox and I, who were not from Newton, looked at him in amazement. Fr Sullivan and the others averted their gaze. After a moment's silence I said, 'What do you mean that you have nothing? What about the £20 to £25 from the weekly collections? Where has that disappeared?'

'The collections don't bring in that much now,' said Fr Sullivan, flushing, 'and they're used up by the considerable running costs.' I asked him to look at the presbytery accounts and see how the normal and extra income were spent. Fr Sullivan said the ledgers had been destroyed in the fire, so it couldn't be done! The fire was blamed for everything. But neither I nor Fr Fox believed his story, because the other books were saved. Surely the ledgers would have had first priority. The two Newton lay brothers and I were convinced that either accounts hadn't been kept or they didn't want them known. Frs Fox and Luck said nothing, knowing there was no point in asking for information or an explanation. Frs Downey and O'Gara sided with Fr Sullivan. Fr Sullivan then proposed the purchase of the quarter of an acre section on which the presbytery had stood, for £450, not including the cost of title. He also proposed building on the site a presbytery of reinforced concrete or brick large enough to house six or seven people, with room for expansion, at a total cost of £1500. When asked where the money would come from he replied, 'I request that Fr Vaggioli's savings of £206 and Fr Fox's of £1300 from their respective missions go towards the costs.' They all agreed, but I said, 'I agree that the £206 I sent you be used for buying a piece of land, on condition that the Newton community pays for my return to Europe.' The monks said that was fair and reasonable. Fr Sullivan promised that were I to return, he would pay. I then asked him in whose name the property would be registered.' He replied, 'Fr Downey's, Fr O'Gara's and mine.'

I said that Fr Fox's name should also be included to avoid any confusion later, and more particularly because he was the one who had contributed the most. Fr Sullivan didn't want Fr Fox as a joint-owner, but knowing how much our superior messed things up, I insisted that his name be included. Fr Sullivan replied that he had no difficulty with the proposal, but saw it as a demonstration of a lack of faith in one's confrères. I countered that it wasn't out of mistrust, but from the awareness that they weren't capable administrators. It was then agreed that the joint owners would be Frs Sullivan, Downey and Fox. But not even Fr Fox was able to prevent the property from being saddled with a mortgage of £1400 on the house and section. This happened a year after my departure. Our mission was completely and irreversibly ruined!

4. The abbot-general, having received my letter and Dr Hovell's medical certificate, replied immediately. He would have received my letter about the beginning of June 1887. He said he would honour the permission he had given me in 1885 and I could return to Europe as soon as possible, that he would be delighted to see me again and to take good care of my needs, etc. He also granted me permission to stay two or three months at my mother's and thence to proceed to Rome and Subiaco. I immediately informed Fr Sullivan that I intended to take up this permission. But he had already had a letter from the abbot-general. Realising that he could not prevent my departure, he searched for another stratagem for blocking me. He wrote that he didn't have any money for my trip and that I would have to get my parishioners to pay. I replied that I would do nothing of the sort. If they gave me money, I would accept it, but I wouldn't request any. He was obligated to pay for my trip. He had promised to do so on condition I sent him the £206 in February. He made no further comment at the time. In July, however, when I demanded that he purchase a ticket for me from Auckland to Marseilles in France, he refused. I then said I would get the money from the bishop and leave it to the general to decide who should pay for the trip. With his back to the wall, he purchased me a first-class ticket for £64. All other expenses, including the trip from Marseilles to Rome and Subiaco, were paid for out of money given me by parishioners and Protestants. I also paid for Br Joseph's trip two years later.

5. When I had the general's permission, I notified the sisters and some parishioners that at the beginning of July I would be leaving Coromandel to return to Europe. Immediately the news spread. My parishioners and the majority of the Protestants were extremely upset. Only the Masons were pleased, relieved that their lies would no longer be exposed. But the ones who were most upset about my departure were the three sisters. They had grown very fond of me, realising that all the time I was in Coromandel I had always sought their spiritual and material well-being, helping them in every way I could. I too was upset at leaving them, because they had acted so well, carrying out their duties as nuns and teachers. And I was afraid that after I left, they would slip back. I made the announcement of my departure as late as possible, only two weeks before I was due to go. I did this to avoid a collection or presentation being made for me. I knew how poor the parishioners were and I didn't want

them making sacrifices on my behalf. However, they wanted to give a formal farewell and wish me bon voyage and present me with a customary purse of gold coins. I begged them not to do anything. But they would not be deterred and a special committee was formed for this purpose.

When the Protestants learnt that the Catholics were going to make a formal address and presentation to me, they asked if they could join in and come to the occasion, as a testimony of their respect and affection. Such a demonstration by Protestants for a Catholic priest had never occurred before. The committee did not know what to do. One group of parishioners wanted to make their own collection. Another group was happy to have the Protestants demonstrate their affection towards the Catholic priest. In their confusion, they decided to consult me, since a lot of people were involved. I advised them that it would be better not to accept a Protestant contribution. It could otherwise later be said that without them the Catholics would not have been able to raise a collection for their priest. This is certainly what the Masons and the few Protestant bigots would say. This would add to the gossip around my departure and would disturb parishioners and affront their sense of devotion to their priest. I thus suggested for them not to accept a Protestant contribution and to tell the Protestants that if they wanted to make a collection they do it on their own behalf. Parishioners regretted that there was insufficient time to present me with an illuminated parchment address, which would have to be ordered from Auckland, costing £15. They begged me to delay for this purpose. I told them not to throw their money away. An address on plain paper would do. I could not delay my departure since I had arranged to leave New Zealand before the end of July. They concurred.

6. The Protestants did not abandon the idea of making an offering, as I would have thought, but decided to take up their own collection. They said nothing about it to me or my parishioners. I thought they had completely given up the idea, but not so. They formed a three-man committee of the most influential members of the Protestant community, comprising two Anglicans and a Methodist. Since time was pressing, they approached only non-Mason Protestants in Coromandel and Kapanga, collecting all they could in three or four days. They wrote a warm address, regretting that poor health obliged me to leave Coromandel, thanking me for all I had done for the district and the people, and wishing me a safe trip. They prayed that God would restore me to good health and that I would return to continue my fine work.

At about 11 a.m. on the Thursday before my departure (I was due to leave on Monday), the three committee members knocked on the presbytery door. I invited them into the drawing room, not knowing what they wanted. They sat down and I asked them how I could help them. The leader pulled out a sheet and a purse and said he came on behalf of the Protestant community to present me with a farewell address. He said that the great majority were very upset about my ill-health and departure, and he hoped that I would soon return to them, etc. He then stood up and read me out a brief but beautiful address on behalf of the Protestants, signed by the committee. At this point, he handed me a purse containing their offering. He said that given the shortness of time the collection was somewhat meagre, because they had only been able to call on a few of my admirers for a contribution. He concluded by saying, 'We are sure that you will kindly accept this small token of our sincere affection for you and sadness at your departure. But we all hope that when your health is restored, you will soon return to us. Meanwhile, on behalf of us all, we wish you a safe voyage and, even more, a happy return.'

I warmly thanked the committee and begged them to convey to all my sincerest thanks for the address and offering presented to me on behalf of the good Protestant community, and said that I would retain everlasting affection for them and that they would always be remembered in my prayers. I was doubtful that I would make a full recovery, but that if I did, and it was the Lord's will for me to return to New Zealand, I would happily return to Coromandel. I said that their affection was extremely precious to me, and finally I begged them to convey my kind regards and sincere thanks to all, especially for their generous collection. They then wished me a safe trip and departed. There was £14 in gold coins in the purse.

7. The Catholics, too, hurriedly collected as much as they could from the parishioners. I think they collected about £30. They didn't have enough time to approach everyone because Coromandel's Catholics were scattered far and wide. On Sunday after the 11 a.m. Mass, Mr Lynch, the Catholic leader, read me out an address on behalf of the parishioners. It was full of praise, affection and recognition of my efforts on their behalf. They deplored the grave loss of my departure and were distressed that ill-health necessitated my leaving the colony. They thanked me for all I had done and wished me a safe trip, a complete recovery and a speedy return if at all possible. I was deeply moved and thanked them for their kindness and generosity. I said that I had only done my duty. I was sad that ill-health forced me to leave them. I mentioned that I would remember them in my humble prayers and asked them to pray for me. I urged them to be steadfast in their faith and duty as Catholics. If we were not to meet again on Earth, I hoped to see them all in a better world. Many were weeping openly. Others had tears in their eyes. All were sad and upset. Since no other priest was coming for the time being, I gifted the sisters my hens and other personal superfluous possessions I had in the presbytery, which could prove useful to them.

8. Meanwhile on Sunday morning at the first Mass at Kapanga, instead of an explanation of the Gospel, I gave the congregation my farewell address, exhorting

them to remain true to their religion, and not to back down, even in the face of persecution, etc. In Coromandel, in the evening at vespers, which was attended by Catholics and Protestants, I gave my final farewell, mentioning the same things as I had at Kapanga. On Monday at about 9 a.m., accompanied by many Catholics and several Protestants, we went to the steamer anchored at the wharf. They were distressed at my departure, and all wanted to embrace me and kiss my hand.* I said a few words of comfort and then Br Joseph and I boarded and the boat departed. For several minutes they waved a final farewell with white handkerchiefs.

I thus bade adieu to Coromandel. In the approximately thirty months I was there, I managed to save more than £100. With the last offerings of about £40, I decided to put aside £150 for the printing of the *Storia della Nuova Zelanda*, which I would try to write on my return to Europe. The rest of the money would be used for my trip to Italy, etc. After my departure, Fr Dom Raphael Wissel, a Bavarian, was sent to Coromandel, but he was there for only a short period. Then the bishop sent a secular priest, but he behaved very badly, causing grave scandal. He was removed not only from Coromandel, but from the diocese. Of the Coromandel sisters, the one who shared the superior's spirit of independence caused some scandal and decided to depart with her superior for the United States of America. The Auckland superior sent down two replacements to join the remaining nun.

PART 8. BOUND FOR AUSTRALIA

SUMMARY. – 1. Which route to take to return to Europe? Poverty compels me to take the cheaper. – 2. I leave New Zealand forever.

1. It took three hours for us to reach Auckland from Coromandel. I was joyously greeted by old Catholic friends and fellow priests. Fr Sullivan decided that Br Joseph would remain in Auckland when I returned to Europe. The return trip cost the same price, whether one went via Australia and Suez to London, or via San Francisco, connecting by train to New York and then on to London. I wished to return via America, having come to New Zealand via Suez and Australia. I could then say I had travelled right around the world. Tickets for both passages were bought from a British shipping company at the same cost of £70. I reflected that if I travelled through the United States of America, I would want to stop in San Francisco, Washington, New York and two other large cities for a couple of days to see the sights. I had gathered information from people who had been there and I realised that staying in hotels would cost at least twenty-five francs a day, even if I had second-class accommodation and saved as much as I could.

---

* The reference is to a traditional practice of kissing a priest's hand as a mark of respect.

For ten days that would amount to 250 francs. I also thought that I would want to spend a few days in London to see the metropolis. That would cost me another 100 francs at least. The trip from London to Genoa would bring the cost to more than 300 francs. I asked myself if it was worth the effort to incur such a large expense, and whether it went against my vow of monastic poverty. After weighing everything up, I decided to return the way I had come as the more economical measure.

Having reached this decision, I wondered which travel company to select. I made enquiries in Auckland, and chose the French Messageries Maritimes Company for the trip from Auckland to Marseilles. It allowed a small ten per cent discount for missionaries and, as well as meals, it provided beverages such as beer and wine. British shipping lines did not do this, and in fact charged a lot for alcohol, as I had experienced in coming to New Zealand. I concluded that travelling on a French company steamer I would save more than 200 francs on drinks alone, without taking into account the ten per cent discount on my ticket. Having made my decision, I asked Fr Sullivan to get me a first-class ticket for £64. He said that the parishioners should have given me the money for my trip and I could pay for it out of that. I told him that they had given me some money, but it was insufficient. I would be able to pay for incidental expenses and for the journey from Marseilles to Subiaco. The money I had would just cover these costs. Fr Sullivan prevaricated. I simply told him he would have to borrow the money from the bishop if he didn't have it and someone would have to pay the bishop back. He then discovered that he could buy me the ticket, as already mentioned.

2. The bishop, Fr Sullivan, the clergy and local Catholics were very upset about my leaving the mission, but since I had become ill, I couldn't continue. Mons. Luck gave me an excellent reference and a letter for a family in Marseilles with whom I could stay. Fr John Lenihan (who succeeded Mons. Luck as Bishop of Auckland)* gave me a silver snuff box as a testimony of his affection, which I later gave to my brother. The secular clergy gave me about £20 towards my expenses. I received the bishop's blessing the day before my departure and I went to say farewell to the sisters and priests of the town. The vicar-general had died about two months previously, leaving an inheritance of Bank of New Zealand shares worth £10,000 (250,000 francs) to the bishop for Catholic education. On 25 July 1887 at 3 p.m. I took my last leave of my Newton confrères and, accompanied by Fr Sullivan, I went to the steamer. Several priests came to wish me bon voyage. At 4 p.m. the steamer cast off and, with final farewells, I bade the town and New Zealand goodbye.

* In fact, Fr George Michael Lenihan, Bishop of Auckland 1896–1910.

NOTES

1   Vaggioli, Dom Felice, *Storia della Nuova Zelanda e dei Suoi Abitatori,* vol. 2, Parma, 1896.
2   Mostardi, Faustino, in *I Monasteri Italiani della Congregazione Sublacense (1843–1972), saggi storici nel primo centenario della congregazione,* Parma, 1972.
3   Ibid., p. 422.
4   Vaggioli, 'Le Avventure di un Refrattario Descritte da lui stesso', unpublished manuscript, Praglia archive, 1908–1911.
5   Vaggioli. His *Storia della Nuova Zelanda e dei Suoi Abitatori (History of New Zealand and Its Inhabitants)* is in two volumes, a natural history (vol. 1) 1891, and a social history (vol. 2), 1896.
6   Galletti, Dom Angelo, personal communication, 22 November 2000.
7   Ibid.
8   Vaggioli, 'New Zealand correspondence', unpublished, file 5, 4, 1, Library Santa Maria della Castagna, Genoa.
9   Vaggioli, 'Lettere e copie di cose più importanti dal 1879 in poi' (uncatalogued), Praglia archive.
10 Whareherehere, Hemi Waikato Tainui Taupiri (kaumatua), interviewed 30 September 1998.
11 Ruka, Pat (kaumatua), interviewed 11 October 1998.
12 Songs, laments and prayers (Maori).
13 Mostardi, ibid., p. 419.
14 Ibid., p. 420.
15 Ibid., p. 414.
16 Vaggioli, 'Le Avventure ...', etc., Book Four, p. 297.
17 Ibid., p. 301.
18 Ibid.
19 Ibid., Book Five, p. 255. Vaggioli comments that he recovered through sales less than half his publication costs.
20 Mostardi, op. cit., p. 425. Mostardi speculates that Vaggioli was telepathic, having premonitions regarding his mother's death and accurately predicting in 1908 that he would die some twelve years later.
21 Cronaca dell'Abazia di s. Giorgio Maggiore, Venice, vol., XII, 1 June 1909–12 December 1935, p. 170.
22 Vaggioli, op. cit., Book Two, preface.
23 The reference is to the 1866 law of suppression.
24 Vaggioli, ibid., Book Five, chapter 10, p. 131.
25 Vaggioli, ibid., Book Five, p. 214, chapter 12, 'I am available'.
26 Ibid., Book Five, chapter 10, p. 152.
27 Vaggioli, Gisborne correspondence, op. cit., Gisborne, 29 December 1881.

28   Vaggioli, 'Le Avventure ...' etc., chapter 11, p. 200.
29   Vaggioli, 'Letter e copie ...' etc., op. cit., Praglia archive, Letter from Mr Jennings,
     Gisborne, 21 April 1883 (uncatalogued).

FELICE VAGGIOLI AND COLONIAL CATHOLICISM

1   *New Zealand Freeman's Journal*, 27 December 1879.
2   Ibid.
3   E.R. Simmons, *In Cruce Salus: A History of the Diocese of Auckland 1848–1980*,
     Auckland, 1982, pp. 142-3.
4   Similarly, Vaggioli's account of Pompallier's niece seducing a priest can be traced
     to the Auckland Sisters of Mercy, who were repaying old scores, having suffered
     from similar scurrilous tales about themselves a decade earlier. E.R. Simmons,
     Pompallier: Prince of Bishops, Auckland, 1984, pp. 189-90.
5   See the entry on Croke in the *Dictionary of New Zealand Biography*, vol 2 (1870–
     1900), Wellington, 1993, pp. 104-5. For a less critical view of Croke's Auckland
     career see Mark Tierney, *Croke of Cashel*, Dublin, 1976.
6   This explains Croke's decision to remove the Franciscans from Thames, making it
     his mensal parish. Simmons, *In Cruce Salus*, p. 109.
7   Viard to Favre, 28 February 1867, Viard Papers, Wellington Catholic Archdiocesan
     Archives.
8   For similar conflicts between bishops and religious orders, see John Hosie, *Chal-
     lenge: The Marists in Colonial Australia*, Sydney, 1987.
9   *A Deserter's Adventures*, p. 18.
10   S. Gilley, 'The Roman Catholic Church and the Nineteenth Century Irish Diaspora',
     Journal of Ecclesiastical History, 35 (1984), pp. 188-207.
11   It was said of Cardinal Cullen that he 'converted the Irish to Christianity'. D. Bowen,
     Paul Cardinal Cullen and the Shaping of Modern Irish Catholicism, Dublin, 1983.
     Emmet Larkin, 'The Devotional Revolution in Ireland 1850–75', *American His-
     torical Review*, lxxvii, 3 (1972), pp. 625-52.
12   Croke to Kirby, 10 July 1871, Kirby Papers, Irish College Rome.
13   Moran to Kirby, 13 March 1871, Kirby Papers, Irish College Rome.
14   'We understand that the Roman Catholic community are taking steps to get Auck-
     land created an archdiocese. Of course the Catholic Bishop of Auckland would
     then become the metropolitan bishop.' *New Zealand Herald*, 25 October 1886. The
     Auckland Catholic Diocesan Council were 'all united in deeming that the claims
     of Auckland should be put as forcibly as possible to the Holy See irrespective of
     the Bishop's own personal feelings.' Minutes of Diocesan Council, 28 August 1886,
     Auckland Catholic Diocesan Archives.
15   The decision went against the recommendations of the first plenary council of the
     Australian and New Zealand episcopacy, held in Sydney two years earlier. Red-
     wood to Grimes, 29 January 1886, Marist Archives, Wellington. *New Zealand Tab-
     let*, 27 July 1887.
16   John Redmond was member for New Ross, William for Wexford, the latter being
     elected while he was in Australia. *New Zealand Freeman's Journal*, 20 July 1883.
17   'I always have been, and am, a warm admirer of the faithful, generous and long-
     suffering Irish nation, and a true and earnest sympathiser with them in their many
     crying wrongs and the gross injustices they have so often to contend with.' Luck to

Auckland Hibernians, 5 March 1883, cited in *New Zealand Freeman's Journal*, 23 March 1883.

18 *New Zealand Freeman's Journal*, 23 March 1883.

19 *New Zealand Freeman's Journal*, 23 March 1883. Luck deprecated politics 'interfering with the bond of charity which ought to unite Catholics of all nationalities in the peace and harmony of the Catholic Church.'

20 'Dr Luck is an Englishman, with anti-Irish prejudices, of which his letter affords ample evidence.' *Bathurst Record*, 15 May 1883. 'Dr Luck is an Englishman, and he evidently shares his countrymen's incapacity to understand Irish feeling and Irish nature.' *Nation* (Dublin), 9 June 1883. The Irish nationalist press considered Auckland 'peculiarly Irish', not least because it had been the see of T.W. Croke, the current hero of the Irish nationalist campaign.

21 Luck had earlier attended two public lectures given by C.H. Bromby, a Tasmanian politician, on 'the English in Ireland'.

22 Despite Vaggioli's claim to the contrary (*A Deserter's Adventures*, p. 163). Luck confirmed this in his letter to the *New Zealand Herald*, 20 November 1883. Moran was out of town for the meeting in Dunedin, but called on the delegates and took them for drives around the city. Hugh Laracy, 'The Life and Context of Bishop Patrick Moran'. MA thesis, Victoria University of Wellington, 1964, p. 126.

23 *New Zealand Herald*, 28 November 1883. Goold also prohibited the use of Catholic schoolrooms 'for other than legitimate purposes', a stance repeated by Luck. *New Zealand Herald*, 1 December 1883.

24 At various times the Vatican declared against boycotting, the tribute to Parnell, and the later phase of the Irish Land War, the 'Plan of Campaign'. See the two volumes by Emmet Larkin, *The Roman Catholic Church and the Creation of the Modern Irish State 1878–1886*, Dublin, 1975; *The Roman Catholic Church and the Plan of Campaign 1886–1888*, Cork, 1978.

25 'It was this [Irish] scheme which nearly ruined the English province so completely that its survival must remain a source of astonishment.' David Parry, *Monastic Century*, Ramsgate, 1965, p. 73.

26 Vaggioli and four other Auckland Catholic priests attended Redmond's lecture at the Theatre Royal, when the speaker mocked those who had expected to hear 'an excited recital of exaggerated wrongs'. *New Zealand Freeman's Journal*, 12 October 1883.

27 Redwood claimed to be the first Catholic bishop to appear publicly in support of the Irish Land League, speaking in its favour in both Ireland and New Zealand. *New Zealand Tablet*, 23 March 1888.

28 Redwood to Grimes, 18 July 1887, Grimes Papers, Christchurch Catholic Diocesan Archives.

29 Wellington's *Evening Post* (14 June 1886) called Gladstone's Home Rule Bill of 1886 'one of the greatest national reforms which ever statesmen essayed.'

30 Luck incurred renewed Irish disfavour by removing Fr Walter McDonald from his postion as cathedral administrator in early 1886. 'There seems to be a national, as well as religious, sentiment involved,' commented the *Evening Bell* (29 April 1886). In 1888 Luck declined to agree to an Irish lecture being announced in the Catholic churches until he was assured that its object was 'for the purpose of affording relief to the distressed in Ireland'. *Evening Bell* (25 April 1888). Luck attended the lecture.

[31]   Diary for 1895, Michael Davitt Papers, Trinity College Dublin. Bishop Cowie re-
       marked of Davitt, 'I always respect and admire any man who suffers for conscience.'
       New Zealand Tablet, 20 December 1895.
[32]   *A Deserter's Adventures*, p. 89.
[33]   Ibid., p. 196.
[34]   Bishop Moran had stood unsuccessfully for the Otago Peninsula seat in 1883.
[35]   Vaggioli's view of Freemasonry reflected that held by many colonists of his own
       church: a politically-inspired movement intent on world domination by secret means.

Index

Also by Dom Felice Vaggioli and translated by John Crockett:

HISTORY OF NEW ZEALAND AND ITS INHABITANTS

First published in Italy in 1896, and translated and published in English for the first time in 2000, this is the second volume of a two-volume work written by Vaggioli after his sojourn in New Zealand as a missionary priest. It is notable for the independent stance he took on the impact of British colonisation on Maori society.

'A frank appraisal of the exploitative nature of colonialism.' *Choice (Current Reviews for Academic Libraries)*

paperback, 368 pp, illustrated, $49.95, ISBN 1 877133 52 3